THE PADDOCK
THAT GREW

THE PADDOCK THAT GREW

Keith Dunstan

The Story of the Melbourne Cricket Club

Third edition

HUTCHINSON AUSTRALIA

Century Hutchinson Australia Pty Ltd
89–91 Albion Street, Surry Hills, New South Wales 2010

Sydney Melbourne London
Auckland Johannesburg
and agencies throughout the world

First published 1962; second edition 1974
This revised edition published 1988

National Library of Australia
Cataloguing-in-Publication Data

Dunstan, Keith.
  The paddock that grew.

  Rev. ed.
  Includes index.
  ISBN 0 09 169170 2.

  1. Melbourne Cricket Club. 2 Cricket —
Victoria — Melbourne. I. Title.

796.358'06'09451

Typeset by Abb-typesetting Pty Ltd, Victoria
Printed by Impact Printing Pty Ltd, Victoria

CONTENTS

FOREWORD

As Keith Dunstan relates in the first chapter of this fascinating volume, it was on November 15, 1838 that Messrs F. H. Powlett, R. Russell, Alfred Mundy, C. F. Mundy and George B. Smyth met and actually formed the Melbourne Cricket Club and documentary evidence to this effect still exists.

I have often wondered what motivated these five gentlemen to get together and to act as they did. I suspect that they merely wished to play cricket on a more or less regular basis, and thought the best way to achieve this was, in the first place, to form a cricket club. I am quite sure they had no idea whatever of the tremendous influence that their quite simple transaction would have over the next 150 years, not only on so many aspects of the life of the community but also on the birth and development of international cricket.

We today who have affection for, or interest in, the Melbourne Cricket Club should feel extremely grateful to our "progenitors" of that bygone era for the courage, wisdom and initiative that they displayed—albeit possibly unconsciously.

From that day in 1838 the Club has thrived and expanded until today it is firmly established as part of our national identity and tradition, and in this the third edition of *The Paddock that Grew* Keith Dunstan maintains the high standards of the first two editions as he weaves the history of this great Club into the background of our developing society, right up to 1988, the Club's 150th birthday year.

Here we can read of great sporting, political and business personalities of the last century and a half—of great social and technological changes that have affected us all—of great cricket games and of other famous sporting events—of military tattoos, royal welcomes, religious crusades, pop concerts —of problems and difficulties that have had to be faced, such as the admission of women to full membership, a rival stadium, industrial confrontation, the Olympic Games saga, troubles with the wicket—and of duels, balloon ascents, wartime billeting, grandstands, floodlights, scoreboards, trustees, dinners, sporting sections, great administrators, great members and great office-bearers—and of many other events, both large and small, in the history of the Club, all recorded not only with perception and realism but also, obviously, with great affection.

The Melbourne Cricket Club is in the unusual—but not unique—position of being a private club with public responsibilities, and here we also read how, over the years, the Club has discharged these responsibilities conscientiously, intelligently and practically and with integrity and dignity, despite much criticism and even calumny from time to time.

I have known Keith Dunstan for well over 50 years since we were at school together for a short time. He has had a distinguished career as a journalist, and is one of Melbourne's best known columnists, diarists and correspondents, with a particular interest in social history. Although never a very keen participant in active or contact sports himself, he and his wife Marie have ridden their bicycles over many parts of the world—a subject on which Keith has written widely. He is a cricket "buff", with an encyclopaedic knowledge of the game, he was the founder of "The Anti-Football League" in Melbourne, and he has been a long time protagonist of the Melbourne Cricket Club, to which he was admitted as a junior member on December 16, 1939—and thus next year he will join the distinguished band of "Fifty Year Members".

No one could be better qualified or suitable to be the official historian of the Melbourne Cricket Club, and I congratulate him most sincerely on the successful completion of this the third edition of *The Paddock that Grew*—which now covers the whole 150-year history of the Club. With its superb illustrations, and its "easy to read" format, this book should be compulsory reading for anyone who has any interest in the Melbourne scene over the last century and a half, but more particularly, of course, for those connected with the Melbourne Cricket Club.

I recommend it unreservedly.

DONALD CORDNER
President, M.C.C.

INTRODUCTION

THE M.C.G. is not a beautiful ground, nobody would call it that. Maybe it was in the last century, when Dr. W. G. Grace talked of its elm trees and the well that provided such cool, clear water. Alas, these things have gone, but something else has taken their place. The M.C.G. has all the atmosphere of the big time, and little that's great takes place in Melbourne without the M.C.G. being part of it. Even when Mr. Stephenson's England XI played at the M.C.G. on New Year's Day, 1862, it was considered the best-equipped cricket ground in the world. That situation has never altered.

The cricketer who walks on to the M.C.G. knows he has arrived, and for the newcomer it is not always easy. Bill O'Reilly used to say that unless you have been out there in the middle it is impossible to understand. The actor on the stage is confronted by a great wall of eyes. How much more so on the M.C.G. The cricketer has the wall all around him. It engulfs. Furthermore the comments of the spectators, kind and unkind, can be heard with astonishing clarity.

But to see the Melbourne Cricket Ground at its best the stands must be full. A yacht makes no show unless it has a full spinnaker, a full spread of canvas. When the stands are full at the M.C.G. then it is alive. Such an occasion was February 11, 1961, the Fifth Test between Australia and the West Indies. The crowd was 90,800, the biggest attendance in the history of cricket.

It was fascinating to listen to the moods of this crowd, the ohs and the ahs, that would well up and down as if controlled by the stops of an organ, or perhaps the explosion of cheers, that could be heard miles away. Yet, far more awe-inspiring were the silences; the truly expectant, excited silence, for example when Wesley Hall started his long run to bowl to Colin McDonald. Yes, 90,800 people not making a sound was something to hear.

This was a big day for the M.C.G., but there have been others. The M.C.G. saw the first match against New South Wales in 1856, the first match against an XI from England in 1862, and the first England-Australia Test Match in 1877. All the great English players from George Parr and Dr. Grace to Jack Hobbs and Len Hutton have played there.

There have been so many performances to remember. Take 1879 when the Demon Spofforth with his flailing arms took the first hat-trick in a Test Match against England, or the day in 1898 when Clem Hill, still not 21, saved Australia with an unforgettable 188. Some like to remember Jack Hobbs' and Wilfred Rhodes' 323 opening partnership in 1912, or the biggest scores against England on the M.C.G.—Don Bradman's 270 in 1936, Bob Cowper's 307 in 1966 or for sheer fun the day in 1946 when Keith Miller hit Toshack three times over the fence in one over.

Behind all this has been the Melbourne Cricket Club, which must lay claim to being the oldest of all clubs in Victoria. It started in 1838. Its influence on sport has been extraordinary. It was an M.C.C. member who first launched the idea of Australian Rules football. He was looking for some way of keeping his cricketers fit during the winter. The M.C.C. fostered the first tennis matches, and the club actually sponsored the first intercolonial tennis matches against New South Wales. The club was a prime mover, too, in establishing baseball in Australia. What else? Whole chapters could be written on the M.C.C.'s interest in bowls, lacrosse, rifle shooting, club and country cricket. In the days when there was no such thing as a Board of Control the club sponsored its own international tours. Vernon's tour to Australia in 1887 cost the club a loss of £3,500.

The M.C.G. always has had a dominating part in the life of Melbourne. Few great events have passed it by. There was Queen Elizabeth's visit in 1954, the Olympic Games in 1956, and March 15, 1959, when 130,000 came to hear Billy Graham.

The club continued to grow, to evolve, to adapt to changing times and conditions. In 1977 it celebrated the centenary of Test Cricket between England and Australia. The President, Sir Albert Chadwick, invited every living Australia/England Test player to come to Melbourne to witness a Centenary Test Match. What an occasion it was; how marvellous to see together such grand adversaries: Percy Fender, Jack Ryder, Harold Larwood, Don Bradman, Bill Voce, Alan Davidson, Denis Compton, Bill O'Reilly, Peter May, Clarrie Grimmett . . .

Oh, there were shocks. It was painful for some to see the old mechanical scoreboard disappear for ever. It had sported names from Trumper to Bobby Simpson. The new creature was really a small television station, an electronic wonder with a giant screen, and so the instant replay became a part of our life. A batsman as he walked back to the pavilion could see again his own humiliation. One day cricket arrived and many of the old hands thought the game was going to ruin; but they had great difficulty in explaining this ruin to

84,153 people who turned out for an England-Australia match on January 24, 1983.

The next shock was the admission of women as club members. Some female journalists thought portraits of ancient presidents would turn pale and drop from the walls when provisional women members first entered the Long Room on July 2, 1983. However the pictures remained intact, and apart from a few grumbles from the long occupied seats in front of the great windows, the change went through with surprising ease.

The acquisition of lights was not so easy. The club became the innocent victim of political warfare between Government and unions. For six months the Melbourne Cricket Ground was virtually under siege and housed its own police station. But then came the triumphant moment on December 3, 1984 when the Premier, John Cain, threw a switch and in the space of seven minutes darkness was turned into day, and a new era of night sport had begun. Nothing like it had been seen since an ill-fated football match under electric light on August 12, 1878.

Another triumph came in November 1986. The Prime Minister, Mr R. J. Hawke, opened the Australian Gallery of Sport, destined to become one of the world's finest sporting museums, where one could see the bat Walter Hammond used to score 203 runs for England in 1932, or maybe the spikes John Landy wore when he ran his sub four-minute mile in 1949.

Unquestionably the club was in good hands. In 1988 it celebrated its 150th birthday, an extraordinary achievement when one considers it was only 50 years younger than its close relative, the Marylebone Cricket Club of London. Robert Russell, the planner of Melbourne, was a founder of the Australian M.C.C. in 1838. If only he could drive his carriage today down Wellington Parade, along Brunton Avenue and up to the Melbourne Cricket Ground, he would, no doubt, have cause to be proud.

KEITH DUNSTAN

CHAPTER ONE

The Beginning

CRICKET and the Melbourne Cricket Club came to Melbourne in 1838 when the town was only three years old. It wasn't a place for the meek or the weak. A Port Phillipian needed a great capacity for enduring discomforts, he needed the mind of a visionary, and, just possibly, he needed a unique capacity for rum.

The settlement put on strength like a hefty young calf, but there was little to take the eye. Admittedly there were brick buildings and a weather-board here and there, but mostly Melbourne consisted of wattle and daub huts roofed with sheets of bark or coarse shingles. These houses had fences, and the front gardens now facing very famous streets grew cabbages and potatoes. Yet one outstanding impression seemed to remain with all those who could remember the time—mud. Flinders Street was a swamp. One wouldn't dare cross parts of Collins Street unless equipped with thigh boots and the idea was seriously canvassed of using a ferry or a punt in Elizabeth Street.

There were logs of wood and tree stumps in the main streets. Then there were those dreadful places where a stump had been removed. The hole left behind a well of soft mud, a likely place on a dark night for a man to fall in up to his armpits.

The west end of Little Flinders Street was the promising place of business, followed by Collins, Elizabeth and Bourke Streets. Swanston Street, the main artery today, was nothing at all. It was a town of young people, scarcely anyone was over 30. The men wore blue serge suits, no coats, cabbage tree hats, belts supporting tobacco pouches and sometimes pistols, breeches, high boots and spurs.

Aborigines, practically naked, wandered everywhere. They did odd jobs, they helped cart water, but already they had been degraded by the white man's habits, rum and tobacco. They begged constantly for money and food. Then at nightfall, followed by their dogs, they retreated to their camps outside the town.

There was no mail delivery and no public water supply. If anyone needed water then he walked down to the Yarra with a bucket. It was difficult even to know the time of day, because until 1843 there was no public clock. There were two or three watchmakers in the town, but they disagreed constantly about the time, and sometimes their claims could vary by an incredible margin.

Yet the surrounding countryside was lush and very beautiful. On the river and around the swamps there were great numbers of swans, pelicans and wild duck. Kangaroos hopped through the long grass, and John Batman reported that quail flew past in great clouds, 1000 at a time.

It was John Batman who on June 8, 1835, sailed his ketch 6½ miles up the Yarra, where he found good, fresh water. Then making his way through the scrub and ti-tree to what is now the corner of Collins and Market Streets, he declared that this would be the place for a village.

When Robert Russell, a 28-year-old surveyor, came from Sydney a year later there were 15,000 sheep and 200 settlers in the district. In 1837 Russell drew up the plans for Melbourne, under the orders of Governor Bourke and the Lands Commissioner, Robert Hoddle. He laid it out in the beautifully precise system of rectangles that we know now. Even then he must have realised that he was designing a great city.

But Russell's enterprise spread in many directions, particularly on sporting matters. He was said to be a first class gun shot. He potted duck on the marshes around Middle Park and he shot kangaroo on the river bank there by the Gardens and Alexandra Avenue.

He raced a horse in the first race meeting and he played in the first cricket match. It would be nice to be able to report that cricket was the first sport played in the colony. However, some aggressive gambling traits in the Australian character were uppermost even then.

Racing came first, and the meeting took place in March 1838 on the west side of Spencer Street near Batman's Hill. Now it is the site of Spencer Street Railway Station. Yet as more Government officials, more military men and graziers came to the settlement, naturally, attention turned to an even more gentlemanly sport, cricket. Robert Russell had the idea that there should be a village cricket club and he became one of the foundation members of the M.C.C.

On November 15, 1838, five gentlemen met and drew up a document agreeing to form a cricket club to be called the "Melbourne Cricket Club", subscription one guinea.

The signatories were:

F. A. Powlett,

R. Russell,

Alfred Mundy,

C. F. Mundy,

George B. Smyth.

They all paid their guinea and on the same day the first secretary, Mr. D. G. McArthur, bought two bats, balls and stumps for £2/0/3.

It was interesting that this primitive settlement, only three years old, should be in a position to start a cricket club. A research group at the Melbourne Cricket Club Library Dr. Ray Crawford, R. Grow, A. Bachelder, H. Webber, N. Sowdon, G. Hibbins and R. Harcourt — have produced a paper on the influence of Anglican public schools in Australian sport. They point out that the driving force in the Port Phillip Association was the banker-financier, Charles Swanston, a director of the Derwent Bank, the most influential bank in Australia. Swanston actively touted for British capitalists to invest in the new colony. So among the new arrivals from Britain were young middle class gentlemen, almost certainly educated at public schools. They were civil servants, military officers, engineers, doctors, architects, writers. The squatters, too, came from respectable middle class families and they all expected to reproduce the life they had led in England.

The first thing they did was to establish private clubs, so in quick order they formed the Melbourne Cricket Club for cricket, quoits and skittles; the Melbourne Club for exclusive social activities and the Melbourne Racing Club (later the Port Phillip Turf Club) for horse racing and related activities.

Frederick Powlett was a founding member of all three clubs and the first president of the Melbourne Cricket Club. Powlett, Robert Russell, Mundy and G. B. Smyth, signatories of the document which launched the Melbourne Cricket Club, also attended the first meeting of the Melbourne Club at the Lamb Inn on January 1, 1839.

Port Phillip was a small settlement, but the founders of the M.C.C. were key men. F. A. Powlett, the first president, was the Crown Land Commissioner of the Western Division of the Port Phillip Settlement and also the first Police Magistrate. It is almost certain that he was a descendant of the Rev. Charles Powlett, who took such a part in the founding of the Hambledon Club, the first cricket club in England. For years he was the best cricketer in the colony and there is one thing nobody can take away from him—he made the first century and he took the first hat-trick. He has another neat distinction. He

3

shares with T. F. Hamilton the honour of being one of the two presidents of the M.C.C. who have represented their State or Colony at cricket.

Alfred Mundy and C. F. Mundy worked for the Melbourne Insurance Company. Later they went to Adelaide. G. B. Smyth was a captain of the 80th Regiment and he was appointed captain of Mounted Police.

After the first five there were other interesting members, such as D. C. McArthur. He came from Sydney to open the Bank of Australasia, Melbourne's first trading bank. It opened on August 28, 1838, in a two-roomed brick cottage on the north side of Little Collins Street, between Elizabeth and Queen Streets. An armed sentry and two mastiffs formed the guard. He was president of the M.C.C. from 1868 to 1877.

There was Captain Bacchus of the 18th Light Dragoons. He became a grazier at Bacchus Marsh. There was William Highett, first manager of the Union Bank, Redmond Barry, a young barrister, and, of course, the irrepressible Peter Snodgrass. Never will we forget Mr. Snodgrass, for it was he who fought the first duel in the colony.

Snodgrass was a very excitable man. His father was a lieutenant-colonel, and apparently he had inherited some of the old man's enthusiasm for military customs. On New Year's Day, 1840, he was at the Lamb's Inn, the hotel which was to become Scott's. He had a furious argument with a grazier from Yering, named William Ryrie. A challenge to a duel was issued and accepted. The time was to be dawn the following morning on the cricket field—yes, the racetrack by Batman's Hill. It would have been more convenient to hold it later, but everyone felt dawn was the traditional hour for duels. Seconds were appointed. Lt. Vignolles of the 28th Regiment for Mr. Snodgrass, the challenger, and Mr. T. F. H-lt-n for the challengee. Garryowen, the historian who records this duel, didn't mind giving the full names of the others, but apparently he was a little bashful about Mr. T. F. H-lt-n.*

The time already was 11 p.m., when they realised that they had no duelling pistols. The Melbourne Club had none, and it was impossible to go hunting around the town for pistols without giving warning to the Police.

Then Mr. H-lt-n remembered that he knew a Mr. Hawdon at the village of Heidelberg, eight miles away. Mr. Hawdon had an excellent pair of hair-trigger duelling pistols. Mr. H-lt-n had a fine speedy horse, so he offered to ride there at once. This offer was met with great cheers and applause.

At 1 a.m. Mr. H-lt-n returned galloping down Collins Street, waving a pistol

---

* Obviously T. F. Hamilton, who became M.C.C. President from 1859-1868 and an original Trustee of the M.C.G.

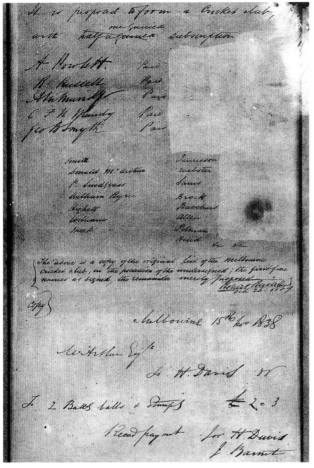

The ingenious Mr R. C. Bagot
designed both Flemington Racecourse
and the Melbourne Cricket Ground.

in either hand. Once again there was uproarious applause. It was then that they realised another fearful difficulty was upon them—no powder, no ammunition. They couldn't go to a store, because on a previous Christmas there had been an explosion in the market reserve which blew up the only sporting emporium.

Of course, Captain Smyth, the military commandant, and a good M.C.C. member, was the man. Captain Smyth lived in the officers' quarters at the west end of Bourke Street. It was decided that Mr. Snodgrass' second, Lt. Vignolles, should go and see him at once. This, Lt. Vignolles flatly refused to do. It was easy to see his point. No lieutenant likes to rouse his senior officer out of bed after one in the morning. It seemed then that it might be a good idea to postpone the whole thing until another time.

But, lo, in again stepped Mr. H·lt·n. Rather than let the very good fun fall through, he would take the risk of calling on Captain Smyth himself. For the third time Mr. H·lt·n earned the cheers of the company.

It must have been well after 2 a.m. when he made his way to the Captain's house. The Captain stepped wearily out of bed, and after much hesitation he finally agreed to help. So Mr. H·lt·n's large coat pocket was turned into a powder magazine.

Meanwhile Mrs. Smyth, in her nightdress, was peering through the partly opened door. She thought it was some sort of a stick-up. She rushed out, grabbed Mr. H·lt·n by the collar and demanded to know what he had hidden in his pocket. Mrs. Smyth grabbed at the pocket, Mr. H·lt·n tore himself free and in one movement his coat was ripped right up to the shoulder.

This time Mr. H. returned a trifle tattered, but nevertheless he had triumphed. The next move was to get a doctor. They dug out a Dr. D. J. Thomas of Bourke Street, who was said to be a surgeon of considerable skill. By the time they got to Batman's Hill it was broad daylight and a lovely, fresh summer's morning.

The usual formalities took place. The principals took up their positions and everything was almost ready. However by this time Mr. Snodgrass was almost bursting with excitement, so much so that his hair-trigger went off and he shot himself in the foot. Mr. Ryrie, a perfect gentleman, fired into the air and honour was satisfied.

Everyone rushed over to Mr. Snodgrass, who was lying stretched out. He wasn't terribly injured except for a slight loss of blood and the loss of a toenail. Thereupon the party decided to dispose of the remaining ammunition and powder. They did this by putting Dr. Thomas' new bell topper on a tree stump and riddling it with bullets. It was still too unfashionable an hour to go to the Melbourne Club so they returned to the Lamb Inn, where they celebrated for most of the day.

You might imagine this was the end of Mr. Snodgrass' duelling career, but it was not. In August 1841 he clashed with Redmond Barry, the young barrister, and also an M.C.C. member. Barry had written a letter to a friend, who unhappily showed it to Snodgrass. Seeing that there were a few points about Snodgrass in the letter, he took action immediately.

Once again the duel took place, correctly, at dawn. This time on a spot midway between the Sandridge (Port Melbourne) Pier and the Albert Park Railway Station. Redmond Barry arrived, superbly attired, as if he were all ready for a Royal levée. He had on his belltopper, he was strap-trousered, swallow-tail coated, white-vested, gloved, cravated; all was perfection. He made sure the distance was correctly paced out. He placed his hat most carefully on the ground. He drew off his gloves, pulled down his spotless wristbands and bowed with great dignity to Mr. Snodgrass. Then he took his pistol and adopted a majestic pose while waiting the command for action.

Poor Snodgrass. He was a very different type from Barry. He fussed and fidgeted. It wasn't that he was frightened, he was just anxious to get it over. No ceremonial nonsense about Snodgrass. But it was all too much. Again he discharged his pistol before the signal was given. Fortunately no damage was done. Barry, magnanimously, fired his pistol in the air. Both men did well after this. Snodgrass became a capturer of bushrangers, a member of parliament and a "voluble if not eloquent" chairman of committees in the Legislative Assembly.

Redmond Barry went on to be Victoria's first Solicitor-General. As Sir Redmond Barry he became a Supreme Court judge and the first Chancellor of Melbourne University. Then just before he died he was the judge who sentenced Ned Kelly to death.

There was one more duel. In 1842 Mr. F. A. Powlett fought Mr. Hogue, a merchant. The site was Flemington Hill. They each exchanged two shots. Hogue missed altogether, but Powlett sent a bullet through Hogue's clothing. This, up to the time of going to press, is the only occasion when a President of the Melbourne Cricket Club has ever engaged in a duel.

CHAPTER TWO

The First Cricket Matches

T HE inaugural meeting of the M.C.C. was on November 15, 1838. The first cricket match was a week later on November 22, 1838. They played on a paddock which is now the site of the Royal Mint in William Street. It was one of the few clear pieces of land in the town, but later the M.C.C. men found something better, a cricket ground west of Spencer Street, the home of the future Spencer Street Railway Station.

This first match was between the civilians and the military. Robert Russell, who lived until his 92nd year and died in 1900, said as an old man that he could remember little about it, except that no uniform was worn and the civilians won. But the *Port Phillip Gazette* of December 1, 1838, gives this report:

> Pleasure and recreation are absolutely necessary to relieve our minds and bodies from too constant attention and labour with truly gratified feelings there. Did we not witness the gentlemen of the district assemble last Saturday week on the beautiful pleasure grounds around this fast rising town, to bring into practice one of the most elegant and manly sports that can be enjoyed? Yes, it was pleasurable to witness those whose mental and enterprising minds had turned this, but short time since wilderness, into a busy emporium of traffic, relinquishing for a time their occupations and writings. These efforts to establish sports such as these.
>
> During the week arrangements had been made by the gentlemen civilians of the district to play a match at cricket again at the military. Captain Smyth, with the enthusiasm natural to him, and desirous of forwarding everything either really beneficial or of useful amusement, was joined by many of those who had retired from the Services, but whose hearts are still with it, mustered on the ground a company with which they would have attempted a more stirring contest.
>
> It was a heartening sight to witness from an adjacent hill the ground as it was laid out. Camps pitched, banners tastefully arranged, and all the enlivening smiles of beauty that would have graced a far-famed tournament of other time, formed a scene which we trust often again to witness.
>
> At 12 o'clock precisely, a signal called the players to their post, when the

game commenced, the Military taking the first innings. We have not the par-
ticulars of the game before us and can therefore but briefly notice those who
particularly distinguished themselves.

After a duration of some hours, it concluded by a triumph on the part of the
civilians. Mr. Powlett, Mr. D. G. McArthur's bowling and Mr. Russell's batting
attracted universal applause.

On the whole, the game was played with an esprit de corps, a judgment and
an activity that a first-rate club in England might be proud of.

So the Melbourne Cricket Club won its first match.

The Melbourne Cricket Club did not have all the good cricketers. There
were the retailers, the tradesmen and the artisans. They banded together to
form "The Melbourne Union Cricket Club." So on January 12, 1839, the
gentlemen of the M.C.C. played the tradesmen. The tradesmen beat the
gentlemen so mercilessly that as a point of honour it was necessary to have a
return match on January 19. This time the gentlemen won comfortably. The
M.C.C. president, Gentleman Powlett, scored 120 runs, the first century to be
scored in the colony. The star of the tradesmen was Mr. Thomas Halfpenny, a
strapping mountain of a man. He did well both at batting and wicket-
keeping.

The greatest problem of all was to organise suitable matches. There were
only two cricket clubs. They couldn't continue interminably playing each
other Saturday after Saturday. So the committee members had to think of
matches that were a trifle different. They played the Benedicts v. Bachelors.
The husbands won, and Husband Powlett scored a total of 101 out of 180.
There were more matches between the military and the civilians, alphabetical
games — the first half of the alphabet against the second half—and a match
which caused great interest was the Whiskers v. Clean Shaven contest. It took
the Gold Rush of 1851 to bring the beard to its full glory of goatee, mutton
chop, squatter's gap, Lord Dundreary, or the unlimited growth as exhibited
by Dr. Grace. Before then the majority of the men in the colony were clean-
shaven. The beards won by seven wickets. As for Mr. Powlett, history does
not record how many runs Bearded Powlett made.

The next club to be formed was at Brighton. It was a good area, some very
fine villas were being built at this fashionable resort. Their cricket team was a
good one, so good that the M.C.C. did not have one victory against Brighton
between 1842 and 1845. For example, on Easter Monday, March 24, 1845,
there was a splendid turnout of the fashionable world at the Batman's Hill
ground. The match was played in the presence of Superintendent La Trobe,
Crown Prosecutor Croke, Deputy-Sheriff McKenzie and Crown Solicitor
Gurner. In the first innings Melbourne made 70, Brighton 62. Then there was

a spell of half an hour, when there were plenty of good old-fashioned colonial refreshments. Melbourne returned to make only 55 and Brighton 70. Brighton's bowling was so skilful that according to one cricket authority it would "do honour to Kent any time."

One fascinating story has gone into history about this game. One of the players was a Mr. John Highett. He was a gentleman "whose purse never ran below the low water mark." This time he had £500 in bank notes in one of his top pockets, which was a vast sum of money when you think that even £5 a week was a large wage. Well, Mr. Highett put down his jacket, complete with the £500, and went out to play cricket. At dressing time when he returned, the coat, £500 and all, was gone. Mr. Highett had to return home coatless.

The next day the coat was found all nicely tied up in a parcel and addressed to the Chief Constable. But there was no clue to the identity of the thief or the whereabouts of the money. Garryowen comments primly: "There can be little doubt that the paper money was promptly placed in the melting pot of the publicans and thus put into speedy liquidation."

The forties was a tough period for the M.C.C. The price of wool and wheat had fallen disastrously and they were known as the "Hungry Forties." There are blank spaces in the minutes where the club very nearly went out of existence, only to be revived again. On November 1, 1841, there was an election, the first that gives us a complete list of office-bearers.

President: F. A. Powlett,
Vice-President: H. F. Gurner (Crown Solicitor).
Honorary Secretary: G. Cavenagh.
Honorary Treasurer: W. V. McVittie.

Cavenagh was to become a powerful force in the club. He was president from 1846-49, 1850-54, and he won the batting average for the 1846-47 season. He was a man full of energy. In 1836 he was joint editor of the *Sydney Gazette*, but he wanted to get out on his own. So he came to Melbourne, where he started as sole proprietor of the *Port Phillip Herald*, first published on January 3, 1840. He imported staff and an editor, William Kerr, from England, and he put in the first steam printing press ever used in Victoria. In 1849 his newspaper became the *Melbourne Herald*.

Entrance fee remained at one guinea, and by 1847 there were 127 members. Some of them were interesting. There was Mr. W. C. Haines, for example, who in 1856 became Victoria's first Premier under responsible government. There was Dr. Patrick Cussen, president of the first Medical Association, and almost certainly a relative of Sir Leo Cussen, who was later a great president of the club. Dr. Cussen was famous, too, for performing the first surgical operation in the colony. He successfully removed the hand of a soldier whose fingers had been blown off in the discharge of a blunderbuss when firing a salute to Lady Franklin on the occasion of her visit to the colony in 1839.

In 1847, also, there was the cricket match against Geelong. This was something of an endurance test. Now Geelong is an hour's drive. For the 1847 M.C.C. team it was different. They embarked on the steamer "Asphrasia," then sailed for eight hours so that they could start the match in Geelong on time at noon. For the return match the teams got together in the evening at the Shakespeare Hotel, at the corner of Collins and Market Streets.

In 1848 the club moved to a site on the south bank of the Yarra, between the river and Emerald Hill (now South Melbourne). It was the paddock where John Pascoe Fawkner in 1836 raised the first wheat in the colony. The club secretary, Mr. Alex G. Broadfoot asked Superintendent La Trobe for use of the land, and supported his request with the suggestion that Sir George Gipps had granted a similar request to the Australian Cricket Club in Sydney. Furthermore, Sir George had even supplied them with a team of convicts to help turf the wicket. Mr. Broadfoot did not receive any convicts, but he did get the 10 acres of land. Immediately the club put up a wooden booth, a vast improvement on the tent it had at Batman's Hill. A four rail fence went in at a cost of £30/13/4, and the club turfed part of the area for £24/13/6.

On August 1, 1850, the Colonies Bill passed through the House of Commons in London, which gave separation to the Port Phillip Settlement from New South Wales. Victoria was to be a brand new colony. Naturally this intelligence had to come to Australia by ship, and the news did not reach Melbourne until the morning of November 11.

After months of rumour this was it. Melbourne went cockahoop; that's the only way you could describe it. There was a 21-gun salute in the Flagstaff Gardens, which was answered by firing the guns of all the vessels in the Bay. Immediately after the salute His Worship the Mayor, Cr. Nicholson, released a balloon which carried the great Separation news written on sheets of parchment.

At sunset the Mayor fired a beacon on Flagstaff Hill, which was answered by bonfires on hill after hill throughout the settlement. There was a display of fireworks and rockets on Punt Road Hill, South Yarra, which the *Argus* described as the greatest ever seen in the Colony (presumably N.S.W.). Furthermore, this was an occasion that would go down in the history of the world. The Mayor declared that Thursday, Friday and Saturday were to be public holidays when no work was to be done. The newspapers by agreement took the unprecedented step of not publishing for four days. They gave the reason that not a single worker should be left out of the celebrations. The *Argus* pointed out that even though this was happening perhaps the sun would continue to rise.

On Wednesday, November 13, it was the city of 100,000 lights. There were tar barrels blazing in the streets, which continued until a shower of rain put them out at 9 p.m. Every business, every hotel, had a sign up announcing WELCOME TO SEPARATION. Mr. Cashmore, the Collins Street draper, had a transparency which depicted one balloon marked MELBOURNE above another balloon marked SYDNEY. Sydney was saying: "We can't hold on any longer." And Melbourne replied: "Let it go, then—we can take care of ourselves."

There were dinners, there was a big gymnastics display at Emerald Hill, there was free beer, and on the Friday there was a procession watched by 10,000 for the opening of the new Princes Bridge, an occasion long awaited in the settlement. The celebrations continued for nearly a fortnight.

Although the new Act did not come into effect until July 1, 1851, the M.C.C. could hardly wait to launch an Intercolonial Cricket Match. So they decided to issue a challenge for the gentlemen of Port Phillip versus the gentlemen of Van Diemen's Land, the match to be played at Launceston on a date to be arranged and depending on the steamer *Shamrock* to arrive at that place.

Mr. H. A. Smith offered to take the M.C.C. team of 13 to Launceston and back on the *Shamrock* for £5 a head. A special general meeting of the club agreed to this, and they fixed the date for February 11, 12, 1851. It was proposed by G. E. Bell, seconded by Dr. Ford, who was the first vaccinator in the colony, that the M.C.C. should have a special uniform for the big match. The committee talked it over for some time, then decided to adopt the colours red, white and blue. That was well over a century ago, and they have been the official colours of the M.C.C. ever since.

It was a very serious business. The committee appointed Messrs. Campbell, Bell and Powlett selectors. They fixed Tuesdays, Thursdays and Saturdays for practice. Furthermore, it went into the official minutes that if any member selected, living within two miles of the town, absented himself more than one day in the week out of the three set apart for practice, without being able to give a satisfactory reason in writing for his absence, then he would be fined one guinea. Sadly, Mr. Powlett sprained his ankle and could not play, but what with players like W. Philpott, T. F. Hamilton and C. Lister there was no question the Port Phillipians would be too strong for the Islanders.

At this time the population of Port Phillip was 77,345 and the population of Melbourne 23,143.

It was just as well that the match took place at Launceston, for there was a heat wave over Victoria and the colony was suffering from disastrous bush-fires. The *Argus* reported that the whole sky was red, and from the city it was possible to see the flames of the Dandenongs. In the town of Dandenong only one building was left standing and that was the Dandenong Inn. But the fires were everywhere, and Portland reported temperatures ranging between 112 and 116.

Meanwhile in Launceston there was another disaster. The Van Diemen's Land team won by two runs with three wickets still intact.

The Islanders were very decent about it. It was reported: "As a mark of kindness and good feeling of the Tasmanians towards the Port Phillipians, not the slightest breath of applause escaped from the multitude, numbering over 1500, but a marked silence ensued as though they had committed a breach of hospitality to their guests. This generous and manly feeling will not soon be forgotten by those who witnessed it."

While the M.C.C. team was there it had a marvellous time. Indeed, it was even suggested, judging from some members' play, that it was too good. After the match they went for the day to the William Field Enfield Estate at Bishopsburne, and also for a trip by coach to Hobart. The players stayed at the Cornwall Hotel. This same hotel was actually the birthplace of Melbourne. It was there that John Batman and a party of graziers laid their plans for an expedition to Port Phillip in 1835. Then on the night of February 11, 1851, 100 gentlemen of Port Phillip and Van Diemen's Land sat down to dinner. After the dinner there was a ball.

This was one newspaper report:

> No sooner had the *Shamrock* discharged her passengers at Launceston than the whole town was in a buzz, each and every person trying to outdo his neighbour in every kind attention which the most genuine hospitality could suggest. Everybody invited everybody, and the difficulty was to partake of all that was offered. From the time of landing to the time of embarking, the same spirit continued—dinners, balls, musical parties, picnics, and every description of entertainment was got up to give a hearty welcome to the strangers from Port Phillip. On the morning of the departure from Launceston, and as an indication of the good fellowship and friendly feeling displayed, the Launceston Band volunteered their services to enliven the scene and cheer the return of the cricketers. It accordingly formed past the Cornwall Hotel, the headquarters of the Victorians, and played several tunes in first-class style—amongst them *Home Sweet Home*.
>
> The Tasmanian cricketers also met them, and the two elevens, with their friends, walked arm in arm to the steamer, the band playing before them. On their arrival at the wharf, *God Save the Queen* was played, and Mr. Philpott, in a few brief remarks, thanked the assembled multitude for their unbounded kindness, and especially for the last pleasing demonstration at parting. The

Victorians assembled on the deck of the *Shamrock* echoed the feelings of Mr. Philpott with a thrice renewed explosion of cheers—a compliment loudly reciprocated on the shore.

As for the cricket, it was played on the old racecourse and the ground was almost incredibly rough. This could partly explain the low scores. The Port Phillipians were baffled by the very slow and peculiar bowling of the Tasmanians, whereas the Tasmanians did not know how to handle the fast bowling of the Port Phillipians. This was the score sheet:

1st Innings	PORT PHILLIP	2nd Innings	
Cooper, b. McDowell	4	Hamilton, lbw., b. McDowell	35
W. Philpott, c. Maddox, b. McDowell	17	Brodie, c. Tabart, b. Henty	5
Hamilton, b. McDowell	10	Hall, lbw., b. McDowell	6
Lister, run out	10	Lister, c. Maddox, b. Field	3
Thomson, b. McDowell	1	Thomson, b. Henty	0
R. Philpott, b. Henty	12	W. Philpott, run out	3
Antill, stumped Marshall	0	Cooper, b. Henty	0
Brodie, c. Henty, b. McDowell	17	R. Philpott, c. Westbrooke, b. Henty	1
Marsden, b. Henty	2	Marsden, b. McDowell	2
Hall, not out	6	Harvey, c. McDowell, b. —	1
Harvey, b. Henty	0	Antill, not out	0
Byes	1	Byes	1
Leg Byes	2	Total	57
Total	82		

Time: 2 hours 5 minutes. — Time: 1 hour 20 minutes.

TOTAL for two innings 139

1st Innings	VAN DIEMEN'S LAND	2nd Innings	
Du Croz, b. Antill	27	Du Croz, b. Antill	6
J. Marshall, c. Lister, b. Antill	13	Giblin, b. Antill	1
Field, b. Antill	0	Westbrooke, c. Cooper, b. Antill	4
Maddox, b. Antill	1	Tabart, not out	15
Gibson, b. Hamilton	8	Field, c. Thomson, b. Brodie	1
Westbrooke, b. Antill	10	Gibson, b. Antill	1
Arthur, b. Antill	1	Marshall, c. & b. Antill	0
Tabart, b. Hamilton	2	Arthur, c. Harvey, b. Antill	0
Giblin, not out	7	McDowell, not out	4
Henty, b. Antill	0	Byes	3
McDowell, c. and b. Hamilton	11	Wides	2
Byes	10	Total—7 (dec.)	37
Leg Byes	6		
Wides	8		
Total	104		

Time: 2 hours 40 minutes. — Time:

TOTAL for two innings 141

After the match the Melbourne team presented £5 to the Launceston Church of England Grammar School, the oldest public school in Australia, as a donation towards its building fund. It was then five years old. In return the headmaster, Mr. Kane, sent the M.C.C. a map of Van Diemen's Land as a gift from himself and the boys.

And the Launceston *Chronicle* very kindly printed this:

> We are much gratified by the visit of these gentlemen, as fine a specimen of mankind as could be seen in the world. Everyone is speaking in the most enthusiastic terms of them. The opinions of the people are highly complimentary, having heard so much of the Melbournites as being a rough set, blue shirts and black pipes being invariably coupled with the names of the Port Phillipians. The contrary is obviously the case.

The Victorians were keen to return the hospitality of the Tasmanians as soon as possible, but it wasn't easy. They hadn't reckoned on the discovery of gold. The first gold strike was at Clunes in July 1851, followed by strikes at Warrandyte, then Ballarat, which was to become one of the richest surface goldfields ever known.

La Trobe, the first Lieutenant-Governor of Victoria, wrote on October 10, 1851:

> Within the last three weeks the towns of Melbourne and Geelong and their large suburbs have been in appearance nearly emptied of their male inhabitants; the streets which, for a week or ten days, were crowded by drays loading with the outfit for the workings, are now seemingly deserted. Not only have the idlers—and day labourers in town and country —thrown up their employment and run off to the workings, but responsible tradesmen, farmers, clerks and not a few of the superior classes have followed. Cottages are deserted, houses to let, business is at a standstill, and even schools are closed. In some of the suburbs not a man is left, and the women for their own protection group together to keep house. The ships in the harbour are in a great measure deserted, and we hear of instances where even masters of vessels, foreseeing the impossibility of maintaining control over their men otherwise, have made up parties among them to go shares.

The *Melbourne Morning Herald* said:

> The whole city is "gold mad." Richmond is a deserted village, so far as the lords of creation are concerned, only one grey-headed old gentleman of some seventy summers being left . . .

So you can imagine, in such a state of chaos, the difficulties of trying to play cricket. The return match did not take place until March 30, 1852. Then it proved an almost impossible problem to get canvas for the public tents. All the canvas had gone with the diggers to the goldfields. Yet eventually they did get a large marquee and a tent.

Play was due to start at 11 a.m. sharp, and any player who was not at his post was liable for a fine of £2. Whatever the state of the game lunch was to be taken at 1.30 p.m. Mr. Yewers, the caterer, was under contract to furnish a luncheon including three dozen bottles of champagne each day, the wine to be approved, he taking the change of a greater or lesser number. Even though there were seven breweries in the colony at the time, it was the custom in those days for gentlemen cricketers always to have champagne at lunch and apparently French champagne too. This continued right up until the eighteen-eighties, when standards slipped. The M.C.C. made a ruling and the cricketers switched to beer.

For the big match His Excellency and suite, both the Judges, and most of the elite of Melbourne were present. There were several thousand spectators. The ground on the south side of the river was in perfect condition and well-rolled. According to the reports, the large marquee for the use of the members contained a table loaded with the good things of life, to which a large party, including a great number of ladies, sat down at luncheon and did ample justice to the viands. It was said that at times the popping of champagne corks drowned the conversation. The players dined in the wooden shed used by the club in their matches. After toasting each other in champagne they resumed the game.

This time Victoria made the score even. They had a victory of 61 runs, by making 80 in the first innings and 125 in the second. Tasmania made 55 in the first innings and 81 in the second. Hamilton made 42 runs in both innings for Victoria and Powlett made 1 and 33.

CHAPTER THREE

The M.C.G. is Born

O N September 12, 1854, the first railway train in Australia ran from Melbourne to Sandridge (now Port Melbourne). The engine was a 6-wheeled tubular boiler of 30 horse-power and the newspapers talked of this iron horse that could achieve a speed of 25 m.p.h. It had three carriages. For the inaugural run it also pulled a third class open carriage, which took the band of the 40th Regiment. All the leading citizens of the colony travelled on the first run, and when the train reached Sandridge after travelling at a speed of 15 m.p.h., there was a banquet in the engine shed, a vast affair of zinc. The banquet was particularly noted for the fact that there were 20 speeches. Not one of these speeches mentioned the fact that this remarkable railway line passed right through the middle of the M.C.C. ground.

It had been a sad shock. The Melbourne Cricket Club in its short career already had suffered one move and the south of the Yarra ground was to be the permanent home. Admittedly it was low-lying and one time the flooding Yarra washed away the players' shed, but the club had spent several thousands of pounds on grading, turfing, fencing, and already there was a small pavilion. As a cricket ground it was something to see.

Yet there was no question, Melbourne had to keep ahead of Sydney with a railway, and it was only natural that the first stretch of track should go from the city to the port at Sandridge, so the line passed through Melbourne's cricket ground. As compensation Governor La Trobe offered the club two alternative sites in the Police Paddock, and the Committee of Management chose a plot 250 yards in diameter "in the hollow to the right of the footbridge leading across the paddock."

The secretary of the M.C.C. on August 15, 1853, wrote to the Superintendent, asking for "permission of His Excellency to erect a cottage as well as to remove such trees as may be necessary. The Committee of Management would further take leave to represent that the ground now in occupation be ceded to the Club, such compensation from the Company for improvements to the Ground to be left there, the removal of which to a new site would entail considerable expense to the Club." On September 23, 1853, His Excellency agreed to the enclosure of the 10 acres in the Government paddock under permissive occupancy for five years. His Excellency would also sanction the erection of such buildings as may be absolutely necessary. It is to be understood that no carriageway to the ground is to be allowed. The exact area enclosed was 9 acres, 1 rood, 37 perches, and was to be used for cricket and no other purpose. This is the present site of the Melbourne Cricket Ground.

As the first trees were being chopped at the Police Paddock to make way for the Melbourne Cricket Ground, Melbourne had all the atmosphere of a wild frontier town. The young Lord Cecil had written in his diary that the streets and hotels were "clamorous with drunken revels which now and again culminated in crimes of audacious violence." A writer who visited the Queen's Theatre in 1853 wrote that at the end of the performance in place of bouquets for the actors there was a shower of nuggets, some more than half an ounce.

Immigrants were pouring in, sometimes at the rate of 3000 a week. There was nowhere to house them. By Emerald Hill near the site of the old cricket ground a new town sprang up. It was laid out in streets, but all the shops, houses, and official buildings were of canvas. In 1853 over 5000 people lived there, and judging by the number of empty bottles and gin jars that have been dug up in the area ever since, Canvastown must have had its interesting moments.

There were still some reminders of the older days. A tribe of aborigines camped not far from Princes Bridge, there was wild duck to be had and there were fish in the Yarra. On both sides of the river there were kangaroos and wallabies. The Police Paddock itself was a lovely place, full of wattle, wildflowers and heath. The Richmond end was thick with timber. A man who was handy as a cut-throat used this timber as a hide-out to catch the travellers as they made their way down to the punt across the river at Punt Road hill.

The first year was devoted to hard work. It is clear from the records that right from the beginning the committee had one ambition—to make the M.C.G. the finest cricket ground in the colonies. In 1855 Richmond Park was described as "a delightful promenade which is becoming quite a place of fashionable resort." The M.C.C. with its picturesque ground and lodge used to invite the Band of the 40th Regiment to go there on Saturday afternoons and the park, invariably, was filled with the gentry.

The gold rush was very good for the club. Not only did it bring cricketers, but in four months in 1855 the club gained 200 members. The secretary recorded: "No club in the world ever increased its practical and numerical

17

strength so rapidly as the M.C.C." In the midst of all this confidence the entrance fee to new members went up from one guinea to two guineas.

The new members needed entertainment, so in January, 1856, the M.C.C. put advertisements in all the newspapers issuing a challenge to play any eleven in the Australian colonies for nothing or anything up to £1000. New South Wales accepted the challenge and decided to play for nothing on March 27. William Tunks, a great figure in the history of N.S.W. cricket, was the force behind the N.S.W. team. He was a publican, and his hotel was a rendezvous for all the best cricketers of his day. But the story goes that both Tunks and Mrs. Tunks disapproved of cricketers drinking beer, so they always received tea at the hotel. For the intercolonial match at Melbourne a large barrel of tea, complete with a tap, was placed on the ground. This caused considerable astonishment among the Victorians, who were accustomed to drinking beer even for breakfast. It astonished an eagle-eyed police constable, who at once took it for granted that here was beer being sold without a licence. History records that he had a very ugly shock when he tasted the contents of that barrel.

Admission was 1/-, ladies free. An excellent German band was in attendance; furthermore, there was a printing machine in a marquee which printed cards of the match on the fall of each wicket. Judging by the rate of fall of wickets, the printing machine must have taken an apoplectic fit before the day was done.

The homely look of the N.S.W. players, plus the dear, old under-arm style of their star bowler, McKone, caused great amusement amongst the spectators. Betting, of course, was one of the chief attractions of cricket at this time and the books were giving 2/1 on Victoria.

At the start each team nominated an umpire, and these gentlemen tossed for the choice of innings. Victoria's umpire won the toss and at once the Sydney men objected. They said this idea of tossing was absurd. It was accepted everywhere that the visitors always had the choice whether or not to bat first. The Victorian captain, Mr. Philpott, politely agreed; even so, the N.S.W. captain, George Gilbert, sent him in to bat. Back in the eighteen-fifties this was the smart thing to do. You sent in your opponents, noted carefully how they shaped, how many runs they made, then you adapted your play accordingly. This was the situation until 1858, when Tommy Wills, the Victorian captain, who had learned his cricket in England, introduced the tossing of the coin.

McKone as he went into action with his underarms had to listen to the giggles of the crowd, but he was deadly. He took 4/25 in the first innings and 5/11 in the second. Victoria made 63 and N.S.W. scored 76 in reply. After the first day there was a lavish ball. It is unknown to this day whether it was the superb skill of the Sydney bowling or whether it was a tribute to the gaiety of the ball, but in the second innings next morning Victoria was all out for 28. Then N.S.W. lost seven wickets before the team had the necessary 16 runs required to win.

R. Driver top-scored for N.S.W. with 18. He went to Melbourne just to umpire, but as the side was one man short, he stood in as an emergency. Later he was to become the first president of the N.S.W. Cricket Association. After the match there was a row over the cricket ball. The Victorians presented it to Driver as a memento, and Driver kept it. On October 21, 1856, the N.S.W. team passed a resolution that Driver be requested to give up the ball, so that it could be deposited with a suitable description, in some place in the colony. Driver refused, and it wasn't until 1907 that Beatrice Driver, his niece, presented the ball to the N.S.W. Cricket Association.

So the first Victoria v. N.S.W. match ended with a victory for N.S.W. At the dinner after the match William Tunks said in his speech that there was a probability that the good fellowship arising through the matches would lead to a better understanding between the colonies. After all, it had not been good to date. He could remember when the Victorians refused to give more than 19/- for a Sydney sovereign.

In 1857 there was a return match against the "homely" New South Welshmen. Apparently the Victorians thought them homely because they didn't wear correct cricket flannels. They wore drill pants, guernseys and caps, and most incredible of all, they played either in bare feet or socks. Yet they beat Victoria again.

Scores: Victoria, 63 and 38.

        N.S.W., 80 and 86.

This match should be remembered because it meant the return of T. W. Wills. He took 6/28 in the first innings and 4/40 in the second, and scored only one run in two excursions to the wicket, but that is immaterial; Wills was to have an incalculable effect on Victorian and Australian cricket.

His father, Horace Spencer Wills, settled at Ararat in 1839. Obviously he was a very wealthy man. In 1852 he sent young Tommy home to England to be educated at Rugby. Tommy was a sporting natural. He was captain of both cricket and football at Rugby, and at Cambridge he was considered one of the most promising young cricketers in England. He returned to Australia in

December 1856. In 1860 his father sold his property at Ararat and bought a station near Moreton Bay in Queensland. Together they set out with 10,000 sheep, and it took them 10 months to get there.

The aboriginals at Ararat had always been friendly, but at Moreton Bay they were wild, difficult to manage. The great quantities of provisions that the Wills brought with them fascinated the tribesmen. On October 17, 1861, only seven weeks after the expedition arrived, the aboriginals attacked, hiding their weapons under possum skin belts. It was noon, the hottest time of the day. All the station hands were dozing in the sub-tropical heat. It was a complete surprise. Wills senior had time only to fire one shot from his revolver before he was knocked down and killed. Everyone on the station, employees and their families, all died, 19 in all.

This is the worst massacre in aboriginal history. The blacks ransacked the camp. They made a total wreck of everything, then vanished.

Young Tom Wills was the only one to escape. A dray had broken down two days journey off and his father had sent him out to bring it in. He managed the station for several years after this, then he returned to Victoria in time to play against Parr's English XI in 1864.

It is hard even to guess at his value to cricket in Australia. For years he was the "Grace" of the colony, and there's no question that his coaching of young players helped put Australia on equal terms with England.

He was a founder, too, of Australian Rules football. Perhaps he even started it. When he was the 20-year-old secretary of the M.C.C. during 1857-8 he wrote his famous letter to *Bell's Life*, suggesting that the M.C.C. should form a football club to keep the players fit during the winter. The grounds were too hard for Rugby tackling, therefore new rules were necessary. With his cousin, H. C. A. Harrison, he worked on the rules of a new football game that was to have quite an effect on the M.C.G. He had a tragic end. In later years he became an alcoholic, and in 1880 he committed suicide with a bayonet.

Wills, before he set out for Queensland, won back Victoria's reputation at cricket, so much so that by 1860 the score was three matches to Victoria, two to N.S.W. In one match Victoria achieved the score of 238, a massive total, equal to at least 1000 these times. Wills was the hero with 61 not out. Then he followed this by taking 5/25 in the first innings and 3/34 in the second. He was sadly missed when the time came to play the first match against a team from England on January 1, 1862.

Left

F. A. Powlett: not only the first president, but he also took the first hat-trick and made the first century.

Below

The original plan of the Melbourne Cricket Ground.

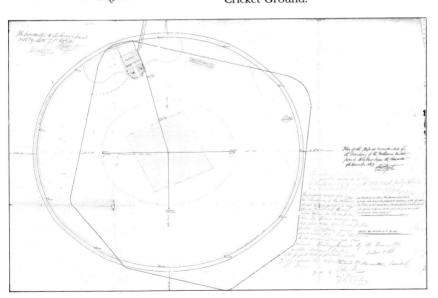

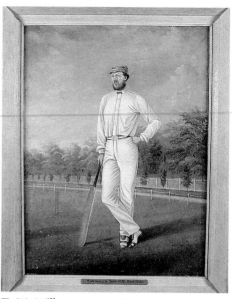

Robt. Russell.
[M.C.C. - 1838].

Robert Russell, artist, surveyor to the
infant settlement of Port Phillip, and a
founder of the Melbourne Cricket Club.

T. W. Wills, secretary 1857–1858,
captain of the Victorian XI, and prime
mover of the establishment of
Australian Rules Football.

CHAPTER FOUR

Mr. Stephenson's XI v. Melbourne XVIII

B Y 1860 the clubs were becoming ambitious. They wanted to test their strength against a team from England. But how was it to be done? England was 12,000 miles away, two months away by steamer, and any visit by a team could be disastrously expensive. There was a suggestion that each colony should put up £3000, but they were not prepared to take the risk. There was an attempt to float a company with the Governors of two colonies as patrons and a 100 per cent. dividend promised to the shareholders, but no shareholders came forward.

It seems hard to believe now, but it was a catering firm that brought out the first English team, Messrs. Spiers & Pond, the proprietors of the Cafe de Paris in Bourke Street. Originally they planned to bring out Charles Dickens. The great man refused to respond, so as second best they gambled on an English eleven. It wasn't England's best team by any means, but even so it was a good representative side, led by H. H. Stephenson, captain of Surrey.

The team embarked on the steamer *Great Eastern* on October 18, 1861. The *Great Eastern* was built in 1846 as a six-masted schooner. Now it was a three-masted steamer. It had carried 44,000 soldiers to the Crimean war and regiments to the Indian Mutiny, so maybe it was fitting that it should carry these troops to another kind of battle.

When the *Great Eastern* arrived at Sandridge (Port Melbourne) there on the wharf was an arch of welcome and 3000 people. The cricketers rode to town on a coach drawn by eight magnificent greys. A shoal of lesser vehicles encircled them and all the way they were cheered to the city. The Melbourne *Herald* felt that there hadn't been an arrival to compare with it since ancient times when the Athenians arrived in Corinth.

The *Argus* sounded a note of warning: "The game of cricket has no heartier admirers than ourselves, but we might imagine from the super-abundant effusion which the approaching contest has excited that some tremendous crisis was at hand, or that some trial which is to make us or mar us for ever is approaching."

But it was Christmas in Melbourne. Money was slightly tight, according to the newspapers. Female servants were demanding an impossible £25 a year and the law clerks had the nerve to ask for three days leave over Christmas, but still it was interesting to run one's eye over the price lists at the market.

Geese were 10/- a pair, hens 5/- a pair, ducks 6/- a pair, turkeys 20/ a pair. In 1861 there was no faltering—one bought everything in pairs. Eggs were 2/- a dozen, butter 1/- a lb., ham 6d. a lb., tobacco 1/7 a half pound. Beer was 8/- a dozen, port and sherry 3/- a bottle, champagne 4/ a bottle, whisky 3/-, gin 2/6, brandy 4/ and claret 18/- a dozen.

Just in time for the holidays there was the opening of the extension of Brighton railway line from Bay Street to the beach. Said the *Herald:* "The advantage of this extension will be greatly felt. Brighton has long been a favourite resort for picnic parties. The scenery along the line is very pretty, passing through gardens and thickly timbered paddocks along the entire distance."

Meanwhile, so that he wouldn't be mobbed by enthusiasts, Mr. Stephenson trained in secret with his eleven, seven miles out in the bush. Almost at once there was a crisis. The original plan was for Mr. Stephenson's eleven to play *twenty-two* Melburnians. Mr. Stephenson objected. His team had been at sea for 60 days. How could they be fit for such an encounter? He refused to have more than 18 in the Melbourne team.

The *Herald* attacked at once. Mr. Stephenson had played against 22 in New York and Canada. "Are the cricketers in Victoria so much superior that the Eleven of England cannot play 22 of them?"

Mr. Stephenson won the day. The Melbourne team was cut to 18, and for the time being they hid the news that for the Geelong match the plan was for his men to compete against *forty-four* players.

Other entertainments were taking place in the city. At the Anatomical Museum Dr. Bowman was lecturing on the "Origin of Species and the Characters which Distinguish Us from Monkeys." The "Puss in Boots" Pantomime was showing at the Cremorne Gardens, and on December 26, 27 and 28 the Grand Caledonian Games took place on the Melbourne Cricket Ground. There was archery, quoit throwing, fencing, tossing the caber, a football match, a running high jump, in which one gentleman cleared 5 ft. 1½ in., and such events as the footrace, in which a gentleman with a man on his back competed over 50 yards against a gentleman without jockey over 100 yards.

New Year's Day was blessed with perfect weather. The M.C.G. was in perfect condition. The new grandstand, 700 feet long, was completed for the occasion, to accommodate nearly 6000 people. Mr. Stephenson was astonished when he arrived, for here was a ground better than anything in England, and certainly there was no cricket pavilion in the world to compare with Melbourne's new grandstand.

The whole of the underneath of the new stand was given over to publicans, who advertised that they would have 500 cases of beer. The *Herald* on the day commented that cricket was the stuff of which life itself was made, and that when a Macaulay came to write a history of the colony the match would not pass unnoticed. By 11 am. the roads to the M.C.G. were packed with every kind of vehicle from buggies to bullock waggons. These times you would say they were bumper to bumper. There were horse patrols every 50 or 60 yards to control the traffic.

Outside the ground there were fruit and sweet stalls, Aunt Sallies, shooting galleries, hurdy-gurdies and small boys sold cards which had pictures of the players on one side and a panel for the scores on the other. The *Herald* put the crowd at 25,000, but some said it was as high as 30 or 40,000. Certainly it was the biggest cricket crowd on record.

There was even a painter with a long ladder for hire. For one shilling spectators could borrow his ladder to climb into the branches of the trees around the ground. He was a crafty fellow, this painter. Unless his customers paid him another shilling he refused to bring back the ladder so that they could climb down again.

George Marshall was captain of the Melbourne and Districts team. His XVIII wore straw-coloured shirts with red spots and round dove-coloured hats trimmed with magenta ribbon. Mr. Stephenson's XI wore white shirts with blue belts and white caps with blue stripes. And there was an interesting innovation, almost as good as our present light system on the scoreboard. Each English player had a different-coloured ribbon tied around his arm. To identify their man the spectators had only to check the ribbon colour on their score cards.

The Governor, Sir Henry Barkly, was there. His box was a blaze of crimson with the Royal coat of arms on the front.

George Marshall won the toss. However, in this very first match against an England XI, it is sad to report that for us the toss was the only thing that went according to plan. Our 18 men were all out for 118. Bryant 11 and George Marshall 27 gave the team a good start, but the remaining almost interminable batting list produced six ducks. Griffith of England, bowling "very swiftly," round-arm, took 7/30. Bennett, bowling round-arm with "considerable breaks," took 7/53. When there are 17 wickets to fall it helps bowling averages.

Mr. Stephenson's XI replied with 305. W. Caffyn, "Terrible Billy" of Surrey, made 79 and Griffith "the Lion-Hitter" made 61. In the second innings the XVIII made only 92, including *ten* ducks.

One reporter commented: "To institute any comparison between the play of the opposing teams was out of the question. The Englishmen were immeasurably superior to their opponents at all points of the game except in the case of long-stopping by Butterworth. The best Victorian fielding was bungling compared to the English, and before Victoria can hope to equal their opponents they must practice to stop balls, as it leads to idleness and bad feeling to depend upon nets." After the match Mr Stephenson's men appeared on the veranda and took the cheers of the crowd. The takings were £5000 gate plus £1000 from refreshment booths.

MELBOURNE & DISTRICTS
XVIII

First Innings		Second Innings	
J. M. Bryant, l.b.w., b. Bennett	11	J. M. Bryant, b. Sewell	0
G. Marshall, c. Iddison, b. Griffith	27	G. Marshall, C. Mortlock, b. Sewell	0
J. Sweeney, l.b.w., b. Griffith	16	J. Sweeney, c. Lawrence, b. Sewell	0
C. Mace, st. H. Stephenson, b. Griffith	5	C. Mace, b. Sewell	20
J. Huddleston, c. Sewell, b. Bennett	6	J.Huddleston, c. Iddison, b. Sewell	18
R. W. Wardill, run out	0	R. W. Wardill, c. Lawrence, b. Griffith	18
C. Makinson, b. Bennett	0	C. Makinson, run out	0
T. Morres, b. Bennett	0	T.Morres, run out	0
S. Cosstick, c. Mudie, b. Bennett	8	S. Cosstick, c. Iddison, b. Griffith	11
J. B. Thompson, ht. wkt., b. Bennett	17	J. B. Thompson, run out	0
G. Elliott, b. Griffith	4	G. Elliott, c. Iddison, b. Sewell	3
T. F. Wray, c. and b. Griffith	3	T. F. Wray, c. H. Stephenson, b. Iddison	0
S. S. Rennie, l.b.w., b. Bennett	9	S. S. Rennie, c. Lawrence, b. Iddison	0
J. Conway, run out	0	J. Conway, st. H. Stephenson, b. Caffyn	1
J. Stewart, b. Griffith	1	J. Stewart, b. Iddison	0
S. Hopkinson, run out	0	S. Hopkinson, c. Bennett, b. Caffyn	18
G. O'Mullane, not out	0	G. O'Mullane, not out	0
B. Butterworth, c. and b. Griffith	0	B. Butterworth, c. Iddison, b. Sewell	0
Extras	11	Extras	2
Total	118	TOTAL	91

24

Bowling

	B.	M.	R.	W.
Caffyn	36	2	23	—
Bennett	148	10	54	7
Griffith	116	12	30	7

Bowling

	B.	M.	R.	W.
Caffyn	28	5	5	2
Griffith	41	4	9	2
Lawrence	44	1	31	—
Sewell	104	16	20	7
Iddison	88	12	24	3

H. H. STEPHENSON'S XI

G. Bennett, c. Butterworth, b. Conway	11
E. Stephenson, b. Conway	34
W. Mudie, b. Elliott	22
G. Griffith, c. Butterworth, b. Cosstick	61
W. Caffyn, c. O'Mullane, b. Stewart	79
R. Iddison, b. Conway	31
H. H. Stephenson, b. Conway	2
C. Lawrence, c. Conway, b. Bryant	20
T. Sewell, b. Stewart	3
W. Mortlock, not out	11
T. Hearne, b. Stewart	8
Extras	23
Total	305

Bowling

	B.	M.	R.	W.
Conway	205	20	60	4
Cosstick	124	19	31	1
Bryant	195	18	33	1
Stewart	153	9	50	3
Elliott	101	7	48	1
Morres	25	—	9	—
Marshall	16	—	8	—
Makinson	60	1	43	—

The match did not go the entire three days, but as a grand finale that enterprising pair, Messrs. Spiers and Pond, had organised a balloon ascent, the first ever made in the colony. The balloon was called "All England," and it was immense. On the outside were pictures of Queen Victoria and the English cricketers. The aviators in the balloon were Mr. and Mrs. Brown and a Mr. Deane. Mrs. Brown received a special round of applause for her courage.

Mr. Hutchinson of the Melbourne Gas Company supervised the inflation, and at 2 p.m. it took off over the M.C.G. First with ropes it was steered towards Sir Henry Barkly's box. The band played "See the Conquering Hero Comes," a photograph was taken and the crowd went wild. Then at 4.30 p.m., with the trio aboard, the balloon was released. It rose rapidly, with the wind taking it in all directions. At 4.37 it was over Fitzroy Square. At 4.42 it was over the Botanical Gardens. They made their first attempt to land between Hawthorn and Richmond, but the wind changed and they returned the way they came. Eventually they landed in Albert Street, East Melbourne, after a voyage of 35 minutes over a distance of seven to eight miles. Their greatest altitude was 7000 feet.

When all was done, Mr. Stephenson announced that he had vastly enjoyed his Christmas and New Year in Melbourne. He complimented the Melbourne Cricket Club on the splendid state of the ground; it would only require another invitation and his Eleven would be happy to return to the colony in another two or three years time. One wonders if Mr. Stephenson fully realised exactly what he was starting.

The team travelled through Victoria, N.S.W. and Tasmania. William Caffyn wrote later that they had high jinks everywhere. Scarcely a day went by when they were not entertained to champagne breakfasts, luncheons and dinners. They played 15 matches against 22-man sides and only twice were they defeated, once by a united Victoria-N.S.W. team playing 22 in Sydney and once by Castlemaine.

Castlemaine, to its eternal glory, on March 14, 15 and 17, 1862, was the first team to defeat an English Eleven on Victorian soil. Castlemaine played 22 and defeated England with three wickets to spare, amidst intense excitement. There were 5000 people with crowds of bearded miners to cheer the local team to victory. The locals played fine cricket, although it was hinted that the lobster and champagne overnight, just possibly, might have been a contributing factor.

The members of the English team each received £150 plus their expenses, but there were bonuses to be had, including a gift of 100 sovereigns from the members of the Melbourne Cricket Club. As for Messrs. Spiers and Pond, their one adventure away from catering proved to be immensely profitable. They covered all their costs, £6000, with the first match. Their clear profit from the tour was £11,000. Considering what they did for cricket, and all that came after, it is hard to begrudge them the money.

Roger Iddison when he returned went down in history as the first Englishman to venture an opinion on the Australian as a cricketer:

"Well, o'i doant think mooch of their play, but they are a wonderful lot of drinking men."

CHAPTER FIVE

'Terrible Billy' Teaches

A T the end of the 1860–61 season the M.C.C. was suffering from those troubles that all clubs inevitably suffer. Club liabilities amounted to £323/19/6 and £500 was owing from overdue subscriptions. The committee decided that the club should "no longer be allowed to remain in the state of impecuniosity which has of late characterised it, and that strenuous efforts should forthwith be made to remove the stain by which it has too long been marred."

The committee decided that it would pass on some of the stain to the members themselves. Any member who hadn't paid his subscription of two guineas by November 1 would have his name put on the notice-board for all to see. This toughness went right through the club rules. Any playing club member who left the ground before a match was over was liable for a half-guinea fine. Any member who disputed an umpire's decision, or any member who pitched a wicket on ground set apart for matches also was to be fined half a guinea.

Half a guinea was real money at this time. For example, the secretary put on a man whose one job it was to stand at the gate of the pavilion and stop non-members from entering the club rooms. The club minutes stated that his salary was not to exceed six shillings a week.

The club also hired Sam Cosstick, who was said to be a very fine bowler. Sam's job was to keep the ground in order, to play in all the club matches when required and to bowl to the members every afternoon from 2.30 p.m. until 7 p.m. His salary was £3/10/- a week.

Mr. R. C. Bagot, the man who designed Flemington racecourse, took the job of redesigning the M.C.G. He altered the shape of the ground to make it a perfect oval, he put drainage pipes underneath, he re-planted, he re-turfed. He did such a brilliant job that the grateful M.C.C. made him a life member. Bagot had the help of Baron Von Mueller. What a team. Dr. Mueller was the man who designed the Botanic Gardens. He presented Bagot with 400 choice trees to plant between the inner and outer fences.

At this stage something definite had to be done about the club's tenure of the M.C.G. We know that Governor La Trobe in 1853 gave the club the use of ten acres in the Police Paddock. But what were the terms? Was it for ever? Melbourne was growing fast; something more was necessary. So in preparation for the Crown Lands Act in December 1861 the club chose four trustees. They were the Hon. W. C. Haines, the first Premier; John Goodman, T. F. Hamilton, the club president, and F. A. Powlett, the first president from back in 1838. The Government immediately confirmed their appointment.

Then in the Government Gazette for December 10, 1861, this notice appeared:

Metropolitan Cricket Ground

In pursuance of the Fourth Section of the Crown Lands Act 27, Vict. No. 177, it is hereby notified that it is intended to permanently reserve from sale the Crown Land herein described, upon the expiration of one month from the date hereof, and to convey the same to the trustees on condition that the rates of admission of the public be subject to the approval of the Government, viz., the Metropolitan Cricket Ground, formerly designated by the name of the Melbourne Cricket Ground, containing nine acres (as set out in the Crown Grant).

C. GAVAN DUFFY.

Eight years later the club found this wasn't good enough. The Deed of Grant mentioned only the word cricket. So the M.C.C. had to go to the Government and ask that the ground should be available "for holding athletic sports meetings and for other purposes of public recreation and amusement." So later under this heading of "public recreation and amusement" came many events, even grand finals between Melbourne and Collingwood.

Yet nothing drew the crowds like a cricket match, and in the year 1863 we had a visit from another All England XI. It was a better team than the side brought out by Mr. Stephenson. Much note was taken of the fact that Mr. Stephenson's men, surprisingly, had not been drowned at sea, nor had they been eaten by the Antipodean natives, and even more important they had returned with money in their pockets. So the great George Parr himself consented to lead a side.

George Parr was the leading batsman of his day. William Caffyn, the only player to return for a second trip, wrote of him that he could use his feet when he went out to drive a ball. He could cut hard and well in front of the wicket. His late cut was almost unique, a hard chop that actually struck the ground at the same time as the ball. However, always would he be remembered as a leg-hitter. There he had few equals. There were other famous names in the team: Dr. E. M. Grace, older brother of W. G. There was "Tear-Em" Tarrant

28

the fast bowler, Bob Carpenter the champion back-player of the century, George Anderson the big hitter and, of course, Julius Caesar of Surrey. One would expect vast things of a cricketer with a name like this, and he was a dashing cricketer, undoubtedly the Harvey or Denis Compton of the eighteen-sixties. Caffyn said of him that he was a boxer, yet rather a nervous man. He did not like sleeping alone in a strange hotel room because he feared that somebody might have died there some time or other.

The team travelled again on the *Great Britain*, and made the trip in the excellent time of sixty days two hours. Captain Gray, as usual, received a testimonial of thanks from the passengers plus "a very handsome present." The passengers were due to go ashore at Sandridge on December 16, but they arrived in time for the worst flood in the history of the colony.

The *Argus* reported that after two terrible days of storms, when Melbourne was as black as midnight, the Yarra burst its banks. Indeed the full title of the river was Yarra Yarra, and now the citizens were forced to remember that it was an aboriginal word meaning *Ever Flowing*.

The damage must have been appalling. The *Argus* described how the city was a collection of hills rising above the lakes. Great stretches of Richmond, Abbotsford, Collingwood, Hawthorn and Toorak were all under water. The barque *Dunedin* was washed up on the beach at Sandridge, St. Kilda Road had ceased to exist, and a weatherboard house had floated down the Yarra to lodge near Princes Bridge.

In Punt Road, near the M.C.G., the water was up to the tops of the verandas. By the Jolimont Railway on the other side it was most interesting to observe the variety of furniture that was floating in the water. One could observe a vast, oak four-poster bed that moved past like a steamer. The Sir Charles Hotham Hotel in Spencer Street was in difficulties, but the proprietor kept up an excellent trade by running a special boat service for his clients. At Toorak Road it was reported that a Mr. Marsden fled from his house after first putting his piano in a safe position on top of the dining room table.

Into this chaos came George Parr, a red-faced, solid gentleman with chestnut-coloured moustache and whiskers. He couldn't bring his team ashore at Sandridge, the entire Sandridge railway line being under water, to say nothing of the old M.C.G. Instead the team landed at Williamstown, and from there they went by train to Spencer Street.

There was nothing doing at Williamstown, but despite the floods a great crowd was waiting at Spencer Street Station, plus the team coach drawn by six handsome greys. George Parr called out each name, whereupon the man climbed into the coach to the applause of the crowd. Then there was a triumphant procession through the city. The crowd was thick along the foot-path, people waved from the upstairs windows. The coach went along Collins Street to Elizabeth Street, where it turned left to Bourke Street and finally round the block to the hotel in Swanston Street owned by the former Victorian skipper, George Marshall.

They had arrived much earlier than Mr. Stephenson's XI, so they had a good fortnight to attend the daily parties, the Mayoral dinners and such. The favourite pastime was quail shooting, and one day, just out of Melbourne, they shot 40 brace.

By January 1 there was no thought of floods. The day was pleasantly warm without being uncomfortably hot, and an "immense crowd of 15,000" came to the M.C.G. The Englishmen looked very fine in their uniform of white helmets and white flannel shirts with a red spot. George Parr won the toss from the local captain, Ben Butterworth, and sent Victoria in to bat.

Once again, obviously the Englishmen were superior. This time there were 22 players in the Victorian team, a frightening assignment for any modern scoreboard. Yet Victoria was all out by 5.30 p.m. for 146. W. Greaves was top-scorer with 34. England replied with 176, including 61 to Haywood. Victoria made 143 in the second innings, which left England 114 runs behind. George Parr's XI was 4 for 105, only nine runs to score with six wickets in hand, when stumps were punctiliously, indeed provokingly, drawn, according to Billy Caffyn, at 6 p.m.

George Parr's XI had a marvellous tour. They went all over the goldfields of Victoria, to N.S.W., to New Zealand, and although they played against 22-man sides they never lost a match.

Caffyn recalls that on April 7, 1864, they boarded the steamer *Wonga Wonga* at Sydney to return to Melbourne. Outside the Heads they collided with a sailing ship called the *Viceroy*, which sank immediately. The *Wonga Wonga* lowered a boat and the crew was saved.

Caffyn wrote: "Poor George Parr was utterly dazed and paralysed with alarm. Tarrant quite lost his head. The first thing he did was to rush down below to get together a collection of curios which had been given to him—at different times during our visit. Then when the boat was lowered he endeavoured to get into it, and was told by the sailors to keep out of the way, in very choice language. Julius Caesar, on the other hand, behaved in a manner worthy of his name, and doing all he could to assist the crew."

The tour made a profit of £7000. Each man received £500, but what they made on the side is anybody's guess, because they all sold a great deal of cricket material at a good profit.

Charles Lawrence remained behind after the first English tour to coach N.S.W. After the departure of George Parr and his men, William Caffyn stayed in Melbourne to coach the M.C.C. The Club engaged Caffyn at a salary of £300 a year "as coach and general instructor of members."

If a cricketer did not have a nickname in those days he did not rate. William Caffyn was known as "Terrible Billy" or "The Surrey Pet." He was a fine all-rounder, a neat, dapper little man with side whiskers.

There are many who think that Billy Caffyn, Charles Lawrence and, of course, Tommy Wills, laid the foundation of Australian cricket. Without that trio there would have been no Trumpers, Spofforths, Armstrongs, Trumbles and Kippaxes. After a year in Melbourne Caffyn and his wife went to Sydney, where they opened a successful hairdressing business in George Street. Mrs. Caffyn was never happy. The climate did not agree with her. She had four children, three boys and a girl, but two of the boys died in Sydney. Finally in 1871 they returned home to England.

But Caffyn saw some big changes, and he was in Melbourne through the height of the overarm controversy. Overarm bowling became legal in 1864, but before that the rule read:

"The ball must be bowled, not thrown or jerked, or if any part of the hand be above the shoulder at time of delivery, the umpire shall call 'no ball'."

Caffyn was not impressed with this fancy new style of bowling. He said the new over the shoulder bowling was mainly straight down the wicket or on the off side. It meant the end of the superb leg-hitting which was one of the greatest joys of cricket. Furthermore, the overarm men did not have the brilliant length or change of flight of the round-armers. And what about the shooter?

Said Terrible Billy: "There is one ball which is denied to the modern bowler, which was a terror to all us old batters—the shooter. Oh, those shooters at Lord's. One or two balls as high as your head, then perhaps one in the ribs, and then a shooter! No wonder when we stopped one of those we were greeted with a round of applause."

Arguments for and against the rule were hot on all sides. Before the rule change, raising one's arm above the shoulder was as villainous an act as "chucking". Indeed, the *Cricketer's Guide* printed a story expressing sympathy for J. Boak of Richmond, the fastest bowler in the colony. He could not moderate his pace without bowling over his shoulder. Umpires were forever in strife. They were glad to see the change.

But cricket at last was making progress. Billy Caffyn said that even between his two Australian tours of 1862 and 1864 he could see the difference. He wrote: "They were delightful pupils to teach, even as far back as the 'sixties'—always willing to be shown a new stroke and quick to do their best to retrieve an error, never taking an offence at having their faults pointed out and never jealous of one another. When I remember all this it is not so much a matter of surprise to me to see what Australian cricket has become today as perhaps may be the case with some people."

The Surrey Pet died in 1919 at the age of 91. Until the time of his death he was convinced that modern cricket was deadly dull compared with what it used to be, and he was far from convinced that the cricketers of the 20th century were in any way superior to the cricketers of the eighteen-sixties.

Billy Caffyn left the M.C.C. in 1865, just before one of the most fascinating stories in the history of the club—the formation of the Aboriginal Cricket Team. As time goes on, what with all the problems over aboriginal affairs, this story becomes more and more impressive.

It began with Mr. W. R. Hayman, who lived on a property in the Lake Wallace District of Victoria. He was the first to notice that the local aboriginals were marvellous, natural athletes. If they could run, jump and throw boomerangs why couldn't they use a bat or throw a cricket ball? He began to teach them cricket. They had been playing together for three years when Tommy Wills, the Cambridge educated star of the M.C.C., went to Edenhope to give them some expert coaching.

The Melbourne *Herald* said: "The men are well built and most intelligent looking fellows, far superior in appearance to the natives whom we have been accustomed to see from time to time."

On Boxing Day, 1866, Wills brought his team to the M.C.G. and led the aboriginals in a match against an M.C.C. club team. The *Argus* commented that the blackfellows had such a fearful reputation that the M.C.C. elected the noted bowler James as a playing member only two days before the match. Nobody thought that a club of such standing would have found such an action necessary. It was hardly cricket, according to the *Argus*.

The scoreboard on the day must have looked fascinating. Here was the aboriginal line-up: Johnny Cuzens, Billy Officer, Bullocky, Johnny Mullagh, Jellico, Tarpot, Sundown, Dick-a-Dick, Paddy, Peter, with emergencies Lake Billy and Wattle. Wills, of course, was captain.

Over 10,000 people turned out at the M.C.G. and another 2500 stole a free look from the trees outside the ground. This would have been a good crowd even for an international match.

The aboriginals were soundly beaten. The M.C.C. made 100 in its first innings. But the aboriginals, even with the help of Wills, could make only 39 in the first innings and 87 in the second. Johnny Mullagh was the aboriginal star. He made 16 and 39.

The *Argus* said the spectators showed their sympathy for the blackfellows by cheering everything they did, but the occasion obviously was overwhelming for them. It was the first time they had appeared before such a crowd.

The *Herald* wrote: "That they have been made thoroughly acquainted with the various points of the game was made manifestly evident by the manner in which they conducted themselves in the field. Mullagh and Bullocky showed themselves to be no mean batsmen. They not only stopped balls but hit them, showing good discretion and strong defence. The fielding was very fair."

After the match there was a sports meeting. Johnny Mullagh threw a cricket ball 111 yards. Then he jumped 5 ft. 4 in., an incredible leap for 1866 and it remained a record for many years. Tarpot won the 100 yards by a clear 20 yards. . . running backwards. His time was 14 seconds, and undoubtedly this stands as a running backwards record for all time at the M.C.G..

The team went on tour throughout Australia, then with some changes it went to England. Charles Lawrence, the Sydney professional, was captain and W. T. Hayman the manager. The first Australian team to tour England was a black side, and it helped to foster the idea in London that all people from the colonies were the same colour.

It was a remarkable piece of enterprise that the team went at all. Johnnie Moyes in his book "Australian Cricket" makes this comment: "One cannot but be fascinated by the thought of these men, many of whom lived in humpies on local properties near Lake Wallace, taking the field at Lord's, the first Australians to do so. I often wonder how they felt when playing against a team which included the Earl of Coventry, Viscount Downe and Lieut.-Colonel Bathurst, who incidentally fell twice without scoring, each time to Cuzens. Johnny Mullagh in that Lord's match scored 75. His record for the tour was 1670 runs and 245 wickets.

After each match Johnny Mullagh gave an exhibition of boomerang throwing, and a cricket historian records this story: "One day a gust of wind deflected the boomerang and it struck a gentleman on the head, severely injuring him. When he had sufficiently recovered he remarked that although he had expected to see something out of the common he was not prepared for such a striking performance."

Dick-a-Dick used to hold his shield and challenge the Englishmen to hurl cricket balls at him from a distance of 12 feet. He was so good with that shield never once was he hit.

Sadly the tour resulted in a loss of £2000. Maybe it is a cynical comment, but if only the tour had made money then there would have been many more aboriginal tours. And so the white man would have taken more interest in the aboriginals as sportsmen.

On the banks of Lake Wallace at Edenhope, Victoria, there is a monument with this plaque:

IN THIS VICINITY

THE ABORIGINAL CRICKET TEAM
FIRST AUSTRALIAN CRICKET TEAM TO TOUR ENGLAND
Trained Prior to Its Departure in 1868
Matches Won, 14
Matches Lost, 10
Matches Drawn, 19.

On November 30, 1870, there was another historic first for the M.C.G.— the first combined public schools' sports. Three schools took part—Wesley College, Scotch College and Melbourne Church of England Grammar School. This was an excellent idea, according to the *Argus*. After all, for years now, the schools had been putting on public demonstrations at their own grounds of the advances they had been making in physical education; why not do it together?

Their advances in physical education covered quite a range. On the programme there was running, vaulting, jumping, hurdle racing, bicycle races, leaping, throwing the hammer and kicking the football. The newspapers said it was an excellent afternoon, but what a pity the schools did not have the foresight to provide a band. Spectators at the M.C.G. always looked forward to the music provided by a quality band, and there's no doubt that it would have added to the pleasure of His Excellency Viscount Canterbury.

Melbourne Grammar took the first combined sports title with 11 wins, Scotch was second with 10, and Wesley scored six. The newspapers did not record any times, but they did give these results. T. Riddell (M.G.S.) won the football kicking with 185 ft. 8 in., J. F. Hamilton (M.G.S.) won the long jump with 17 ft. 1 in., and W. Wearne (Wesley) won the running high jump with 4 ft. 9 in. Wearne also won the cricket ball throwing with 287 ft. 6 in.

Naturally there was an Old Scholars' Cup. The old boys competed for this over three events, the 100 yards, 440 and 880, all in the one afternoon. Mr. Daniel, a Wesley old boy, won the cup.

He must have had more stamina than some of the old scholars who came 90 years later.

CHAPTER SIX

The Year of Grace

D URING the eighteen-sixties cricket lost its optimism and sparkle. The M.C.C. was in debt and no English side came to Australia for nine years. There were those who said cricket was on the way out, a dying sport which held no interest for the public. But the enthusiast who studies the records will find an interesting cycle here. Every decade has its Jonahs who forecast the early death of cricket. We had them in 1842 and we had them in 1960. Yet, remarkably, the dear old game managed to survive.

The dear old game was surviving splendidly in 1871. The dream of all cricketers was to bring out a team, led by the greatest of all players, Dr. W. G. Grace. The M.C.C. wrote to London, and Dr. Grace replied that his personal fee would be £1500, exclusive of all expenses. This was overwhelming. No such fee had ever been paid to a cricketer. Even more startling to the M.C.C. committee, Dr. Grace was a member of the Marylebone Cricket Club, and the finest of amateurs. Would not an amateur take rather less than a professional?

So the M.C.C. postponed the idea. But it would be absurd to bring out an All England XI without Dr. Grace, so in 1872 the M.C.C., the East Melbourne and the South Melbourne cricket clubs formed a committee of management, which conducted the negotiations. These were the terms: £1500 for W. G. Grace plus extras, and £170 for each of the professionals plus expenses.

Dr. Grace wrote to say that he had succeeded in getting together a very strong side, and if they lost a single match against any 22 side, then all he could say was that "Your cricket must be a good deal stronger than we play in England."

He was in for a surprise. Cricket in Australia had come a long way since George Parr's visit nine years before.

There were great improvements at the M.C.G. in preparation for the match on Boxing Day, 1873. There was a new sloping embankment in the outer "where patrons, even though sitting, could gain an uninterrupted view over those in front." There were seats all around the ground and the trees provided by Baron Von Mueller were giving excellent shade. There was a new grandstand built by Messrs. Halstead, Kerr and Co. The underneath included a great public dining room, bars, oyster stalls and fruit stall, plus one special innovation—an electric telegraph room. Now it was possible, not only to send telegrams to neighbouring colonies, but also one could send telegrams to England. Londoners could read in *The Times* of the exploits of the All England XI the morning after the event.

The promoters were very optimistic. To prevent crowding there were 10 ticket boxes around the ground. Then for the convenience of spectators the names of the batsmen were put up in two places, and the order went out that the Governor's carriage and the drag for the cricketers would be the only vehicles allowed inside the Richmond Paddock gates opposite the Parade Hotel. Yet best of all, workmen were making a bitumen road in Wellington Parade. Melbourne *Punch* commented that normally bullock teams had to stand by to pull the carriages out of the mud in Wellington Parade, so this was one small benefit that was being bestowed upon us by Dr. Grace's visit.

Boxing Day, 1873, was a sunny, cloudless day with, according to the *Argus*, "an atmosphere of the purest transparency." Even at the last minute there was no captain for the Victorian XVIII. There was bitter feeling between the club elevens, and Melbourne was in two camps . . . one for Conway, captain of South Melbourne, the other for Robertson of the M.C.C. Conway was the best cricketer, but there were those who said he had been involved in some unfortunate incidents on the field.

So the cricket match had to wait while the Victorian XVIII held an election. The *Argus* said the team went into committee like a solemn conclave of cardinals. One almost expected a puff of smoke to rise from the pavilion with the announcement that they had found a Pope. Eventually they elected Robertson, 12 votes to 6.

Robertson won the toss and Victoria batted. From the start the Victorians "collared" the bowling. B. B. Cooper scored 84, Conway 32 and the total was 266. The *Argus* said the Victorians did so well, stories were afoot that Dr. Grace was making use of the new telegraph to advise his friends in London to lay off some of their bets.

The batting line-up of 18 Victorians was impressive enough, but when all of them took the field it was frightening. Look what happened when Frank Allan came on to bowl. He was a six-footer, a fast left-hander, and the most effective bowler in the colonies. There were so many fieldsmen grouped behind the wicket, including six slips and assorted long stops, it was impossible to see how any ball could get past. Yet even with this regiment Robertson on one occasion had the courage to ask if he could field a substitute. Dr. Grace

Victoria, at last! The first victory over New South Wales in 1858.

The Victorian Intercolonial team of 1860.

Standing Left to Right: G.MARSHALL. T.MORRES. W.J.HAMMERSLEY. A.BURCHETT. J.RHODES (Umpire).
B.GRINDROD. G.ELLIOTT. J.THORNTON. J.BRYANT. T.WRAY.
Seated: T.WILLS. J.B.THOMPSON (12ᵗʰ Man). W.FAIRFAX (Scorer). E.WHITLOW.

The arrival of Mr Stephenson's team, 21 November 1861.

refused. The combination of Harry Boyle, Frank Allan and Sam Cosstick dismissed the English XI for 110 and again for 132, to win by an innings and 26 runs. On both occasions the Doctor was the man to see. In 1873 he was only 25, but his reputation was huge. It was still possible to discern a face behind his beard, his middle had not begun to thicken, and he was very athletic. He was a little crusty perhaps, and some of the country clubs noted that he was not over-anxious to attend their functions.

Said the *Australasian* of his second innings: "As a judge of a run and for speed between the wickets he is unequalled in the world. He makes safe runs where we would not dream of even stealing them. The ease and power with which the leviathan played the bowling, the shooters and bumpers, met equally coolly, not hitting the ball over the moon, but making runs simply and rapidly without apparent effort, showing, when opportunity offered, brilliant cutting and driving, defence impregnable—all this was as near perfection as it is possible to be."

He must have been a crowd pleaser, for he performed one little trick, which has been a beloved cliche with cricketers ever since. He played a ball from Allan hard down and he was caught close to the wicket. "The crowd was frantic with 20,000 hurrahs and the great man walked out very downcast." But then, of course, he walked back. The ball had hit the ground. It was a good match for Dr. Grace. He scored well in both innings and he took 10 wickets for 58.

However it was far from being a happy tour. It was poorly organised, and to make matters worse this was the first Australian tour which included both amateurs and professionals. The friction was obvious. And there was the Press. The colonial press was highly competitive, and in the eighteen-seventies, as vocal as a barracker shouting over the fence. The Sydney correspondent of the *Australasian* after one match described Dr. Grace as a "bumptious and overbearing captain."

Yet it was accusations about the quality of the cricket that rankled with Dr. Grace. After the first match many of the journals accused him of bringing out a weak team, far inferior to the sides led by Stephenson and Parr. The *Australasian* cricket writer said at least four of the XI should have been left at home, and asked: "After W. G. Grace who is there?" One could have answered that there was the very gifted G. F. Grace, W.G.'s 23-year-old brother and the third of the three Graces. But the *Australasian* man did not like him either. "He has a cramped, ugly style and he hits across the ball."

W.G. replied that the colonial cricket writers knew little about their task, and he said that he would like to see a Victorian team perform at its best in

England after 40 days at sea. The *Australasian's* reply to this was that the All England XI had a fortnight to practise before the first match. Admittedly the cricketers did undergo some heavy hospitality, hardly suited to athletes engaged in a game of skill, yet these cries of being out of form came curiously after the match. Nobody heard them before.

There was the match at the M.C.G., then the Grace XI went on a country tour that must have been appallingly rugged. They played 22-man sides at Ballarat, Stawell and Warrnambool, yet some of the familiar faces like Allan, Cosstick and Wills kept appearing for every contest. At Ballarat England made 470—W. G. Grace 126, G. F. Grace 112. The heat was shocking. Sam Cosstick complained that at one stage there seemed to be a whole vast family of Graces. Frank Allan suffered from sunstroke and the team put his head under a tap. The ground was only small, and with 22 men in the field, sometimes the grabbing of the ball was like a football scrum. The local cricket writer summed it up: "The sun shone infernally, the eleven scored tremendously, we fielded abominably and all drank excessively."

From Ballarat to Stawell they had a harrowing 12-hour journey across a 72-mile bush track in a ricketty Cobb & Co. coach. Perhaps their bruised bones were soothed by the appearance, four miles out from Stawell, of two brass bands. The Stawell wicket was only three months from being a ploughed field. The local club had nurtured it, watered it daily, put hay over it to protect the grass from the burning summer sun. The story goes that Dr. Grace walked out on to the ground and asked where was the wicket? They told him, to his obvious horror: "You're standing on it."

Every reporter complained of the wicket. Some said that the Stawell club would have done better to have supplied a strip of bitumen, or even concrete, which had been used most successfully for cricket matches in America. In the first innings the Grace XI was all out for 43 and the Stawell XXII won by 10 wickets. This was unbelievable; the might of England beaten by a country town.

The *Australasian* commented that many were saying the match was squared. This was nonsense. The reasons for the defeat were bad ground and good liquor. Some of the professionals were unable to perform their tasks because of the hospitality offered to them. It was said too that Dr. Grace gave his men a warning about drinking while matches were in progress.

The All England Eleven had three defeats on the tour, but there were times when the men of Grace deserved more credit. There was a good win over a combined N.S.W.-Victorian XV at Sydney, and they had their revenge by beating a Victorian XV. Undoubtedly the event to watch was a special match at the M.C.G., Dr. Grace v. a Victorian XI in the field. This match was designed especially to show off the doctor's batting skill against a normally placed field, and on this day he must have been superb. Grace scored 100 in 58 minutes and he went on to make 126. He opened with Jupp, who made 45. Jupp did well to score his 45 in 45 minutes, but by that time Grace already was 95.

The *Argus* commented: "No other cricketer in the world could have accomplished such a feat." He hit one ball over the fence, over the crowd on to the Ladies' Reserve. "It was a very sweet hit." This earned Dr. Grace five runs. In 1874 there was no such thing as a six.

Sam Cosstick was involved in an incident with Dr. Grace. Sam already had caused a stir in the Combined XV match at Sydney. Sam claimed the wrong umpire had given him out and he refused to budge. Dr. Grace marched off the field with his team behind him and he refused to play until Sam succumbed. On this occasion the *Argus* reported: "Cosstick, apparently disgusted at being hit all over the field for the amusement of the public, deliberately shied three balls at Grace, the missiles passing near enough to the Leviathan's body to make him wince. Cosstick immediately was taken off. Whatever his grievance may have been it was unfair to take it out on the batsman. There was a short adjournment for refreshments, and it seemed as if Sam were placated at the interval, for he returned to his place as bowler and misconducted himself no more."

The newspapers even had leading articles on the third match at the M.C.G. It promised to be a beauty. Victoria had won the first, England the second. Sadly it was washed out by rain when the Grace XI had a slight advantage on the first innings.

There was one remarkable incident. The English umpire, Mr. Humphrey, feeling unwell retired, and he was replaced by a Victorian, Mr. H. Budd. According to the *Argus*, Newing drove a ball off Lillywhite with such force that it went to the chains in front of the grandstand and rebounded on to the turf. Budd signalled a four. But G. F. Grace called that he had stopped the ball. It was not a four, it was a two. The crowd began to hoot. "W. G. Grace took the part of his brother and spoke in such an insulting manner to Mr. Budd, the umpire, that he refused to remain in the field any longer and he walked off." Mr. Humphrey had to come on again. The following night, March 12, 1874, there was a farewell dinner to the English XI. This was supposed to be a glittering affair for the Englishmen, the Australians and the public. One important group failed to arrive—the English professionals. All the speeches had the same pained note of embarrassment.

The tour promoter, Mr. W. C. Biddle, said ever since the tour started that he had always been on the best of terms with Dr. Grace. It was unfortunate that the professional portion of the team was not present tonight. All he could say was that they had been invited "a little more specifically than the others." He knew of no cause for their absence and he could not account for it.

Dr. Grace said he was unable to offer any explanation either. Mr. Biddle had done everything in his power to make their stay a pleasant one. He then attacked the press for the very hard treatment they had given him throughout the tour. As for the incident the day before, he had said nothing offensive to Mr. Budd and if Mr. Budd was offended then he apologised. G. F. Grace also commented on the incident. All he could say was that in England it was the custom for an umpire to accept a gentleman's word.

The following morning there was a storm. The leading newspapers retaliated. "Does Dr. Grace expect us to lie down for him and never to utter a word of criticism." Yet the most interesting item was a letter to the *Argus* and this explained a good deal. Lillywhite, the leading English professional, had put his views. Lillywhite explained their terms for coming to Australia, how the amateurs travelled first class and the professionals second. He wrote:

> Eventually the players signed an agreement to come out and return second class, which they repented after being three or four days at sea, it being bad accommodation and bad living. Upon arriving at Melbourne that distinction which has caused so much feeling was immediately commenced—namely, the gentlemen sent to one hotel, the players to another, and so on through the whole chapter. Even when stopping at the same house, apartments were reserved for the gentlemen in every instance except Stawell, and there it was because they couldn't get them.
>
> In Melbourne and Sydney the professionals have been satisfied with their hotels; in other instances they have not. In one place they were let out like a horse and trap at 7/6 a day and in others have been neglected, and a long way from satisfied. . . . It has been stated that Mr. W. G. Grace is the cause of this wretched second class business, but, I am much deceived in the man if it is through him. Let the promoters send us home first class and the professionals will have at least one kindly recollection of them."
>
> Yours truly,
> *James Lillywhite,*
> One of the English Eleven.

The reply came from the promoter the following morning.

> ". . . a very silly letter, scarcely worthy of notice. Mr. Lillywhite has forfeited any claims he might have by his offensive and unusual manner of demanding

them. I am sure your readers must deeply sympathise with this unfortunate man in his prospects of second class passage to England by P. & O., and trust that when next he goes aboard he will be able to secure as means of transport something more suitable to his merits and deserts.

Yours truly,

W. C. Biddle."

Dear Sir,

The reason the professionals did not attend the farewell dinner was a remark heard by Humphrey. Mr. Pickersgill (not Josh) said second class was plenty good enough for us; at home we travelled third class and were glad to get a glass of beer; we could not appreciate champagne given to us by these liberal-minded men.

I can assure you that the professionals will be very glad when they have fulfilled their agreement with these stuck-up persons, and they thank the public of Melbourne for the kind treatment they have received during their stay here.

Yours truly,

Jas. Lillywhite.

We have omitted some of Mr. Lillywhite's adjectives.—Ed. *Argus.*

Some of Mr. Lillywhite's adjectives were so strong it was presumed that never would he visit Australia again. But he was back as leader of his own team within three years and he was to make three more tours of Australia.

There was no answer to James Lillywhite's final letter. The team departed for South Australia, where W.G. found some wickets and endured some coach rides even worse than those in Victoria. Yet the Year of Grace was a success. It did much to liven interest in cricket, and although the colonials had yet to realise it, now their cricket almost was on equal terms with England. No longer was there any need to put these armies of 18 and 22 men into the field.

CHAPTER SEVEN

The First of the Tests

A T the approach of the eighteen-eighties the M.C.C. was gaining a few comforts. Every member now received two ladies' tickets, and much was done to improve the ladies' reserve. As the records put it, the Ladies' Reserve "is now a place where the fair visitors can see and be seen to advantage, and when tired of watching the sterner game, can turn to the quieter attractions of croquet and flirtations." There was an old cow shed in the outer reserve. The club turned this into a skittle alley. Skittles—80 years before the arrival of indoor bowling—was all the rage in Melbourne. There were alleys up and down Bourke Street, there were alleys in the new Eastern Market, and the M.C.C. skittle alley proved very popular with the older members.

The club held a special general meeting, and rule xii was altered to read:

"That a paid Secretary be appointed to the Club. The Secretary shall be appointed by the Committee, the salary to be determined by them, such salary not to exceed £250 per anum."

So the new paid secretary, Mr. Curtis Reed, received just under £5 a week. This was rather less than the wages that had been paid to Sam Cosstick, the professional bowler. Sam used to receive almost £7 a week.

For James Lillywhite's tour of 1876-77 the club built a new grandstand for £4678. This was a stand in the true English tradition. It faced both ways and it held 2000 people. At the end of the cricket season it would be reconstructed so that the seats faced the other way. This meant that during the summer the spectators could watch the cricket in the M.C.G., then in the winter the football out in Richmond Park. In 1876 the club did not tolerate football on the sacred turf of the M.C.G. Few seriously believed then that a ground could be a sea of football mud in August and a cricket playing wicket in September.

Yet during the winter of 1877 there was a football match between the Melbourne and Carlton clubs which added £95/12/8 to the club funds, and the ground did not appear to suffer any damage. This bore out T. W. Wills' idea, when he wrote his letter to *Bell's Life* suggesting that the M.C.C. should form a football club. He wrote that it would be of vast benefit to any cricket ground to be trampled upon, and it would make the turf firm and durable. However, the club permitted just this one match. The M.C.G. still was not ready for regular football.

There were signs in the late 'seventies and the early 'eighties that cricketers were becoming more sober people. Not that Melbourne was quietening in any way, the free-spending land boom was yet to come, but there were strong moral influences at work. For example, the Sabbatarians were immensely vocal, and barely a day went by when they did not complain of some piece of wickedness that was taking place in Melbourne. They protested against the shameful running of railway trains on Sundays, and there was a deplorable case in 1874 when 1500 railways employees went on a train excursion to Mt. Macedon, where drinks were sold. Their toughest fight was over the opening of the National Gallery on Sunday. This was not as harmless as you might think, for in 1883 Chloe, now in Young & Jackson's saloon bar, the nude painting by Lefèbvre of Paris, was put on display. The Sabbatarians were horrified.

There was a debate in the *Argus*. The artists McCubbin and Longstaff nobly defended Chloe, but a father replied: "Would any of the gentlemen trustees permit a nude picture of their daughter or sister to be hung there, and, if not, why anyone else's daughter?" Said a mother: "Can it be right that a mother cannot take her young daughter to a public gallery, never to speak of her sons, without feeling her cheeks tingling with shame?"

Anyway the Melbourne Cricket Club was doing its bit. The committee decided that champagne lunches, which always had been inseparable from intercolonial matches, in future would be plain but substantial. Beer would replace champagne, but at the finish of play there would be a grand dinner for the players. The players, oddly enough, did not complain, and there was no deterioration in the standard of play as a result of the switch from champagne to beer. But one wonders whether James Lillywhite was saddened by all this. He returned with his All England team of professionals at the end of 1876. He had shown in his letters to the *Argus* that he was not above an interest in champagne.

From the start Lillywhite's team was struggling. It was beaten by a Victorian Fifteen once and by N.S.W. teams twice. Melbourne *Punch* became so cocky that it described the likely tour of England ten years hence when an Australia XI would be asked to compete against an All England XV. In a third England v. N.S.W. match England thrashed the New South Welshmen, and there could have been a victory by an innings only for lack of time. The

43

Australian spirits were a trifle deflated, yet the Victorian Cricketers' Association decided that the two colonies at last were ready for a match on even terms—a combined N.S.W.-Victoria XI against the All England XI. This came to be recognised as the first Test match. It started on March 15, 1877.

The Melbourne Cricket Ground was the choice for the match, and as an intercolonial compromise it was agreed that the XI would include six from N.S.W. and five from Victoria. The troubles began at once. Evans, the great Sydney bowler, could not play because of "pressure of business." So the Sydney six became Bannerman, Spofforth, Garrett, Nat Thompson and the two Gregorys, Dave and Edward. For 100 years a Sydney team was not complete without a Gregory.

Then Spofforth announced that Murdoch was the one wicket-keeper who understood his type of bowling. Unless Murdoch were included in the XI he would not play. The *Australasian* said: "Spofforth, apparently considering his success was due to his wicket-keeper and not his own merit, and fearing he would be shorn of his lustre if another who 'knew not Joseph' were behind his sticks, declined to play unless his own special wicket-keeper was selected. As this could not be arranged, this modest gentleman had to remain behind."

Whatever happened, Victoria would not give up John Blackham. He was the first man to stand up to the wicket for fast bowling. He visited England eight times with Australian Elevens and he was acknowledged alike by English and Australian cricketers as the greatest wicket-keeper in the world.

So the great Spofforth had to go and the representation from Sydney dropped to five. Things were becoming desperate, but there was still Frank Allan of Victoria, "the bowler of the century." Allan, who worked for the Lands Department at Warrnambool, consented to play, the department gave him leave; all was well.

The match was to start on Thursday. On Tuesday he sent a telegram to advise that he was not available. This was the last straw. For the first time Australia was to meet England on even terms and the team had lost players the equivalent of say, Davidson, Miller and Lindwall. The Richmond bowler Hodges replaced Allan. "A very poor substitute," snarled the *Argus.* Indeed Hodges' elevation was astonishing. At the beginning of the season he was playing for a minor club in the Junior Collingwood group.

Allan excused himself by saying the Warrnambool Fair was taking place that week-end. Many of his friends would be in town, whom he would have no other chance to see. This not very strong excuse brought down the fury of the press. Several newspapers suggested that he should be retired at once and never again be called upon to play for his country. Said the *Argus:* "It may interest Mr. Allan to know that his withdrawal has been attributed to fear."

Melbourne *Punch* was merciless and this was one example:

1.   Once upon a time a great match was to be played. And the greatest bowler for one side hid himself in the woods. A deputation waited on him and said, "O, great bowler, bowl for our side," and the great bowler said, "I will bowl."

2.   And when the deputation had departed, the great bowler was sorry, for he said to himself, "What is the honour of bowling to me? I will not go, but will stop in the woods and play with the little boys, even Tommy, Jimmy and Billy, for I can bowl them easily." And he did so.

3.   And when the day came, and everybody was expecting the great bowler to come and bowl like winking, behold, he never came. And all that could be heard of that great bowler on that great day was a telegram and a beautiful white feather.

Meanwhile the Englishmen also had their troubles. Their wicket-keeper, Pooley, a near indispensable man in the team, had been detained in New Zealand. He was involved in an assault case that arose out of a bet. Eventually he was acquitted and his friends gave him a watch and a purse of sovereigns, but Pooley played no more with the team. Even so the English team seemed far too powerful, and the newspapers gave the colonials very little hope, so much so that only 1000 people turned out for the start.

Every day there was a change in the playing times. On the first day play did not start until 1 p.m., there was a half-hour break for lunch at 2 p.m., which spread to 40 minutes, then there was stumps at 5 p.m. As one critic put it, this was a spendthrift waste of a beautiful autumn day.

The choice for captain was between Cooper of Victoria and Dave Gregory of N.S.W. Mercifully "no silly intercolonial rivalry was to be allowed to interfere with the prudent conduct of the match," and Dave Gregory was elected.

Gregory won the toss and batted. The Australian openers were Charles Bannerman and Nat Thompson. The English bowlers were Shaw, Hill and Ulyett. Lillywhite was banking heavily on Ulyett, a hefty Yorkshire man, who was considered the fastest bowler in England. His short-pitched balls rose viciously and all the batsmen took a battering round the body.

There were no eight-ball or even six-ball overs; the four-ball over was the thing, and even at that the umpires found it difficult to keep track. One umpire, Mr. Terry, made repeated mistakes. He gave Shaw a five-ball over, but then it could be argued he was merely making up for his error when later he gave him only three balls in an over.

45

Nat Thompson was out bowled Hill for 1, but Charles Bannerman stayed firm. The good news spread as it did many years later in the Bradman era; the crowds began to flock to the M.C.G.

The numbers grew from 1000 to 4000. Bannerman hit two fours off Shaw in one over, and at times he was scoring off almost every ball. Batsmen came and went, yet Bannerman remained and by stumps he was 126 not out in a total of 6 for 166. At last Melbourne began to realise that the combined eleven had a chance, and the next day 12,000 people were waiting at the M.C.G. to see Bannerman continue his innings.

It seemed certain that he would bat right through when at 165 a rising ball from Ulyett hit him on the hand, split a finger and he was unable to continue. But for this injury he could have been the first cricketer to make 200 in a Test match. Even so he scored 165 out of Australia's total of 245, an extraordinary achievement when you consider that no other Australian made more than 20 in either innings.

The *Argus* was so excited that it asked for a Charles Bannerman subscription even before the match was over. "We should not grudge him a jot of the honours won even if he did come from Sydney." James Lilly white said he had seen as good a display of batting in England but never better. Even W. G. Grace himself could not have batted with more resolution.

At this distance it is not easy to judge the quality of Bannerman's batting on that day. Stanley Brogden in his book "The First Test" wrote: "It is doubtful whether there was ever a finer innings in Test cricket, for Bannerman was batting without great traditions behind him, and without Test experience, which counts so much with modern Test batsmen."

England replied with 196, which included 63 by Jupp. Billy Midwinter, a big-hitting all-rounder, took 5 wickets for 78. Midwinter was to make a name for himself as the only man ever to play Test cricket for Australia against England, then for England against Australia. He toured England with the 1878 team and he returned to Australia in 1881 as a member of the visiting English side, a name to be remembered ever since for cricket quiz programmes.

Australia's second innings was a disaster. Bannerman tried to bat with his hand in bandages, but he could not stand up to Ulyett and he was clean-bowled for 4. Lillywhite's men were no world beaters as batsmen, but the speed trio of Shaw, Hill and Ulyett was formidable, and they went through the Australian side for 104 runs. England needed only 155 to win and it seemed all over. The crowd certainly thought so for there was a miserable attendance of 3000 for the final day. Yet this was one of those days when a bowler was born for the occasion. Tom Kendall, a left-hander, bowled practically unchanged throughout the innings. His was the bowling performance of the match. He took 7 for 55. Never again did he bowl so well, and but for this First Test he would be completely forgotten. He was not chosen to tour England in 1878. But on this day, to the astonishment of all, he routed the Englishmen for 108 and the combined side won by 45 runs outright. Kendall was clapped and cheered off the ground.

The joy throughout the two colonies was overwhelming. The *Australasian* was careful. While they were overjoyed at the victory, perhaps it would be a good idea not to "blow" too much at this stage. But the *Daily News* in Sydney saw it as epoch-making:

> Up to this year England had at least led the world in cricket. An American or Australian Twenty-two might play an English Eleven with a fair chance of not being defeated, but to be defeated in a cricket contest man to man by the natives of an island comparatively lately discovered is too much, and yet a well-known bust in the headquarters of the game is not reported to have shed tears, nor has any other omen been observed at Lord's or The Oval. For all that the sceptre has passed away so to speak, the flag is struck. It may console them to note that the English race is not degenerating and that in the distant land and on turf where lately the blackfellow hurled his boomerang, a generation has arisen which can play the best bowlers of the time.

Melbourne *Punch* was so thrilled that it put the story of the match into verse. These were the final stanzas:

> There came a tale to England,
> 'Twas of a contest done:
> Australian youths in cricket fields
> Had met the cracks and won;
> They fell like sheaves in autumn,
> Despite the old-world dodges.
> Their efforts vain the runs to gain
> Off Kendall or off Hodges;
> Then rose a shout Australian
> That echoed to the main,
> 'Twas confident, not "blowing,"
> "Again we'll do the same!"

Moral. Presented to Messrs. Allan, Evans and Spofforth with the compliments of the cricketing world:

When bowling cracks of little mind
Prove beggars upon horses,
Australia is compelled to find
Fresh strength and new resources.

For Allan, Evans, Spofforth
She does not care a snuff,
Since Kendall, Mid., and Hodges prove
Themselves quite good enough.

So patriotic A., E., S.,
Next time, 'tis we will strike;
Henceforth go play with babes,
For like should mate with like.

AUSTRALIA

First Innings

C. Bannerman, retired hurt	165
N. Thompson, b. Hill	1
T. Horan, c. Hill, b. Shaw	12
D. W. Gregory, run out	1
B. B. Cooper, b. Southerton	15
W. E. Midwinter, c. Ulyett, b. Southerton	5
E. J. Gregory, c. Greenwood, b. Lillywhite	0
J. M. Blackham, b. Southerton	17
T. W. Garrett, not out	18
T. Kendall, c. Southerton, b. Shaw	3
J. Hodges, b. Shaw	0
Sundries	8
Total	245

Fall of Wickets: 2, 40, 41, 118, 142, 143, 197, 242, 245.

Second Innings

C. Bannerman, b. Ulyett	4
N. Thompson, c. Emmett, b. Shaw	7
T. Horan, c. Selby, b. Ulyett	20
D. W. Gregory, b. Shaw	3
B. B. Cooper, b. Shaw	3
W. E. Midwinter, c. Southerton, b. Ulyett	17
E. J. Gregory, c. Emmett, b. Ulyett	11
J. M. Blackham, l.b.w., b. Shaw	6
T. W. Garrett, c. Emmett, b. Shaw	0
T. Kendall, not out	17
J. Hodges, b. Lillywhite	8
Sundries	8
Total	104

Fall of Wickets: 7, 27, 31, 31, 35, 58, 71, 75, 104.

Bowling

	O.	M.	R.	W.
Armitage	3	—	15	—
Hill	23	10	42	1
Lillywhite	14	5	19	1
Shaw	55.3	34	51	3
Emmett	12	7	13	—
Southerton	37	17	61	3
Ulyett	25	12	36	—

	O.	M.	R.	W.
Hill	14	6	18	—
Lillywhite	1	—	1	1
Ulyett	19	7	39	4
Shaw	34	16	38	5

ENGLAND

First Innings		Second Innings	
H. Jupp, l.b.w., b. Garrett	63	H. Jupp, l.b.w., b. Midwinter	4
J. Selby, c. Cooper, b. Hodges	7	J. Selby, c. Horan, b. Hodges	38
H. Charlwood, c. Blackham, b. Midwinter	36	H. Charlwood, b. Kendall	13
G. Ulyett, l.b.w., b. Thompson	10	G. Ulyett, b. Kendall	24
A. Greenwood, c. E. Gregory, b. Midwinter	1	A. Greenwood, c. Midwinter, b. Kendall	5
T.Armitage, c. Blackham, b. Midwinter	9	T. Armitage, c. Blackham, b. Kendall	3
A. Shaw, b. Midwinter	10	A. Shaw, std. Blackham, b. Kendall	2
T. Emmett, b. Midwinter	8	T. Emmett, b. Kendall	9
A. Hill, not out	35	A. Hill, c. Thompson, b. Kendall	0
J. Lillywhite, c. & b. Kendall	10	J. Lillywhite, b. Hodges	4
J. Southerton, c. Cooper, b. Garrett	6	J. Southerton, not out	1
Sundries	1	Sundries	5
Total	196	Total	108

Fall of Wickets: 23, 79, 98, 109, 121, 135, 145, 145, 168, 198.

Fall of Wickets: 0, 7, 20, 22, 62, 68, 92, 93, 100, 108.

Bowling

	O.	M.	R.	W.		O.	M.	R.	W.
Hodges	9	—	27	1	Hodges	7	5	7	2
Garrett	18.1	10	22	2	Garrett	2	—	9	—
Kendall	38	16	54	1	Kendall	33.1	12	55	7
Midwinter	54	23	78	5	Midwinter	19	7	23	1
Thompson	17	10	14	1	D. Gregory	5	1	9	—

The Victorian Cricket Association also was thrilled. Every man received a gold medal. Dave Gregory's medal, of course, for the purpose of sound discipline was a trifle larger than the others. The subscription for Bannerman brought £87/7/6 and another for Blackham and Kendall £23/5/-.

A fortnight later there was a return match on the Melbourne Cricket Ground. Oddly enough, neither Sydney nor Adelaide was even considered. Melbourne was Australia's biggest city, so it was the logical place for the big match. Cooper, Horan and E. Gregory were dropped. Kelly, Spofforth and Murdoch came in. However, Spofforth, "the modest gentleman with the personal wicket-keeper," had not triumphed. Murdoch won his place as a batsman.

Charles Bannerman could not repeat his performance of the First Test. He made 19 in the first innings and 30 in the second. Australia's total was 122 and England scored 261, a lead of 139 on the first innings. In the second innings Gregory's men made a game fight back with 259, including 43 not out by the captain himself. But it was not enough. Ulyett, the Yorkshire fast bowler, made 63 not out, and England won by four wickets.

The score was even, and while the colonial press offered its congratulations, this time the comments were rather more restrained. Melbourne *Punch* did not record the occasion in verse.

CHAPTER EIGHT

The Roaring 'Eighties

IF one had to choose a time other than the present for living in Melbourne, then surely the choice would be the eighteen-eighties. This was a time of booming expansion, when all was optimism and money seemed hardly important.

The first cable tram ran to Richmond in 1887, the hydraulic lift was invented, and, glory be, buildings were going up to six and seven stories high. The greatest building of all was the Exhibition Building, an incredible structure, 50 years ahead of its time. It covered nine acres. On October 1, 1880, the opening day of the great International Exhibition, the ships of five navies fired their salute from out in the Bay. There was a procession through the city and a choir of a thousand voices sung a specially composed cantata. In 1888 there was the Centennial Exhibition, which has made all Australian exhibitions since look like garden fetes. For this exhibition the buildings, permanent and temporary, covered 39 acres, and the exhibit that everybody had to see was Mr. Edison's phonograph.

But Melbourne at this time had enthusiasm and zip. It had a reputation for fine music halls, a gas-lit gaiety; every visitor expressed astonishment that such a go-ahead city could exist at the antipodes. The reputation for stolidity did not come until the 'nineties.

The first telephone exchange, the property of the Melbourne Telephone Exchange Company, opened in June 1880. This was progress, because Alexander Graham Bell did not invent the telephone until 1876. The first telephone directory consisted of 23 names, which included Messrs. Sands & McDougall, James McEwan & Co., the *Daily Telegraph*, the *Argus*, the *Age*, Howard Smith & Sons, Messrs. Swallow & Ariell and John Danks, Esq. The Victoria Racing Club had the telephone on from the office to Flemington Racecourse and to Mr. R. C. Bagot's house at Ascot Vale. Seeing that Mr. Bagot was both secretary of the V.R.C. and a life member of the M.C.C., undoubtedly he reported on the value of this instrument, and the Melbourne Cricket Club bought an Edison-Bell telephone in 1881.

The M.C.C. was interested in all the new inventions. In August 1879 there was an experiment with electricity—the first night football match. It is true that some city buildings were lit for the Duke of Edinburgh's visit in 1867. Yet little progress was made with the invention, and almost certainly the night football at the M.C.G. was Melbourne's first commercial use of electricity. There were two matches. The first drew a crowd of 12,000, and although it was a great financial success the footballers were little more than shadowy ghosts in the blackness. The promoters promised to borrow a light of 7000 candle-power from the Gipps Land Railway Workshops. This, they said, would increase the illumination by 50 per cent. So the match for August 12, between Melbourne and Carlton, was heavily advertised. The game was due to start at 7.30 p.m., but the electricians had their problems. It was not a mere matter of throwing a switch. First they had to stoke the steam engine until it had sufficient power to drive the generators. The crowd shivered for an hour until "the stream of electric light came on at 8.30 p.m." Yet the light was a disappointment. It was difficult for the spectators to see the players, and there was even some doubt as to whether the players could see each other.

The *Australasian* said: "Sixteen each of Carlton and Melbourne took the field and a motley crew they were, scarcely two of a side being similarly attired." The players used a white ball, which was very attractive, but after only five minutes it blew up. This was something nobody had predicted, so they had to continue with an ordinary tan-coloured ball. This made play difficult, and only when the ball passed through the banks of light could they see it. After 20 minutes Carlton scored a goal, and much to the relief of everyone the promoters produced another white ball.

The Carlton men adapted themselves with rare skill to the dark. They scored two more goals and had an easy win. Summing it all up, the *Australasian* said there were three things wrong with this entertainment. For one thing it was the wrong time of the year. Watching football at the M.C.G. on an August night was a chilling, uncomfortable experience. For another thing, the foot-ballers would need brighter uniforms, and for a third, somehow, some way, there would have to be a vast improvement in the lighting arrangements.

"In any case, all things considered, I am inclined to think the game under such circumstances will always partake more of the nature of a show than a trial of skill."

The Carlton and Melbourne clubs were over 100 years ahead of their time. Night football was not played on the M.C.G. again until April, 1985, although in recent years there have been the regular night premierships at the South Melbourne ground.

But in the 'eighties there was a love for doing things in the grand style. Take

The "Old" Pavilion: completed in 1861 for the arrival of Mr Stephenson's XI.

The first international cricket match: Mr Stephenson's XI v. the Victorian XVIII.

J. McCarthy Blackham "The Prince of
wicketkeepers". He played 35 Tests
against England.

F. R. Spofforth, the first of the demon
pacemen.

December 7, 1882. Murdoch's team had just returned from its triumphant tour, which included the famous match at The Oval, where Spofforth took 14 wickets for 90 runs, which caused the *Sporting Times* to publish its obituary notice to English cricket:

> In affectionate remembrance of English Cricket, which died at The Oval on 29th August, 1882. Deeply lamented by a large circle of sorrowing friends and acquaintances. R.I.P. The body will be cremated and the ashes taken to Australia.

A team that had received such a tribute deserved a proper homecoming. The first part of the programme was a torchlight procession composed of 700 firemen from Melbourne's fire brigades. They assembled at the Burke and Wills monument in Spring Street at 7.30 p.m. Then at 8 o'clock they lit their flambeaux and the march started. The Australian Eleven and some members of the Victorian Cricketers' Association occupied two drags in the middle. There were crowds all along the footpaths, the upstairs windows of the houses were filled, and there were even people on the roofs.

There were bands. There was the band from H.M.V.S. *Cerberus*, the strength of the Victorian Navy; there were the bands of the Emerald Hill, Sandridge and West Melbourne Brigades, and the band of the Fitzroy Lifeboat Crew. The procession moved down Collins Street to Elizabeth Street, up to Bourke Street, then back to Spring Street, and so it proceeded down to the Melbourne Cricket Ground. "Peace hath her victories no less than war," said the *Australasian*, "and the view from Jolimont, the procession with glittering points of light, as it wound its way from Spring Street down the steep descent was especially imposing."

At the Melbourne Cricket Ground all was ready. The Electric Light Company kindly gave a special display of electric light, all provided by an eight horse-power engine. Mr. Tillett, the fireworks expert, was there with some marvellous equipment. When Richie Benaud's team returned triumphant from England in 1961 there was merely a gentlemanly reception at the Town Hall, but at 9 p.m. on December 7, 1882, Murdoch's men drove into the M.C.G. The volunteer bands struck up *See the Conquering Hero Comes,* and Mr. Tillett lit a device which crackled out WELCOME HOME in huge luminous letters.

The players made their grand tour of the M.C.G., then they stopped in front of the main grandstand. Here Mr. E. S. Watson of the Victorian Cricketers' Association presented each man with a gold medal. This medal was the size of a five shilling piece. It had the words Victorian Cricketers' Association and the Victorian coat of arms on one side and on the other was the formal inscription, for example:

> Presented to Mr. F. R. Spofforth,
> In commemoration of the brilliant
> performances of the Australian team
> in England, 1882.

The crowd cheered after each presentation, then came the fireworks display. There were rockets, catherine wheels, stars, and "the heavens were laced with streams of gauzy fire." There was one device that displayed SUCCESS TO CRICKET and another which wound up the show, GOOD NIGHT. The entertainment finished just after 10 p.m.

While Melbourne was putting up buildings at a rate which was not repeated for 70 years, the Melbourne Cricket Club also was enjoying the boom. In 1880 there were 908 members, and the club was gathering new members at such a speed the committee decided to place a limit. At a special general meeting the members passed a new rule that membership should not exceed 1500. Obviously it was time to build a new grandstand.

During 1881 Prince Edward and Prince George of Wales were visiting Australia on H.M.S. *Bacchante*. Would it be possible for them to lay the foundation stone? So at very short notice the offer was made and generously accepted. When this pavilion was pulled down in 1927 to make way for the present members' stand the stone was given the place of honour it now occupies in the club's main hall.

The club made Prince Edward and Prince George honorary members. Indeed, the Rear Admiral and all the officers of the squadron in the Bay were made honorary members and the crews were admitted free to the ground on all occasions.

Prince George visited Australia again in 1901 to open the first Federal Parliament. Afterwards he became His Majesty King George V. His brother, Prince Edward, became the Duke of Clarence.

The Princes later published a book titled *The Cruise of Her Majesty's Ship "Bacchante," 1879-1882*. Under the date July 4, 1881, they wrote:

> In the afternoon we went to lay the foundation stone of the new pavilion in the Melbourne Cricket Ground. The Hon. (now Sir) W. J. Clarke, president of the Club, and many members were there. We find that the bats and balls are not made in Victoria, although there is a heavy duty of course on the import of these foreign articles from England.

After laying the stone Eddy called for three cheers for the club, of which we both today became honorary members, and carried away two silver trowels in memory of the occasion. We saw a sketch and plan of the building as it is to be when completed by December 1st: it will cost nearly £5000.

By the end of 1881 the new two-story pavilion, designed by William Salway, was ready for use. According to title records of the day, "on the ground floor there was a refreshment room large enough to accommodate 150 in comfort. There was a secretary's office. There was a refreshment bar complete with liquor and oyster counters. There was a billiard room brilliantly lit, with two tables, whilst on the second floor there were reading rooms and visitors' dressing rooms. There was also a veranda and a balcony which could accommodate 350 people, and, seeing that the roof was flat and galleried, here was standing room for another 200, and this position commanded a magnificent view of the suburbs and surrounding country. Speaking tubes were connected throughout. The exterior of the building was composed of dark brick and the woodwork was beautifully varnished. It was considered the finest cricket pavilion in the world."

Yes, the club was greatly impressed with its progress. The skittle alley now had padded seats and it could "bear comparison with any skittle alley in the country." Early in 1881 the club put in sight boards. They were small by present standards, 6 ft. by 12 ft., but it was felt that this innovation would help the batsmen to see the bowler's arm and the ball more distinctly.

For a Test match the following year the club built a two-story wooden building for the scorers, press and telegraph operators. The building had everything that was modern. The walls were padded to keep out the heat, and there were speaking tubes from the press up above to the scorers and telegraph operators below. Pressmen could send telegrams without moving from their seats. "This was a convenience greatly appreciated by the gentlemen of the press."

Yet one could say, quite accurately, that this period was not all beer and skittles for the M.C.C. At 9 o'clock on Sunday morning, August 31, 1884, Mr. McAlpine, the club curator, made his inspection and nothing was amiss. At 9.15 one of his children came running. He could see smoke and fire coming from the double-sided grandstand, the stand that was built for watching cricket on the M.C.G. and football out in the Richmond Paddock. Mr. McAlpine turned on a hose, but there was no chance. In 20 minutes the stand was blazing from top to bottom.

The look-out man in the tower at Eastern Hill saw the fire as soon as it was reported. In the eighteen-eighties there was no such luxury as a State fire brigade. The insurance companies sponsored the Assurance Brigade, which was the most efficient, then there were all types of company and local brigades. The Assurance Brigade did not acquire a proper steam fire engine until 1886. Yet the Assurance men were first to arrive at the M.C.G., followed by the Fitzroy Temperance Brigade, the Richmond, East Melbourne, Collingwood, Simpson's Road brigades, the Carlton Brewery, Prahran Yorkshire Brewery, Windsor and Shamrock Brewery Brigades. "Very soon," said the *Argus*, "there was a large crowd of people, the majority in negligent Sunday morning attire, gathered on the football ground outside."

The water pressure was miserable, and the vast collection of firemen stood by virtually idle while the stand burnt to the ground.

"From a purely architectural point of view," said the *Argus*, "it was not a very elegant building, but its plainness was more than counterbalanced by its usefulness."

Nobody ever discovered the cause of the fire. The popular theory was that it started in the skittle alley. The alley was closed from 6.30 p.m. on Saturday, but there was a thick layer of sawdust on the floor. Perhaps some one dropped a cigar stump and there it smouldered with the sawdust slowly burning until it lit one of the walls.

The *Herald* on Monday afternoon had a thundering leader. It castigated the useless crowds that gather at fires, trample on the hoses and interfere with the work of the firemen. "Why should anyone turn out of a comfortable bed or leave a house merely to witness the destruction of property, when he knows that he can't be of the slightest assistance we have never been able to understand. The presence of women too at these fires is like the gladiatorial shows of Rome or the bullfights."

Nor was the *Herald* pleased about the lack of water pressure in winter and of all times on a Sunday morning. "The gallant colonel, unattached, who now controls the Water Supply Department will have to satisfy the public with something more than the customary stereotyped excuse."

The stand was insured for £3000, and the Indemnity Insurance Company paid £2900 within a fortnight. The club thought this highly satisfactory, and the committee asked William Salway to design another stand, at a cost of £11,490. The new pavilion provided accommodation for 1500, plus 450 in the section for the ladies. The plans provided for cast iron columns of 11 inches in diameter at a distance of 20 feet, a vast improvement over the massive brick and cement pillars which were such a conspicuous feature of the old stand. This stand was torn down to make way for the new Northern stand built for the Olympic Games in 1956.

Yet the big feature of this period was the number of cricket tours. Cricketers were for ever packing their bags. Between 1877 and 1890 there were 15 tours, including that crazy season of 1887-88 when there were two English elevens touring Australia at the one time.

To be accurate, the touring sides were invariably twelves, which makes one think those cricketers must have been men of iron. Their tours were long and tough, including as many as five Test matches. The tours of the nineteen-sixties call for 16-man parties, and the keen newspaper reporter who wants to give his public a complete coverage, must also have a practical knowledge of medicine, so that he can give all the news of the bad knees, ailing backs and strained muscles:. But in the eighteen-eighties with only 12-man touring teams cricketers could not afford to go sick. There was one compensation, after a touring side was first put together there were rarely any selection problems.

Between 1877 and 1890 England was the stronger cricketing country. The score was 17 Test wins to England, 11 to Australia, with 4 drawn. Our first representative side went away in 1878 and Dave Gregory was captain. There were all the big names—Charles Bannerman, Frank Allan, Murdoch, Spofforth, Blackham, Midwinter and Boyle. They were received with great hospitality, yet there was curiosity in England as to what sort of people came from the Antipodes. George Bailey, the Tasmanian representative, was congratulated for the English he spoke, and he was asked if also he could speak Australian. On the other hand, G. Alexander, the Australian who made two trips to England, remarked one time: "I think it's absurd that all those historic castles should remain unroofed while corrugated iron is so cheap."

The first Australian touring side did not play a Test match, but the team had a history-making win over a Marylebone Cricket Club team which was virtually an All England Eleven. Spofforth and Boyle dismissed the M.C.C. for 34 and 19.

Those years had their moments. Lord Harris brought his XI to Australia in 1878-79, and in a match against Victoria A. N. Hornby, the great English amateur, bowled 12 maidens in succession. He specialised in a type of ball which was known as the "Sydney Grubber." It was a fast underhand delivery aimed directly at the middle stump, and at no stage did it ever leave the ground. The M.C.G. spectators became angry. First they chanted "Why don't you have a go?" and when the impossibility of scoring off Hornby became obvious they switched to "Take him off." It is surprising how little barracking has changed at the M.C.G. in 110 years. There was one Test match and Spofforth created another piece of history for the M.C.G. He bowled the first

Test hat-trick. He took 13 wickets for 110 runs, and in the first innings he dismissed Royle, McKinnon and Emmett with successive balls.

In 1882-83 the Hon. Ivo Bligh brought his team to Melbourne. The Australians loved Ivo Bligh and this was the happiest of all tours. The Australians won two Tests and the Englishmen won two Tests. Indeed it was an even match all round, for Ivo Bligh married an Australian girl. Later he was to become Lord Darnley. The amateurs of his team received nothing but their expenses and the professionals took £200 each.

Ivo Bligh's men had to contend with George Bonnor. George was the greatest hitter Australia has produced. He was 6 ft. 6 in., 17 stone, and he had a flowing blond beard. There are no end of stories of his big hits in England, including one that went through the secretary's window at The Oval and another that went right over the pavilion. In 1881 George hit a ball from the Englishman Bates 150 yards over the skittle alley and 20 yards beyond into the Richmond Paddock. Gerald Brodribb in his book "Hit for Six" wrote that once Bonnor was asked for the names of the three world's best batsmen: "Well," said George with careful thought, "you can't get away from W.G., and Murdoch is not far behind. I would rather you did not ask me to name the third."

In the First Test against Bligh's Eleven George scored 85, and he hit four balls into the Ladies' Reserve. This display caused some agitation for the Ladies' Reserve to be wire-netted to prevent injury to the fair occupants. In the return match on the M.C.G. W. Bates took a hat-trick for England. He dismissed McDonnell, Giffen and Bonnor with successive balls.

At a full meeting of the members in March 1884 there was a big decision, the club decided that it should send a team to England. This was the first time the M.C.C. had tried such a venture, and it was largely on the advice of the English amateurs Lord Harris, A. S. Hornby and Hon. Ivo Bligh. They suggested that an M.C.C. team would be better received in England than a team sent over by a private promoter. It went in 1886.

Major Ben Wardill, secretary of the Melbourne Cricket Club, always a snappy figure with his moustache and black bowler, was the manager and J. H. Scott was the captain, but it was not one of our most famous tours. Out of 39 matches played only nine were won, eight were lost and 22 were drawn. Australia lost all three Test matches.

The 1887-88 season was the disastrous time of the two Australian tours. The M.C.C. had invited G. F. Vernon to bring out a team under the captaincy of Lord Hawke and Lillywhite also had arranged to bring out a team under C.-A. Smith, now better known as Sir Aubrey Smith, the actor. The two tours killed all interest and the M.C.C. lost over £3000. Lord Hawke in his reminiscences wrote: "There was never such a prominent case of folly. . . The fact was that it had nothing to do with us at home at all, and arose from the rivalry then existent between the Melbourne Club and their neighbours at Sydney. The Melbourne Club had endeavoured to collect a side from the mother country in the previous winter, therefore it had merely been postponed, whereas the Sydney authorities asserted that for all they knew when they wanted an English eleven to take part in the celebration in New South Wales, the Melbourne project had been abandoned."

Lord Hawke was referring to the centenary celebrations of the first settlement in Australia. Sydney celebrated with a cricket tour. Melbourne celebrated with the huge Centennial Exhibition and imported the full London Philharmonic Orchestra. Lord Hawke was not here for long. His father died and he had to return to England, but like James Lillywhite he ran into the old amateur-professional problem. The newspapermen noticed that the amateurs and the professionals were not staying in the same hotels and, as Lord Hawke said, they threatened to take it up as a grievance. Lord Hawke wrote: "It is rather curious that the Australians themselves do not realise that our professionals prefer to be on their own off the field rather than to be in the same hotel as the amateurs. Indeed, I know that some of our professionals would prefer to have second-class passages on board ship rather than having to dress each night for dinner. This is not in the least diminishing the perfect accord between English amateurs and professionals. . ."

Meanwhile the Melbourne Cricket Club was keeping careful control over manners. Why, complaints were even made that gentlemen had been seen smoking in the grandstand. The committee promised that steps would be taken to stamp out this undesirable practice when ladies were present.

In 1886 Mr. Frank Grey Smith became president, and he held this post until his death in 1900. The club, perhaps, will never fully realise how lucky it was to have him at this time. He was chief manager of the National Bank, and it was his wise banking knowledge that steered the club through the financial miseries of the 'nineties when many of the trading banks closed their doors.

He had to deal with one financial crisis even before that. The Melbourne Football Club was in a sad state. The standard of play was poor and the numbers of spectators could be counted in dozens. It was obvious that unless something was done quickly the club that began Australian football would cease to exist. The M.C.C. committee examined the position, and Major Wardill reported that the club's liabilities could be met for £400. The Melbourne Football Club agreed to all the conditions imposed, and the M.C.C.

agreed to take over the liabilities and manage the club in the future. Frank Grey Smith personally guaranteed the overdraft.

But if Melbourne was failing there was nothing wrong with the other football teams. The M.C.C. let the ground for a match between South Melbourne and Carlton on August 2, 1890. The attendance was 32,595, which the club claimed as the largest crowd ever recorded in Australia or Great Britain.

It was under Frank Grey Smith's presidency also that the M.C.C. won an agreement to take over the Warehousemen's Ground in St. Kilda Road. The club rebuilt the fence, ploughed and relaid the playing surface and at the same time prepared another important comfort for the members—a licence for the sale of wines and spirits. The Warehousemen's Ground was to become the Albert Ground, one of the Melbourne Cricket Club's most important playing fields.

The roaring 'eighties came to an end with a triumph for an M.C.C. committee member. In the 1879-80 election for office Donald Wallace topped the poll for the committee. One would like to think that 10 years later, on November 4, 1890, some of his glory was shed on to the M.C.C. Mr. Wallace was the owner of Carbine. The *Age* of November 5, 1890, recorded:

> As the clerk of the course escorted him back to the weighing yard, winner of the most valuable handicap race ever run in the world (10,000 sovs.), the scene was one to be remembered. Inside the enclosure his popular owner was receiving the hearty congratulations of his friends and acknowledging the cheers of the assembled thousands.
>
> By his great triumph in the Melbourne Cup Carbine has broken more than one record in connection with that famous event. He carried 10 st. 5lb., a weight never previously borne to victory in a Melbourne Cup, and beat the best time previously recorded for that race (3 min. 28½ sec.) by a quarter of a second, whilst it is also worthy of remark that the number of starters for the Cup (39) had never been equalled in any previous year. Indeed, the more this last great run of Carbine's is considered the more phenomenal does it appear.

CHAPTER NINE

The Return of Grace

THE tide of enthusiasm in the 'eighties rose and by the 'nineties it was ebbing fast. Yet in June 1891 it wasn't all over. Sarah—the divine Sarah —Bernhardt appeared at the Princess Theatre. It is difficult to describe the size of this event, for she was the greatest actress of the age and nobody of her stature lives today. Sarah, of course, was French. Few people in Melbourne could understand her English and even fewer could understand her French, but that did not matter—just to be able to say that one had seen the great Bernhardt was enough. Mr. J. C. Williamson paid Miss Bernhardt £20,000 plus £5000 expenses for a 13 weeks tour of Sydney and Melbourne theatres. Miss Bernhardt had to pay some of the cast out of this, yet the price was staggering, and everyone wondered how Mr. Williamson managed to do it. As it happened he did rather well. At one stage seats were so sought after they were sold by auction.

On the opening night a great crowd had gathered by 5 p.m. at the Princess. Melbourne *Punch* records that men and women fainted, some had hysterics, some lost portions of their attire, children were in danger of being trampled to death, and there were such scenes as had never been witnessed at a Melbourne Theatre.

Sarah was one great figure to come to Melbourne, Dr. W. G. Grace was another. There had been no English tour since the disastrous twin tours of 1887–88, and so much money had been lost on these tours that the promoters were not anxious to try again. But that same cycle was back and the critics were claiming that Australians no longer were interested in cricket. Why, in the eighteen-nineties the young people were much interested in tennis and this dashing new sport of surfing. So the M.C.C. invited Lord Sheffield to bring a team for the season 1891–92. Dr. Grace agreed to tour as captain, his first visit after an absence of 18 years. The club did ask him to come with Vernon's team, but he wanted £2000 plus expenses. This time Dr. Grace asked for and received £3000 plus expenses for himself and his wife. It makes one wonder if the figure has ever been equalled. That kind of money would be worth a huge amount today.

The visit of W.G. was important, but Lord Sheffield's decision to bring out the team was a great honour. This man loved the game. He was cricket's greatest patron, and the Melbourne newspapers described him as the very personification of John Bull. When the Earl first arrived at the M.C.G. the band played *That Fine Old English Gentleman,* and the M.C.C. granted the ground free of charge to show how much the club had appreciated his hospitality for entertaining so many touring Australian Elevens at Sheffield Park.

Lord Sheffield's Eleven first landed at Adelaide, where the team beat South Australia by an innings and 62 runs. Then on November 25 the Englishmen arrived at Melbourne's Spencer Street Station aboard the Adelaide Express. Major Ben Wardill, J. Worrall, Harry Boyle and Dr. J. E. Barrett, all of whom had played against Grace, were members of the welcoming party. "There was a storm of cheers when the heavy bearded face of the old warrior was first seen on the platform." The Englishmen went off first to a reception at the Union Club Hotel given by the Victorian Cricketers' Association, and then to a Lord Mayoral reception, and as they went they were a sight worth seeing. The drags were decorated in the colours of Lord Sheffield and the horses were dressed in matching harness. The Doctor did not say much in his speeches. He was a doer not a talker, he said, but this was the best cricket team ever to come out of England.

With Mrs. Grace, Miss Grace and Master Grace he stayed at the Oriental Hotel, and that night Major Ben Wardill took them to see *The Gondoliers* at the Princess Theatre, where they sat in the Vice-Regal box.

When Dr. Grace arrived at the M.C.G. he struck a wistful note, so much had changed in 18 years. He said: "Where are the grapevines which climbed over the wall and the wooden pavilion, and provided the players with luscious grapes. . . and where is that famous well into which a bucket was lowered and players drank copious drafts of icy cold water after practice?"

Yes, the age of brick and iron had succeeded the age of wood, and the grape-covered wall went with the old pavilion. But then the membership 18 years before was just 400, now it was 3000.

The match England versus Victoria at the M.C.G. was a triumph for W. G. Grace. His beard was thicker, his middle was larger and he was 43. Said the *Australasian:* "Taking his years and his weight into consideration, it must be admitted that he is still a marvel." The week before, he told the newspapers that far too much time was wasted in Australian cricket. There were so many unnecessary stops for refreshments. At 4 p.m. on the first day the bell rang for the usual adjournment. Grace ignored it and shaped up for the next ball. The players started to move off the field, but Grace refused to go, and everybody was so much in awe of the man they came back and play went on. The crowd gave him a cheer—spectators do not always get their money's worth.

Grace opened for England and he batted right through the innings undefeated for 159. There were only 12 fours, and according to the newspapers he did nothing extravagant. This was a different, quieter Grace. His timing was faultless and every reporter commented on the uncanny way that he could place the ball. He would not face the bowler until all the fieldsmen had settled in their places, and it was obvious that always he was making an exact mental diagram of where each man was standing. He was still quick enough to change his mind about playing forward or back while the ball was in the air, and a pile of runs came from his favourite stroke—a late cut just clear of point's left hand. The big crowd cheered him off the field. The Englishmen won by an innings and 117 runs.

The First Test started on January 1, 1892, at the Melbourne Cricket Ground. Even at this stage the economy was cracking, and Victoria was on its way to the worst depression it has known. On a day when the *Argus* would have had a thoughtful leader on the undoubtedly splendid chances of the Australia Eleven this appeared:

> It will be appreciated by every observer of current events that the people of Melbourne have faced the disasters and difficulties of the financial depression reasonably and manfully. There has been no such blind or unreasoning fear as could be called panic. Though it has been shown over and over again that directors were careless and officers of public companies have been guilty of gross frauds and frittered away the money of shareholders in their own pleasures . . .

Punch put it more simply: "We're stony, motherless broke."

The Land Boom bubble had burst, and in the worst year, 1893, Melbourne was to see soup kitchens in the suburbs for the hungry unemployed. One of the popular songs of the day gave an insight into the situation:

> Good-bye, Melbourne Town,
> Melbourne Town, good-bye;
> I am leaving you today
> For a country far away;
> Though today I'm stony broke,
> Without a single brown,
> When I make my fortune I'll
>   come back and spend it
> In dear, old Melbourne town.

Then while Lord Sheffield's men were playing cricket during the First Test a gentleman living in Salisbury House, Nicholson Street, took a revolver and put a bullet through his head. He was an Australian representative for English brewing interests, and his friends reported that he had been in a bad mental state for three weeks over the collapse of the share market. The man who heard the shot and found the body stretched over the bed was a Mr. Isaac Isaacs. He was to become the first Australian-born Governor-General.

Despite the financial troubles big crowds went to the Melbourne Cricket Ground. There were 20,000 on the first day, 22,000 on the second day, and it was like old times. Even the Governor, Lord Hopetoun, was there. Normally he was a devout racegoer, and it took a cricket match of vast importance to attract him to the M.C.G.

John Blackham was appointed the Australian captain, and the *Argus* reports this story:

> Blackham fossicked an old and battered penny out of his pocket which bore evidence of having been tossed many a time and sometimes heavily. He spun it and Grace called "man," but as the penny was Blackham's lucky one it turned "woman"—and the English captain, looking at it with an air of disgust, said, "Well that's a pretty sort of a coin to toss with. You have to toss first then take it into the light to see whether it's man or woman."
> Then he tossed it experimentally to see if it always came down the same way. However, the battered brown enabled Blackham to say. "We bat, Doctor," and sent the Englishmen unwillingly to field.

That was the end of the battered brown—Dr. Grace refused to let him produce it for the Second and Third Tests.

As the newspapers said, "the game was a melancholy slow affair, and nothing but the magnitude of the issue could have sustained the public interest. On so good a wicket 250 should have been got on the first day". Indeed, the Australians got only 191, finishing with 240 on the next day.

The Englishmen always scored faster. Between lunch and stumps on Saturday they scored 240 in the same time that it took Australia to make 139. Dr. Grace made 50 in the first innings and 30 in the second. "It is doubtful if the crowd saw him under anything but his very best." England forced a lead of 24 runs on the first innings, but Australia went on to win by 54 runs.

Australia won the first two Test matches and England the third. It was far from being a happy tour for Dr. Grace. Not that there was anything wrong with the quality of his cricket—the newspapers and sporting magazines took up their old feud just where they left off in 1874, except that this time they were tougher. With the possible exception of Jardine and Larwood no English cricketer ever had such caustic treatment from the press in Australia. The *Australasian* writer, for example, summing up the tour, said that always he had followed the viewpoint that Dr. Grace was not as bad as he was painted, but his patience was at an end. He wrote:

> As captain, W. G. Grace was not popular with his team, especially since the Second Test match. Grace is admittedly a bad loser, and when he lost two of the Test matches in succession he lost his temper too, and kept on losing it right to the finish. Since that match Grace seems to have developed a condition of capriciousness, fussiness and nastiness strongly to be depre-cated . . .

On the other hand, there was never any official criticism of Dr. Grace, and John Blackham on several occasions came to his defence, saying that W.G. was a perfect sportsman. Certainly not all the attacks seemed to be justified. Two unfortunate articles appeared that did not help at all. A Sydney Sunday newspaper printed an article which it claimed was a criticism of Australia made by Dr. Grace in 1874. The Melbourne *Argus* reported that this was nothing but a hoax that had long since been exposed, but it caused the great Doctor to be jeered on the Sydney Cricket Ground during the Second Test.

Then there was the article that appeared in the January 1892 issue of *Blackwood's Magazine*. *Blackwood's* had a big reputation in Australia for being one of England's leading magazines. The Australian newspapers at once quoted the article in full and it is worth quoting here:

> With this parting shot we may take leave of the professionals and turn to another exciting or, as some think, disturbing element in the cricket of recent years—namely, the Australian visits. The first of these took place so far back as 1878, and we can remember even now the excitement and curiosity that pervaded the public mind as to the probable appearance and manners of these strangers. Australia was (and probably still is) associated with Botany Bay and Norfolk Island in country districts, and it was supposed by many rustics—especially by those whose grandfathers had disappeared about the time of the assizes—that our visitors were the lineal descendants of impenitent thieves, even if they were not doing a flourishing trade in bushranging on their account. It was supposed also that their complexions would be of a dusky hue, and the rising generation confidently expected that they would appear in war-paint and flourish boomerangs instead of cricket bats. The sanguine expectations were not altogether realised; but it must be confessed that many members of the colonial teams were forbidding and almost truculent in their aspect. The features of the great Spofforth himself (whose looks, however, entirely belied his character) often wore a scowl of deadly hatred as he deliv-ered the ball, followed by an almost fiendish smile of satisfaction as he bowled

65

his man. Their manners, again, scarcely indicated that they belonged to the highest classes of Australian society, who (if we may believe Mr. Froude) are in the highest degree cultured and refined. There was even a suspicion, amounting in some cases to a certainty, that several members of these teams, although a "Mr" was prefixed to their names on the score-sheets, could hardly be classed as amateurs in the English sense of the term. Their visits to this country were believed to be prompted not so much by ideas of glory as of gate-money, and it was openly stated (and so far as we know this statement has never been contradicted) that every Australian received a large sum, on one occasion amounting to as much as £800 per man, in addition to his travelling expenses. Again, their manners in the field were often the reverse of what one expects from gentlemen, especially in the seasons of 1878 and of 1886. Not only did they wrangle amongst themselves and give free-spoken and unusually unseasonable advice to their captain; but if they were caught at the wicket or given out "leg-before," they audibly invoked malediction on the umpire's head and both suggested at the time, and wrote letters to their friends, distinctly stating that our English professionals—men of unimpeachable honesty and integrity—gave wittingly unfair decisions. In short, it was sufficiently patent to all who watched the colonial matches in England that, in many instances, the Australians were deficient in the temper and self-control which enable gentlemen and sportsmen to show the same equanimity in defeat as in victory. Furthermore in Australia itself the game is entirely in the hands of speculators and bookmakers, who regard it simply as the vehicle for heavy betting, just as the "ring" regards horse racing in England. On great match days at Sydney or Melbourne the grounds are filled with roughs or rowdies, while the pavilion is occupied by the great bookmakers and the sporting contingent, who one and all have backed their own side for large amounts, and, if they lose, are apt to vent their feelings in a manner that is more forcible than pleasant. No wonder that under these circumstances the highest class of Australian society keeps aloof from the cricket grounds, or that of recent years cricket itself should have lost much of its popularity both in Victoria and New South Wales."

"Oh dear! Boy, bring me a couple of bags of salt," said Melbourne *Punch.* "Amusing and amazing," said the *Argus.* "The article contains reflections on Australian cricket which our present visitors will be able to state are totally undeserved and which for the sake of good feeling should have been omitted."

Many of the troubles arose because this was a very hard-fought season. In the first two Test matches Australia came from behind to win. And there were those who could not understand Dr. Grace. Like many a captain who came later, both English and Australian, he was tough, unyielding and above all, he played the game relentlessly to win. As the *Australasian* put it: "It is scarcely a matter for wonder that W. G. Grace should be somewhat autocratic in demeanour considering how long he has been the idol in English cricket."

There was a surprise when the Australian team was chosen for the Second Test at Sydney. Moses, the star Australian left-hander, was in and the brilliant Syd Gregory was 12th man. Moses injured his leg so badly in the Melbourne Test that few expected he could play again that season. The newspapers reported that Dr. W. G. Grace was determined to win this match, and he did not intend to allow the Australians a single point more than they could claim. Furthermore, he warned Moses that if his leg broke down again he need not expect a substitute. Indeed, speaking as a medical man, he felt that Moses had no right to take the risk.

Moses tested his leg. He ran on it, he jumped on it, he batted at the nets. He declared himself completely fit. He did look fit, too, as he batted on the first day, running speedily between the wickets. But after scoring 20 odd runs he started to hobble with pain. From then on his only hope of scoring was to go for the boundary. He did not dare to run. His innings was the start of a bad day. He was out for 29 and Australia was all out for 145.

The situation was most uncomfortable. Grace said nothing and Blackham said nothing. After the Doctor's warning Blackham could hardly ask for a substitute. Moses had to field. The *Herald* reported: "It was a pitiful sight yesterday to see Moses limping about the field. He had to creep and crawl to the slips at each change of ends, and the crowd were loud in their expressions of indignation at Grace in not providing a substitute for the Sydney man."

The next day Dr. Grace "very amiably" called on Blackham and offered him a substitute. Several newspapers reported that he was under considerable pressure from Lord Sheffield to do this, and *Punch* went even further—there were threats that the G.O.M. would be sent back to England.

Yet if there was tension over substitutes it was understandable. The cricket match was a thriller. In reply to Australia's 144 England made 307, and the opening bat, R. Abel, played right through the innings for 132 not out. So Australia was in bad trouble. What about Moses? Harry Moses was taking a course of electric baths in the city and he was surrounded by a squadron of medical men. Some said that he must not bat, he could do himself fearful injury. On the other hand, an old friend, Dr. Springthorpe, sent this telegram from Melbourne: "TRY HOPPING TODAY. MUST BAT. EVERY RUN WANTED."

Then, if Australia was not in enough trouble. R. McLeod's brother Norman died suddenly in Melbourne. The news came through early on the Tuesday morning. It was a great tragedy for McLeod—could they in all decency ask him to bat? Finally it was decided that for the sake of Australia they could. After all, the Melbourne Express did not leave until that night, so he could not get away before then, whatever happened. The team, respectfully, wore black crepe and McLeod batted. He made 18 runs and he caught the train that night.

But his departure left another problem that was almost too embarrassing to be true. Blackham had to ask Dr. Grace for another substitute. The *Argus* said: "The Australians asked that Hutton, a Melbourne University man, might field in his place. Grace was candid, "Is he a better field than McLeod?"

"Yes," said Blackham with equal candour.

"Then get someone else," replied Grace.

So the Australians found Donnan, an arrangement that gave no cause for grumblings.

Despite all the entreaties and special electric baths, it was impossible for Moses to bat in the second innings. Yet, when all looked hopeless, Alick Bannerman and J. J. Lyons took to the deadly Lohmann, who had taken 8 for 58 in the first innings. Bannerman made 91 and Lyons 134. It was an incredible comeback with 391, and the next day England was dismissed for 156. Australia had won the Ashes.

The *Argus* reported:

> There was such a scene as perhaps has never been witnessed before at the Sydney Cricket Ground. Straw hats, a popular summer wear in Sydney, were thrown in the air a thousand at a time. The ladies who crowded the reserve smashed their parasols on the seats and battered umbrellas were kicked about the lawn.

When all was over John Blackham was courteous: "I would like to refer to some ugly rumours which have gained currency about Dr. Grace's behaviour. Before Moses broke down he was running between the wickets as well as his partner, George Giffen. Dr. Grace came up to me after the Moses accident and said, 'Jack, you can have a man to run for Moses if you like.' I did not approach Dr. Grace on the subject, he came to me. All the rumours about Dr. Grace's sharp tactics are untrue."

Yet perhaps the most awkward incident came in the match England v. N.S.W. There was an appeal against the N.S.W. batsman, Charlton, for a catch behind. Umpire Briscoe called "not out." There were several versions of the incident. One was that Dr. Grace said to Briscoe: "You would not give anyone out, it's unpardonable. We might as well go home to England."

Grace on the other hand commented that all he said was: "I wish you would pay attention to the game. We all heard the catch."

This Troedel print reveals the gracious
Melbourne Cricket Ground in 1864.

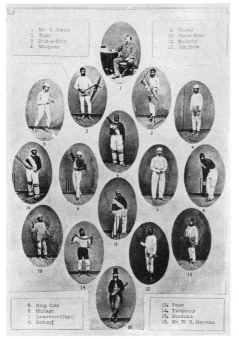

1. Mr. G. Smith
2. Tiger
3. Dick-a-Dick
4. Mosquito

9. Cousins
10. Henry Rose
11. Bullocky
12. Jim Crow

5. King Cole
6. Mullagh
7. Lawrence (Capt.)
8. Redcap

13. Peter
14. Twopenny
15. Sundown
16. Mr. W. R. Hayman

Left
Australia's first touring team: the
Aboriginal side that went to England
in 1868.

Right
The founders of the M.C.C. Tennis
Club in 1879.

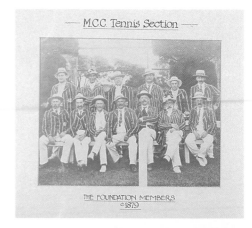

M.C.C. Tennis Section

THE FOUNDATION MEMBERS
c1879

Below
Night football between Melbourne
and Carlton, August 1879. This was
the first commercial use of electric
light in Victoria.

Anyway Briscoe walked off and refused to umpire further. After a long delay Charles Bannerman agreed to take his place and the match continued. Briscoe made a formal complaint and Grace in a letter replied:

"I did not insult Mr. Briscoe, nor did I think him a cheat. The umpiring question will have to be gone into thoroughly, and some new system adopted, or cricket will not be worth playing under the present system of umpiring. Believe me, yours truly, W. G. Grace."

Admittedly at times he was prickly. For example, in the Third Test at Adelaide, when there was disagreement over the state of the wicket, he called for an inspection every 15 minutes. Yet he was a great personality. He drew the crowds, and there is no doubt that it was the presence of W. G. Grace that caused a revival of cricket in Australia.

Nor could anyone criticise him for the quality of his cricket. The Australians worked him almost to death. He even had to play matches against East Melbourne, and Malvern at Malvern, where the reporters complained bitterly about the facilities for the press. Dr. Grace, at 43 years, topped the averages for the tour. For eleven a side matches his average was 41.8 as against 38.8 for Abel and 37.5 for Stoddart. For all matches his average was 32.89 compared with 31.09 for Peel and 30.00 for Stoddart.

He promised that he would return to Australia the following year with an even stronger team, but Dr. Grace had made his last tour of Australia. Yet he was still opening for England against Australia four years later, and he made 66 at Lord's before he was bowled by Giffen. His last Test against Australia was at Nottingham in June 1899. He made 28 in the first innings, 1 in the second innings. He was in his fifty-first year.

Lord Sheffield returned home leaving many friends behind him. While in Australia he spent lavishly, and the newspapers speculated at length on how much the tour and his generosity must have cost him. His grandest gesture was the donation of the Sheffield Shield. Strangely enough, it did not cause much comment at the time. There were a few lines printed here and there after the First Test announcing that on January 12 Major Ben Wardill had informed the ordinary meeting of the Victorian Cricketers' Association that Lord Sheffield had made an offer of 150 guineas "with the intention of its being devoted to the advancement of cricket in the colonies."

Later the Australian Cricket Council passed these regulations:

1. That the donation be devoted to the purchase of a silver shield to be called the Sheffield Shield, and to be given for competition by the colonies New South Wales, Victoria and South Australia.
2. That the competition be confined to intercolonial matches.

So Lord Sheffield never has been forgotten. Victoria was the first to win the Shield in 1892-93. Queensland came into the competition in 1926-27 and Western Australia in 1947-48.

Lord Sheffield's bust stands in the Long Room at the M.C.C. and, just as the newspapermen wrote, in 1891, he does look remarkably like John Bull.

CHAPTER TEN

The Cricketing 'Nineties

L ORD Sheffield and Dr. W. G. Grace went home to England, and Melbourne settled down into the financial miseries. Victoria had enjoyed
the greatest spree, so it was hit the first and hardest. All but one of the
Victorian banks failed. The Sydney *Bulletin* on November 18, 1893, made a
merciless attack on the misdeeds of Melbourne's financial set and the land-
boomers:

> Federation these times would mean tainting the Continent with Victoria's
> foulness, and a general taking over of the bulk of Victoria's stink. Isolation
> would be the best thing that could happen to the Cabbage Garden just now. If
> it were denounced as a plague-spot and officially apologised for in a haughty
> manner by the neighbouring countries the honest portion of the population
> might at least perceive the folly of not making an effort to stamp out their
> disease.

The Melbourne Cricket Club also was in trouble. The club's debt was
£2336/8/6, and its bank, the City of Melbourne Bank. Like the others, the City
of Melbourne Bank was caught in the famous run on the banks in June 1893,
and it closed its doors never to open again. Two things saved the M.C.C.—
Frank Grey Smith, the club president, arranged a £500 overdraft with the still
surviving National Bank, and cricket was booming. Yes, cricket was booming
at such a pace that when the day came for the official liquidation of the City of
Melbourne Bank the M.C.C. paid its debts in full.

And that was the fascinating situation. At a time when the colony was
"stony, motherless, broke," cricket at the M.C.G. was drawing bigger crowds
than ever before. Nor were the prices cheap—five shillings a head for a Test
match. Yet it was not merely good fortune, the 'nineties produced cricket at
the M.C.G. good enough to make one's mouth water. There were so many of
the young, new stars—Albert Trott, the schoolboy Clem Hill, one of the most
famous of all M.C.C. members—Hugh Trumble, Syd Gregory, Victor
Trumper, Joe Darling, Monty Noble, just to mention a few. Then from
England there was the youthful Archie Maclaren, Prince Ranjitsinhji, Tom

Richardson, A. E. Stoddart, George Hirst and the amazing off-spinner, John Thomas Hearne.

The visit of A. E. Stoddart's Eleven in 1894-95 was the tour that pulled the M.C.C. out of debt. It meant a profit of £3349. One touring member was Archie Maclaren, aged 23 years. He was included because the selectors considered him to be an amateur of promise. Archie very quickly made that promise a fact, and he proved to be one of the best half-dozen batsmen ever to come out of England.

On November 16, 1894, in the match between England and Victoria on the M.C.G. the *Argus* reported:

> When the Englishmen walked out at 6 p.m. the crowd pressed around the pavilion gates to cheer Maclaren. The score stood at 394 for 4, Maclaren 220 not out. He gave only one chance, when about half-way through his second hundred, and it is doubtful whether an innings of equal length both in runs and time has been seen on the M.C.G. marred by fewer bad strokes. He abjures almost entirely lifting them, but nothing could be better than his hard skimming hits along the turf, and he has the invaluable quality in a batsman of being able to hit equally well around the wicket. He batted for 5¾ hours, hitting 22 fours.

It was a good start for the Englishman Archie Maclaren, but at the same time it was a marvellous tour for the 21-year-old Australian Albert Trott. He achieved a Test average of 102.5, something which has never been beaten, not even by Don Bradman. Before the Fifth Test the *Argus* wrote: "The popularity of Albert Trott is such that if he died at this moment—which Heaven forfend!—there would probably be an irresistible demand for his immediate canonisation. Saint Albert Trott would look well in a coloured window." Unbelievably, the selectors did not choose him for the next tour to England, so Albert packed his bags and went there on his own account, where he won great fame playing both for England and Middlesex. Most enthusiasts remember him with affection for being the man who hit a ball right over the pavilion at Lord's. Anyone who has seen the pavilion could only presume that Albert must have used a trench mortar rather than a cricket bat. The incident took place in 1899 off the bowling of M. A. Noble. It is said that the ball went so high it struck a chimney outside the ground.

The 1895 series worked up to a beautiful climax. By the Fifth Test England and Australia were two Tests each. Cricket had never created excitement like it. The newspapers every day headed their stories "THE HISTORIC MATCH." Of course there was no radio, so great crowds gathered around the newspaper offices in all the capital cities. Nor was it any different in London.

According to one English journal, all cables were being delivered immediately to Queen Victoria, "who is sharing the same interest which is enthusiastically being exhibited by her subjects."

In Melbourne it was like Cup Week, and 400 came by train from Adelaide and 600 from Sydney, just for the cricket. Both the Adelaide and Sydney expresses had to be divided to cater for the crowds. Even a boundary rider from Blackall in outback Queensland made the trip. Cable trams ran to the M.C.G. at the rate of one a minute, carrying full loads of passengers at three-pence a fare.

"This was a Niagara of a crowd," said the *Herald*. On the first day there was a crowd of 17,500 and on the second 28,000, a world record for a cricket match. Maybe football had drawn bigger crowds, but the charges for cricket were higher. The *Argus* described the scene:

> The people were literally banked up around the rink, the great trees appearing to grow out of a vast bed of straw hats. The pavilion enclosure and the terrace in front were so packed that hundreds of people seated on the parapet gave the illusion of an unbroken plane of faces from the fence to the top of the rear wall. And the pavilion enclosure could not have held another man and given him even a glimpse of the wicket.
>
> A wise Government, to improve our credit abroad, might do worse than to send away thousands of photographs of the scene on the M.C.G. on Saturday. There appears to be an idea somewhere else that there is a depression here. To the spectator on Saturday that word had no meaning.

The *Herald* also talked of the trees that grew out of a sea of heads, particularly a circle of 11 elms darker and larger than the rest. These were the trees planted by each member of Mr. Stephenson's All England XI in 1862.

George Giffen, the South Australian, was the Australian captain. John Blackham, who used such perilously thin wicket-keeping gloves, injured a hand during the First Test and he did not play again. So ended an amazing career. He played in the first of all Tests in 1877, he made eight tours to England, and in 18 years he missed only three Test matches.

The newspapers reported that "the historic match" began when the beaming Major Ben Wardill, secretary of the M.C.C., walked on to the ground with a captain on either arm. It was said that George Giffen had a devil-may-care look about him and responsibility hung lightly upon his shoulders. Yet one had only to look more closely, especially when he brought out the coin for the toss. His hands were trembling. As for the coin, earlier that morning a fellow—South Australian, a Mr. James Marshall, —had presented George with a battered shilling. "Take this, George, and toss with it—it's the coin I always win drinks with." Such a recommendation was quite sufficient for George.

The captains chatted about the weather, about the rolling of the wicket, and Ben Wardill's nerve was the first to crack. "For Heaven's sake," he said, "toss and get it over with." "Keep cool, Major," replied Mr. Stoddart, and as George tossed he called "heads." But Mr. Stoddart called incorrectly and George made a delighted jump in the air. There were cries of "Giff wins easily," and in the midst of the congratulations Mr. James Marshall made a desperate attempt to recover his shilling, for, as the *Argus* said, "the dry weather was by no means over." But he had no chance; the coin was now historic and George was keeping it for all time.

The Australians wore dark blue caps with blue sashes around their waists. It was the custom always to wear the colours of the host colony, and dark blue was the colour of Victoria. But the system had proved a failure. The sky blue caps of N.S.W., for example, turned grey almost at once in the sun; then all the top batsmen had their favourite, lucky caps. They would not dare go to the crease in some foreign, new creation. The hazards of batting already were great enough without that. However, the gossip in the dressing room at the M.C.G. on March 1, 1895, was that All-Australian colours had been suggested. They would be olive green with gold braid.

At the end of the first day Australia was 4 for 282 with Syd Gregory and Joe Darling undefeated for 70 and 72. The cricket writers felt that there was no question, both men on the Saturday would carry on for their centuries. Darling's father was so proud of his son's performance that he promised him a 25-guinea gold watch if he reached three figures. The offer must have been too much. Next morning Syd Gregory was out almost first ball and Joe added only two runs.

But what a match it was. Two Tests all, the sun shone in the exact manner that it should for such an occasion, and neither side could get the upper hand. Australia made 414 in the first innings, then England replied with 385, including a lovely 120 by Archie Maclaren. Regrettably, while this was going on it was reported that in one of the best seats in the grandstand a lady was seen reading a novel, "without the least pretext of being interested in the game," and Charlie Hobbs of South Australia, one of the greats of his colony, overheard a lady remark, "Oh, now I know what byes really are, but you haven't told me how many byes make a goal."

Australia in the second innings scored 267, and some of our finest, like Albert Trott, went for nil. Tom Richardson, bowling "faster perhaps than he had ever done in his life," took 6 for 104. Yet even on Wednesday, the fifth

74

and final day, no one dared to forecast the result. In the city it was difficult to concentrate on the business at hand, no more so than in the courts. At one court James Ball appeared on a charge that on Tuesday evening he did assault Thomas Bailes near the Melbourne Cricket Ground, striking him a violent blow on the face.

The prisoner admitted that the altercation took place, but it wasn't really his fault. They were discussing the relative merits of Australian and English cricket . . . "You see, it was only a snick, Your Honour."

Whereupon a witness remarked: "Snick! It was a regular boundary hit. Had a lot of devil in it, too."

The prisoner appealed: "I meant no harm, Your Honour. Give me another innings and it won't happen again."

Said His Honour: "You have had enough innings already. This time you're in for six months."

His Honour then drew the stumps at 12 noon so that the Court could rush to the M.C.G. for the climax of the historic match.

And it was a climax. Undoubtedly by the time His Honour arrived Stoddart already had gone for 11 runs, l.b.w., bowled by Harry Trott. Australia virtually had the match won, and the *Herald* reported that when J. T. Brown came in the situation for England was perilous. He almost went after the second ball, but then, suddenly, from across the other side of the ground came the thin tune of *Rule Britannia* played on a tin whistle. Whether Mr. Brown was truly stirred by this, history does not record, but from that moment on he crushed the Australian attack. He scored 140 . . ."a dashing, forcing game, made when the runs were most wanted."

So England won by six wickets and Mr. Stoddart took home the Ashes. He was a popular captain, the matches were so closely fought no one grudged him his win. Indeed, Melbourne *Punch* went even further than that:

> There went a tale to England,
> 'Twas of the Test match won,
> And nobly had her cricketers
> That day their duty done.
> They didn't fail like funkers,
> They kept up England's tail,
> They kept their pros. from off the booze
> And knew they could not fail.
>
> Then wrote the Queen of England,
> Whose hand is blessed by God,
> "I must do something handsome

For my dear victorious Stod.
Let him return without delay
And we will dub him pat—
A baronet that he may be
Sir Andrew Stoddart, bat (? Bart).

One man who did not make the Test team in 1895 was Clem Hill. At the time of the First Test he was only 17. Yet even at 17 he was a mighty cricketer and on the way to becoming the greatest left-hander in the world. While at Prince Alfred College in Adelaide he made 360 in a match against St. Peter's College. Even then he played for South Australia, and he scored 150 against Stoddart's men, batting against Tom Richardson, considered by some to be the father of swing bowling. The Melbourne Cricket Club saw him for the first time that year in the annual Victoria-South Australia match. He charmed the crowd with a very well-made 33. But there was an incident in this match which charmed the crowd even more. "Jonah" Jones, the South Australian fast bowler, played a ball from Trumble which lodged in his shirt. Instead of asking one of the Victorians to take it out, he did it himself and naively handed it to a fieldsman. There was an appeal and the umpire gave him out for handling the ball. Since then the rule governing this has been amended, and a ball that lodges in the clothing of a batsman or an umpire is dead.

Clem Hill forced his way into the team for England the following year, but some of his finest cricket was to come during Stoddart's tour of Australia in 1897-98. By this time Australians were suffering from an inferiority complex. They had not seen the Ashes for seven years. However, the prospects were much brighter, Australia won two of the first three Tests and the fourth was on the Melbourne Cricket Ground.

The start by Australia was appalling. Six wickets went down for 58 runs— McLeod 1, Darling 12, Gregory 0, Iredale 0, Noble 4 and G. H. S. Trott 7. One paper commented: "If misery loves company, McLeod, Darling, Gregory, Iredale, Noble and Trott should have banded together in a back room for company. Charley McLeod came off, looking all broken up and crippled in spirit. He was like a man who had lost father and mother and wife and family and all his aunts in a railway smash and was wondering how he was going to raise the funeral expenses, but seemed to be saying, "I know just how it is—I am a melancholy failure. Make no excuses for me, please, but just let me get away to a quiet place where I can kick myself."

Hugh Trumble came in when Australia was 59 and when he left the score stood at 223. He made only 46 of the difference, while 20-year-old Clem Hill scored the rest; but the pair went down into history for a record seventh wicket partnership that still stands for Test matches between England and Australia.

The cricket was so remarkable that the press agencies, to get ahead of one another, were sending urgent cables to London at the rate of 13/9 a word, which would make newspaper proprietors wince even today. The news was hitting London 20 minutes after the actual event.

At the end of the day Hugh Trumble had gone but Clem Hill was undefeated with 182 not out, and a very shy man he was when he returned to the pavilion. The *Argus* reported:

> Cricketers are more superstitious than sailors. One of the superstitions is a firm conviction of the bad luck which attends a batsman who, with a big overnight score, has a photograph taken before continuing the next day. When Clem Hill scored 200 in Adelaide against the Englishmen in their first match there this season he was taken in several poses and, on again going out to bat, he failed to get another run. Darling on scoring 178 in the last match against England was extremely anxious to avoid the photographers. He was untimely persuaded against his better judgement. The same thing happened to him. When Hill carried his bat at the M.C.G. a perfect battery of lenses was being got ready to "pot him" as he came in. He managed to dodge behind the backs of the fieldsmen, and they shielded him as he made for the pavilion, and he said, "I've had my luck queered that way before this season."

Yet some rascal must have taken a picture somewhere, for the next day he added only another six runs before he fell to Hearne. He batted for 4 hours 40 minutes and he hit 21 fours. Once again *Punch* was lyrical:

> I would like to sing
> A little thing
> About young Clement Hill,
> Whose plucky play
> On Saturday
> Completely filled the bill.
> He pasted Richardson about,
> And Hayward, too, in turn,
> And fairly knocked "the devil" out
> Of clever Johnnie Hearne.
> Did Clement Hill
> Whose batting skill
> Has often made the lion ill.
> He saw our boys
> Go down like toys,
> He did not catch the blight,
> But pegged away
> Throughout the day

> And whacked 'em out of sight.
> He was not, as some batsmen were,
>   Content to make "a score,"
> One score is neither here nor there—
>   He knocked up nine and more,
>   For Hill a whoop;
>   He worked a scoop,
> And pulled us all from out the soup!

The weather became hotter and hotter and it was 107 in the shade. Frank Allan (remember "the bowler of the century") brought a bundle of vine leaves for the Australians to wear inside their hats. There were bad bushfires all around Melbourne, so much so that there was a heavy cloud of smoke and the sun glowed like a Chinese lantern. Prince Ranjitsinhji remarked that Australia was probably the only nation on earth that was prepared to set the country alight, merely to win a Test match. There was nothing in the cricket rules about appealing against the smoke.

England fared very little better than the first six Australians. Hugh Trumble was the chief wrecker with 4 for 56, and Australia went on to win by 8 wickets.

There was a rival show taking place in Melbourne, the big convention for the Federation of the colonies. Several of the newspapers criticised the public for having no interest whatever in this birth of their nation and devoting all their attention to a cricket match. The public could hardly be blamed. The convention had dragged on for months and months and months. It could almost be said that the wrangle had gone on for 50 years, through referendums, conventions, and millions of words, often loaded with local jealousies and self-interest.

But one weekly came to the defence of cricket:

> It is implied that in neglecting their politicians for their cricketers, the people have discredited themselves. We think not—we think that they have merely given expression to their very reasonable sentiments towards the larger proportion of the 50 delegates who have met with the avowed object of creating a new united Australia, and have done little since but advertise their utter contempt for Federation, or at least their inability to entertain the true Federal feeling.
>
> Our cricketing eleven forms the best example of Federation yet achieved. In the team that has beaten the Englishmen in three Test matches out of four, Australia is truly united, and we believe Harry Trott and his ten good men and true have done more for the federation of Australian hearts than all the big delegates put together.

Actually many of the "big delegates" were guests at the farewell dinner to

78

Mr. Stoddart and his men in the M.C.C. pavilion. Mr. Frank Grey Smith was in the chair. He had Lord Brassey, the Governor, and Prince Ranjitsinhji on his left, and Mr. Stoddart on his right. The president presented the Prince, J. R. Mason and W. Druce with badges, making them honorary life members. A. E. Stoddart and A. C. Maclaren already were life members, but there was a special presentation of another badge, to Mr. Stoddart. Mr. Grey Smith pointed out that on one occasion during this present tour a thief, unkindly, relieved Mr. Stoddart of his watch and chain, to which was attached his M.C.C. life membership badge. With Federal Convention delegates present, the president, tactfully, did not say where this ungracious deed took place, but he let everyone have a good guess. It happened in "a neighbouring northern colony."

The next day all the committeemen went down to Spencer Street to wave them farewell on their way to Adelaide. Mr. Stoddart left the Ashes behind, but he had one consolation, he won £1500 in an Australian lottery and Archie Maclaren won an Australian bride. As for the Prince, he left behind broken hearts. As one social journal pointed out, Melbourne would now be able to return to normal conversation. Every woman in Melbourne seemed to adore the Prince. At every function it was Prince this, Prince that. "Indeed, one became quite tired of it."

But the M.C.C. was not tired of him. The club profit for the tour was £3875, and as the century came to a close the M.C.C. could look back on its efforts with pride. Up to 1899 the club had brought out English touring sides in 1879, 1882, 1887 and 1891. In 1894 and 1897 it was a joint arrangement between the M.C.C. and the Trustees of the Sydney Cricket Ground.

Then in 1899 the M.C.C. sponsored a tour to England under Joe Darling, with Ben Wardill as manager. In any age this would have been a superb cricket team with men like Noble, S. E. Gregory, Hill, Trumper, Trumble and Jones. It was Victor Trumper's first tour, and he came in only as extra after all the others had been selected. So as the new boy he was virtually on half-pay without the opportunity to share in the profits. The club still has a copy of the agreement.

But after he arrived in England the new boy obviously was so good, the players put him on the same profit-sharing basis as themselves. Darling topped the averages with 1941 runs at 41.29, Noble made 1608 and Trumper 1556. Hugh Trumble not only scored 1183 runs but he topped the bowling averages with 142 wickets at 18.43 runs apiece. This last of the 19th century tours was one to remember. Although they won only one Test, four were drawn, and it was the first time that the Australians had won a series in England since the mythical Ashes were created back in 1882.

CHAPTER ELEVEN

Edwardiana at the M.C.G.

A T five minutes before midnight on December 31, 1900, there were 15,000 gathered around the Town Hall and Post Office clocks in Swanston and Bourke Streets. The city was blazing with light and, incredibly, all the leading stores were still open. And the noise! There were tin whistles, toy trumpets, and real musical instruments that would blast out with a Wagnerian weirdness. But as the big hand on the Post Office clock drew closer and closer to XII, the revellers one by one ceased their noise and a reverent hush descended over the city.

First came the 16 bells that herald the striking of the hour. No longer could the crowd wait; there was a burst of deafening cheering. The 20th Century had arrived. A man with a cannon on the veranda of a shop opposite put a match to the touch hole, but the boom was hardly heard in all the noise. A beacon was fired on the top of the Post Office and all the buildings were bathed in a crimson glow.

"Then came the chime again," said the *Argus*, "this time with the National Anthem, and the crowd reverently bared their heads as they picked up the tunes and joined in the fervent hymn of the British people. At its last note the pent-up feelings of the crowd gave way. From buildings on either side of Bourke Street came showers of sparks from Roman candles. . . . Above the ringing of the bells and the laughter of the girls sounded the blare of horns and trumpets. The crowd moved forward and backward until an early hour, and it was not until after 2 o'clock that the last line of patriotic youths made their way out of the city with the strains of the ever popular *Soldiers of the Queen* still rising unsteadily from their jaded throats."

This was a time of vast change. That day, January 1, 1901, saw in Sydney the proclaiming of the Commonwealth of Australia. Then three weeks later on January 23, the Queen died. Business came to a standstill in Melbourne. The newspapers ran black borders for 10 days and some had black borders around every single column. The cricket match Victoria versus Tasmania was abandoned for the day. All the stores in the city put up black draperies. The gentlemen wore black hat bands and black ties and many of the ladies went into full mourning. The doctors in Collins Street draped their brass plates with black and the clubs respectfully pulled their blinds.

This was a time of change also for the Melbourne Cricket Club. Earlier, on May 1, 1900, the club president, Frank Grey Smith, died suddenly, at the age of 73. He had attended a committee meeting only a few days before, but he had suffered some difficult years, a serious operation in 1898, and he had never fully recovered from the strain of the years of the financial crisis when the National Bank had to be reconstructed.

He had been a club member since 1849, and could remember the days when the M.C.C. played cricket at Batman's Hill. He became a vice president in 1879 and succeeded Sir William Clarke as president in 1886. He deserves to be remembered because he guided the M.C.C. from the time when it was a small shaky club to the years when it became so powerful that often it was accused of running cricket all over Australia. Nor was it only cricket—the M.C.C. was dominating football, bowls, rifle shooting, even to producing champion skittles players.

Mr. Frank Grey Smith knew as much about the young footballers and cricketers as he did about the customers of the National Bank. It was said that from the day he took office the prosperity of the club became immediately more apparent. He used to watch every important match right through from the time the first ball was bowled. He would sit in his regular seat in the pavilion and always it was the done thing for a visitor to pay his respects.

It was never just Mr. Smith; invariably he used his two Christian names, Frank Grey Smith. He was clean-shaven and faultlessly dressed, usually in grey. And as he sat there in the pavilion he was an austere figure. He had an air of gravity about him, which did not seem entirely in keeping with his surroundings, but he knew both his cricket and his football, and he did not miss a point in either. The club was very distressed at his death. Mr. Roderick Murchison took over as President.

Also it was a new era for cricketers. In February 1900 the M.C.C. scored 141 against South Melbourne. South replied with 6 for 609 and a hefty young colt named Warwick Armstrong made 270. He was to be a power in Victorian and Australian cricket for the next 20 years. He did not stay long with South Melbourne. He switched to the M.C.C., and in his first match against his old club he made 45 in a total of 485. In his first interstate match against South Australia he made 118, and on January 1, 1901, the following year, when the 101-gun salute was being fired in the Domain to announce the new Commonwealth, he made 120, again in the South Australian match.

For the new century the club bought a typewriter. Price: £52. It proved such a success the committee decided to invest in another. The weather was so hot that an ice-box was acquired for the committee room, and at last the stands were lit with electric light. The new lighting was of enormous benefit to the Monday night concerts. From November to April the club held weekly concerts at the M.C.G., and they were quite the thing for Melbourne society. There would be a dozen or so singers with a good band, like the Victorian Railways Military Band. The crowd of 3000 to 5000 would sit in the stands or, if they wished, "promenade on the turf." The concerts always made a good profit, and one year the proceeds went to patriotic funds for the Boer War.

Occasionally there were extra attractions. For example, on January 13, 1902, the club showed moving pictures from a cinematograph. They were brief pictures on a continuous reel of film, yet "very interesting," according to the *Argus*. "The subjects ranged from 'The Quick Change Dancers' to the attack on a mission station by the Boxers and a gallant rescue by the blue-jackets. Various war pictures were shown, the effect being made more striking by appropriate interjections of cannonading and volleyfire."

There was just one trouble with the night concerts: the rattle of the railway trains could spoil the fine singing and sometimes there was the inclement weather. On the Monday before the showing of the cinematograph films the rain proved awkward in a most cruel fashion. Mr. Walter Kirby was singing *Alice, Where Art Thou?* He came to the line "When silvery rain falleth, just as it falleth now," when indeed the silvery rain was proving how it could falleth quite markedly. The audience laughed so much Mr. Walter Kirby was unable to continue.

The year 1901 was the year of the most sensational of all the Austral Wheel Races. Perhaps that does not sound a great deal now, but at the turn of the century the Austral Wheel Race was the richest professional bike race in the world. It attracted the world's finest bike riders, and the man who had not competed in an Austral on the Melbourne Cricket Ground was a nobody. The people of Melbourne were among the pioneers of the bicycle and, particularly in the 'nineties, the craze for cycling knew no limits. All newspapers carried pages of cycling notes, including the social magazines like *Table Talk*. Cycling, according to the enthusiasts, was the cure for all diseases from sciatica to weaknesses of the lung. Also, according to the cycling publications, it was good for the ladies and it certainly did not produce any masculine tendencies. The lady cyclist gained perfect health and at the same time remained as sweet and as refined as ever.

The first Austral was on the M.C.G. in 1886. There were £214 in prizes, and

82

the first prize for the three-mile race was a grand piano valued at 80 guineas. For four years it was an amateur event and in 1890 it turned professional. Then it really grew. The professionals rode the penny farthing bicycle, which was known as the ordinary or high bike or even "spiders' legs." And on these high bikes there were some phenomenal performances. Some Australs had as many as 50 competitors in the one race, and it must have been a sight to see, 50 cyclists on penny farthings high-revving past the pavilion. The old pictures show that the riders were bearded, they wore long, tight white pants, striped shirts and schoolboy caps.

Mr. H. C. Bagot, a relative of Mr. R. C. Bagot, who designed Flemington and the M.C.G., introduced racing silks and satin peaked caps, so that the cyclists looked for all the world like jockeys. Nor was this done without some forethought, because the Austral was run over two or three Saturdays in November, and it was beginning to outshine the Melbourne Cup, book-makers, betting and all. All the ladies of fashion turned out for the Austral, and there were times when the first day of the wheel race was actually before the Cup. The first of the new season's fashions then appeared not at Flemington but at a professional bicycle race on the M.C.G. So they were featured by all the fashion writers, who recorded what was worn by the vice-regal party and the society leaders.

The high bikes, some of which weighed 46 lb., disappeared towards the end of the 'nineties, and by 1901 all the riders were using the dashing "safety bikes" that we ride today. The 1901 event received a big build-up because it featured the Irish-American champion, "Plugger" Bill Martin. Before the final Plugger Bill already was backed for a fortune. The ordinary punter, too, had good reasons for backing Plugger. Not only was he a good rider but, look here, he arrived in Australia aboard a steamer named the AUSTRAL, and where was he staying?—at the AUSTRAL HOTEL, no less. The Austral Hotel was at the corner of Bourke and Russell Streets.

On Saturday, December 14, 1901, there was a crowd of 30,000 at the M.C.G. and the takings of £1307 were a record at the ground for any sport. Plugger Bill rode a remarkable race. He won by 15 yards and he was only the third rider in the history of the race to win from scratch. He was introduced to the Lieutenant-Governor, to the new Prime Minister of the Commonwealth, Mr. Edmund Barton, and to the president of the Melbourne Bicycle Club, Sir Malcolm McEacharn, M.H.R. But there was an outcry. The rider F. S. Beauchamp was disqualified immediately and the recommendation went in to the League of Victorian Wheelmen that he be put out for life. The charge was that he had acted as a pacer for Martin. Nine other riders were on charges of not having tried to win, and were told to report for an inquiry at the Port Phillip Club Hotel. The betting on the race was said to have been greater than on any other bike race in the world. The pay-out on Plugger Bill alone was £8000.

Letters poured in to the *Argus*:

> Sir,—As a member of the M.C.C. of long-standing, I cannot help expressing my feelings of disgust at the events that have been taking place in our ground during the past three Saturdays.
>
> Generally speaking, the members of the M.C.C. are jealous of the reputation of their club, and in conversation with several members this morning the opinion was freely expressed that it would be far better for the club to refrain from making any further engagements with the bicycle authorities if the opportunity for the raiding of their ground by the bookmaking fraternity with all the attendant evils cannot be done away with.
>
> Yours, etc.,
ANTI-BOOKMAKER.

> Sir,—Outside the grandstand, as if by way of a grim joke, was a notice prohibiting betting, but on emerging from the corridor under the stand the place was simply alive with bookmakers, from the foot of the steps right down to the front fence, offering a physical and noisy impediment to the passage of ladies through and up to the third row back in the stand. Where I sat the din was unbearable and the smoke like that of a bushfire.
>
> Boys were betting as well as adults. There was one free fight that lasted over 10 minutes. I have never seen such sights at Flemington. This is the first Austral I have seen for three years and unless some radical alteration be made it will be the last.
>
> Yours, etc.,
COUNTRY VISITOR.

> Sir,—I was in the grandstand on Saturday, unfortunately accompanied, as it turned out, by a lady. I have never enjoyed myself less. The deafening clamor of the barrackers, the degrading antics of the "ticktackers", the absence of true sport, thoroughly disgusted me. Sport! More sport could be found in watching a mosquito and far more excitement. There was a last straw, though. After seeing the big race, my companion and I naturally felt tired, and in making our way out of the pandemonium we had to discover a way through the labyrinth of bookmakers who had taken possession of the enclosure in front of the stand. Our way was blocked by a burly member of the ring, who, in a loud voice, was indulging in a tirade, which for blasphemy and filth stands alone. It was horrible to the masculine ear, but——!
>
> Now, Sir, is it possible that respectable people can be expected to patronise this sort of thing?
>
> Yours, etc.,
HAWTHORN.

There was a meeting of the Melbourne Cricket Club and another letter appeared in the *Argus*:

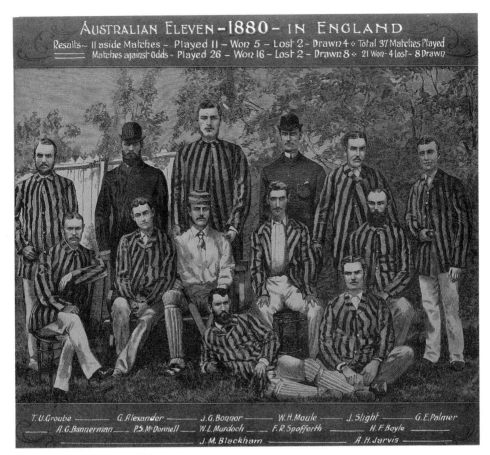

The Australian team, 1880.

George Bonnor, the biggest hitter the game ever knew.

Dr H. J. H. Scott, captain of the 1886 Australian touring side to England.

"Unless in future some means can be devised calculated to prevent such an exhibition of betting as characterised the recent Austral Wheel Race meeting the ground should not be again let for such a purpose.

Yours, etc.,

H. ATKINSON, for Sec. of M.C.C.

Plugger Bill's purse of £400 was temporarily held over and he commented: "I've decided I ain't goin' to start in any more competition events. I'm tired of bein' pulled up in front of the crowd like a small boy every time that some fellow that's lost a few shillings opens his mouth."

The nine accused riders were summoned to appear before the inquiry. Each rider was asked whether he received money in connection with the running of the race. The *Argus* reported: "The winner, W. Martin, was also in attendance, and each time any of the officials appeared he asked, 'When am I going to get my £400?'"

But the inquiry came to nothing, and eventually Plugger Bill received his £400 just as he was about to serve a writ.

It seemed as if the Austral was finished, but the M.C.C. relented, and it was on again the following year, much purer, with no betting. Betting returned in 1904 and 1905 in a more careful form with licensed bookmakers, but the Austral already had lost its glamour. No longer was it a great international event.

In 1908, when bike riding was going down, the Melbourne Bicycle Club tried to compensate by getting into the air. To help draw the crowds to the Austral the M.B.C. staged a balloon ascent on the Melbourne Cricket Ground. Messrs. John Rinaldo and Christopher Sebphe went aloft and reached a height of 5000 feet. Rinaldo came down by a scarlet parachute and landed in a tree in the Fitzroy Gardens. Mr. Sebphe came down with the balloon, which landed on the roof of a house in Queen's Parade, North Fitzroy. Sebphe said when he landed on the top of this house he startled the lady inside "quite a bit."

For the Austral of 1909 clearly the M.B.C. had to go one better. It hired Miss Mollie Mostyn, the American lady aeronaut, and Captain Penfold, the Australian balloonist. Captain Penfold would ascend first and perform his sensational act of descending to earth by parachute mounted on a bicycle. Then Captain Penfold and Miss Mostyn would ascend together in the biggest balloon ever seen in Australia and they would race to the ground by parachute.

The ballooning had to be postponed for a week because of bad weather, but the next Saturday at the M.C.G. Molly Mostyn and Captain Penfold were ready. The captain first made his solo flight. The balloon took off very slowly and did not reach any great height, so he did not make his sensational descent as scheduled by parachute on a bicycle. The balloon came down on top of a fence in Vere Street, Collingwood. But he still had his bicycle, and it proved most convenient for riding back to the Melbourne Cricket Ground.

Then came the moment for the great double ascent. The Lady Mayoress, Mrs. Burston, christened the big balloon "The Austral" by throwing a bottle of champagne against its side. However, just as the ropes were being cast off, the balloon split from top to bottom. Fortunately, the Lady Mayoress had just moved away. A second balloon was requisitioned, but this developed a hole in the canvas from which smoke began to pour. Miss Mostyn, splendid in a drummer's uniform of blue with gold facings and parachute attached, was not daunted. She still wanted to go aloft, but Captain Penfold was not having any. Reluctantly Miss Mostyn put on her coat and the attempt was abandoned.

For 1910 what was left? The M.B.C. decided to stage an aeroplane flight right out of the M.C.G. Not only would such a thing be a remarkable feat at any time but it was only two months since Harry Houdini, the world famous escapologist, had made his historic flight at Diggers' Rest. He reached a height of 100 feet, covered a distance of between three and four miles and remained off the ground for 3 minutes 45 seconds.

The aeroplane chosen was a little Bleriot monoplane piloted by Mr. G. Cugnet. From the start, obviously it was a most dangerous operation, and Mr. Cugnet refused to take off until the weather conditions were just right. When the weather conditions were just right the cycling was long over and it was almost 7 p.m., so late that most of the Austral crowd had gone home.

Melbourne *Punch* said: "The machine looked like that formidable monster we called a horsestinger in our juvenile days. It had two wings and a long tail, and the tail resembled that of a crayfish."

The crowd waited a very long time before Mr. Cugnet appeared. When he did come he waved his arms in an agitated manner, and it appeared that he wanted the scoreboard removed. This was not altogether possible, so the tension mounted and the announcer told the crowd to hold its breath. A large gentleman swung the propeller of the Bleriot. It raced across the grass on tip-toes, changed its mind, stopped and sat down. Mr. Cugnet got out. Stakes were moved, ropes were moved, and this time said *Punch* with vicious sarcasm, it appeared he wanted the pavilion and Government House removed.

There was more delay. The propeller was swung again, and once more the Bleriot raced across the grass on tip-toes. "It was like a drunk being propelled from a pub by the seat of its pants." It rose into the air, ducked, tried to side-step the scoreboard, then dived into the tennis-court. Mr. Cugnet was unhurt, but his Bleriot was hideously wrecked, and *Punch* unkindly printed two photographs, one titled BEFORE, the other AFTER, and commented, "Neither Wright, Paulhan, nor Latham would have attempted such a thing. The risks of aeroplaning are sufficient without looking for trouble."

The wreckage of the poor little Bleriot was carted away from the tennis court and that was the end of the Austral at the M.C.G. Like the Bleriot, no longer could it get off the ground.

The Edwardian age may have been a sick time for professional cycling, but there was nothing wrong with cricket. A. C. Maclaren should have arrived with his England team in 1900, but because of the Boer War this was not possible. He arrived a season later, in November 1901, and right from the beginning Melbourne provided some novel weather. At 6 p.m. on November 14, 1901, there was the worst hailstorm on record. It was described as the sort of hailstorm that one reads about only in scientific journals. The majority of the stones were an inch in diameter and slightly flattened at either end, but the larger stones were as big as eggs.

The hail came down with a deafening clatter, and on the roofs it sounded like an artillery barrage. The damage was appalling, particularly to sky lights and glasshouses. Cole's Book Arcade was soon a pretty mess with broken glass and water pouring on to the books, and the beautiful Royal Arcade between Little Collins and Bourke Streets was a complete scene of devastation, knee-deep in glass. The hail caught the peak hour homegoers. One gentleman in Collins Street was struck by an egg-sized hailstone that bounced off the neck of his horse, and he received "as fine a specimen of a black eye as would grace the ring of the Democratic Club." Of all the home-goers the hail treated most harshly the crowds on the uncovered platforms of Flinders Street Railway Station. The newspapers said it was deplorable that in a modern city travellers had to put up with such primitive conditions, and the hail only served to highlight how badly Melbourne needed a new station. However, the unfortunate travellers had to wait another seven years before they received the building that now occupies the site.

There was another immediate, pressing problem. Would play be possible the following morning on the Melbourne Cricket Ground for the match between Victoria and England? Major Ben Wardill told the press that hail would not hurt the pitch. It was too hard. You could batter it with brickbats.

Yet next day the pitch was a rare sight. It looked as if it had been attacked by smallpox. It was so odd that even the Governor-General, Lord Hopetoun, and the Countess of Hopetoun went out to inspect it. Victoria sent England in to bat, but Maclaren's men showed their traditional skill on difficult wickets and made 166. In the second innings Victoria was all out for 89, and the great S. F. Barnes took 7 for 38. England won by 118 runs.

England won the First Test in Sydney by an innings and 124 runs, so there was great alarm and forebodings about the Second Test, particularly when New Year's Day 1902 arrived and it was obvious that there would be another wet wicket. Australia was all out for 112, with ducks from Trumper, Noble and S. E. Gregory. Barnes took 6 for 42 and Blythe 4 for 64, and they bowled unchanged throughout the innings. It was disastrous, the first time Melbourne had seen the Test side in the new All-Australian colours of green and gold and this had to happen. But then Noble and Trumble went into action and bowling unchanged like Barnes and Blythe they routed England for SIXTY-ONE runs. The newspapers were ecstatic. Noble was the greatest all-rounder, the greatest bowler in the world. Never before in a Test match had a bowler turned in such figures—7 wickets for 17 runs. Hugh Trumble took 3 for 38. Australia was all out, England was all out, but still the day was not over. Gregory sent in his nightwatchmen, but by stumps he was five down for 48. For the man who goes to cricket to see the falling of wickets it could hardly have been more delightful—in one amazing day 25 wickets fell. Johnnie Moyes has recorded that in the Third Test against the West Indies in Adelaide in 1952 22 wickets fell on the first day for 207 runs. He said: "We thought this was a record, and no one mentioned that famous day in Melbourne in the 1901-02 season."

It was Warwick Armstrong's first Test, and seeing that he was an M.C.C. man he received a big cheer when he went out to bat. There was such a line up of Australian stars his turn did not come until seventh wicket down and he scored 4 not out. In the second innings he was last man in and he made 45 not out in a 120 tenth wicket partnership with Duff. It was a lovely match for Duff. It was also his first Test match, and some of the newspapers had criticised the selectors for their amazing imbecility in picking him. He made 32 in his first innings and 104 in the second. It was his heavy scoring plus 99 from Clem Hill that helped Australia to win by 229 runs. England was all out for 175 in the second innings, and what a match it was for Noble—13 wickets for 77 runs. Then at the finish Hugh Trumble got a hat-trick. He took the wickets of Gunn, A. O. Jones and S. F. Barnes with successive balls.

With a splendid all-star cast of Hill, Noble, Trumble, Armstrong, Trumper and Gregory, Australia won the rubber four Tests to one.

The star-studded team went to England in 1902, managed again by the "never-stop-running" secretary of the Melbourne Cricket Club, Major Ben Wardill. Not only did he manage most teams that went to England, he managed also many of the English teams that came to Australia. He must have had a happy year in 1902. This was possibly the best team ever to visit England. Under the captaincy of Joe Darling it won two Tests, lost one and drew two. But seven batsmen made over 1000 runs for the tour—Trumper, Noble, Hill, Duff, Armstrong, Hopkins and Darling. Trumper made 2540 runs. He enraptured the English critics. He was described, with no argument, as the finest batsman in the world. He had the highest average, 48.49, and he had made the greatest number of runs in an Australian tour to date. Trumble was hailed as the finest bowler in the world and Noble the best all-rounder.

When they returned, the club gave them a dinner at Menzies Hotel, attended by the Governor, Sir Sydenham Clark. The M.C.C. president, Mr. Roderick Murchison, said it was the first time Australia had ever won two Tests in England. What a year it had been. Australia had to welcome home the winners of the Kolapore Cup (much prized at the time for rifle shooting), the champion sculler of the world, George Towns, and Madame Melba had returned to us as the acknowledged Queen of Song.

Triumphant as the homecoming for the Test side was, it could not be compared with Nellie Melba's return. She returned two months earlier, her first visit in 16 years. On September 27 an enormous crowd gathered outside the Melbourne Town Hall, three hours before her concert was due to begin, and the police had to fight through the night to make way for the traffic. Major Ben Wardill would have admired the financial arrangements. For nine concerts, five in Melbourne, four in Sydney, Nellie Melba netted £21,000.

In 1903 for the first time the Marylebone Cricket Club arranged and managed a cricket tour to Australia. To use the vernacular, neither the English nor the Australian press thought the team was worth a crumpet. Archie Maclaren refused to go, so did the Hon. F. S. Jackson, C. B. Fry and S. F. Barnes, who had been such a success on the previous tour. But the famous pair from Yorkshire, G. H. Hirst and Wilfred Rhodes, was there. Rhodes was not the bat he was to become, but he was the world's greatest left-hand bowler on a wet wicket, and there was a good deal of water available that Australian summer. Then there was B. J. T. Bosanquet, the inventor of the Bosey or the wrong-'un. Often his length was all over the wicket, but when he was accurate the Australians did not know what they had struck. R. E. Foster was another, just a name to the Australian newspapermen, yet he made 287 in the First Test at Sydney, a Test record.

Australia was beaten in the First Test, and the beautiful confidence of December changed to the desperation of January. Who would bowl against Mr. Pelham Warner's powerful team? Hugh Trumble was urged to come out of retirement and did so. Over 32,000 people saw the first day, when England somewhat laboriously made 221, then increased it to 315 the next day. Then came the wet and Australia had to bat on a bad wicket. The Merri Creek soil had a famed reputation. When it was bad, it was not merely bad—it was shocking. The day, the weather, the wicket, seemed to have been designed for the benefit of Wilfred Rhodes.

He started with six men within seven yards of the bat and made the big-name Australian batsmen—Noble, Duff, Clem Hill and Armstrong look like Saturday morning cricketers. Rhodes took 7 for 56, and without Victor Trumper the innings would have been all over in an hour. He made 185 not out in the previous Test, but there were club members who claimed this was the finest of all the Trumper innings and the most skilful ever played on the Melbourne Cricket Ground.

He made 74 out of a 122 total in 1 hour 52 minutes. He opened the batting and he was the last man out. Just to gain some idea of the quality of this innings it should be remembered that at no time did he have a reliable partner and constantly he was trying to save an end to face the bowling. At times he scored off almost every ball, and when the situation looked blackest of all he hit out. Frequently he sent the ball bouncing into the Ladies' Reserve. Towards the end of the innings he walked down the wicket to Rhodes and hit him right over the sightboard for five. There were still no sixes in Test cricket.

He was the only batsman who knew how to use his feet on this sticky wicket, and by walking down the pitch he knocked Rhodes off his length. The cricket writers talked of his amazing quickness of eye, of his remarkable reflexes, of the way he could take a second look and change his mind in the middle of a stroke. The end of the innings, and the end of Trumper, came in worthy style. Tyldesley caught him on the fence.

England did no better in the second innings with 103, but the first innings advantage was too much. Wilfred Rhodes finished with 15 wickets for 124 runs and Mr. Pelham Warner had another easy win.

Yet Melbourne had not seen all that could be done with a wet wicket at the M.C.C. The 1904 match between England and Victoria was a classic. Victoria started well by making 299 against England's 248, and it was considered that should the weather turn bad then this 51 runs was a nice advantage, just enough to make the game interesting. Over the week-end it poured, and it became obvious that anyone who wanted to see the Victorian batsmen in action needed to be there bright and early. The innings lasted only 45 minutes and they were all out for 15 runs. Rhodes bowled 37 balls and took 5 wickets for 6. Arnold bowled 36 balls and took 4 wickets for 8.

There were six Victorian ducks. Harry Trott with 9 runs made the top score, but as one newspaper said, "Let him not be overcome with pride over this, because he gave two chances during those nine runs, one of which robbed Rhodes of a hat-trick. Rhodes bowled McAlister with his third ball, Armstrong with his fourth, and Trott should have gone with his next, but Bosanquet missed a catch." The *Argus* went to a great deal of trouble over statistics. "This was the worst score ever by an Australian team against English bowling. It is not the world's worst score. Oxford once scored 12 against the Marylebone Club and Notts once got 13 against Yorkshire, but Victoria comes a good third."

The 15 runs still remains the lowest score ever made in a first-class match in Australia, and the batsmen could not blame it all on the pitch because batting on the same wicket England had no trouble in scoring freely.

Australia won the next Test at Adelaide and England won the Fourth Test at Sydney, so by the time the Fifth Test came to Melbourne it was all over. Yet the public was still fascinated with the series. During Test match time in the pre-radio days one of the greatest problems was to find out the score. The telephone was still a luxury and newspaper information was quickly stale. So the *Argus* ran a news agency system. As a public service the newspaper posted the latest telegrams outside all the leading suburban news agencies. So if mother wanted to know the Test score she had merely to send junior down to the local newspaper shop.

Once again it was a wet weather affair, but this time it rained for Australia, and the Australians won by 218 runs. In the first innings England was all out for 61. Noble took 4 wickets for 19 and Albert Cotter, the new find as a fast bowler, took 6 for 40. But the second innings was the one to remember, and it was the sort of finale to a great cricket career that a Test bowler could only dream about. England made 101 and the wrecker was Hugh Trumble. He took 7 for 28, including the hat-trick—Bosanquet, Warner and Lilley—with successive balls. Mr. Pelham Warner was captain, so he could not use that charming Patsy Hendren trick of blaming his captain for sending him out to bat in the middle of a hat-trick.

There have been only six hat-tricks in Test cricket between England and

Australia; Trumble has taken two of them, and four have been on the M.C.G. J. T. Hearne had, perhaps, the most brilliant of them all. His hat-trick sent Hill, Gregory and Noble back to the pavilion.

Hugh Trumble finished his cricket as a Test hero. His score of 141 Test wickets was a record against England, made at a time when English amateur batsmen were supreme—Stoddart, Maclaren, Prince Ranjitsinhji, Hon. F. S. Jackson and C. B. Fry. He stood 6 ft. 4 in., and like Bill Johnston he could give the ball a strange trajectory, and it invariably dropped shorter than expected. His long arms stretched out like a barbed wire entanglement and he was a magnificent slips fieldsman. In one match he threw out an arm and caught a swallow in full flight, which is the only time the bird life has been worried that way on the M.C.G.

At the start of the series a fine compliment came from C. B. Fry: "I should prefer not to see Hugh Trumble against me in flannels for the simple reason that he is the most long-headed, observant and acute judge of the game, a perfect master of the whole art of placing fieldsmen and changing bowlers. It is his head—that long solemn head—I should fear were I Warner, not his bowling arm, spinning fingers, deft as they are. It is the head, the best of the side, that Hugh Trumble makes most difference to the Australians."

This was a great time for Warwick Armstrong. In a match Melbourne versus University at the University in March 1904 he made 438. He gave difficult chances at 210 and 411 and made his runs in 6 hours 35 minutes, better than a run a minute. On the tour to England in 1905 he topped the batting average with 2002 runs at 48.42 and the bowling, 130 wickets at 17.6. And when he came home there was a lovely match—Melbourne against Williamstown. He made 200 not out in 144 minutes. He hit 6 sixes, 1 five and 20 fours. Then there was the 1906 match against Essendon, when he made 251 runs in 180 minutes, and twice he hit the Essendon bowler Forsythe right out of the ground, something that had been done only twice before. George Bonnor hit the English bowler Peate into the Richmond Paddock in 1881, and Bill Howell, the Bathurst bee farmer, hit Jack Saunders right over the grandstand in 1901.

The club let in another 1000 members, raising the total to 4497, and in February 1906 Mr. Thomas Bent, the Premier, laid the foundation stone of the Grey Smith stand. As soon as it was built, again it was reported that gentlemen were seen smoking there, something very distasteful to the ladies, so the committee ordered that "No Smoking" signs be displayed. Another stand was built to cater for the public in the outer, but apparently no complaints about smoking came from there.

92

Early in 1907 Mr. Roderick Murchison resigned his position as president to go abroad and Mr. Justice Cussen became the new leader of the M.C.C. He was to be president for 26 years.

Mr. A. O. Jones brought out a team for the Marylebone Cricket Club for the 1907-08 season. Australia won four out of the five Tests, and the new stars were Vernon Ransford for Australia and J. B. Hobbs for England. For those who like to be wise after the event it is always fun to read the pre-match forecasts. Take the Second Test match played at the M.C.G. It was generally agreed that while Hobbs had played two good innings in N.S.W., was this man up to Test match standard? There were two candidates for selection, Hobbs and Hayes, but seeing that Hayes could also bowl, any sensible captain would go for Hayes. Oddly enough the selectors did not take this shrewd advice and they selected Jack Hobbs. He scored an 83 that was "full of confidence and forceful batting." It was the only Test in the rubber lost by Australia and then by one wicket.

The Fourth Test at the M.C.G. Australia won by 308 runs, but there were two fearful shocks, disasters that hit the nation at once like losing two battleships in a naval engagement. Victor Trumper went for a duck in both innings. This was something that had never happened to Trumper before and mercifully never happened again. Much space was devoted to the calamity. As one newspaper said: "Before the contest nobody would have dreamed of such a remote contingency as the great Victor Trumper making two duck eggs in a Test match. Any man who had cared to gamble on such a thing would have received fantastic odds." No doubt it would soothe any cricketer to know that a match has been remembered by posterity for the one reason that he did something so extraordinary as to fail to score in both innings, yet it must have rankled at the time. In the final Test he gave one of his most Trumperish displays. He scored a dazzling 166 runs.

Australians were making names for themselves in 1908. Norman Brookes was the world champion tennis player and Frank Beaurepaire was just beginning to startle the world with his swimming achievements. Melburnians were crazy for sport. On Boxing Day, 1908, there was the important Victoria-N.S.W. match on the Melbourne Cricket Ground, but at Rushcutters Bay there was a counter-attraction that was a little too powerful. The M.C.C.'s only hope of attracting spectators was to provide a running telegram service on everything that was happening at Rushcutters Bay, round by round.

December 26 was the day of the long-awaited Tommy Burns-Jack Johnson bout for the heavyweight championship of the world, the only such contest ever to be fought in Australia. The next morning the *Argus* printed an astonishing photograph, not of the fight but of the scene outside the *Argus* office in Melbourne. The photograph went right across the spread of the broadsheet on the main news page, a daring thing to do in those days of non-pictorial journalism. Collins Street was choked with people, the sort of crowd one would expect for the announcement of the Armistice or the burning of the Town Hall. In the centre of this crowd were several cable trams, unable to move because of the crush of gentlemen in their straw boaters.

The *Argus* reported that the crowd was there for no other reason but to read the telegrams posted outside the office of the news of the fight. And this crowd was bitterly resentful towards Johnson. The telegrams told how this black monolith of a man towered over Tommy Burns, how he thrashed him for round after round, enjoying the murder far too much to knock him out. The telegrams, too, told how Johnson was so much in command that he was able to taunt Burns constantly, and even the crowd could hear.

" 'Come on now, Tahmy—Jewel won't know you when she gets you home'. . . 'That's right, Tahmy, feint away, you'll fight directly perhaps'. . . Then he would grin, show his gold teeth, pat Burns on the shoulder and say, 'Poor little guy.' "

The *Argus* reported: "Hardly a cheer greeted the reports of Johnson's successes, and the air was heavy with resentment. One man said, 'If Johnson is licking him so badly why doesn't he knock him out?' " But Burns was never at any time capable of touching the negro. Johnson thrashed him to the edge of insensibility, and at the 14th round the bout was stopped. Johnson was the new champion and Burns announced his retirement from the ring.

Meanwhile Victoria thrashed N.S.W. at the M.C.G. Victoria made 369 and won by an innings and 47 runs. Vernon Ransford was in a hitting mood and he made 94 runs.

Every year the M.C.C. gave exhibitioners' tickets to promising young cricketers from the public schools. This was something that had been done, since 1875, and many of the young exhibitioners later played for Australia. The exhibitioners received honorary membership for two years. After that time they had to revert to the waiting list, unless, of course, they proved to be exceptional cricketers, then, under the rules, the ballot could be opened. The same system still applies today. If the talent is there, exhibitions are available for each of the six original public schools and four of the associated grammar and new public schools.

For the 1909-10 season the club awarded exhibitions to E. F. Herring of Melbourne Grammar, R. L. Park of Wesley College, and A. E. V. Hartkopf of Scotch College. Two of these boys played cricket for Australia. E. F. Herring,

94

later Sir Edmund, and Victoria's Lieutenant-Governor and Chief Justice, was an exceptionally fine schoolboy bat. He, too, perhaps, could have played for Australia, but there was too little time for cricket. He went to Oxford as a Rhodes Scholar in 1911 and his next assignment was the 1914-18 War. Like Roy Park, he was a lovely cricketer to watch—there was perfection in the timing of his strokes.

The late Dr. R. L. Park won the M.C.C. first eleven batting average while he was still at school, the only time it has ever been done by a schoolboy. He did not pick a lucky year either; in the club were men like Warwick Armstrong, Ransford and Vaughan. On leaving school he went to the University and, of course, had to play with that club. He was a good wicketkeeper and a change bowler, but his career was spoilt by bad luck. He was selected to go to South Africa, but the tour was cancelled because of the war. He played again in 1919, and his big chance came when he was selected for the Second Test against England in 1920 on the M.C.G. The crowd loved the little doctor, and when he went out to bat they rose and gave him probably the greatest reception a cricketer has ever received on the M.C.G. He was out first ball. Maybe the reception from the crowd was too much, but Harry Howell, the Warwickshire fast bowler, got him while he was still looking for concentration. It was a sad day too for Mrs. Park. She was knitting in the grandstand and just as Roy Park shaped up to the first delivery she dropped a ball of wool. She bent down to pick it up and by the time she looked again she had missed her husband's entire Test career. Australia won the Test by an innings, but Park never again played in a Test match. A man had to be almost superhuman to earn a safe place in the Australian Eleven. Roy Park made nine centuries for Victoria, all within a short period, but still he was not good enough. Yet cricket was not all; he was an outstanding Australian Rules footballer. He played for the Melbourne Football Club, and he represented Victoria against South Australia. Maybe the finest tribute he received was the year he finished at the head of the goal-kicking list; the Richmond barrackers lifted him on to their shoulders and carried him in to the pavilion. All those with any knowledge of Melbourne football will realise such an occurrence is even more remarkable than Mr. Trumper scoring two duck eggs in a Test match. But Roy Park was a great sportsman and cricket remained in the family, for his daughter married the Australian Test captain Ian Johnson, later secretary of the M.C.C.

A. E. V. Hartkopf also became a doctor, and he too played in only one Test match. The selectors seemed even more contrary this time, because he made 80 runs and then was dropped. The selectors were not looking so much for runs as for wickets, and here Hartkopf had a bad time. He took one wicket for

134 runs. Yet he had a successful Sheffield Shield career, he was a great athlete, a fine oarsman, a top-class Australian Rules footballer, and many experts
believe he was the best all-round athlete ever to go to a public school in
Victoria.

The first touring side of South Africans came to Australia for the 1910-11
season. Their bag was only one Test out of five, but they were much better
than that. They had Aubrey Faulkner, who scored a Test average of 73.2,
including two centuries, and David Nourse, the big left-hander, hit five centuries in first-class games. It is rare for famous cricketers to have equally
famous cricketing sons. While David Nourse was playing in the match South
Africa versus South Australia, A. D. Nourse junior was born. Nourse then
showed a brand of courage not possessed by all fathers. While his wife was
afar off in South Africa he named the boy after Lord Dudley, the State Governor, and that was the very first time that Australia heard about Dudley
Nourse.

The Fourth Test at the M.C.G. was an Australian scoring spree. The Aus-
tralians made 328 in the first innings and 578 in the second. There was
something in the pie for everybody, Bardsley, Ransford, Armstrong, Hill and
Trumper all made big scores, but the South Africans never really got going.
They did not know what to make of H. V. Hordern, the young Sydney dentist.
He was the first Australian to develop Bosanquet's wrong-'un. Mailey and
Grimmett were to follow, and some claim he was a more accurate bowler
than either, but dentistry stopped him from giving much time to cricket.

On the Saturday this Fourth Test provided rather a different kind of drama.
W. L. Murdoch, a solicitor, was there. But more than that he was the G.O.M.,
the W. G. Grace, of Australian cricket. Nor was there much between them.
When Grace was Grace and Murdoch was Murdoch, Grace had a Test average
of 32.29 and Murdoch had an average of 32. Then there was the day he made
321 for N.S.W. against Victoria, a record that stood for 47 years until Bradman beat it with 340 not out. Well, the great man watched the match that
morning, then he had lunch with the committee. He was troubled because
earlier he had made a forecast that five South African wickets would fall
before lunch. As soon as he said it those wickets fell one by one and he
remarked, "I'll never make another prophecy again—I've brought bad luck
on those boys."

After lunch he was talking to a friend, when he complained of being ill.
Suddenly he nosed forward on the table. Obviously he was very ill indeed. Dr.
Ramsay Mailer, a committeeman, saw that he was suffering from a stroke and
ordered his immediate removal to hospital. W. L. Murdoch died that after-

noon, and while the match was still being played all the flags at the M.C.G. were lowered to half-mast.

The *Argus* said: "News of his death under any circumstances would have created profound regret, but on such an occasion, in such surroundings, the event was infused with a note of tragedy and pathos that made a very deep impression."

The newspapers recalled the days when Murdoch was just a young wicket-keeper for New South Wales, how John Blackham got the job in the First Test match, and the Demon Spofforth refused to play because he wanted Murdoch "his own personal wicket-keeper." John Blackham became the "prince of wicket-keepers," so Murdoch had to find another outlet for his talents. He became the great Australian batsman of the 19th century, and forever will he be remembered as the first Australian captain to defeat England on English soil. He was only 54 when he died.

M. A. Noble took a team to England in 1909 and captured the Ashes, but by the 1912 season, for some, there was little time left for big cricket. It was the last big season for Victor Trumper, Clem Hill, Tibby Cotter and Vernon Ransford, a season that was to be full of frustration, anger and bitterness. Sadly Pelham Warner became ill after the first match and Johnny Douglas had to take over. But this was a good team, and with the bowling pair of Barnes and Foster it was very nearly the best in the history of cricket.

For the Second Test the M.C.C. had a new grandstand—the B. J. Wardill stand, which was opened by the Governor, Sir John Fuller. Major Ben Wardill, "the popular M.C.C. secretary," retired in February, 1911. In the countless references to him in the newspapers he was never just the secretary of the M.C.C.; always he was "the popular secretary," and one suspects he must have been. Immediately the committee made him a life member, and, as he was retiring because of ill-health, he received a pension. Yet the greatest honour of all was the new stand, and this was completed within a year of his resignation. S. M. Tindall was the new secretary, but he was there only nine months. On November 30, 1911, Hugh Trumble took over, and for many years he was to apply "that long solemn head" to the problems of the M.C.C.

Australia won the First Test, and the Second Test began at the M.C.G. on January 1, 1912, and the result was awaited by the crowd of 26,390 confidently and in a state of happy contentment. When Clem Hill won the toss there was even a sporting feeling of sympathy for the Englishmen. It was obvious that there would be a large score on such a wicket, and the English would do at least two days of leather hunting.

Foster opened the bowling and the first over was a maiden. Bardsley played the first ball from Barnes on to his foot and from there to the wicket. He was out. Those who went into the bar to recover from this awful shock returned only to find that Kelleway had gone l.b.w. to Barnes and then Clem Hill, clean bowled by Barnes. The score: 3 wickets for 8 runs, Barnes 3 for 1.

This could not possibly go on. But it did. Warwick Armstrong remained for only 4 runs. He was caught Smith, bowled Barnes. The score was 4 for 11, Barnes 4 for 1. Then came Trumper. Ah-h, now with Victor Trumper at the wicket the crowd looked forward to one of those typically brilliant Trumper innings, where he would bravely thrash the bowler off his length. Alas, he did not. Barnes drove him back against the stumps, so that he was defending, pushing, poking desperately. At lunch the score was just 32 runs—Trumper 13, Ransford 8.

Theoretically a good lunch should have made everything right once more, but it did not. Trumper failed to add another run. He was bowled by Foster and Sid Barnes bowled Minnett. At this stage it is recorded that Barnes said nothing. He folded his arms and, with great happiness, he looked at the scoreboard which almost looked like a misprint—Australia 6 for 38, Barnes 5 for 6. Take the wicket, take the batsmen concerned, then those figures were recording the greatest bowling performance ever on the M.C.G.

Some commentators said the wicket was a "little over-ripe," that some dampness came through after the covers were removed, which caused the ball to bite; but under no circumstances could it be described as a bad wicket. This was the day of the "Barnes-Dance." From the very first ball it was obvious that the batsmen were in for some great unhappiness. Barnes quickly proved himself unplayable, sending down medium-paced balls that turned viciously from the leg, with an occasional fast, straight one. Then every so often he brought back a ball from the leg without any apparent change of action.

Vernon Ransford made 43 and the tail-enders did far better than the star batsmen. Particularly when Hordern and Carter hit the ball about, the crowd began to cheer. Barnes, very foolishly, resented this. He was about to begin an over, when suddenly he stopped and threw the ball down. The crowd broke into roars, groans and yells. "Take him off." The angrier Barnes became the more they yelled. When Barnes finally was persuaded to go on bowling he was rattled and he was unable to find a length. His figures at the last were 5 for 44, but they could have been much better. England won by 8 wickets.

Australia did not win another match in this series. In the Fourth Test at the M.C.G. the Englishmen completed the picture by setting some records of a different kind. Rhodes for the previous tour was last man in. This time he opened with Jack Hobbs, and everybody was most interested to see how he would shape. They had a good opportunity, for he was there all day, and the opening partnership provided 323 runs. Hobbs made 178, Rhodes made 179. The partnership lasted 268 minutes. The *Argus* said:

> They helped themselves to runs almost as they pleased; the weakness of the Australian attack was completely and mercilessly exposed. Some 31,795 paid £1442 for the privilege of seeing their countrymen flogged about the field. Not for many a day has an Australian Eleven been so badly whipped. Those who consider cricket apart from country—possibIy only a small minority—witnessed some very remarkable batting. Hobbs by his achievements this tour has proved himself to be the greatest living batsman. Rhodes was stolid rather than masterful. As his bowling declines so his batting improves, not at all an uncommon experience in cricket.

England with 589 runs on the board naturally had only to bat once and won by an innings and 225 runs.

It was not a good match for the Australians, and what with Edwardian fashions it was not always a good match for the spectators. This letter appeared in the *Argus*:

> Sir,—May I on behalf of many fellow-sufferers protest against the abnormal size of the hats worn by the majority of the women at cricket and football matches. A stand has been made against this nuisance by theatrical managers, and the matinee hat is now a thing of the past.
>
> Why cannot a similar stand be made by the managers of open-air entertainments, and the huge hat be classed with dogs and perambulators as calculated to cause inconveniences to the general public, and as such be refused admittance to circumscribed enclosures.
>
> During the Test match today my view for the greater part of the match was completely blocked by three women with enormous creations of flowers, feathers and whatnot on their heads. In vain I tried to see round, above or below; every way was equally futile.
>
> The practice of wearing these monster hats is both stupid and selfish, and the sooner the wearers are made to realise that they are a public nuisance the better for everyone.
>
> Yours, etc
> ST. KILDA.

Then this appeared:

> There are seven reasons why women go to cricket at the M.C.G., good and sufficient all of them—to women.

Firstly, because they meet their friends;
Secondly, because they meet their enemies;
Thirdly, because they wish to see other women's dresses.,
Fourthly, because they want other women to see their dresses;
Fifthly, because a Test match is a correct thing to see;
Sixthly, because their husbands or lovers go;
Seventhly, and far from leastly, out of curiosity.

And on the question of sitting out a whole match, no woman has ever done it, unless she was in love with one of the players. Once it is said that a woman did undoubtedly see the first ball bowled and the last wicket fall, but the statement lacks confirmation.

Under these attacks, and after the passage of more than 50 years, women have continued to wear big hats to cricket matches and they still have seven excellent reasons for going to the M.C.G.—bless them.

Lord Sheffield's team of 1891–1892.

The Australian team, 1893.

A Melbourne Cricket Club team in the mid 1890s.

CHAPTER TWELVE

The 1912 Overture

BEFORE 1912 the Melbourne Cricket Club dominated cricket in Australia. In the other States there was no equivalent to it in power or prestige. In Sydney the Sydney Cricket Ground was run by trustees and there was no counterpart to the M.C.C. The controlling body in Victoria was the Victorian Cricket Association, yet the M.C.C. was the real force. The M.C.C. backed the tours of England teams in Australia, and in turn the club sent Australian sides to England. The V.C.A. was nearly penniless and it had to depend on assistance from the M.C.C.

At the height of the 1912 controversy Joe Darling, the old Australian captain, said: "The M.C.C. has done more in the past for Australian cricket than the N.S.W. and Victorian associations have ever done or are ever likely to do." He spoke from tbe heart, and most of the players, past and present, agreed with him. Of the many disputes that took place between 1904 and 1912 nobody will ever know who was in the right and who was in the wrong. Time and again in 1912 the M.C.C. was accused of being the villain, trying to corner Australian cricket. But after 1905 most M.C.C. members realised that the club could not remain the benevolent dictator of cricket and there would have to be another form of control.

The struggle with the V.C.A. started as early as 1888-89. For that year the leading colonies decided to play just one match against each other. N.S.W. refused to go along with this agreement. It wanted two matches against Victoria as always, but as a result of the wrangle the M.C.G. was left without the traditional Boxing Day match. The M.C.C. stepped in, and of its own authority agreed to stage the intercolonial matches with N.S.W. for the next five years. The V.C.A. was livid. The Association met and stated that if the M.C.C. continued in this then V.C.A. members would refuse to meet the M.C.C. on the cricket field. The club resigned from the V.C.A., but later there was a private conference, the V.C.A. resumed control of the intercolonial matches and the M.C.C. rejoined the V.C.A.

In 1905 there was the move to form the Australian Board of Control. There had been an organisation called the Australian Cricket Council, a short-lived, ineffective body, which proved unpopular with the players. Maybe the M.C.C. saw the same thing happening again, maybe after its long experience in international cricket it was jealous of losing control; but whatever the motives the M.C.C. opposed the formation of the Board, and on February 4, 1905, it sent out a circular to all clubs explaining why it was unnecessary. Circulars then were very much the fashion. Anyone who disagreed with anything produced a circular. During the 1912 controversy all the leading players and officials produced circulars, and after the 1905 M.C.C. circular the V.C.A. brought out a circular in reply.

The circular said it was incontrovertible that control of international cricket in Australia should be in the hands, not of a single club however great and wealthy, but in those of various associations already governing interstate cricket.

At the height of the controversy, in April 1906, the club withdrew from the V.C.A. and joined with other clubs like Caulfield and Elsternwick in forming the Victorian Cricket League for the purpose of introducing and playing district cricket. The V.C.A. accused the M.C.C. of offering these clubs cash bribes to join. Furthermore, how could the M.C.C. play district cricket? It did not have a district.

Yet when the controversy was at its most bitter point and the V.C.A. almost ready to go out of existence, suddenly the fight ended. The V.C.A. introduced its own scheme for district cricket. The M.C.C. would play in the matches, but seeing it had no district it would not compete for the pennant. Then best of all, as far as the club was concerned, it would have a delegate on the Board of Control. The M.C.C. joined the V.C.A. and it dropped its opposition to the Board. It seemed that all the troubles of Australian cricket were over, and on May 6 the Board of Control had its inaugural meeting at Wesley College. The first honorary secretary was Alderman William Percy McElhone, a future Lord Mayor of Sydney. Nobody knew it then, but here was a man who was to be caricatured in Melbourne almost as often as Billy Hughes.

The great dispute of 1912, which was the end of dozens of friendships and was to cause great bitterness for years to come, started quite suddenly. The Board of Control met just before New Year's Day, 1912, to discuss arrangements for the coming tour to England. Almost at the end of the meeting, Colonel Foxton, the Queensland delegate, introduced this resolution:

"That a representative of the Board be appointed by the Board to accompany the Australian Eleven to England in 1912. That the duties shall be to keep the books of account relating to the tour and generally supervise all matters relating to or incidental to the tour; such a representative to be allowed a salary of £400, to be paid by the Board, together with all travelling expenses as enjoyed by members of the Eleven, which shall be charged against the expenses of the tour."

It looked innocent enough as resolutions go, but every line was radioactive. Only two delegates voted against it, the South Australian man and Mr. Aitken of the Melbourne Cricket Club.

The resolution was a deliberate attempt to get rid of Frank Laver, who managed both the 1905 and the 1909 tours to England. Managers had to earn their money in those days. He not only managed and did the administration but he played as well. Laver always bowled better in England and his 1909 tour was a beauty. In the Manchester Test he took 8 wickets for 31 runs. Yet apart from his cricket, he was a personality, an efficient manager and the players adored him.

At this meeting of the Board of Control the delegates accused him of mismanaging the tour and of being disloyal to the Board. There was the matter of the books. Repeatedly the Board had asked him for a full accounting of the tour and Laver refused to produce the books.

Laver had no chance to defend himself at the meeting, but he made a long reply to the newspapers. He said the treasurer of the tour was Peter McAlister, and it should have been his job to look after all the figures. Certainly, he had kept books, but they contained personal information about the players and he did not intend to hand them over. In turn he accused the Board of bungling the financial arrangements, and he made it obvious that he had written a letter to Mr. McElhone, now chairman of the Board, telling him to do everything but "go jump in the lake." Frank Laver had many other qualities, but one of them was not tact. And he had another black mark against him. Originally he was made manager through the Melbourne Cricket Club.

However, there was more to it than this. Under the constitution of the new Board of Control, clause nine stated the players had the right to appoint their own manager, subject to confirmation by the Board.

The outcry in Melbourne was ominous. The *Australasian* cried: "Is there no such thing as respect for principle in public life? Mr. Lawyer Foxton and Mr. Lawyer Hughes in the artifices they devise to transgress the bounds are absolutely indistinguishable."

The battle divided into two camps. On one side there was the Board of Control and the cricket associations of Tasmania, Victoria, Queensland, New South Wales and the Sydney press. On the other was the South Australian

Cricket Association, the Melbourne Cricket Club, most of the players everywhere and the Melbourne press. Perhaps the fury was greatest of all in South Australia. The brilliant Australian captain, Clement Hill, the leader of the rebels, was a local Adelaide boy. Any attack on him was akin to an attack on the Royal Family, Lord Kitchener, Nellie Melba and Colonel Light all of a piece. The players had yet to show their hand, but already the suggestions were loud that if Frank Laver were not appointed manager many of the leading players would refuse to go to England.

The Board's first move was very subtle. It would send a representative of the Board with the team, who would supervise all matters. He would be paid £400 by the Board, plus all travelling expenses, and this money would come out of the Board's share of the tour. Thus the players would profit. Admittedly there was clause nine in the constitution, but if the players still wished they could take their own manager, but would he not be rather unnecessary?

Unnecessary was hardly the word. It was obvious to the players that the Board representative would hold the stick, and there was no hope for Frank Laver.

On January 7, Mr. McElhone, the Board chairman, said: "The attitude of the Melbourne press comes as no surprise to me, because it has been hostile to the Board from its establishment, evidently, rightly or wrongly, holding the opinion that the control of cricket should have remained in the hands of the Melbourne Cricket Club. This attempt to bring certain cricketers into conflict with the Board is no doubt done with the object of bursting up the body so that management of international cricket would again revert to the M.C.C."

Mr. E. F. Mitchell, K.C., for the club, said that never at any time in M.C.C. circles had there been the slightest mention of "bursting up the Board of Control." Mr. McElhone had the M.C.C. on the brain.

On January 25 six players sent an historic letter to the Board of Control. It said that under the rules of the constitution the players must be allowed to appoint their own manager. . ."Failing compliance with our request, we have to inform you with much regret that none of us will be available for selection or to play if selected."

Yours truly,
C. HILL, W. W. ARMSTRONG, V. TRUMPER, V. RANSFORD,
A. COTTER, H. CARTER."

Those names meant the cream of Australian cricket—four of the best batsmen, the best fast bowler, and the best wicket-keeper. For the cricket lover the shock was almost too much to bear.

104

The Board of Control replied:

> The Board has in no sense abrogated clause nine of its constitution, but has only expressed its opinion that as a representative of the Board will accompany the team the appointment of a manager is unnecessary, so it feels that if this opinion is not voiced by the majority of the players they can still nominate a manager acceptable to the Board. Personally I don't see why the position cannot be filled by one person.
>
> Whilst the Board is anxious at all times to send the best team possible, at the same time I am sure it will not permit any number of cricketers to dictate terms or conditions on which a visit is to be made or, if a manager is appointed, the terms and nature of the engagement.
>
> Yours truly,
SYDNEY SMITH, JUN.,
Hon. Sec., Australian Board of Control.

If the situation already was delicate then there was dynamite on the way—the February 3 meeting of the selectors in Sydney. Their job was to pick the team for the Fourth Test in Melbourne and the team to leave for England in March. Two of the selectors were Clem Hill and Peter McAlister. Clem Hill was the captain of Australia. Peter McAlister of Victoria, a friend of the Board, went to England on the 1909 tour and, judging from his performances, he was lucky to get the trip.

Before the selectors' meeting Clem Hill sent this telegram to McAlister:

> Macartney all right. Think must have left-arm bowler. Suggest Macartney and Matthews in place of Whitty and Minnett. Minnett twelfth.

McAlister replied:

> My team as forwarded yesterday. Still opposed Macartney's inclusion. If Iredale agrees with you, favour YOURSELF standing down and not Minnett.

One can only imagine Hill's reaction when he received this telegram. HIMSELF stand down indeed. He had just come from making 98 in the Adelaide Test. The effrontery of the suggestion was quite something.

So they met in Sydney with the other selector, F. A. Iredale, the Test batsman of the 'nineties, and the secretary of the Board of Control, Sydney Smith.

As they sat down the atmosphere was uncomfortable because of the McAlister telegram. Immediately Hill said that Frank Laver ought to be in the Fourth Test. The mere mention of Laver was enough to annoy McAlister. Far better, he said, to have Kelleway and Minnett. Hill said he didn't think much of either of them.

And so the argument progressed, and it became the most bitter, the most violent, selectors' meeting ever held in Australia.

The next day was Sunday. Hill handed in his resignation as a selector. Then McAlister and Iredale picked the team for the Fourth Test and 10 certainties for the trip to England, by themselves. All those who took part in the meeting agreed that for the good name of Australian cricket no word would ever be mentioned of what had happened.

That Monday Hill and McAlister caught the express to Melbourne. There was a great gathering of newspapermen waiting for them at Spencer Street Station. Both were determined to say nothing whatever to the press.

But it was difficult. The *Sydney Morning Herald* representative pointed out, "As McAlister stepped from the Sydney Express and walked along the platform there was no disguising the fact that he had been engaged in a bout of fisticuffs. His nose was cut and there was a bruise under the left eye and numerous scratches disfigured his face."

Then the newspapermen used an old technique which bowled both batsmen first ball. They suggested to Hill that McAlister already had stated that the attack was cowardly and he had punched him while his arms were folded. To McAlister they said Hill already stated that the punch was thrown only after long provocation and repeated warnings.

Such suggestions were too much for either man and obligingly they "blew" the whole story.

"I told him," said Hill, "that if he kept on insulting me I'd pull his nose. He said I was the worst captain he had seen, and as he had aggravated me beyond endurance—a man is only flesh and blood—I gave him a gentle slap on the face. He rushed at me like a mad bull and then I admit I fought him. Messrs. Iredale and Smith held me back, and as I went out he called out that I was a coward, but as others prevented him from leaving the room the matter ended."

McAlister said that Hill gave him no warning whatever and struck him a violent blow on the face. "I wouldn't have minded so much if he had invited me to come outside, as I would have known what to expect. I admit that I rushed at Hill when he hit me and I admit that the others locked the door and placed their backs against it after he had gone and would not let me get at him. You see that my face is scratched in several places; it must have knocked against the table and walls."

Several newspapers printed photographs showing the size of the adversaries. The Melbourne *Age* reported that Hill was not as tall as McAlister, but then he was heavier and more powerful. Said the *Age*: "Hill had the better of

106

the fisticuffs. If the engagement had been fought at the Stadium he would have secured a verdict."

The meeting of the selectors was not the only Sydney meeting. There was also a meeting of the Board. Clem Hill took over Frank Laver's books for the 1909 tour, the books which had started all the trouble. He showed them to Mr. McElhone and said that if he wished he could take them to any licensed auditor and have them checked, but Mr. McElhone was not interested. He said: "I do not doubt Mr. Laver's honesty in any way. Our objection to him is that he was disloyal to the Board."

Meanwhile the Board appointed its much-disputed representative-manager for the tour. He was a most careful compromise—Mr. G. S. Crouch of the Woolloongabba Club in Brisbane. He had never held an official position with the Q.C.A., but he had been a member of the Queensland State side, and he was the type of man to whom there could be no possible objection on personality grounds.

The Victorian delegates to the Board were Messrs. H. R. Rush and E. E. Bean of the V.C.A., and Dr. Ramsay Mailer of the Melbourne Cricket Club. Rush and Bean voted for the appointment but Dr. Mailer made a passionate appeal. He urged that the players be allowed to keep their legal rights in appointing their own manager. If this were permitted, then why couldn't this manager meet with the Board and be told precisely what the Board wanted of him during the tour, and be told, too, that there would be serious penalties if its wishes were not carried out?

Dr. Mailer said later that the Board turned down his suggestion. After that he refused to have any part in the choice of a Board tour representative. Furthermore, he insisted that he had no part in it, and that this be put down in the record.

The 14 players for the tour received their invitation letters from the Board of Control. Although one of the 14, Clem Hill did not receive his letter until some days later. Maybe this was an effort to separate him from the others, to stop him from being the ring-leader. All the letters said that the players had 10 days to give a definite reply.

Ten days! Cape Canaveral was unthought of in 1912, but those 10 days must have seemed like the count-down for the big blast-off. The deadline was midnight, Wednesday, February 21. Mr. Pelham Warner, the English captain, made a last-minute appeal as mediator. For the sake of cricket, for the sake of the Marylebone Club, and particularly for the success of the triangular contest that was to be played between England, Australia and South Africa, surely something could be done? On the 10th day there was a report that the

Governor of N.S.W., Lord Chelmsford, had intervened, so too did Mr. J. S. T. McGowan, the N.S.W. State Premier.

Mr. McGowan put forward this proposal:

1. Laver to be taken as a member of the team whether as player or manager.

2. That cricketers submit two names of persons to be their candidates for the position of manager and let the Board of Control take one of the two.

It seemed like a chance of compromise, but the players rejected it. They would not give in and they would not turn their backs on their friend Frank Laver.

The six rebels all returned identical letters. They accepted the Board's invitation to play in the Australian side, but in accepting the invitation they reserved "the right to withdraw such acceptance if anything should arise, prior to the departure of the team, rendering such withdrawal necessary."

This heavy phraseology, of course, meant "No Laver, no go." As soon as the replies arrived the Board sent back letters withdrawing the invitations, and replacements were named at once. The first letters came from Armstrong, Trumper and Cotter. They were replaced by Gregory, Hazlitt and McLaren. Carkeek replaced Carter. Then came Vernon Ransford's letter, and finally the letter from Clem Hill. They were replaced by C. G. Macartney of N.S.W. and Dave Smith of Victoria.

It had happened. The *Argus* announcement sounded as gloomy as if Paris had fallen:

> The worst fears of the supporters of cricket were realised on Saturday night, when it became known that the selectors of the Board of Control had completed their team for England and Australia's best men had been replaced.

Shock gave way to anger. Newspaper leading articles described Billy McElhone as a Napoleon, a dictator. One man sent a cheque for £100 to the *Argus.* He said this was the start of a fund to send an independent team to England, which should be chosen by Hill, Trumper and Armstrong. The money poured in and within three days there was just on £1000 in hand.

Melbourne *Punch,* which always liked to put matters of extreme moment into verse, produced this:

THE CRICKET COCONUT
The reason for the Milk of Human Kindness that is inside.
When the Board of Control
Was appointed, the whole

Was supposed to have cricket at heart,
To leave self-conceit
To the man in the street,
Letting interstate envy depart.

But out in the bone
Of the tribe McElhone
Will come what is born in the child,
And undying hate
Of each rival State
Ran hot in the veins it defiled.

And quickly one head
In diameter spread,
Like a beggar's upon a steed's back,
Till—woe to the man
Who came under the ban
Of the fierce hydrocephalous Mac.

Mac smiled and "sat," tight,
When the people in might
His action arose to assail,
Demanding the "why?"
With a wink of his eye,
He grunted "My choice must prevail."

"Let the Lion, Springbok,"
Or any old crock
Knock the 'over-tailed' Kangaroo stark;
Let folks fume and fuss—
What matter to us,
If the Melbourne Club we can but 'nark!' "

The current cartoon joke was that Billy McElhone should go to England himself. After all, what a cricketer—he had dismissed six of the finest players in the world with one blow.

Yet opinion in Melbourne was not unanimous. One man, who signed himself "Old Cricketer," wrote: "I am sure there are thousands of cricketers who follow the game in Australia who recognise that the outcome of the dispute will be a splendid thing. It will teach men no matter how good they may be at any branch of sport, they still must be amenable to some kind of authority."

North Melbourne, East Melbourne, South Melbourne, Fitzroy and Prahran cricket clubs gave their support to the Board of Control, and North Mel-

bourne Cricket Club passed a resolution congratulating the Board and sym-
pathising with the Victorian delegates, Messrs. E. E. Bean and H. R. Rush, and
the selector, Peter McAlister, who had been "subjected to spiteful and most
unjust criticisms at the hands of the Melbourne press, which throughout the
trouble had persisted in presenting a garbled and absolutely one-sided view of
the situation."

The storm still gathered. An organisation called the Citizens' Cricket Committee was formed, and the C.C.C. had protest meetings in Adelaide, Melbourne, Sydney and Hobart. But for Melbourne all meetings were chaired by
the local Lord Mayor. They passed angry resolutions. In Hobart, for example,
there was a demand for the immediate resignation of Mr. McElhone.

In Melbourne the meeting was at the Athenaeum Hall. The doors were
advertised to open at 7 p.m., but at 6.45 the crowd poured in, sprinting for the
front seats. Both the upper and lower Athenaeum halls filled to capacity, so
the conveners then had to organise a third protest meeting in the Baptist Hall
nearby. Even at that, thousands of people were turned away. An orchestra
was there and they played a parody on a popular tune: "What's the matter
with Laver?—he's all right." Mr. W. L. Baillieu, M.L.C., Australia's top finan-
cier, was in the chair, and with him was Mr. W. J. Carre-Riddell, chairman of
the Board of Works. The committee names made up an all-star cast, including
even Mr. Norman Brookes, the champion tennis player.

At the meeting it was said that £10,000 could be had within 24 hours, if
necessary, to send away an independent team, and little notice was taken of
the warning in the *Argus* several days before that an unofficial team would
never be accepted in England and there would be no hope at this late stage of
organising matches. The major move of the evening was a decision to send a
cable to the Marylebone Cricket Club asking it to protest against the Australian team because it was not representative.

Next morning this notice appeared in the Sydney *Daily Telegraph* and the
Sydney Morning Herald:

> With regard to the meeting of protest held in Melbourne on Thursday night
> Mr. Sydney Smith, jnr., has received the following official telegram from
> Melbourne:
> "Indignation meeting last night convened by members of Melbourne
> Cricket Club. Admission by tickets issued members, who were admitted by
> private entrance. Hall full Melbourne Club members before doors open.
> Ninety per cent. members Melbourne Club. Meeting regarded as dying effort
> Melbourne Club and members to smash board and give club boss-ship
> cricket."

Edmund Jowett, one of the conveners of the meeting, could hardly have been more angry. He demanded to know who this "official" was. It was nothing more than an attempt to stir up Sydney-Melbourne rivalry in the hope of embarrassing the Citizens' Committee. He said the meeting had not been dominated by M.C.C. members. Admission was free and the only tickets issued were for the stage. And he fumed: "The telegram is one of the most monstrous falsehoods I have ever seen in print."

From the M.C.C. there was an official denial:

"Sir—I desire to say that any statement to the effect that the Melbourne Cricket Club or its committee had anything to do with the calling of a meeting recently held at the Athenaeum Hall is absolutely devoid of the truth.   Yours, etc.,

L. F. CUSSEN, President of M.C.C."

The telegram was described as official, so who sent it? Donald Mackinnon, president of the V.C.A., said it had nothing to do with his association. Then the Sydney newspapers solved the mystery. The telegram was sent to Sydney Smith, jnr., by Mr. E. E. Bean, the Victorian delegate to the Board of Control. Mr. Bean, when he was exposed, was magnificently unrepentant. He repeated his charges that the protest meetings were all plots by the M.C.C. He said the conveners at the Athenaeum were both M.C.C. men, Edmund Jowett and Frank Guthrie. He gave their club numbers, 2686 and 2098. Furthermore, he said, all but two of the speakers reported at the meeting were M.C.C. members.

There were some last-minute moves. The Board made a fresh approach to Vernon Ransford and Victor Trumper, but they remained unrelenting. There was a move in the South Australian Cricket Association to take out a High Court injunction to prevent the team from leaving Australia, but it came to nothing.

The final blow to the Citizens' Committee was the reply from the Marylebone Cricket Club:

"The committee today considered your telegram, but felt it was impossible for the M.C.C. to interfere in any way on the selection of a team to visit England."

What else could the club have done?

There was a farewell dinner to the team at the Vienna Cafe on March 19, which was attended by the Prime Minister, Mr. Fisher. The next day the team sailed from Port Melbourne Railway Pier on the R.M.S. *Otway*. There were 2000 people to cheer them off, and as the ship sailed away someone called

"Three cheers for Clem Hill." The response was tremendous, but there was a touch of pathos about it.

The struggle went on for another six months. Frank Laver produced a pamphlet, the V.C.A. produced a pamphlet, the M.C.C. produced a pamphlet. The fight now has long since been forgotten, and the Board of Control, the V.C.A. and the M.C.C. are on such happy terms it is hard to believe they ever had a cross word. In 1912 undoubtedly there were faults on all sides. The players were presumptuous, but then surely the Board of Control did not have to be quite so heavy-handed?

Johnnie Moyes, who lived through the crisis and even attended the Adelaide protest meeting, has this to say in his book *Australian Cricket:*

"Back in the days of the big fight my sympathies were with the players, for Clem Hill was our hero in Adelaide. I believed they had justice on their side and they were not well treated, but at the same time I could see that some Australia-wide control of cricket was essential. The Board at that time knew it must win or die and it fought bitterly. . . The Board would have become defunct or merely a museum piece if it had not won at once. It needed a knockout blow, not a points decision."

But it was a sadly weakened team that went to England. Except for stars like Bardsley, Macartney and Hazlitt the players did not shine. The triangular series of Tests were not a success and it was many years before they were attempted again. Australia won two Tests against South Africa, lost one and drew two against England. The score for the tour was eight games lost and nine won. Time and again cricket was made miserable by bad weather.

As Melbourne *Punch* pointed out at the time: "This bad weather undoubtedly will be put down by the Board of Control as a plot conceived by the Melbourne Cricket Club."

CHAPTER THIRTEEN

The Years of War

IN 1912 Melburnians were becoming more daring. Perhaps it was the dashing influence of the motor car, for there were plenty to be had, and Australians were amongst the most motor-minded people in the world. Any newspaper of the day carried advertisements for 20 or more different brands of imported vehicles—the Lanchester, the Siddeley-Deasey, the F.N., the Bianchi, the Waverley and the Hurtu. Ladies, for street wear now were almost showing their ankles, and what they were wearing on the beach was enough to make a gentleman's blood churn. Bathing suits were above the knee, and on some secluded beaches men had been seen bare to the waist. *Punch's* comment to this was that a man might as well wear a fig leaf.

Camping suddenly had become immensely popular, no doubt through the influence of Lord Baden Powell. Many thought this outdoor way of spending a holiday was an excellent thing, but moralists saw dangers for young people. It could easily lead to loose living. Yet camping was not as bad as mixed bathing. What young men and women did together in the water could only be imagined.

Costs seemed to rise every year. A lady's skirt was 18/-, straw boaters were 7/6, a two-passenger Hupmobile cost £230, a sports Buick £285, and cigarettes were 1/- for a packet of 20. This could be expensive for a heavy smoker, but always there was the bonus of a cigarette card and a man stood to win a free picture of Victor Trumper or Clem Hill. One could buy a suit for 75/-, but it was better to go for that extra quality and pay £5/5/-. The Melbourne Cricket Club was trying to keep costs down, but in 1912 reluctantly it informed members that club blazers from now on would be 25/- instead of 22/6.

The 1912 football grand final at the M.C.G. drew a record crowd, and the *Australasian* commented:

> Surely if ever there was any doubt in anybody's mind as to which is the national game of the land, the attendances and the money taken at the finals of both League and Association on the last day of the season should be

enough to dispel any illusions that may have previously existed. The Melbourne ground is the Mecca of all League football pilgrims at this time of the year, and they literally poured in in thousands from midday until 3 p.m. The enclosure was packed, and in the event of a League final taking place some day, with no counter attraction at North Melbourne (Association final), the ground accommodating as it is, will be unequal to the strain imposed. There were 84,000 people present at the two matches, and it is difficult to see how the present conveniences can furnish room for more than 60,000 persons. The bank will have to be extended to the fence, or else buildings must be erected in the outer ground from goal to goal.

The record gave great cause for satisfaction, because a recent Rugby match between N.S.W. and New Zealand on the Sydney Cricket Ground set an Australian record crowd of 52,000. For this grand final between Essendon and South Melbourne the crowd was 54,463. Essendon defeated South Melbourne 9-8 (62) to 5-11 (41).

The M.C.C. must have taken the *Australasian's* advice, for in 1913 the committee came to a drastic decision. This was to cut down the finest trees on the ground, the 11 lovely old elms planted by Mr. Stephenson's Eleven in 1862. Not only were the trees large and shady but they stood for the first English team ever to come to Australia. Yet they had to go, and more than anything else this meant the end of an era at the M.C.G. No longer was it like a country ground, now for ever it was to be a big sports arena. So for the Grand Final of 1913 there was more room, and hence a new record of 59,479 people. Fitzroy defeated St. Kilda, and ever since St. Kilda has been battling to get back into a Grand Final.

There were some new names coming into cricket. There was a tall, very lean young man named Jack Ryder. He looked as if he could do anything. In 1913 he was a presentable opening fast bowler and he had an early flair for big run-getting. He did not show it quite early enough in his first match against N.S.W., for he did not score anything, but he went on to take 6 wickets for 44 in the second innings. Jack Ryder was to settle down as the sporting King of Collingwood, a marvellous dual monarchy—Jack Ryder in the summer and Syd Coventry in the winter.

Then there was Bert Ironmonger. Hugh Trumble, now secretary of the M.C.C., went on a Queensland tour and he found him at Ipswich. Trumble did not hesitate. He thought Ironmonger had the makings of a first-class cricketer, so he asked the committee to appoint him as a ground bowler at the M.C.G. For a man who had just been passed over as a Test selector, he had a shrewd eye. Bert Ironmonger went on to break the record for interstate wickets—313 at an average of 22.35.

114

It was a poor time for a man to be reaching his peak as a cricketer. On August 4 the cable news came through:

> At a late hour on Thursday night it was officially announced by proclamation in London that a state of war existed between Great Britain and Germany. The war proclamation was read from the top of the broad flight of steps leading up to the Royal Exchange, and simultaneously the mobilisation of the Army was proclaimed. Great enthusiasm prevailed among the crowd.

Meanwhile Melbourne was equally enthusiastic. The *Age* reported on August 4:

> Scenes of wild enthusiasm were witnessed outside the newspaper office last night. All day long and throughout the early part of the evening there was always a crowd extending out on the roadway reading the cables as they were posted up, but as the hour grew late, so the crowd grew denser and spread right across Collins Street. It needed only a single voice to give the opening bars of a patriotic song and thousands of throats took it up, hats and coats were waved, and those who were lucky enough to possess even the smallest of Union Jacks were the heroes of the moment and were raised shoulder high as the crowd surged hither and thither. *Rule Britannia, Soldiers of the King* and *Sons of the Sea* were sung again and again. The National Anthem had a sobering effect from time to time, and woe betide anyone who failed to remove his hat without hesitation. Suddenly a Frenchman got up on the steps and commenced singing the Marseillaise. The crowd grew frantic with enthusiasm. He was lifted bodily in the air shouting "Vive L'Australia! Vive La France!"
> About 11.20 p.m., in response to the persistent cry of "We want more news," a notice was put up stating that there would be no more news till morning. "We won't go home till morning," shouted someone and every voice took up the chorus. Suddenly two blue jackets arrived on the scene. They were pounced upon. A procession formed and they were carried up and down the street to the tune of *Rule Britannia, Boys of the Bulldog Breed* and *Sons of the Sea*. Finally the procession or part of it marched up the steps of the office, deposited the jovial tars on the counter and asked,"Is there more news?" The notice already posted was confirmed and the crowd gradually dwindled away.

The next night, according to the *Australasian,* a mob of 300 larrikins attacked the German Club in Victoria Parade. They barged through the gate and they lashed at the windows with sticks. Then they set a piece of rag alight, which they announced was the German flag, and while it was burning they jumped up and down on it, hooting threats against the Germans. They finished their little patriotic display with an all-in fight against 20 police from Russell Street.

115

The 1914 cricket season was just about to start, but there seemed little point in interfering with it. The team for the 1914-15 cricket tour of South Africa had been chosen with the M.C.C. man Warwick Armstrong as captain. It included such men as A. G. "Johnnie" Moyes, R. L. Park, Jack Ryder and Charles Macartney, but the tour had to be abandoned. Nobody, however was concerned at this stage. There was no reason why the war should not be over very quickly. The Board of Control discussed the matter. Mr. Sydney Smith moved, Dr. Ramsay Mailer seconded, that the international cricket programme simply be put forward 12 months. The Australian team could then go to South Africa for the 1915-16 season.

The 1915-16 season was a different affair altogether, and those who played sport played only with a sense of guilt. On July 10, 1915, the *Australasian* said the past two months had been the shattering of a dream . . . "That frightful landing in Gallipoli, the desperate fight against fearful odds to hold the positions so hardly won, the tragic tale told by the succession of casualty lists, the mourning in thousands of Australian homes—these things have burned themselves into the hearts and brains of the people."

The Sheffield Shield season was abandoned. District cricket went on in the form of "matches for exercise only"; there was no pennant. In 1915 football was not easy. It did not look good for healthy men to be fighting for a premiership when the wounded were coming off the ships in batch after batch. According to the press, some footballers could have joined up a little more quickly, and many players "who were no doubt anxious to serve their country found their glorious aspirations barred by a hammer toe or bad teeth." There was criticism because the V.F.L. at the beginning of the season did not suspend payment to players. Men who were earning good money were not so anxious to join up.

The *Australasian* said:

> The atmosphere in the dressing rooms is very different from what it was a month ago. The men are more serious, and the usual light-hearted gaiety had practically disappeared. In common with the rest of the country, footballers will fill gaps and prove worthy sons of the Empire."

For the 1916 season Melbourne, Essendon, South Melbourne, Geelong and St. Kilda all pulled out. The competition was left with just four teams—Carlton, Collingwood, Fitzroy and Richmond. If this left the competition rather restricted there was the compensation that they could not possibly drop out of the final four.

At the annual meeting of the M.C.C. in September 1915, the president, Mr.

The cricket immortal, Hugh Trumble. He took 141 Test wickets against England.

The Melbourne Cricket Ground, 1904.

M.C.C. baseball team, 1907.

Justice Cussen, said that cricket and sport generally had been thrown into comparative insignificance owing to the crisis through which they were all passing. Already nearly 400 members were on active service, and of these 21 had lost their lives in battle. The very well-known member A. M. "Joe" Pearce, one of the most popular and manly sportsmen he had ever known, had been killed on the very first day of the Gallipoli landing. He had been full back for Victoria in the first Australian Rules football carnival on the M.C.G. in 1908. The President said that all interests arising from sport were very properly put in the background by the greater consideration of the war. The duty of the club was not to honour those who had excelled in sport, but to honour those who had served and were serving their country. It was decided to forward to those members on active service the greetings of the annual meeting.

The best cricket of the war years came from patriotic matches. During the Christmas holidays of 1915-16 the M.C.C. and the V.C.A. decided to stage big cricket to help the wounded soldiers' appeal. They would have a real inter-state match between N.S.W and Victoria, just like old times. Warren Bardsley, Charlie Macartney and M. A. Noble all were available in Sydney. The N.S.W. Cricket Association would have nothing to do with it. Such a match would interfere with recruiting. So Victoria had no choice but to go it alone. The first match on Boxing Day was titled "Fifteen of Victoria v. the Sheffield Shield XI," and the second match on New Year's Day was "Victoria v. W. Arm-strong's Eighteen."

Everything was done in fine style. On Boxing Day there were three bands, the Richmond City, the Prahran City and the Fitzroy Citizens Band. Captain Harrison flew over the ground from the direction of Werribee in his BE2 biplane and "he met with a most hearty reception." There were some good performances in the matches—Bert Ironmonger took 5/74 and 7/59 in the one match, Warwick Armstrong made 102 for his eighteen, Jack Ryder 83 and 4/17, and Dr. R. L. Park 96.

Yet the big effort for the appeal was the auction of cricket relics and curios, which took place at Scott's Hotel, and the piece de resistance was the cricket ball presented by the greatest of wicketkeepers, John McCarthy Blackham. As relics go, nothing could compete with this. It was the ball used in the last innings of the 1882 Test at the Oval, the day when all looked hopeless and Australia dismissed England for 77 runs, the day when Spofforth became the "Demon" and took 7 for 44, the day when the Ashes were born, the day when Australia had her first Test win on English soil.

Just so that people would appreciate the huge significance of this auction,

Tommy Horan, who played in the match, and now a war veteran, wrote of the game: "The excitement was so tremendous and long-sustained that one man dropped dead, some fainted, and one man made deep notches with his teeth in the top of his umbrella. The vast crowd rushed the ground, patted the Australians on the back and cheered them to the echo, with cries 'Bravo, Australia.' That was the only time I saw W. G. Grace looking a bit downcast over cricket. He said to me, 'Well, well. I left six men to get 30 odd runs and they couldn't get them.' "

In all this excitement Mr. Blackham still had the marvellous presence of mind to quietly put the ball in his pocket.

It was decided that it would be sacrilege for the ball to pass into the hands of a private individual. One of the organisers, Mr. Mat Ellis, had an idea. Why not auction the ball for the National Museum? Every subscriber who gave £1 or more would have his name recorded in an album which would be on display with the ball. Hugh Trumble set a minimum price of £500. Finally the ball went for £617, the most expensive cricket ball in history. It is now on loan to the M.C.C. Museum by the V.C.A.

There were other relics. There was the score book of the 1882 tour, and Tommy Horan said you could sense the drama of that famous Oval Test match just by looking at the handwriting in this book. Peate, bowled by Boyle for 2, was the last man out, but the handwriting at this stage was so wriggly with emotion the scorer could have been writing anything. The score book went for 33 guineas. W. L. Murdoch's bat fetched 70 guineas, Clem Hill's bat 20 guineas, Trumper's bat 35 guineas, an autographed Trumper bat 55 guineas and a bat autographed by all the 1909 Eleven 24 guineas. There were photographs of cricketers, commemoration plates, and even a letter written home by Spofforth from England. The matches and the auction were a big success. The grand total for the appeal from all sources was £3255/7/10.

On June 25, 1915, Victor Trumper died of Bright's disease. Frank Laver and M. A. Noble called on him when he first went to hospital, and they reported back that his case was hopeless. Yet then he seemed to respond to treatment, so much so that he left hospital and went home. It was only a respite. He had a relapse and within a week he was dead. Tributes came in from all over the world. Pelham Warner said: "Trumper was the most unassuming cricketer in the world, and at one time was its finest batsman; but he spoke as if he had never made a run in his life." And London's *Sporting Life* wrote: "No other batsman has played cricket with greater grace and more

118

attractiveness. Even his shorter innings were masterpieces of artistic cricket." There was a big funeral in Sydney. The pallbearers were Noble, Cotter, Carter, S. Gregory, Bardsley and Armstrong.

Then on October 31 Gerry Hazlitt died. He was an M.C.C. exhibitioner from Haileybury College, and at one time he looked like becoming the great-est cricketer Australia had ever seen. He played for Victoria when he was 17 and still at school, and he was a Test cricketer by the time he was 19. He was third in the bowling averages for the 1912 tour and, even if this tour did have its difficult moments, he had the lovely satisfaction of taking 7 wickets for 25 at Lord's. He died at King's School, Parramatta. He was only 27, and it was said that 10 years before, when he was a brilliant 17-year-old player, even then he had a weak heart.

The links with the past were disappearing. Albert Trott, Harry Trott, Dr. Grace, Tom Horan, all died, and in 1917 "Tibby" Cotter was killed in action fighting in the Middle East. Then on October 15, 1917, Major Ben Wardill died at the age of 75. He became club secretary in 1879 when there were 572 members, and by the time he retired in 1910 there were 5353. He was known as the Major and he was into everything. He took part in all Melbourne's activities, and it is a wonder that he was not known as the "Galloping Major." He took three Australian teams to England on behalf of the M.C.C. and he toured with many of the teams that the M.C.C. brought here, which meant that he could spend all the English summer touring with the Australians, then all the Australian summer touring with the Englishmen. He went all around Australia with the Lord Sheffield-W. G. Grace tour of 1892. He was born in Liverpool and he came to Australia in 1861. He worked as a clerk with the Victorian Sugar Company and then he joined the Garrison Artillery, where, of course, he rose to the rank of major. Apart from being a good cricketer he was a good rifle shot and in 1876 he went on tour with a rifle team to the United States, and he shot at the Philadelphia Centennial Exhibition. Yet perhaps his best achievement was the manner of his retirement in 1910. There was a great public testimonial, and the man who presided over the meeting was the Governor-General, Lord Dudley. It is not often that a man has a Governor-General to look after his retirement day.

These days were the blackest of the war, and there was no shortage of people who were only too keen to accuse others of not doing enough for the war effort. Mr. E. H. C. Oliphant, as a guest of the trustees of the Public Library, gave a lecture in the Latrobe Gallery titled "Do we Deserve to Win?" He attacked the racegoers and the footballers, then he turned his attention to cricketers. "It is not only the footballers who are the disgrace of the community. While N.S.W. has sent nearly all her leading cricketers to the front Victoria has not provided one of her chief players. When one looks at athletic young men disgracing their country and devoting days to cricket and other sports when their country needs them one might again ask whether as a people we deserve to be successful in this terrible war."

Mr. E. E. Bean of the V.C.A. replied that 11 Sheffield Shield players were serving overseas, as well as a vast number of junior cricketers, but Mr. Oliphant stuck to his guns and said that of the victorious 1914 Sheffield Shield side not one had gone to the front. There was just one man, "whose name should be mentioned with honour." R. L. Park had volunteered and later went overseas. However, a few months afterwards Mr. Bean was able to mention in the V.C.A.'s annual report that Captain R. Grieve of the Brighton Club had won the Victoria Cross, the first Australian cricketer to win the honour, and Mr. Justice Cussen in the M.C.C. annual report said nearly 1000 members were in the forces and 109 had been killed in action.

Hope began to rise. Six football teams played in the 1917 season and in 1918 Melbourne was the only club to stand out. Then on a November Monday afternoon, just in time to catch the late editions, the news came through. The Armistice had been declared. The *Australasian* said: "From henceforth November 11, 1918, will be regarded as the greatest day in history." Said the *Argus:* "The end at last! What words can tell adequately of the wave of relief that will sweep the civilised world . . . heads that for years have been bowed with suffering will be raised in thanksgiving."

Everybody came to the city. The crowds rushed into Collins Street so that it would have been impossible to take any more. There were boys up the trees like monkeys, a boy and a girl solemnly sat on top of the traffic sign at the corner of Collins and Swanston Streets. The trams were unable to move and banked up at the top of Collins Street. People swarmed all over them, using the tops as a grandstand.

Everybody was making a noise, letting off crackers, blowing bugles, blowing tin whistles. Some had kerosene tins which they crashed with sticks, and according to one newspaper "youths added to the general music by jumping up and down on top of the tin verandas in Swanston Street." Any soldier in sight was a hero. He was kissed by the office girls and lifted on to the shoulders of the crowd in triumph. Then a mob of thousands of boisterous youths tackled the trams in Bourke Street. They were not satisfied with lifting the tramcars bodily off their tracks, they carried them into side streets. Then they moved into Little Bourke Street and Post Office Place, where they smashed windows. The Government declared November 12 a holiday, and the celebrations continued on with crowds singing anthems and patriotic songs. There was hardly anyone in the city who did not wear a flag.

Before the week was out the cricket administrators were talking of a resumption of interstate cricket, and there was an excellent rumour that N.S.W. was entirely agreeable. The cricket writers said it was remarkable how the declaration of peace seemed to make all the difference. There was a new spirit in the game, and "now supporters are seeing qualities in their favourites undreamt of a few weeks ago." Why, even barracking returned to the M.C.G., and the old pre-war cries were back: "Get on with it, you loafer" and "Why don't ya'ave a go?" One old cricket writer commented that while he failed to see anything humorous in the practice it was good to see the return of the personal element.

The Melbourne Cricket Club suddenly discovered that it had a shortage of members. So an appeal went for all members to bring in their friends. This was something that had not happened for 40 years and has not happened since. The membership was very quickly filled.

Interstate cricket was organised at once, and the series gained extra interest because of a big gesture by two old cricketers. M. A. Noble, who was soon to be 46, agreed to come out of retirement to captain N.S.W., and Clem Hill, who was in his 42nd year, was again the South Australian captain. The first match was on Boxing Day, N.S.W. v. Victoria. After four years out of work it was pure joy for the statisticians. They recorded that 94 matches had been played between Victoria and N.S.W. Of these N.S.W. had won 53 and Victoria 41. The match started at 11 a.m., instead of 12 noon. The players put in a petition of protest. They felt it was far too early for them to be up and about giving of their best.

Then it was the first interstate match with the 8-ball over. Mr. Sydney Smith, jnr., put forward the idea at a meeting of the N.S.W. Cricket Association as early as March 1915, as a suggestion "for restoring the popularity of cricket." There were grumbles as to how the fast bowlers would stand up to this "on a normal 105-degree day on the M.C.G.," and *Sporting Life* in London commented: "It will not brighten the game and it will only save a few minutes, while it will prejudicially affect young fast bowlers. It is hardly worth the candle." Victoria tried it out for the Patriotic Match at the M.C.G. on Boxing Day 1917, and it became general for club matches during the 1916-17 season. There were many grumbles early, but then one cricket writer pointed out a singular thing: how remarkable it was that so many wickets were taken off the seventh or the eighth ball of an over. This won the bowlers' hearts to such a degree it was surprising that they did not ask for a 10-ball over.

So by Boxing Day 1919 the eight-ball over was well-established. Victoria

121

won the match by 216 runs and the takings were the highest for a Christmas match on the M.C.G. for 22 years. Melbourne had not seen M. A. Noble for 10 years, but he was still a great captain and he could teach the younger generation how to play cricket. Maybe he was not quite as brilliant as he was in 1909, but still he made the top score for New South Wales with 52 runs. Another player noticed by the press was a newcomer, A. Kippax. "Kippax, a brisk young batsman, was not in the least dismayed by the conditions and he played first-class cricket." His score was 20.

On New Year's Day Victoria played South Australia, and this was a day out for Warwick Armstrong and Jack Ryder. Armstrong made 162 not out and Ryder 78. Clem Hill made a run for every year of his age. He scored 42.

The best of the post-war matches came on January 16, 1920. The glamour A.I.F. team came home after touring in England and South Africa. The captain was Corporal Bert Collins and the players called him "Lucky." He was never a spectacular cricketer, but like Keith Miller he had a passion for race-horses, and he was shrewd. There was a Diggers' camaraderie in this side, a sort of inspired loyalty, and Arthur Mailey later described it as one of the strongest teams in the history of cricket. Pelham Warner predicted that five of them would eventually play for Australia—Collins, Pellew, Gregory, Taylor and Oldfield—and he was right.

The soldiers had the reputation of being supermen and their early form was ominous. There was a practice match at Fitzroy, and the A.I.F. men scored 550 runs in a day. C. T. Docker and H. L. Collins made 100 in 22 minutes. Docker hit 3 sixes, Murray 6 sixes. Two of Murray's blows went into the bowling green and one, superbly, right over the grandstand. Pellew hit 4 sixes in one over and he scored 10 sixes in three overs off W. Cannon, the Fitzroy bowler.

All this was splendid publicity and the build-up went on. Most of it centred on Jack Gregory, the last of Sydney's famous Gregorys, who had been playing cricket for nearly 100 years. Jack was 24. He was 6 ft. 3 in. in his socks. Already it had been noted that for a fast bowler he had a length of remarkable accuracy and he was as fast as, if not faster than, Tibby Cotter at his best. As for W. A. Oldfield, he had yet to be noticed. "The team has a fair wicket-keeper in Oldfield," was the comment.

It does not often happen, but Jack Gregory proved to be quite as good as his reputation. He had the ball flying up around Warwick Armstrong's chin, and it was a long way up to Warwick Armstrong's chin. He took 7 wickets for 22 runs and Victoria was all out for 116.

Then the soldiers went in to bat. Carl Willis, the Melbourne University man, who topped the averages for the A.I.F. in England, was the man to see. He had a trick which he had borrowed from Dr. Grace. When taking block he knocked a bail hard into the mark with the handle of his bat, and so he made a definite hole, which would stay there for two or three days. "Gamesmanship" experts of today would appreciate a move like that. Carl Willis was demonstrating to the bowlers that he was pitching his camp to stay there for a long, long time. He did, too, for he made 111 runs. The A.I.F. won the match by six wickets. It was good cricket, but even more than the bowling of Gregory and the batting of Willis, there was something else to remember. The *Argus* reported on a ceremony that took place before a crowd of 18,000 on the Saturday afternoon:

> At ten minutes to four play was suspended while the most impressive ceremony ever carried out on a cricket ground was performed with due solemnity. At the time mentioned the Victorians, who were in the field, assembled at the southern end of the wicket, where they were joined by members of the A.I.F. team. Two buglers took up their stand at either end of the ground and, one in front of the pavilion, the other near the Wardill stand, sounded the *Last Post*. For a moment as the large crowd stood bareheaded there was a stillness that was remarkable, and after the first bugler had sounded his call the silence seemed the greater by contrast. The second call sounded as though wafted from far away, and added considerably to the impressiveness of the ceremony. It was a wonderful sight—the vast bareheaded crowd standing motionless while the solemn tribute to those gone West was paid.

In May 1920 there was a visit from His Royal Highness the slim young Prince of Wales, the late Duke of Windsor. Royal visits were no different in 1920. The public curiosity was so immense it was almost too much to bear. The crowds were prepared to wait on street corners by the hour, all night if need be, just to see the young prince. He went to a Royal Ball at the Town Hall. He went to an official reception at Essendon. He went to the Royal Show and he looked at the Grand Parade. Crowds everywhere were so enthusiastic that there had to be official warnings. In particular the public was asked to refrain from jumping on the running board of his car to shake him by the hand. Not only was someone likely to be killed doing this, but it obstructed the view of others.

The biggest show of all was the youth display by 10,000 children at the Melbourne Cricket Ground. The M.C.G. had seen everything from aboriginal cricketers to balloon ascents, but the Prince attracted the greatest crowd ever —70,000 people. One reporter said: "It had to be the largest crowd on record, because there was simply no more room. Even the tops of the stands were occupied." The Prince, accompanied by handsome young Sub-Lieutenant Lord Louis Mountbatten, sat in a box specially built in front of the members' pavilion, the same stand for which his father, King George V, and his late uncle, Prince Edward, laid the foundation stone when they came to Melbourne as midshipmen aboard H.M.S. *Bacchante*.

The spectacular item on the programme was a living tableau titled "In the Heart of Australia." The bigger children formed themselves into a map of Australia. Then across the centre the smaller children made the words "OUR PRINCE." There was a march of 6000 children and 3000 girls gave a physical culture display.

The Prince said it was the finest thing he had seen since he left home. He made himself most popular before he departed by asking that all the children be given not one but two days holiday. He suggested even further that the holidays become an annual affair.

Children with an historical bent could well inquire why they do not receive the two-day Prince of Wales holiday now. The Melbourne Cricket Club made him an honorary life member, as it did for his uncles 39 years before.

CHAPTER FOURTEEN

The Scoring 'Twenties

ENGLISH cricket was devastated by the war, whereas Australia had strength almost as if nothing had happened. The A.I.F. team acted like a paid-up insurance policy. After the factory had burned down the handy reserves were there to put up a new building even better than before. The Englishmen had one great cricketer, Jack Hobbs, who still acted like the best batsman in the world, but he could not win a series on his own. The 1920-21 tour under J. W. H. T. Douglas was the most disastrous in the history of the contests, and England lost all five Tests.

Warwick Armstrong, immense in size, and at 20 stone immense around the middle, stole most of the headlines in 1921. Nellie Melba was the Queen of culture, Billy Hughes was the King of politics, and Warwick, if not a king, was the Roman Emperor or feudal Baron of cricket, the last still playing of the 1912 "terrible six." For 20 years he was an employee of the Melbourne Cricket Club, then in December 1921 he resigned his job and became a special representative for a Scotch whisky firm. The public loved him, but it was a different story with the cricket officials. Here Armstrong was apt to be the Roman Emperor. Warwick had little time for them, and they were anxious to have little time for Warwick, but what could they do? If they had to pick a team to play Mars, on sheer ability alone W. W. Armstrong would have to tour as skipper of the interplanetary eleven.

At the end of January 1921 he went to Sydney to captain Victoria in the match against N.S.W. He had taken a beating about the legs in the Third Test at Adelaide. He did not turn up for practice and he did not announce he was unfit to play until the match was almost due to start. The Victorian selectors were angry. Mr. E. Bean, Mr. P. McAlister and Mr. Mat Ellis met on Monday night, February 1, to pick the Victorian Eleven to play England. It was like 1912 all over again.

On Tuesday the *Herald* ran the story all over page one. W. W. Armstrong HAD BEEN DROPPED. Could one believe it? The great captain of Australia, the captain of Victoria, the world's greatest all-rounder, had been found not good enough for Friday's game. The selectors refused to give an explanation.

Mr. Bean told reporters to ring him at home after dinner. Yet after dinner he was still evasive. He said selectors had never been bound to give any reasons why they showed preference for one man over another, and he refused to give any reasons now.

Mr. H. D. Westley immediately organised a protest meeting, at the old home for cricket protest meetings, the Athenaeum Hall in Collins Street. He did not get the idea until 5 p.m., an hour when it was too late to do any advertising, but still he organised the meeting for that night, and the hall was packed. So at 8 p.m. on Tuesday, February 2, Mr. Westley told the meeting that he had come to raise his voice against the most dastardly outrage in the history of cricket. Armstrong's integrity was undoubted, but this was only a culmination of previous acts of oppression against the players. Mr. Westley moved:

"That this meeting of lovers of sport expresses its condemnation at the treatment meted out to Australia's greatest cricketer, Mr. W. Armstrong, who has been omitted from the Victorian Eleven without even an opportunity to make an explanation."

Then Mr. Julius Sim moved that a "monster meeting" be held outside the M.C.C. on the Saturday afternoon at 3 p.m.

At this stage, no doubt, Shakespeare would have said, "Alas, poor Warwick. I knew him well." The newspapers ran every item of information they could glean. They listed all his big scores, tallied up his batting and bowling averages, retold the full story of the 1912 controversy. They also, somewhat acidly, balanced the cricket records of Messrs. Bean, McAlister and Ellis against the record of W. W. Armstrong. Peter McAlister did not come out of it too badly. Apart from his brief Test career he had played for East Melbourne for more than 30 years and he had scored 10,000 runs for his club. Yet no matter what the provocation the selectors gave no statements to the newspapers and neither did Armstrong.

On the Wednesday, when Melbourne was talking of little else, Armstrong drove quietly out to Mentone, where he played the most remarkable match in his long cricket career—Mr. W. W. Armstrong v. 18 Schoolboys of Mentone. It was all the result of a rash promise he had made to Mr. J. J. Fogarty of Naples Road, Mentone. Mr. Fogarty made the most of it. Carefully he selected his boys from all over the district. They ranged from 6 to 15 years, from 3 ft. 6in. to nearly 6 ft., and for weeks he had them practising together at the nets.

When the huge Warwick Armstrong arrived, now 42 years old, he looked like Gulliver among the citizens of Lilliput. He was dressed as if he were ready to step out on the field against England. He drew from his nicely creased flannel trousers his famous American dollar—the very coin with which he had won the toss from Douglas in the three Test matches—and he invited Billy Godby, the smallest boy in the team, to call.

Someone called, "Have a look at the coin, Billy; it's got two tails." Whereupon Billy was most cautious and he had a good look at the dollar. However, Armstrong, as he invariably did, won the toss and he put the Mentone Eighteen in to bat.

The innings was half-way through before Armstrong realised he was up against a representative combination of Melbourne college and school boys. He had only two boys to help him: Bill Tootell, aged eight, and Tom Tootell, six, sons of Mr. C. Tootell, of Elizabeth Street, Elsternwick. He had to do ALL the bowling. Furthermore he had to stick to slow breaks and googlies, for if he attempted fast or even medium paced deliveries on the concrete and matting wicket, somebody would get badly hurt.

It was a hot February day and steadily it became hotter. Armstrong bowled and bowled. He leather-hunted. He perspired. Mr. Fogarty at last showed mercy. Surreptitiously he drafted boy after boy on to the field, so that the perspiring Mr. Armstrong suddenly found himself in possession of a full eleven. Hitting the wicket had been most difficult, and now wickets began to fall—by catches. As the eighteenth man approached the wicket the crowd yelled encouragingly, "That's the last." His bowling figures were 36 overs, no maidens, two no-balls, one wide, 16 wickets for 144 runs.

Mentone made 145, and it was clear to the wise heads exactly what would happen. Armstrong would behave like a perfect sporting gentleman. He would knock up a brilliant 144, then gallantly he would throw away his hand to give Mentone the victory by one run. Yet he did not have to do it all by himself. The rest of his team, Bill and Tom Tootell, with their combined strength of 14 years, made three runs between them. Armstrong opened with fatherly caution, tapping the ball along the few vacant spaces not monopolised by the 18 fieldsmen. He hit two fine boundary shots, then to the shock of all, and Mr. Armstrong in particular, he was clean-bowled by Bill Godby, aged 11 years. The most abashed player on the ground was Godby, and some of the older players looked as if they could have killed him.

His big moment came several minutes later when Armstrong handed him the ball and said: "It's a long time since any man bowled me for so small a score. That ball you bowled me with is the ball that was used in the Test game played at Nottingham, England, in 1909. Keep it, boy, to remind you of the day you got me cheap."

In return, Charlie Smith, the Mentone skipper, gave Armstrong a pipe, "a present from the boys." "Thank you, boys," he replied. "I'll never forget you, nor the happy time we have had together today." There were three cheers for Mr. Armstrong, and, according to the reporters, he drove off in his car looking rather less worried than when he arrived.

Everybody thought that the selectors would relent and Armstrong still would lead Victoria in the match against England on the M.C.G. that Friday. But they did not. So the *Herald* printed a large front page photograph of Armstrong with his latest team—by his right knee Bill Tootell, by his left knee, Tom Tootell.

The big move now was the protest meeting to be held outside the M.C.G. on Saturday afternoon. No longer was it a protest meeting. Mr. Westley was advertising it as the "Indignation Meeting." On Friday, when Victoria made 268, including 54 from Jack Ryder, the stands were nearly empty. The crowds were staying away, for without Armstrong this was like producing *Hamlet* without the Prince.

On the Saturday the V.C.A. was smart. The Indignation Meeting was at 3 p.m., but there would be no pass-out checks, which meant that all those who left to show their indignation would have to pay to come in again. The *Herald* said: "The shadow of Warwick Armstrong seemed to have fallen across the ground. Attendance was well below what it might have been, seeing that there was no racing, no big counter-attraction. It was an unorganised boycott." Boycott or no boycott, there was still a crowd of 17,000, and for those who were keen on their cricket little Patsy Hendren was playing like a man inspired. He made his first fifty in 38 minutes, his second fifty in 77 minutes, his third fifty in 50 minutes, his fourth in 49 minutes and his last fifty in 29 minutes. So there was this incredible choice—Patsy Hendren inside the ground or the Indignation Meeting outside.

Just before 3 p.m. the crowds drained out of the stands, not so much in the outer, for there they would have to pay to get back in again, but there was a real clearance from the members' pavilion. The crowd came and went from the meeting, but at its peak there must have been 8000 people. There was even a blind man who played *Will ye no come back again?* on a tin whistle; undoubtedly a tribute to Mr. Armstrong.

The meeting was immediately outside the ground near the members' reserve, and the speakers stood on top of a lorry. When Patsy Hendren scored his century the people outside could hear the cheering from the stands. Every time the "protestors" or the "indignators" passed a motion the crowds inside could hear the cheers from the crowd outside.

It was a bright but orderly meeting. The accepted description for the selectors was "the three blind mice." Mr. Westley put the same motion as he put to the meeting at the Athenaeum Hall on the Tuesday night. It was passed. He said, "I desire to offer an apology to the English cricketers for the indignity placed on them by the holding of an indignation meeting outside the ground on which they are playing. But the Englishmen are true sports, and I am sure they are in entire sympathy with the objects of the meeting. (Hear, hear.) Dirty washing is being washed in the presence of the visitors, but Armstrong is being crucified without a trial, and such a thing is opposed to the ethics of British justice." (Hear, hear.)

Inside Patsy Hendren continued to murder the bowling and the barrackers had a lovely day. "Put Armstrong on . . . You could do with the big feller now, eh?" . . . And, of course, "Why don'tcha give Ernie Bean a bowl?" Actually Mr. Bean was watching the game, and, according to the *Herald,* "he was subjected to some heckling by the crowd as he walked about. Some of the remarks were distinctly personal and Mr. Bean did not appear to be pleased." Then the story went that one of the members was touring the stand looking for men to make up a scratch match, and everywhere he went he received the same reply, "Look, old man, I know one fellow who isn't doing anything . . . can bat and bowl a bit . . . bloke by the name of Warwick Armstrong."

Patsy Hendren went on and on—off drives, on drives, cover drives, glances to the leg, late cuts placed to perfection, until he was 262 not out and England was 5 for 445. Then, just as stumps were drawn, the pathetic cry came across the ground, "Oh, where's Warwick?"

Hendren finished with 271 and it was an easy win for England. But on the Monday night there was the meeting of the V.C.A., and this time it was rather more than a meeting—it was the trial of Warwick Armstrong with an all-star cast of witnesses. The first to appear was Mr. O'Brien, manager of the Victorian team and prime witness for the prosecution. He said that he took the Victorian side to Sydney and all the time the whereabouts of Mr. Armstrong was a complete mystery. He did not turn up for practice the day before the match. Then, not until five minutes before play was due to start, did Mr. Armstrong announce that he was unfit.

For the defence there was Armstrong himself, Dr. R. L. Park and E. R. Mayne, the Victorian vice-captain. Armstrong explained that during the Third Test at Adelaide (when he made 121) he took a beating from the fast bowlers. He was bruised from the ankle to the thigh on his right leg. He said: "I got a beauty on the knee. But when I left Melbourne I was confident I would be able to play, and I particularly wanted to be in this match, seeing that it was the hundredth between N.S.W. and Victoria. When I got there I spent the whole day sitting in a hot water bath at Coogee trying to clear the bruises. But next morning at 11 o'clock Dr. Park and Mr. Mayne looked at the leg, and it was clear that I couldn't play. One decent knock and I would be out for the Fourth Test."

All this went on with the press, very angry, outside the closed doors. Finally the newspapermen received this statement:

"This Association, having heard Messrs. Armstrong and Mayne and Dr. Park, considers that Mr. Armstrong was justified in not playing in Sydney, but regards that the manager of the team should have been informed earlier of the likelihood of Mr. Armstrong not being able to play. If this had been done the trouble would not have arisen."

This easily could have been the end of the affair, but the indefatigable Mr. Westley was far from done. He called a third protest meeting, this time for February 16 in the Melbourne Town Hall. The newspapers reported that Mr. Westley had a projector and he showed slides of the recent Indignation Meeting outside the M.C.G. There were slides too of the leading Australian cricketers, and when Armstrong's picture was flashed on the screen there were cheers and everybody began to sing, *He's a Jolly Good Fellow.* Mr. Westley called for the sacking of all the cricket selectors, and he told the meeting that if it acted now it could give new life to Australian cricket.

Senator Guthrie moved: "That this meeting refutes entirely the unsatisfactory excuses set forth by the V.C.A. in its report in an endeavour to justify the action of the selectors in excluding Warwick Armstrong from the Victorian Eleven against England."

The Senator was most eloquent. Many people had criticised him for coming to the meeting. They had said it was no place for an Australian Senator. But his reply was this: he did not tie himself to any section of the community. His job was to stamp out persecution and injustice wherever it occurred, and that night they were all present at the Melbourne Town Hall for one reason— because they refused to stand for the persecution of one of their leading citizens by a little clique of dictators. (Cheers.)

Whether all the protest meetings and the hundreds of thousands of words that were written had the slightest effect is a matter for debate. Yet there was a good deal of conjecture as to whether Armstrong would be chosen for the Fourth Test, and many thought that his chances of going to England the following month, and of being chosen as captain, were slim indeed. Even Armstrong himself was not over-hopeful. He let it be known that if he were not picked as captain he would not go. The selectors announced later that

Armstrong would be captain and the choice was unanimous, but many believed the choice had been far from unanimous and he had just scraped home. Mr. Bean himself was one of the Test selectors. So who knows? Maybe the public outcry did have some effect. If Mr. Westley was prepared to turn on three protest meetings just because Warwick Armstrong was dropped from the Victorian side, maybe he would have turned on a riot the equivalent to the sacking of the Bastille had he been dropped as captain of the Australian Eleven.

There were two Tests at Sydney, two at Melbourne and one at Adelaide, and they produced a lively controversy over barracking. Jack Hobbs, just as A. E. Stoddart and W. G. Grace had done before him, complained of the rudeness of the crowd. There were many letters on the subject, and one gentleman even wrote an erudite piece to *The Times*. He pointed out that the English cricketers did not thoroughly understand the nature of Australians. Australian crowds knew far more about cricket than English crowds and the barracking was good-natured, part of the fun of the game. Admittedly to the newcomer it sounded a little merciless, but there was little harm in what they said, and the pointed remarks of the barrackers applied equally to the home side as well as the visitors. The *Herald* had a charming theory that the word "barrack" was derived from the old Arabic "bar" for refreshment booth and "arrack" for strong drink. And seeing that much of the barracking came from areas close to the refreshment booths at the M.C.G., perhaps there was even some truth to the theory.

Throughout the Second and Fourth Tests a barracker called out monotonously, "Why don'tcha put Billy Hughes on?" This was a reference to the remarkable bowling prowess of the Prime Minister. On November 29 last there had been a match at the Albert Ground between the Federal and State Parliaments. As a cricketer Mr. Hughes was somebody to see. The *Argus* reported that he wore "a picturesque if scarcely orthodox cricket costume which consisted of a blue shirt, a striped collar, a flowing silk tie, white trousers well rolled up and tennis shoes."

The State side batted and three wickets fell for 12 runs, but then the batsmen dug in, and when they passed 50 the Federal men became alarmed. "It's time somebody did something," said Mr. Hughes. Whereupon he took the ball and a spectator in the pavilion had the courage to call out sardonically, "Bowler's name?"

The *Argus* said, "The Prime Minister has a peculiar action that is faintly—very faintly—reminiscent of Wilfred Rhodes. He takes three long strides and tosses the ball well up, and then apparently prays for something to happen.

To everybody's amazement his first ball clean bowled Mr. Hannah, the captain of the State side." If the easy catches had been held off his next two balls he would have taken the hat-trick. The Federal Parliamentarians were incredibly inefficient at catching the balls which were hit at them, and this gravely affected the Prime Minister's analysis. He finished with 4 wickets for 45 with six dropped catches. It looked as if a new Australian bowler had arrived, but one of his wickets was open to question. Mr. Hughes appealed for an lbw with such prime ministerial ferocity that the startled umpire felt he had no choice but to give the man out.

Fortunately Australia did not have to call on Mr. Hughes for any of the Tests, for Arthur Mailey was bowling as never before. The Fourth Test match in Melbourne was a good match both for Armstrong and Mailey. The fight with the V.C.A. was just over and Warwick Armstrong was the hero of Melbourne. As he stepped out of the pavilion the crowd at the M.C.G. stood on their seats and cheered him all the way to the wicket. Their enthusiasm was even a little embarrassing. If he played badly or if he were bowled first ball, this would prove perhaps that the selectors' doubts were justified. Nobody need have worried. The first ball from Fender he cut for two, the next he drove for four and he was on his way. At the end of the innings he was still there undefeated for 123 not out.

Arthur Mailey, like a postman at Christmas time, had to work for his money. He took 4/115 in the first innings and he seemed rather an expensive luxury. In the second innings a great deal depended on him because Gregory had a bad back and Armstrong was off the field with malaria. He started superbly by taking three wickets for 10 runs. He added half a century before he took another wicket, and by the time he had taken his fifth he had a full century on the board. Now Collins was a most imperturbable captain. A less brave or less thoughtful man would have posted the expensive Mailey to a nice safe post on the boundary for the rest of the afternoon. But once again he gave him the ball and Mailey broke through to wind up the innings with 4 wickets for six runs.

Mailey's triumph was complete. He had done something which no other bowler had ever done in a Test match; he had taken nine wickets in an innings. His figures 47 overs, 8 maidens, 121 runs, 9 wickets. Such figures could not be compared now with Laker's 9/37 and 10/53 at Manchester in 1956, but still it remains a record for an Australian against England. Unlike Laker, on this day Mailey had little help from the pitch. The newspapers talked of the perfection of his length, how he plotted, how he altered his style for every batsman. For example, as soon as Woolley came in he flighted the

BATSMEN OUT.			FALL OF WKTS.	BATSMEN. RUNS	BOWLERS. WKTS. RUNS		
SANDFORD	S2	23	I FOR 43		Nº6 BOWLING.		
HERRING	C2	66	2 · · 168	LANSDOWN 25			
BROWN	C1	87	3 · · 200	EXTRAS 42	I FACY	2	228
MATHERS	C1	46	4 · · 259 10 OUT FOR 1059		2 NEWTON	2	182
LOVE	C7	156	5 · · 595	VICTORIA	3 DAVIE		97
BAILEY	B6	82	6 · · 792	I" INNINGS 1059	4 GOODRICK	I	14
SCHNEIDER	RO 1	55	7 · · 956	2" INNINGS II I	5 ALLEN	2	154
PONSFORD	C5	429	8 · · 1001	TASMANIA	6 MARTIN	2	161
MULLETT	B5	16	9 · · 1002	I" INNINGS 217	7 LONEY	I	70
GAMBLE	C6	32	10 · · 1059	2" INNINGS	8 SMITH		I I

Above

The first time 1,000 runs were scored in first class cricket, Victoria v. Tasmania in 1923.

Left

The incomparable Bill Ponsford. He made 1,013 runs in four innings in three matches played in successive weeks on the M.C.G. in 1927.

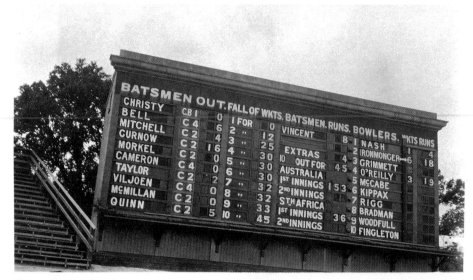

A beautiful day for the spinners — South
Africa all out for 45, Fifth Test, 1932.

Right
Sir Leo Cussen, President, 1922–1933.

ball much more than he had done for Hobbs and Makepeace. Always he was prepared to take risks to get wickets. He was not a bowler who would bottle up the game. It was Arthur Mailey's greatest day and the Melbourne crowd cheered him all the way into the dressing room.

After the Fifth Test Armstrong took the first post-war touring side to England. One could toss up as to which was the greatest team ever to leave Australia—Darling's side in 1902, Bradman's in 1948, but Armstrong's in 1921 would not rate far behind them. It was the first team to go away with a double-barrelled opening fast attack—E. A. McDonald and Jack Gregory. Macartney scored 2335 runs for the tour and Bardsley 2218. Armstrong, the 42-year-old, topped the bowling with 106 wickets, average 14.66, and Arthur Mailey took 146 wickets at an average of 19.78. The team won three Tests and two were drawn.

Fares on the cable trams went up by a shocking 50 per cent., so that in 1922 it was costly to visit the M.C.G. Before the fare was one penny a section, now it cost three-halfpence a section. Yet if trams were too expensive there were other forms of transport. The M.C.C. started a most novel move. Senator George Fairbairn, one of the trustees, supported by Dr. R. B. Weigall, president of the Automobile Club, put a request to the Parks and Gardens Committee that a small area of land between the entrance to the M.C.G. and Jolimont Terrace might be used as a car park while matches were in progress. After all, the parking of cars was becoming a serious problem. There were now 25,000 motor vehicles on Melbourne's roads.

In the New Year's honours lists for 1922 there were some interesting names. The wife of the Prime Minister was now Dame Mary Hughes, and listed among the knighthoods was Leo Finn Bernard Cussen, President of the Melbourne Cricket Club. He was the second President to be so honoured. Sir William Clarke became a baronet in 1882.

The newspapers told the story of Sir Leo's unusual career, the railway engineer who became a Justice of the Supreme Court of Victoria. He was born at Portland on November 29, 1859, and educated at Hamilton College and Melbourne University. He took his certificate in civil engineering with an exhibition in mathematics. Then in 1879 he joined the Victorian Railways and he helped to survey the track for the direct line to Ballarat. Yet after five years he tired of the railways and he went back to the University, where he took his B.A., his M.A. and his LL.B. He set himself up as a barrister and solicitor in 1886. Immediately he was a success in patent and engineering cases. He was elevated to the Supreme Court bench in 1906. Sir Leo loved both his cricket and his football, but maybe cricket was his first love, for, after all, he was a

Melbourne University cricket blue. One wonders if he had time to watch a certain cricket match that took place between Victoria and Tasmania in 1923.

You could only describe this period as the scoring twenties. Bert Luttrell's wickets on the M.C.G. were granite hard and glass smooth. The batsmen seemed to have complete mastery. The team to play Tasmania was a second Victorian eleven, made up of young hopefuls who were on the fringe of the senior side. One of the young hopefuls, who although obviously brilliant, had been passed over again and again. He was a St. Kilda player, Bill Ponsford, aged 22.

Tasmania batted first and made 217 runs. That night, at the close of play, the Tasmanians were astonished to see Bert Luttrell covering the wicket. Mr. Smith, captain and manager of the Tasmanians, asked him what was going on. Bert said that this was the practice now for the Sheffield Shield matches. He admitted that some of the old players were shocked at the idea, but it gave a much better deal to the spectators. Whereupon it is reported that one of the Tasmanians replied: "Oh, so we play drawing room cricket in Melbourne now. I wonder if it would be permissible to plant flowers around the wicket to protect it from the wind."

Next day the drawing room cricket settled down in earnest, and at stumps the score was 5 for 672, with Ponsford 234 not out. The Victorians had made 506 runs in a day. Lesser enthusiasts might have declared the innings at this point, but they went on and on. The *Herald* reported that Ponsford passed records like a fast car shooting past milestones. He passed Armstrong's Victoria v. South Australia record of 250, and five minutes later Victoria's record score of 724 made against South Australia was passed. The next to go was Victor Trumper's Australian record against Tasmania of 292, then F. Woolley's English record against Tasmania of 305. The hours went by and still the records fell, including C. W. Gregory's record Australian score of 383 for N.S.W. against Queensland.

The *Herald* said: "The seventh wicket fell at 956, and once more Ponsford got among the records. When he reached 424 and equalled Maclaren's world record the spectators rose and gave him three cheers. The next objective was 1000 runs for his side, and here his partner, L. Mullett, did a most sporting thing. He was facing the bowling at 999 and could have scored easily, but wishing to give Ponsford the distinction he blocked the over, and then Ponsford with a pat to mid-on got the thousandth run and more cheers. Then realising there were no more worlds to conquer he hit out and was caught. The board showed the remarkable figures 8-429-1001."

Actually, having a four-figure score on the board made things a little untidy. There was no room for the fourth figure and the extra one had to be added with chalk.

Never before had the statisticians enjoyed themselves quite so much. Apart from listing the countless records he had broken, it was demonstrated that Ponsford had scored at the rate of 53 runs an hour, he had been there for three minutes under eight hours, he hit 42 fours and he gave difficult chances at 60 and 116. He was at the wicket for the making of 801 runs, and if one accepted the point that he ran 22 yards for each run, then Mr. Ponsford had covered 17,622 yards.

Bill Ponsford was described as a slim, dark young man, who worked as a bank clerk with the State Savings Bank, a player of icy cold determination, and as far as the newspapermen were concerned, frustratingly modest and reticent. The best they could extract from an interview was this: "After I had been there for such a long time I felt rather sick of it. My feet and hands were all blistered." Later the State Savings Bank presented him with a gold watch and chain and the V.C.A. gave him a miniature gold bat.

However, do not think that Victoria was done with the dismissal of Ponsford. The tail-enders added another 58 runs and Victoria was all out for 1059. Tasmania made 176 in the second innings, so Victoria won comfortably . . . by an innings and 666 runs. If nothing else, this proved that the B.P. era had begun and Bill Ponsford had to struggle no more to get into State or Australian sides. Indeed, Australia came to depend on him when Arthur Gilligan arrived with his team for the 1924-25 season. Ponsford made 110 on the Sydney Cricket Ground in his first Test.

For the Second Test on the M.C.G. interest was tremendous, and at last there was radio. 3AR had been in action for nearly a year, and no longer did one have to stand outside the *Age* or the *Argus* office to get the latest news. 3AR bought the radio rights for the season at the Melbourne Cricket Ground for £75. The new morning daily, the *Sun-News Pictorial"* reported on January 1, 1925:

> Wireless operators will obtain a first-hand description of every incident in the Second Test match which begins today. This is the result of arrangements made by the 3AR broadcasting station. The company has secured the services of the Victorian Eleven captain, E. R. Mayne, and will describe the progress of the game. A special land line has been run from the studio in Elizabeth Street to the M.C.G., where a special observer from 3AR will transmit over the telephone to the broadcasting studio a complete description of the match.
> The enterprise of 3AR marks a new era in the use of radio. The wireless operator in the remotest part of Australia will be able to learn the many turns

135

which the game may take within a few seconds of ihe time at which the spectators on the ground become aware of them. 3LO, the other broadcasting station, will also broadcast the scores every half hour.

The sun shone precisely as the M.C.C. committee would have wanted it to shine, and all cricket attendance and cash records were broken. There was the new world record for a cricket match on the first day, 49,413, then 47,000 on the second day, 48,151 on the third, 33,129 on the fourth, 23,740 on the fifth, and so it went on. Even the new car park provided some records of its own. Nobody had ever seen so many automobiles massed in the one spot. On the first day there were 1770 cars and 2500 on the second.

Then, of course, there was the pitiless, relentless run-getting. Australia made 300 on the first day and 300 on the second, including 128 from Ponsford and 138 from Vic Richardson. Hobbs and Sutcliffe painfully set out after the big score, and at the end of the third day Hobbs was 154, Sutcliffe 123, and England no wicket for 283. This was unbelievable, almost 900 runs scored in three days of cricket and only 10 wickets had fallen. The falling of a wicket was a notable event, something to look forward to, a bonus to be enjoyed only by those who were prepared to put in a full day at the ground. The newspapers were full of suggestions for speeding up cricket, everything from bigger and wider stumps to narrower bats. There were suggestions too that it might be wise to limit the time for a Test match. That surely would force batsmen to speed up their play. However, in this sunny January of 1925 there was little need to speed up anything and the Test lasted for seven days.

It seemed certain that Hobbs and Sutcliffe would carry on to break the 323 opening partnership record made by Hobbs and Rhodes in 1912, but both men were out first thing on the morning of the fourth day and England was all out for 479. It was not enough and Australia won by 81 runs. Although beaten, at times the Englishmen looked very impressive. Maurice Tate, every time he appeared, looked more and more like a great bowler. His boots, too, impressed, so much so that one newspaper published a photograph of the boots without Tate in them. Here was a pair that was almost as large as the famous boots of Mr. W. W. Armstrong. Tate, like Keith Miller, had that trick, done with such perfect nonchalance, of flicking the ball into his hand with the toe of his boot. The crowd always gave this performance a cheer, which Tate always acknowledged with a bow.

As for Sutcliffe, he made 127 in the second innings, which meant that he scored a century in both innings, something that had been done only once before in a Test match—Warren Bardsley at the Oval in 1909. There was an immediate shilling subscription around the members' stand. Even the Governor-General, Lord Forster, and the State Governor, Lord Stradbroke,

136

handed over their shillings. Herbert Sutcliffe received a cheque for £8.

Australia won the first three Tests and so the rubber. Yet when the selectors gave their choice for the Fourth Test there was fury from all quarters. The critics thought it fantastic that once again Kippax, Woodfull and Grimmett were omitted. Kippax was on top of the Sheffield Shield averages with 92 and Woodfull was right behind him with 72. Yet in the case of Clarrie Grimmett it almost reached the proportions of a plot. What did he have to do to be recognised? First he came from New Zealand seeking fame as a bowler. He was spurned in New South Wales, so he moved to Victoria, where he played for South Melbourne. In spite of some remarkable bowling feats, still the selectors would not look at him, so he moved to Adelaide, where at last his ability was appreciated. In 1925 he had the best bowling average in the Commonwealth. He was 32 years old and he was still waiting.

England at the M.C.G. won the Fourth Test, and there could have been few men as happy anywhere as Arthur Gilligan. It was England's first Test match victory since 1912 and it was by an innings and 29 runs. Sutcliffe made 143— no Englishman had ever done so well in Australia. After four Test matches his tally was 712 runs, his average 101.71.

At last Clarrie Grimmett got his break for the Fifth Test at Sydney. It was like the breaking of the drought. Or as the Melbourne *Sun* said: "Cinderella had the last laugh on her ugly sisters when she married the prince and escaped from the groove of drudgery in which they had placed her. In the same way the Australian slow bowler now has the laugh on Edgar Mayne, Victoria's captain, and Ernie Bean, Victorian and Australian selector, who consigned him to obscurity in cricket."

Clarrie bowled as if all the years of waiting were boiling inside him. He took 5 for 35 in the first innings and 6 for 37 in the second innings. It was the clever bowling of Arthur Mailey that had kept him out of the side. But Clarrie bowled so well in this match that Arthur Mailey had only five overs in the first innings and he did not take the ball at all in the second. Alan Kippax also made his debut with 42 runs in the first innings. Australia won by 307 runs.

In 1926 Bob Crockett announced his retirement. It had to come of course, but somehow this was something unexpected. It was like the retirement of a permanent institution, the equivalent of the stopping of the Town Hall clock. Bob Crockett was Australia's greatest umpire, the Chief Justice of cricket. He first umpired cricket matches in 1887. He came to first class matches in 1892 and from 1902 he was a Test umpire. Johnnie Moyes has written of him: "I knew him well and appreciated his skill, his modesty, his love of cricket. There were no mannerisms about Crockett, no sudden turning and bending as the bowler released the ball—a modern invention which must at times distract the batsman's attention—no playing to the crowd. He stood quietly in a position to see, and he gave his decisions. The players loved and respected him."

In January 1926 J. W. Trumble suggested a public subscription. He said that Bob Crockett was famous the world over as a cricket umpire. The respect for his ability was as high in England as it was in Australia. Yet neither Bob Crockett nor his wife had ever been to England. He knew that they would dearly love to go there for the coming Test series.

The Melbourne Cricket Club agreed to handle the subscription and opened the list with a cheque for 100 guineas. At the tea adjournment of the district cricket final between St. Kilda and Hawthorn-East Melbourne Sir Leo Cussen presented Bob Crockett with a cheque for £1043/1/8. Sir Leo said Mr. Crockett had umpired 27 Test matches between England and Australia and five between South Africa and Australia. As a servant of the Melbourne Cricket Club he had given 38 years of loyal and faithful service. All players knew that a Crockett decision on the field was always fair and honest. Mr. Crockett himself might admit that he may have made mistakes, but every player and follower of the game knew that if such mistakes had been made they were very, very few. As the spectators gave three cheers Bob Crockett obviously was overcome. He could say little. As the *Argus* put it: "Mr. Crockett expressed his thanks to the subscribers, but then the routine of a lifetime asserted itself. He suddenly remembered that if he spoke any longer the players would be late getting back on to the field after the tea adjournment." On April 15 Mr. and Mrs. Crockett left for England to arrive in time for the First Test match.

On Friday, December 23, 1926, there were 22,893 people at the Melbourne Cricket Ground, a fair crowd for the traditional holiday match between Victoria and New South Wales. The spectators did not realise that they were to see an unforgettable cricket match, one that will always occupy a permanent place, not only in the annals of the M.C.C. but in the cricket record books of the world. The N.S.W. captain, Alan Kippax, had a young team and he was hopeful, but for reasons of retirement and injury he was without Gregory, Macartney, Kelleway, Oldfield, Collins and Everett. No amount of dreaming could cover up the fact that he needed all the luck in the world.

At 6 o'clock that Friday night here was Victoria's score:

Woodfull, c. Ratcliffe, b. Andrews	133
Ponsford, not out	334
Hendry, not out	86
Sundries	20
One wicket for	573

Ponsford had done what no other player has ever done on the M.C.G.—he had made 300 runs in one day, and he reached 300 in 285 minutes. The labouring New South Welshmen, and particularly Arthur Mailey, who was said to be indomitable in his courage, sent down 64 overs during the innings. The runs came at the rate of 5½ runs an over.

As for Ponsford, the newspapers said that never had they seen such a display of resolute, relentless batting. His stamina was extraordinary. The only occasion he showed any signs of fatigue was during the tea interval, when he had an attack of cramp. Already the match had caught the imagination of Victoria, and the following morning there were more than 22,000 people at the M.C.G., waiting to see what would happen. There was no telling what Bill Ponsford would do. He could make 400, 500, 600 runs, and certainly Clem Hill's Sheffield Shield record of 365 made against N.S.W. would go at once.

There was an almost ecclesiastical calm at the M.C.G. The match was not so important; there was the extraordinary fascination in watching Ponsford break every record in the book. The cricket was slow, but that did not matter. The crowd stayed respectfully silent as Ponsford hit single after single, creeping closer and closer to Clem Hill's record. Then suddenly he was gone, bowled Morgan for 352. If the silence was ecclesiastical before, now the crowd was out of church. There was laughing and cheering and barracking. The crowd had done all it could. No longer was it possible to assist Ponsford in his record-breaking.

This time the statisticians went to work on Ponsford's innings with much greater accuracy. In his 352 runs he ran more than five miles. Ponsford hit 36 fours, Woodfull seven fours and Hendry five fours—or 192 runs out of the total of 614 scored while Ponsford was at the wicket. The other 422 all were scored by running. The pitch was 22 yards long, but in most cases the batsmen ran only 20 yards. But one had to consider spirited dashes when they ran further, or fours that were run right out, so altogether they said Ponsford ran 9000 yards, or about five miles.

Then Jack Ryder went into action in the most brilliant Ryder innings of them all. He scored 295, with six sixes. He scored his first 100 in 115 minutes, his second in 74 minutes and his last 95 in 56 minutes.

The *Sun News-Pictorial* said:

> One of Ryder's sixes, a full toss from Mailey, struck the veranda on the smokers' pavilion, another went into the reserve, while the other four were lovely drives against the wind into the outer ground. The crowd cheered with delight as he hit four after four, but when he began to go for the sixes it fairly roared. In five overs 62 were hit off Mailey and practically all came from Ryder's bat. Later he hit 18 off one over from Mailey. Facing Andrews when

275, Ryder hit the first ball for four, the second for six, the third for four, the fourth for six, and miss-hitting the fifth was caught by Kippax at mid-on.

The ball that hit the veranda of the smokers' pavilion went close to the clock. A practical man might have thought that for such a crime as smashing the clock the batsman could be sued by the M.C.C. for wilful destruction of property. But no, the reverse was the case. One newspaper reported that had Ryder hit the clock he would have won a case of champagne. This was challenged. Indeed, he would not merely have received one case of champagne but six cases. The *Herald* went to the M.C.C. secretary, Hugh Trumble, who said: "Break the clock? God bless my soul, no one has ever done that. Champagne? I've never heard of any champagne being offered. If that were true I wouldn't mind having a go myself. I don't know how the idea started. Once upon a time a chap bet big George Bonnor £50 to nothing that he couldn't hit the clock. That was taking quite a chance, for George was a mighty hitter and he came dashed near to doing it more than once."

The mighty hitting in this match continued until Victoria had made 1107, a world record in first-class cricket, and it has never been beaten. It was all done in 10½ hours. Here was the scoreboard:

Woodfull, c. Ratcliffe, b. Andrews	133
Ponsford, b. Morgan	352
Hendry, c. Morgan, b. Mailey	100
Ryder, c. Kippax, b. Andrews	295
Love, std. Ratcliffe, b. Mailey	6
King, std. Ratcliffe, b. Mailey	7
Hartkopf, c. McGuirk, b. Mailey	61
Liddicut, b. McGuirk	36
Ellis, run out	63
Morton, run out	0
Blackie, not out	27
Sundries	27
Total	1107

Bowling

	O.	M.	R.	W.
McNamee	24	2	124	0
McGuirk	26	1	130	1
Mailey	64	0	362	4
Campbell	11	0	89	0
Phillips	11.7	0	64	0
Morgan	26	0	137	1
Andrews	21	2	148	2
Kippax	7	0	26	0

One thousand one hundred and seven runs. The newspapers printed photographs of the scoreboard and also they put in a photograph of the gloves of A. Ratcliffe, the New South Wales wicketkeeper, the man who had to stay there for 1527 deliveries. It was an iron man performance, almost as great as the batting of Ponsford. He allowed only 27 extras. And how about Arthur Mailey, who bowled 64 overs and took four wickets for 362 runs?

Already Arthur had a reputation for being a humourist as well as a cartoonist, and here are some of his comments that appeared in the *Sun News-Pictorial*:

> This match just finished was certainly one for records. Some caused the breasts of players concerned to well with pride and importance. Other records caused a little embarrassment. In my own case I regret a record that was broken. A well-known Victorian cricket statistician told me this morning that no other alleged bowler has ever had so many runs knocked off his bowling in an innings. He shook my limp hand. I am still wondering whether it was a congratulatory grip or even one of thanks. He is a statistician who makes a hobby of recording uncommon performances.

Arthur explained how very co-operative the batsmen had been in helping him to create this record, and he gave great praise to Bill Ponsford and Bill Woodfull.

> Of the other batsmen Ryder in particular played a splendid innings. He hopped into top gear and left most of us floundering in the dust, blinking at the scoreboard. After he had cruelly hit me into the members' reserve Andrews said, "Put a man there; that's his weak spot."
>
> It was rather a pity that Ellis was run out at the finish, for I was just striking my length.
>
> Very few chances were given, although I think a chap in a tweed coat dropped Jack Ryder just near the shilling stand. Here I would like to thank the spectators who fielded so well. They never let up during their long stay on the other side of the fence.
>
> Of course, we would have done much better if the scoring board had been up to date. There was only room for eight bowlers' names, and I am sure the wicket-keeper, who appeared to be the most agile person on the ground, would have gone right through the Victorian team. But you cannot very well put a man on to bowl if there is no room for his name on the board. For the bowler is like the politician; we like to see our names in print.
>
> To the scoring board officials I humbly apologise. I do hope they were on piecework. If so, "I'm hoppin' in for me cut on pay day."

New South Wales made 221 and 230 and was beaten by an innings and 656 runs. Such a defeat for mighty New South Wales was incredible. When it was all over there were many leading articles. Was cricket a game or just a grim struggle to break records? The Christmas match at the M.C.G. certainly had been fascinating and a crowd pleaser, but were scores of over 1000 runs good for cricket? The *Herald* said: "The bowling of today is unquestionably weak, but even the best bowlers find themselves handicapped by the perfection of the wickets, and their covering. The whole tendency during the past few years has been to make conditions easier for the batsmen and it's high time this tendency was checked." Yet nobody really checked Ponsford that season. His scores were 214, 54, 151, 352 and 108. His average: 175.4.

Membership of the Melbourne Cricket Club went up from 4000 to 5200 and the annual subscription rose to £3. The club was forever growing and something had to give. In October 1927 there was an announcement; the club would build a new members' pavilion at a cost of £80,000. So the wreckers moved in and the old club, built in 1881 at a cost of £5170, began to crumble under the hammers. Many of the old members were bitterly unhappy. If the pavilion at Lord's was the holy of holies in England, then the pavilion at the Melbourne Cricket Ground was the holy of holies in Australia. Every piece of timber, every room, was charged with tradition. The great who visited Melbourne invariably called at the M.C.C. pavilion. The young Princes Edward and George laid the foundation stone in 1881, and only last year, on April 26, 1926, there had been a visit from the Duke of York.

So many cricket matches, so many great players, Grace, Hill, Stoddart, Ranjitsinhji, Trumper, Blackham, Spofforth, Giffen, Laver, Bannerman, Horan, Murdoch, they had left something behind, the pavilion had seen the history of cricket. From the earliest days the room on the right-hand side of the door was the home of the first eleven of the club and, until the advent of the Board of Control, the home for representative sides, the room from which Australian Elevens went out to fight for the Ashes. Then just behind the dressing room was a small room, almost the heart of the pavilion. Here Jim Phillips and later Bob Crockett, the two greatest of Australian umpires, had their quarters. Every evening after stumps there was a little gathering in this room, and Bob Crockett would talk over the day's play. If ever you were invited into the quarters of the Chief Justice then you knew you had arrived indeed.

Nobody, of course, literally owned a seat in the old pavilion, but always the same people could be found in the same places. Perhaps it was one of the 50 seats under the press balcony, others could be found up on the balcony itself, and then there were the roof regulars. J. McCarthy Blackham, the prince of wicketkeepers, always held court up there with a group of his friends. The veteran players all had their picked and loved positions. Now they would have to move elsewhere.

Yet some of the regrets were washed away by the promise of the new pavilion. It was to be the very latest thing of its kind, with accommodation for 3000. There would be a buffet room, a magnificent members' bar on the ground floor, 40 by 72 feet, there would be a splendid long room glazed in for the members' comfort, a committee dining room, special reserves for visiting officials, and the roof would be so arranged that only the minimum of supports would interrupt the view of the members.

And the *Argus* gave some excellent reasons:

> There are now nearly 6000 M.C.C. members and there are 4150 names on the waiting list, and some of them have been there for the past six years. For many years, owing to lack of accommodation, members have wondered whether it really was a privilege to belong to the club, for they found themselves crowded out of their own pavilion by representatives of other bodies. In the new pavilion I understand a notice which has long been disregarded, "Members Only," will be strictly observed. It will make membership of the club what it used to be, a privilege and a pleasure. Now there are so many complimentary tickets that the character of the members' reserve has changed. The pity is that the old building could not have been retained and the new pavilion erected on another site.

On February 25, 1928, Sir Leo Cussen, the President, laid the foundation stone. Sir Leo placed a copper cylinder in the foundation stone. It contained a copy of the last annual report of the club inscribed on parchment, and signed by the president, treasurer and secretary; photographs of the former pavilion, a membership badge, a life member's medallion, a list of the members of the club, a copy on silk of the world record score, newspaper front pages of February 7, and a complete copy of the *Australasian* of that date.

December 16, 1927, was a hot, muggy day at the M.C.G. It was only Queensland's second year in the Sheffield Shield competition, and maybe the Queensland captain was a little fearful of the immensely strong 1000 run Victorian XI. The wicket was a typical, beautiful, M.C.G. wicket, as permanent as the Pyramids. The captains, Leo O'Connor of Queensland and W. M. Woodfull of Victoria, tossed. O'Connor won, and incredibly he sent Victoria in to bat. Ponsford said later: "We were absolutely flabbergasted when we heard the decision. Woodfull was so surprised he actually asked O'Connor three times if Victoria was to go in. He thought there was some mistake and couldn't credit his own hearing."

Why O'Connor put Victoria in to bat was never adequately explained.

143

There was a theory that sometimes the wicket at the M.C.G. was lively for the first two hours, but the theory had little basis in fact. Then there was another possible reason, also hard to credit, that at this stage O'Connor already was playing for a draw. Under the new rules there was a time limit on Sheffield Shield matches. Some critics feared that this time limit would merely cause the dull cricket it was trying to prevent. Timid captains would always go for a draw. So the theory was that maybe O'Connor hoped Victoria would make a huge score, waste too much time, and only gain a win on the first innings. Hence Queensland, at least, would salvage one point.

So Victoria batted. At stumps Victoria was 2 for 400, Ponsford 234 not out and Hendry 129. The next day Victoria's score went to 793 before the last wicket fell, and Ponsford made 437. Until Bradman scored his 452 not out against Queensland in the 1929-30 season this was the highest score ever made in a first-class match. He was at the wicket 421 minutes and he hit 42 fours. The commentators asked: "What is there left for Billy Ponsford to do? He has broken every record in the book. He has broken Clem Hill's Sheffield Shield record of 365, and he has broken his own world record of 429. Yet perhaps there is still one—R. E. Foster's record of 287, the highest score for a Test match. No doubt Ponsford will even break that record when he meets the Englishmen next year."

One of the first telegrams of congratulation came from another expert at marathons, Hubert Opperman, the breaker of world cycling records.

Queensland at the finish showed great fight in an attempt to stave off an innings defeat by making 189 in the first innings and 407 in the second. But the result never was in doubt, and on the last day practically the only spectators were the bricklayers who were working on the new pavilion. It was reported that they enjoyed the cricket immensely.

Yet more and more people were wondering what would be the end to this huge scoring. The *Sun News-Pictorial* commented: "A young batsman made history on Saturday. Now we wonder if there is anywhere a bowler who can also make history—bowling history. He would be very welcome. The season is now well advanced and we still wait in vain the appearance of the super bowler who can deal with the super batsmen. England, apparently, also waits. Opportunity is beckoning to the brilliant bowler, and he is badly needed in both countries."

However, England already had a super bowler in mind, a man who moved with the rhythmical ease of a racehorse, Harold Larwood. Larwood arrived with Percy Chapman's team on October 31, 1928. In Melbourne there was something of the pomp and excitement of the old days, reception committees, cheering crowds, a real Test fever atmosphere. The newspapers were running £100 "Pick Your Test Side" competitions, and everyone from the retired Clem Hill to Mr. Stanley Bruce was being selected. The official reception was very gay. Mr. Donald Mackinnon, president of the V.C.A., said during the previous tours he was fascinated by the initials of the English captain, Mr. J. W. H. T. Douglas. It was always a comfort when he went out to bat to believe that they meant "Johnny Won't Hit Today." Now the new English captain, Percy Chapman, had a fine set—A.P.F. He had given the matter some considerable thought on the previous night, but, alas, he could find nothing that would suit.

Mr. A. P. F. Chapman replied that he was sorry Mr. Mackinnon had spent sleepless nights on this problem, because the answer was simple. They meant "A Perfect Fool."

Mr. Toone, the English manager, said no. "We have 17 handsome fellows —I would suggest 'A Perfect Family.' "

Sir Leo Cussen said, "Or, of course, they could mean 'A Perfect Field.' "

"I beg your pardon," replied Percy Chapman. "Did you say 'A Perfect Fiend?' "

And so it was a bright opening. Nor was there any great alarm concerning the match against Victoria. After all, South Australia had handled the Englishmen very well in a drawn match and Larwood had proved a most amiable bowler. Where were his thunderbolts? At one stage Vic Richardson hooked him for six.

In London that week-end one might have thought, reasonably, that the big news was the flight of the German airship Graf Zeppelin. It flew from Lakehurst, New Jersey, to Friedrichshafen in 72 hours 15 minutes. The Zeppelin arrived over the town at 4.30 a.m. The cables said that the noise of the engines brought thousands of the inhabitants to their doors and windows. Even though there was a mist it was possible to see the lights of the cabins above. The cheering crowds quickly filled the streets, and the passengers received a tumultuous welcome when the airship landed at dawn.

This story was pushed to one side. Larwood's name was on all the London posters. He had routed the Victorians by taking 7 wickets for 51 runs. The *Star*'s streamer headline read: "LARWOOD ROUTS AUSTRALIAN BATSMEN," and the news story read, "The manner in which Larwood mowed down Australia's cricket giants showed that he was obviously being nursed against South Australia." Only Woodfull stood firm. He carried his bat through the innings and he made 67 out of Victoria's 164. England replied with 486 and the match was drawn.

145

Larwood almost repeated his performance in the First Test. Brisbane at last had a Test match, and Larwood not only had his revenge on Woodfull by bowling him for a duck but he took 6 for 32 in the first innings and 2 for 30 in the second. England was happier than ever, and a comment from the *Daily Express* did make one wonder if A. P. F. Chapman was "A Perfect Fiend." It said: "What it comes to is this. This time our men are not going to make a mistake. They are out to give Australia the biggest hiding it has ever had. They are out not merely to keep the Ashes but to double-padlock the urn. Chapman's tactics concealed his deadly, merciless intent to break the opposition. In other words, he is leading his men with the will to win. That is why they went to Australia."

And he won very well. In the First Test it was a victory by 675 runs, in the Second Test it was a victory by 8 wickets and 2 runs, so that for the Third Test at the Melbourne Cricket Ground the Australian captain, Jack Ryder, had worries a-plenty. He had to win or say goodbye to the Ashes. Ponsford was out for the season with a broken finger. The team had no genuine fast bowler, for Jack Gregory broke down in the First Test. The replacement was Ted a'Beckett, aged 21, a former Melbourne Grammar boy, and 20-year-old Donald Bradman was reinstated after being dropped following his low scores in the First Test. Then there was a spin bowler old enough to be the father of these two juniors, Don Blackie. He made his debut in the Second Test when he was 46 years old. He was a St. Kilda player, yet he had not been a regular member of the State side. Why he had never been promoted before perhaps only the selectors knew. If he had shot into Test cricket at the age of 20 like young Bradman, he could have been playing in Tests immediately after the Boer War, along with Trumper, Darling, Hill and co. Yet even at 46 he was a mighty bowler, and it was said that he could appeal as appealingly as any bowler who ever lived. In this match he had the best bowling figures for either side. While the fearsome Larwood took 3 for 127 in the first innings, Don Blackie for Australia took 6 for 94.

It was a see-sawing match with marvellous attendances. On the first day there was a world record crowd of 63,247. Woodfull, Kippax, Ryder, Sutcliffe all got centuries and Wally Hammond made a superb double century. England won by three wickets and one run. Yet at this distance perhaps most interesting was the performance of young Don Bradman. He scored 79 in the first innings, and with his 112 in the second he was the youngest cricketer to score a century in a Test match.

The newspapers talked of his crisp stroke-making, his perfect defence and his almost brash confidence. This was the report of his first Test century:

146

Soon after lunch the lad found himself left to play almost a lone fighting hand. The bowling was definitely mastered and Bradman hit it unmercifully. The bowlers and fieldsmen, overcome by the heat of one of Melbourne's muggiest days, must have prayed for relief from the torture of Bradman. He refused to relax, and when at last he had piled up his first 100 in a Test—he has played in only two matches—the crowd went wild with joy. It was another one of those great demonstrations for which the M.C.C. is famous. For minutes thousands cheered, clapped and stamped, and the tired Englishmen were glad to sit on the grass until it was all over.

R. W. Wilmot in the *Argus* said he still retained some of those crudities in his play which were the result of playing on country wickets. But his confidence! He faced up to Larwood just as if he were merely the best bowler in Bowral. Wilmot recalled a story from the Brisbane Test. The Bowral boy was reported to have asked, "What do you do on a wet wicket—hook them?" It was not so much the question but the confidence, the suggestion that he knew the answer already, that was so characteristic, according to Wilmot.

At this stage England had won three Tests in a row, and Percy Chapman's comment to the Press also was characteristic: "Thank God it's over."

It was an extraordinary period for run-getting in every way, and few days were more extraordinary, than December 25, 1928. This was the third day of the traditional Victoria-N.S.W. holiday match on the M.C.G. Not only was it one of those very rare occasions when cricket was played on Christmas Day, but a record was set that has never been broken. It was the world record for a 10th wicket partnership and the only record of its kind held by the M.C.C.

Victoria made 376 runs in the first innings, which seemed adequate for a good first innings lead. Then Hans Ebeling, a'Beckett and Bert Ironmonger started to go through the N.S.W. side. When seven wickets were down for 58 runs it seemed all over. But then came this incredible last wicket partnership, which lasted all Christmas Day and 45 minutes of Boxing Day. By stumps on Christmas Day N.S.W. were only nine runs behind Victoria and an extra 53 were added next day. Alan Kippax made 260 not out and H. Hooker 62.

Ebeling, a'Beckett and Ironmonger must have had their worst Christmas Day ever. Nothing in cricket is more frustrating than a last-wicket partnership that won't crack, and this was one that endured for nearly seven hours, while other people were drinking beer, eating turkey and plum pudding. It was a partnership that was worth 307 runs.

Kippax played the way he always played, a master of grace and style. He hit 30 fours. Hooker, the bowler, attempted nothing. His object was to stick and few batsmen have stuck better. He took 232 minutes to get his 50 and he added only one run in the last 52 minutes before stumps on Christmas Day.

The *Sun News-Pictorial* commented that before they were separated Kippax and Hooker broke every record known in first-class cricket for a 10th wicket partnership. They passed every record in Interstate cricket and for County games in England. The previous record was 289 made in a first grade club match in Adelaide in 1901.

Kippax thanked the M.C.G. crowd. He said at times it must have been gruelling cricket, but always the crowd appreciated the struggle that was going on. Even at the finish the spectators were giving big applause for every single. The partnership was enough to give N.S.W. a win on the first innings, and as one newspaper said, it virtually gave the New South Welshmen the Sheffield Shield for 1928-29.

On March 1, 1929, there was a return Victoria-England match. But for two things there would be little reason to recall this match: one was the play of Bill Woodfull, the other was an incident with Harold Larwood. Woodfull had a reputation for being dour, and this day he was as dour as a man can be. For the third time during the English tour he batted through the innings, and he made 275 not out in seven hours forty minutes. Len Darling, the young South Melbourne batsman, scored 87, and it all amounted to 572, the best score Victoria has ever made against England.

The incident came at the end of the innings. Bert Ironmonger was the last man in, and, unbelievably, Percy Chapman tossed the ball to Larwood. The crowd was immensely tickled. Here was the fastest bowler in the world coming on to dismiss their Bert. Now Bert, everyone knew, was a very fine bowler, but as a batsman, well, he was just the fellow who sometimes briefly, very briefly, stood at the other end. Here was a sledgehammer being used to crush the egg of a thrush. So there was good-humoured barracking and some fine advice to Larwood on how to get him out.

Ironmonger took his stand at the wicket and Larwood placed a strong off-field. He took a long run and bowled at full speed. Yet instead of the ball crashing the middle stump, Ironmonger, with all the grace of Vernon Ransford, cut it for two runs. The noise of the crowd was redoubled. Larwood further strengthened the off-field and rushed in to attack. This surely was the end. But no, the polished Ironmonger once again cut him for two. Now everybody was standing.

The third ball flew past the off stump, but he was still there, and the noise could be heard half a mile away. People in the reserve were laughing and applauding. Up to this stage all was comedy, but Larwood became rattled. As he ran in to bowl his next ball the noise was unabated. This was too much. As he reached the crease he stopped, he looked at the crowd and he looked at his

148

Bleriot aeroplane prior to crashing into Tennis Courts on take off from M.C.G. 1910.

Above
A Bleriot aeroplane at the M.C.G. in 1910 — shortly afterwards it crashed into the tennis courts on take-off.

Left
Vernon Ransford, a brilliant left-hand batsman who first played for Australia in 1907.

Right
The extraordinary W. W. Armstrong:
he joined the M.C.C. in 1900, and led
perhaps the greatest of all teams to
England in 1921.

Below
Hobbs caught Carter, bowled
McDonald at the M.C.G. 11 February
1922.

captain. Several of the English players sat down. Then he walked over to mid-on where Tate was fielding and he threw the ball to Chapman. What else could Chapman do? He threw the ball back to Larwood and told him to get on with it. So Larwood ran up again, but now the crowd knew he was annoyed and a section of the outer began to bait him, even counting him out. Once more Larwood stopped at the crease and once more the players sat down. This happened three times. Woodfull, the other batsman, had a conference with Chapman, and together they walked over to the storm centre in front of the Wardill stand. Yet the crowd would not let Larwood off, and they continued to jeer. Just when there seemed no way out of what was becoming an ugly incident, Jack Ryder provided a perfect example of cricket diplomacy—he closed the innings.

Chapman said later, "What amazed me was the way in which the crowd treated Woodfull. He had played a wonderful innings and was on the verge of doing what no one has ever done before, carried his bat through an innings against an English team three times in one season. When he and I walked over to the fence in the most friendly manner to ask the crowd to be quiet, they would not listen to their own champion. They were utterly unreasonable, and I don't think they would have listened to the Angel Gabriel himself."

The incident made big news in London. Reuters described the behaviour of the Melbourne crowd as "churlish," and said that here was one of the blackest pages in the history of cricket. Maybe the crowd was irresponsible, but many felt that with a little tact and humour the incident could have been avoided.

England scored 303 runs and had to follow on. The match was drawn.

This, perhaps, was the best team ever to leave England. Percy Chapman won four Test matches in a row, and by the Fifth Test at the M.C.G. it was all well and truly over. Yet the interest was still astonishing, and the final Test was the greatest marathon ever between Australia and England. Unlike the Sheffield Shield matches, there was no limit, and it ran for eight days. Not as prolonged as the famous 10-day Durban Test match, perhaps, but at least this match was fought to a finish. Jack Hobbs made 142. It had not been his best season, but the M.C.C. always has been happy over the fact that this great batsman made his first Test century and his last on the M.C.G. He scored 12 centuries against Australia in Tests, and in 1929 this was six more than any other English batsman had done.

Maurice Leyland in his first Test made 137 and the English total was 519. Yet Australia doggedly came back with 491. Woodfull made 102 and Bradman 123, until finally after the M.C.G. had been occupied from March 8 to March 16, Australia won by 5 wickets and 2 runs. Tim Wall was the man who

149

made the difference. At last Australia had discovered a fast bowler, and in the second innings he took 5 for 66.

After such an interminable Test and after waiting all the season for a win the crowd went berserk. Bradman and Ryder were at the wicket, and the winning run came from a ball to Ryder off Larwood which went for four byes. Twenty thousand people swarmed over the fence. Immediately the English players grabbed the stumps and bails as souvenirs. Ryder and Bradman sprinted for the pavilion. Now Ryder once had a reputation as a sprinter, but this time he was a little too slow. Thousands wanted to shake him by the hand and hundreds wanted to carry him to the pavilion. They hoisted him on their shoulders, but it was like being tossed in a whirlpool and he had a very rough ride. His bat was wrenched from his hand and they tore away his green cap with the Australian coat of arms. As the *Argus* said, this was a winning cap, a precious souvenir, and he made desperate efforts to get it back, but he had no chance. The mob surged and swayed and finally the police had to rescue him at the pavilion gates. So he went inside and later returned on the balcony with Alan Kippax and Jack Gregory. It was almost as if Australia had won the Ashes. Yet it had been a good series. Australia found five good colts in Archie Jackson, Don Bradman, Tim Wall, Alan Fairfax and Ted a'Beckett. Percy Chapman had the satisfaction in producing a Rolls Royce cricket team, well tuned in all departments, and, with Wally Hammond in his prime, he was an answer to a captain's dream. Just look at these Test scores—251, 200, 119 and 177.

There was a sign of things to come in a cry from England. G. L. Jessop, a former Test batsman, wrote: "Stop these torture Tests." He said four days was devoted to a Test match in England, surely five days with 25 hours play would be enough in Australia. Yet Australians are a curious people. Even with eight days of Test cricket the M.C.G. never went short of spectators. It had the same marathon fascination as marathon opera has for the Chinese. Why, the match was so important that the German newspaper *Vossiche Zeitung* at one stage gave the scores for its English readers under the heading, "Great Kriccett Match," and it said, "England 47 for 11 wickets, namely Hobbs." How it worked out those fignres nobody will ever know, but apparently *Vossiche Zeitung* was so impressed by Jack Hobbs, the paper thought he was the entire English cricket team.

CHAPTER FIFTEEN

Leg and other Theories

NEW YEAR messages run very much to a pattern, and the messages printed in Melbourne's newspapers on January 1, 1929, were no exception. This would be a year of achievement, another great step forward for the young nation. It was not to be. The depression was under way even as early as March. While Jack Ryder's men were winning the Fifth Test at the M.C.G., the Lord Mayor, Cr. Luxton, called a meeting of 22 municipalities to discuss ways of providing work for the unemployed. While a cricket match dragged on for eight days the newspapers had leading articles which discussed the merits of a plan for every wage earner to put aside a little of his pay packet to help the out-of-work and hungry.

"Susso" for the sustenance worker was a new word in the language, and the unemployed reached a peak of 30 per cent. of the work force. It was like the 'nineties all over again; thousands left the city and took to the track. Others begged from door-to-door round the wealthier suburbs. Christmas 1930 was wet and miserable. The regular holiday match between New South Wales and Victoria at the M.C.G. would have been a diversion, but because of the rain there was only one day of cricket.

On Christmas Day Mr. Sidney Myer, the city's leading retailer, gave the greatest Christmas dinner Melbourne had ever seen. He fed 11,000 of the poor and unemployed at the Exhibition Building. At first he planned to limit the dinner to 10,000 and he issued tickets, but when it was almost over he walked outside and found 1000 people waiting there, silently, so he invited them inside.

Preparation for the great meal started at 7.30 a.m., and the first sitting went through at 10 o'clock. After that they came in hourly batches of 2000. Many of the guests had not eaten a decent meal for days. Each of them had a plate of ham and corned beef, part of a lettuce, three pickled onions, two bread rolls, two apples, 1 lb. of Christmas cake, 1½ ounces of butter, peaches and ice-cream, coffee and two glasses of beer or orange juice.

Over 300 of the Myer staff helped, shop girls, superintendents, departmental managers and Mr. Myer himself, constantly walked from table to

151

table, making sure that everybody was fed, and they did feed too. They ate, among other things, three-quarters of a ton of ham, half a ton of corned beef, half a ton of butter, and they drank 1000 gallons of beer. One newspaper said: "Mr. Myer seemed disconcerted by the continuous gratitude shown him. At first he fled from the concerted cheering, but then he remained and stood with his head bowed."

The Melbourne Cricket Club survived the crisis remarkably well. General receipts dropped from £40,516 in 1928-29 to £30,165 in 1931-32, yet the club paid off a debt of £11,000 and even declared a small profit. There was an influx of members, and when conditions were at their worst there were 2168 candidates waiting to become full members. Perhaps the most heart-breaking thing was the worry of trying to find jobs for the footballers. Charlie Streeter, the full back of Melbourne's 1926 premiership side, was on the ground staff. He spent his days searching the suburbs for the jobs. There were only so many vacancies at the M.C.G. He had four footballers working on the ground staff with three actually employed at any one time. They were rationed with three weeks on and one week off. In 1932 rationing eased, so that they had only one week off in five. Then by October 1932 the worst of the depression was over and the club ended the rationing system.

In the early days of the depression an old club member died. It barely seemed possible that a man could have lived through so much of the club's history. He was H. C. A. Harrison, and when he died on September 2, 1929, he was 92. He had been a member of the M.C.C. for 68 years and he was vice-president since 1892. In the nineteen-twenties he used to call himself the oldest Melburnian, for when he was at Melbourne Grammar the school was at Eastern Hill and called the Diocesan Grammar School. With his cousin, Tommy Wills, H. C. A. Harrison was responsible for the start of Australian Rules football. In 1858, when they were only 20, they arranged the first game of football, and later they drafted a code which they felt would be more suitable to our conditions. Harrison himself was a great athlete and a mighty footballer. It was on March 8, 1866, when he chaired a committee that settled the rules of the game we play today. So he was able to see the whole amazing development of the game right up to the time when crowds of 60,000 people were watching Grand Finals at the M.C.G., and Melbourne had a special reputation for football madness.

In January 1930 there was a madness of a different kind. The selectors met to consider the touring side to go to England, and Jack Ryder was one of the selectors. On January 30 the team of 16 was announced. There were only three Victorians, Woodfull, Ponsford and a'Beckett, no Bert Ironmonger, no

Don Blackie, no member of the M.C.C., but worst of all, NO JACK RYDER. The critics attacked. This was a young side, inexperienced, and it needed somebody like Ryder. There was brilliance, certainly, but Bradman had never been away, and who knows, with his style of batting he could be a flop on English wickets. Ryder was 41, but he was still batting well, and he topped the Victorian Sheffield Shield batting averages for that season.

The greatest anger came from Collingwood, where Jack Ryder was king. The Mayor, Cr. W. F. Angus, called a protest meeting in the Collingwood Town Hall. It was packed with 800 people. There were apologies from the Prime Minister, Mr. Scullin, and from Mr. John Wren, who sent his cheque for £50 towards a fund that had been initiated by the president of Hawthorn-East Melbourne Cricket Club, Canon Hughes. Some of the resolutions that were passed that night must have sizzled the ears of the selectors.

The protests went on for weeks, yet perhaps the most splendid piece of unsolicited indignation came from the prisoners of B Division at Pentridge Gaol. B Division housed the men who were serving long terms, prisoners who were unlikely to see any cricket for some considerable time. The protest was addressed to the Hon. Tom Tunnecliffe, the Chief Secretary.

> Sir,—Cannot some action be taken to prevent the selected team of crick-eters for England being finalised. We, the members of B Division, feel that the team has been jealously and unfairly selected, and is likely to cause a break if nothing is done to rectify the wrong done to Australia and its only Ryder. Because our support comes from inside the penitentiary, it should not be put out of court. Outside our particular faults we possess as much common sense as most people and evidently more than Australia's team selectors.
>
> A reply at your earliest will oblige B Division.

The Hon. Tom Tunnecliffe himself must have been extremely pro Ryder, because it was rare indeed for B Division's comments on matters of impor-tance to reach the newspapers.

Through all this Jack Ryder kept a dignified silence. One time under pres-sure he admitted: "I was disappointed when my name wasn't there. Who wouldn't be?" But he said he was perfectly happy to accept the decision. The game had given him so much he wouldn't under any circumstances say anything or do anything that would cause it the slightest harm.

He had several newspaper offers to go to England to write about the tour, but he would not accept them. As a former selector he felt it wasn't right that he should go to England and pass comment on players he had helped to choose.

In place of Jack Ryder, W. M. Woodfull was the new Australian captain. He won two Tests, lost one and two were drawn. Bradman, of course, played like a machine. He made 2960 runs at the unbelievable average of 98.61. He made 974 runs in Tests with an average of 139.14. Grimmett topped the bowling with 142 wickets at 16.79.

Only those who can remember the days would believe the hero-worship of Bradman at this time. There were public subscriptions, presentations, and there was hardly a newspaper or broadcasting station in the country that was not after his services. When the touring side reached Adelaide, General Motors arranged for Bradman to fly on to Melbourne. It was announced that the aeroplane would reach Essendon airport at 3.30 p.m., when there would be a big reception. The name of Bradman was enough to draw the crowds even when he was away from a cricket ground. At 3.30 there were 10,000 people at the airport. Aeroplanes in 1930 were rather more vague in their habits than they are now, and Bradman did not arrive for another two hours. Yet this was a cricket crowd, used to waiting, and all 10,000 waited most patiently.

At 5.30 p.m., as the aeroplane taxied up the tarmac, the crowd massed all around. When Bradman appeared at the door everybody cheered and there were shouts of "Good on you, Don." He was unable to move, and mounted police had to come to his rescue so that he could make his way to a lorry. The tray of the lorry was the grandstand and it was draped with an Australian flag. Here Warwick Armstrong, captain of the 1921 Eleven, gave a speech of welcome.

Bradman said: "We have had many great welcomes, but this is the greatest welcome of all." There had been rumours of lucrative offers to Bradman in England and the cry went up, "You are not going back to England?" Bradman said, "Yes I am, or I hope I am, as a member of the 1934 Eleven." (Cheers.)

He then escaped to the official car, and at the head of a long line of cars he made his way to the city.

Next morning at 8 o'clock the Victorian, N.S.W., and Queensland members of the team arrived at Port Melbourne aboard the *Oronsay,* and a crowd of 2000 was waiting to welcome them. According to the *Argus* many of the team members were angry. They felt that by flying on ahead Bradman had stolen their thunder.

During the 1931-32 season the South Africans visited Australia for the first time in 20 years. Yet this was not one of the better South African teams, and they struck Bradman in his most murderous mood. He made a century in every Test in which he batted. He scored 806 runs with an average of 201.35, and his best score was 299 not out. After the South Africans had suffered terrible thrashings in the first two Tests the *News Chronicle* commented from London: "As long as Australia has Bradman she will apparently be invincible, for he always seems able to score the number of runs required in a given time. In order to keep alive the competitive spirit of cricket the authorities might take a hint from billiards. It is almost time to request a legal limit on the number of runs Bradman should be permitted to make." Understandably there was no enthusiastic support for this idea in Australia.

There were many new names, Keith Rigg, Jack Fingleton, Bill O'Reilly. Keith Rigg, later on an M.C.C. committeeman, came into the side for the Second Test and he made 127. Then in the Third Test at the M.C.G. he saved Australia by making 68 when Woodfull, Ponsford and Bradman had gone for 25 runs. South Africa had a real chance of winning this Test match. A beautiful century by Viljoen helped the Springboks to a lead of 160 on the first innings.

Then Bradman came back, and for the first time Melbourne had an example of the extraordinary effect that this cricketer had on the M.C.G. As soon as the word went about on the Monday morning that Bradman was making runs crowds began to pour through the turnstiles. "Bradman was a magnet," said one newspaper, "and there were thousands who could not 1ttend business. Suddenly they discovered they had a most pressing appointment at the Melbourne Cricket Ground." There was another example of the power of Bradman. The Deputy Director of Postal Services, Mr. A. J. Christie, said that the volume of mails was abnormally low and he could put it down only to the cricket. Businessmen were not at their place of work, so they were not writing letters. The crowd on the Monday was 31,786, a record for a Monday.

Nor were the businessmen disappointed. While they should have been attending to their correspondence Bradman and Woodfull turned on a Test record of 274 runs for a second wicket partnership. Bradman made 167 and Woodfull 161, and Australia went on to win by 169 runs.

The South Africans lost four Tests in a row, but the Fifth at the M.C.G. had to be played to a finish. Cameron and his men were leaving the following Thursday, so at the most it was possible to play only five days. Yet to overcome this problem they agreed to play extra hours if necessary. They need not have worried. This was one of the shortest Test matches on record. There were only 1½ days of actual play.

The wicket was soft and wet. Australia batted first and managed to make an awkward 153. Jack Fingleton, a batsman almost as stubborn as Woodfull himself, made 40 and Keith Rigg, his partner, scored 22. The South Africans

155

batted and they were all out for 36. The newspapers were full of eulogies for the bowlers, particularly for Bert Ironmonger, who took 5 wickets for 6 runs off 7.2 overs. The *Herald* said: "For years experts and cartoonists have depicted Ironmonger in terms of patriarchal age, of moths, silverfish and creaking joints. But this Methuselah business has been carried far enough. With five wickets for six runs in a Test match Ironmonger today steps into the gallery of immortals. If his age was 64 instead of 44 he would still rank as Australia's greatest left hand bowler. Ironmonger looks a decidedly young 44. He feels a decidedly vital 32. He must be considered a certainty to play against the Englishmen next year."

Laurie Nash, who was the opening fast bowler, took four wickets for 18. His father, Bob Nash, a great Collingwood footballer of former days, was present. He was immensely proud of his son Laurence. The newspapers did not call him Laurie in 1932. Although he was born in Melbourne he was working in a Tasmanian sports store. At 22 he was described as a fine all-rounder, and it was known that he was more than an average footballer. Yet after Laurence had taken 4 for 18 in a Test match his father said that soon he would have to make a decision between cricket and football. But personally he wanted Laurie to choose cricket; it offered a better and longer career. Yet Laurie had other ideas. As centre half-forward for South Melbourne he was to become one of the greatest footballers Victoria has ever known.

Rain washed out play on the Saturday and the wicket was not fit for a start until 2.15 p.m. on the Monday. In 89 minutes the match was all over. South Africa made only 45 runs. Bert Ironmonger enjoyed himself immensely. Rarely had conditions been quite so perfect for his brand of spin and he took 6 wickets for 18. Laurie Nash took 1 for 4 and Bill O'Reilly 3 for 19.

The South African Tests were one-sided, but they helped to sort out Australia's best team for the appalling, harrowing struggle that was to come—the 1932-33 series against Jardine's Eleven, better known as the "body-line" series. Harold Larwood hated this term. In 1933 he wrote: "It was maliciously coined by a cute Australian journalist for the express purpose of misleading, and for obscuring the issue, which it did with great success. This mere use of the word 'body' was meant to damn me, and damn me it did. Quite as successfully as did any of the batsmen who had to cope with it. The term being brief was very suitable for a sort of war-cry, and that it became."

He resented, too, an extra verse that Cyril Ritchard added to his performance in *Our Miss Gibbs*, at Her Majesty's Theatre in Sydney.

> Now this new kind of cricket,
> Takes courage to stick it,

There's bruises and fractures galore.
　　After kissing their wives
　　And insuring their lives
Batsmen fearfully walk out to score.
　　With a prayer and a curse
　　They prepare for the hearse,
Undertakers look on with broad grins.
　　Oh, they'd be a lot calmer
　　In Ned Kelly's armour,
When Larwood the wrecker begins.

The Test matches that were played created bitter feelings among the players and hostile barracking from the spectators. The so-called body-line bowling was directed at the leg stump with six men clustered on the leg-side. The ball, pitched short, left the batsman no option except to make a shot to protect his body or to back away from his wicket. Of course it was directed against Bradman, to reduce his status to that of an ordinary batsman. Larwood had some success in this, for Bradman was not the tremendous run-getter of the 1930 tour. He played eight innings in the Tests and once he was not out. In the remaining seven innings Larwood took his wicket four times, twice clean-bowled. Yet Bradman still headed the Australian batting averages with an average of 56.57.

The anger boiled over when a ball from Larwood hit Woodfull over the heart during the Third Test at Adelaide. It was then that Woodfull made his celebrated remark to the Englishmen: "There are two teams out there. One of them is playing cricket, the other is not."

After 30 years it is difficult to credit the bitterness of the cables that were exchanged between the Australian Board of Control and the Marylebone Cricket Club. The first cable from the Board of Control on January 18, 1933, read:

> Body-line bowling has assumed such proportions as to menace the best interests of the game, making protection of the body by the batsmen the main consideration. This is causing intensely bitter feeling between the players, as well as injury. In our opinion it is unsportsmanlike. Unless stopped at once it is likely to upset the friendly relations existing between Australia and England.

This was the Marylebone Club's reply on January 23:

> We, Marylebone Cricket Club, deplore your cable. We deprecate your opinion that there has been unsportsmanlike play. We have fullest confidence in captain, team and managers, and are convinced that they would do nothing

157

to infringe either the laws of cricket, or the spirit of the game. We have no evidence that our confidence has been misplaced. Much as we regret accidents to Woodfull and Oldfield, we understand that in neither case was the bowler to blame.

If the Australian Board of Control wish to propose a new law or rule it shall receive our careful consideration in due course. We hope the situation is now not as serious as your cable would seem to indicate, but if it is such as to jeopardise the good relations between English and Australian cricketers, and you consider it desirable to cancel remainder of programme, we would consent but with great reluctance.

There were many comments. One English newspaper said: "Some things are not cricket. One of them is this most undignified snivelling by a section of the Australians because English bowling tactics have defeated their Test batsmen." Lord Tennyson, a former English captain, said: "If cricket is impossible without squabbles and screaming, let us be content with domesticity and glory on the village green."

The *Daily Sketch* said: "Both the Australian protest and our reply show a lack of sense and proportion. If the Australian protest was a little rude our reply was unnecessarily stiff. Surely it was unnecessary to talk about the cancelling of the rest of the tour."

Then Will Dyson, the Australian cartoonist, drew for London's *Daily Herald* a beautiful cartoon of a big, bruised and beplastered Australian cricketer calling at the Secretariat of the League of Nations and saying to an astonished official, "Tell 'em I'm here, cobber. It's urgent."

Millions of words were written and said, yet there was not unanimity of opinion on either side. In England there were many who felt leg theory was unfair. In Australia men like J. W. Trumble and M. A. Noble came out on the side of Larwood.

There were further cables, each of them more gentle than the first. Nobody actually apologised, but both sides obviously regretted their early angry words. After the English team had returned to England the problem was discussed in a calm, reasonable air. A new law came into force that gave the umpire power to stop this type of bowling after he had warned the bowler once. Rarely has it been necessary to bring it into operation.

In November there was the Australian Eleven match v. England at the M.C.G. This was Victoria's compensation for receiving only one Test match and the Englishmen used it to try out their secret weapon. They opened with three fast bowlers—Larwood, Bowes and Allen. Arthur Mailey reported: "Although I have had a presentiment for some weeks that England would depend on a battery of fast bowlers, I thought terrifying leg-stump tactics would be adopted only when everything else failed. On Saturday it was not so. Almost immediately Larwood placed a leg field to Woodfull and began to fire them down at lightning speed straight at the batsman's body. I am not complaining. The press box at the M.C.G. is on the off side, and I am comparatively safe from injury, and I am sure Woodfull is not complaining. A fast bowler, like a slow bowler, has a right to adopt leg-stump theory if he wishes, but Australian selectors will be compelled to think out reprisals or something to combat the menace."

Larwood and Bowes both bowled very fast. Frequently the ball flew over the batsmen's heads and they were punished on the legs and thighs. One ball from Larwood, pitched up a little more than the others, hit Woodfull over the heart and he staggered back from the wicket. At first he seemed to be seriously injured and all Melbourne's newspapers printed pictures of him grimacing in pain and holding his chest. Yet he recovered and went on playing. Larwood sportingly bowled the next ball outside the offstump and Woodfull scored.

The *Argus*, which, perhaps, commented more soberly than other papers, said of the new bowling: "It certainly was dangerous. This latest development in cricket is not to be commended, for, as P. F. Warner says, 'Cricket is a friendly game,' and there is nothing particularly amicable about a fast bowler who attacks the leg stump with a ball swinging into the batsman's body. I do not believe for one moment that any of the English bowlers bowl at the batsman, but the leg-stump attack at a great pace is certainly disconcerting and is fraught with danger."

In this atmosphere, almost as if a state of war existed between Australia and England, it is not difficult to imagine the excitement when the Second Test came to Melbourne. Yet this was the happiest match of the tour, not merely because it was the only Test match won by Australia, but there were no difficult incidents.

Radio helped immensely. It was the first series when radio really took over. The P.M.G. organised the most extensive interstate hook-up it had ever undertaken, and while the Board of Control banned the players from writing for the newspapers there was no ban on talking over the air. So there was the extraordinary situation that after every day's play most of the leading players commented on their own exploits.

There was a wireless in every home and in every shop. Tailors, ironmongers, department stores all put blackboards or score sheets outside. They caused so much traffic congestion that finally the police had to ban them. This was a matter of great joy to the pubkeepers. They merely shifted their radios and notice-boards into the bar, and they found cricket a splendid boost to beer sales. The radio mania reached such a peak that the *Herald* printed this poem from "Dad":

> I reckon (said Dad) that the country's pests
> Is this here wireless an' these here Tests.
> Up to the house and around the door,
> Stretchin their ears for to catch the score,
> Leavin' the horses down in the crop,
> Can you wonder a farmer goes off pop?
>
> There's a standin' crop, an' the rain's not far
> An' the price is rotten but there you are:
> As soon as these cricketin' games begin
> The farm goes dilly on listenin' in,
> Not only the boys and the harvester crew
> But Mum an' the girls gets dotty too.
> An' I reckon (said Dad) that a man's worst pests
> Is this here wireless an' these here Tests.

Yet as far as the Englishmen were concerned the country's worst pests were the barrackers. When Jardine's men arrived in Melbourne there were the usual receptions, and Mr. Pelham Warner hit out. He said: "Do you think it dignified that a match between the two greatest cricketing countries in the world should be interrupted by a certain amount of noise? It is many years since I was last in Melbourne, but one barracker called out, 'Hit him on his bald head, Armstrong.' I am an old cricketer and I have no axe to grind, only the improvement of the game which I love and adore. A great cricket match should be played with great dignity in a great manner. I was glad to see your last team in England. Over and over the players said to me, 'We love your crowds, they are so keen, they applaud with their hands.' "

At this reception the barrackers had a splendid defending barrister, Mr. R. G. Menzies, K.C., then Victoria's Attorney-General. He began by telling the story of two Englishmen, two Irishmen, two Scotsmen and two Australians who were stranded on a desert island for a year. In that time the two English-men had not spoken to each other because they had not been introduced, the two Irishmen spent most of the time fighting each other, the two Scotsmen had formed a Caledonian society and the two Australians filled in time mak-ing speeches to each other.

Mr. Menzies said: "Harrison stand patrons feel the need for self-expression; they must say something or die. Anything they say, of course, would be softened down out of respect for the English visitors. All the effervescence means is that everyone in Australia is tremendously interested in the Test matches and tremendously interested in all the visitors do on and off the field. Whether the batsmen score rapidly or sit on their splice the onlookers insist on barracking; that is their prerogative."

The interest was so great on Friday, December 30, 1932, the queue outside the M.C.G. was half a mile long by 7.30 a.m., and by the afternoon there was a record crowd of 63,993. Woodfull won the toss and decided to bat. It was very clear—this was to be a long, hard day. Jardine dropped Verity, an incredible thing to do in the era of great slow bowlers. It was like going into battle with all battleships and no destroyer escort. He had a quartet of fast bowlers— Larwood, Voce, Allen and Bowes.

The big crowd saw only 194 runs scored that day, one of the lowest all day totals in Test history. Woodfull was there 51 minutes for 10 runs, but the hero was Jack Fingleton. He took a battering all over the body. He ducked his head to the short-pitched deliveries and he stubbornly defended against those of good length. For four hours he held up an end for just 83 runs, but the crowd did not object to the slowness of the cricket. This was an enthralling duel. McCabe, who seemed to have mastered the leg theory in Sydney with 187 not out, went for 32, but the awful shock was Bradman. Bill Bowes bowled him first ball. Bradman tried to hook to the boundary and snicked the ball on to the wicket. Arthur Mailey described it as a shocking long hop and Bradman's stroke as something worse. "It would have been a bad shot even had he connected." Larwood did not get a wicket all day.

Australia next day was all out for 228. England in reply incredibly could manage only 169 runs. Tim Wall took 4 wickets for 52 and Bill O'Reilly 5 for 63. The match was in a beautiful balance at precisely the right time. Even if the script had been written by a promoter he could not have staged it better for the holiday on Monday, January 2.

All Melbourne was thinking over the situation. At 3 o'clock that morning a nightwatchman was making his last round before daylight. He was threading his way through the dark passages below the stands in the outer when he saw two figures crouched on top of the wall. He challenged them but nothing happened. He drew his revolver and fired a shot in the air. The terrified intruders dropped down inside the wall, and while looking down the barrel of that six-shooter they did not dare make a move. The nightwatchman asked them what was their business. Why were they trying to break into the M.C.G.?

"We came in because we wanted to see Bradman bat," they said. It was true; they were extremely well armed—with food. They had their breakfast and their lunch in neat little bundles. It was a sad tale. They were frightened that there would be such an awful crowd there would be no chance of getting a seat. The only thing to do was to be first at the M.C.G. Oh, yes, they climbed in without paying, but the idea was to sleep in the stand until daybreak.

The watchman naturally was pleased to discover that the intruders were not burglars. Instead, here he had Melbourne's most enthusiastic cricket fans. However his heart did not soften to the extent of letting them remain. He marched them straight out of the ground, this time by the front gate.

The poor intruders had lost a splendid advantage, for there was indeed an "awful crowd"—69,724 entered the ground, a new record, and thousands were turned away. It was a day of days, because Bradman played possibly his finest innings in Test cricket. He made 103 not out of Australia's total of 191. It was not so much the number of runs, but the manner in which he handled the unending toughness of the opposition. Nor was it a good wicket. According to Larwood there were cracks in it even before the first ball was bowled.

Here was one contemporary report:

> For sheer grit and courageous steady run-getting it was an innings fit to rank with the greatest in Test history. Australia had lost 2 for 27 in half an hour when he joined his captain, Woodfull, and he set about restoring the chances of his side. From the first moment he was never in doubt, and he hit back everything the English bowlers gave him with interest. He revealed daring without any suggestion of recklessness. His defence was impressive and his hitting tremendous, whether the fieldsmen were placed for leg-theory, or off-theory, or both, he found open places in the field and chose the ball to hit.

When he reached his century salvo after salvo of cheering swept through the mighty crowd, and it was some minutes before he was able to take strike. From the fall of the fifth wicket at 133 he had to nurse successively Oldfield, Grimmett, Wall, O'Reilly and Ironmonger. Between them they contributed only nine runs. Wall's stay of 34 minutes for three runs was the most helpful of all. As one batsman departed after another Bradman fought to keep the strike. He had to ignore singles unless they came at the end of an over and the rest of the time he played for twos and fours. At the finish, still unbeaten, he looked as if he could go on for ever.

All Jardine needed now were 251 runs, and at stumps the score was no wicket for 41. However, cricket is a peculiar sport, possibly the strangest game created by mankind. Just when England was set for victory the side collapsed for 139 runs. The Richmond end of the pitch, where the vast procession of

English fast bowlers had worn their track, was like a road back of Bourke, and Bert Ironmonger took 4 for 26. Bill O'Reilly, "the greatest bowling find in years," was equally happy from the other end. He took 5 for 66. In 1933 he was just beginning to earn his reputation as the Tiger. He bowled with an almost unbelievable determination, and his appeals were loud and often. Or as Johnnie Moyes said, they were not so much appeals, his whole demeanour was the demand of an indignant man for justice.

England lost the Test match by 111 runs, and it seemed that the body-line bogy was finished. Woodfull must have felt like Montgomery at Alamein, but his troubles were only just beginning. There were no more victories, and there is little doubt that both captains were glad when the series was over.

The club President at this time was Sir Leo Cussen, the Acting Chief Justice of Victoria. On May 15, 1933, Sir Leo sat on the bench at the Practice Court. Two days later he was dead. There was great grief at the Melbourne Cricket Club, for he had been President for 26 years, but also the grief was great throughout the community. The Chief Justice of the High Court, Sir Owen Dixon, described him as the best lawyer he had known and one of the great lawyers of the English-speaking world.

The newspapers were filled with pages of tributes. They described the brilliance of his mind, his kindliness and his wit. One time he was asked at the bar how he had fared in an argument before the Full Court. He replied that Holroyd certainly was with him and that a'Beckett had fallen asleep in his favour. One night at a bar dinner the barristers even put their feelings about him into verse:

> Gladly we give, as all agree 'tis right,
> First tribute of the day unto the Knight.
> King George—we speak with one concordant voice—
> Was never pleased to make a better choice.
> We swear by this post-prandial affidavit
> Cussen nil tetigit quod non omavit
> (For seniors rusty in the Latin lore
> Translations will be tendered at the door).
> To him a two-fold greeting we extend,
> We hail him as our joint and several friend,
> While on his merits as a judge we touch
> We have a grievance—that he knows too much.
> We argue ably (sometimes) for our side.
> And when we feel, with glowing conscious pride,
> We've made a case no court could e'er resist,
> He finds the flaws opposing counsel missed.

As for the M.C.C. secretary, Hugh Trumble, he said: "His lovable personality and great outstanding ability endeared him to the committee and the great body of members. His loss is a very sad blow to the club and the community. Personally I shall never see his like again."

Archbishop Mannix sang the Pontifical Mass of Requiem at St. Patrick's Cathedral, then Sir Leo's body lay in state for two and a half hours in Queen's Hall at Parliament House. Sir Edward Mitchell, the vice-president since 1925, became the new President.

He took over in time for the Melbourne Centenary celebrations of 1934. They had a zest about them that seemed to be worth more than the mere remembering of the passing of 100 years. After all, not one in a thousand Victorians had the slightest interest in history. Yes, there was something else to it. This was the celebration of the end of the depression, the opportunity to spend a little money and have fun without the wowsers looking down their noses. There is so much to remember from that year. The Duke of Gloucester came out just for the occasion. Sir Macpherson Robertson made his centenary gift of £100,000 to the State, and so the MacRobertson Girls' High School was established. Then the highlight of the year was the Centenary Air Race. Scott and Black, at an amazing 200 miles an hour, flew to Australia in less than three days. The *Argus* commented: "If the present conquest of speed be maintained at its present rate, an air journey to England in three days will become a commonplace and Australia, that vast land over the edge of the beyond, will become a part of a great world metropolis."

There were centenary medals, centenary mugs, centenary propelling pencils and every conceivable type of centenary souvenir. The newspapers produced centenary supplements which told the story of Melbourne. Carefully they were put away in the bottoms of cupboards and bureau drawers, and many of them are there still.

Melbourne was gay. There were pylons on Princes Bridge and there were standards along the city streets. The City Council solemnly referred to these standards as Venetian Poles, but they were better known to the public as "lolly sticks." It was the thing to do to drive into town to see the illuminations, and after six there was the funeral-like procession of Buicks, Austins, Fords and Chevrolets, loaded with children, staring at it all in wonder. Almost every building had its lights, there were fairy lights and Chinese lanterns in the Treasury Gardens, but best of all was the Carlton Brewery at the top of Swanston Street. One would have sworn that it was on fire with great flames that changed from red to violet to green. The flames came from a huge pyramid of pipes that surmounted the building. The pipes were quite hideous by day, but as soon as it was dark they issued forth clouds of steam, which were lit from below by coloured beacons.

The Duke of Gloucester arrived on October 18 aboard H.M.S. *Sussex*, escorted by H.M.A.S. *Canberra* and H.M.A.S. *Australia*. The Royal Progress into the city was seen by half a million people. That night there was a fireworks display on the banks of the Yarra, said to be the finest Melbourne had seen. It started with an aerial bombing display. Searchlights from the warships out in the bay raked the sky, then an aeroplane, trailing a 40,000 candle-power flare, flew across the city. It attacked the Manchester Unity building, the T. & G. building and the Fire Brigade lookout tower on Eastern Hill. As the aeroplane passed overhead each building let forth clouds of smoke.

Next day the Duke went to the Melbourne Cricket Ground to see a display by 17,000 children. More than 80,000 people crammed into the stands and the outer grounds; thousands more who could not get inside waited around the gates, just for the chance to see the Duke arrive and depart.

The main feature of the display was the formation of a living tableau. Thousands of children, spread out across the arena, made the figures 100—1834-1934. The Duke insisted on leaving the Royal Box to walk on to the ground, and as he did so thousands jumped the barrier into the arena. Police ran forward to clear a path, making what one newspaper called "an avenue of enthusiasm."

Early in the afternoon he left for Flemington to visit the Royal Show, and as he went out the gate there was an announcement over the amplifiers "that His Royal Highness had asked that every school should be granted a full holiday in recognition of the great day," and it was said that the cheering could be heard as far off as Point Lonsdale.

Four members of the M.C.C. went with the 1934 team to England—H. Ebeling, W. H. Ponsford, L. S. Darling and L. O. B. Fleetwood-Smith and for the second time Woodfull brought home the Ashes. Ponsford scored 1784 runs at an average of 77.56 and Len Darling made 1022 runs, average 34.06. Fleetwod-Smith took 106 wickets, average 19.21, and Ebeling took 62 wickets, average 20.83.

But a change was coming over Australian cricket. As soon as the tour was over Woodfull and Ponsford announced their retirement from first-class cricket and the B.P. era was over. They were young—Ponsford was only 34 and Woodfull 37. Cricket fans called them "The Twins" and "The Old Firm." Five times they had been together in partnerships over 200 and 22 times in century partnerships. As they retired already there was new talent on the way.

Early in 1935 a Wesley College boy, Ian Johnson, aged 16, was selected to play for South Melbourne against Fitzroy. The *Argus* described him as an off-spin bowler and a fine stroke player. He received promotion after making 63 for the South Melbourne seconds against Hawthorn-East Melbourne, and he picked a tough day for his debut. The wicket was bad, made to order for the medium-paced deliveries of Maurice Sievers, and South Melbourne was all out for 70. Yet Ian Johnson made the top score with 17 runs, and the newspapers predicted that in a few years he would cause his father, Mr. W. J. Johnson, some anxious moments as a State and Australian selector.

That December the M.C.C. announced a splendid building plan for the Outer, which it was hoped would increase accommodation to 100,000. It was something the club had been planning for years, but always there had been an obstacle in the way, either a reluctance to interfere with the running of the ground, or lack of money. Now that the Centenary celebrations were over there was a great chance to go ahead. During the Third Test match of 1933 there had been angry complaints about overcrowding, and even the Health Commission was called in to make a report. One letter particularly stung the committee. It came from a lady visitor. She said that always she was infinitely more comfortable at, of all places, the Sydney Cricket Ground. She considered that the M.C.G. was a slur on Melbourne. Furthermore, Mr. Cotter, a Labor member in the State Parliament, suggested that if the 1936-37 tour produced another Larwood and there was no extra accommodation in the Outer, then there would be a riot at the M.C.G.

So something had to be done. The new stand would be 1250 feet in length. There would be changing rooms for footballers and cricketers, refreshment booths, casualty rooms, seating space for 35,000 and accommodation for 100,000. Altogether the cost would be £100,000.

Indeed the cost was a big worry, for the club still was paying off the new members' pavilion. The committee had one idea. It decided to call a special meeting for July 10, 1936, the object being to reduce the number of ladies' tickets for each member from two to one and to increase membership from 5200 to 6200. This would help to pay off the £100,000. The ladies' ticket situation was sadly out of hand. There were 14,754 issued, yet there was accommodation for only 11,000. Maybe the subject would never have arisen, but during the 'thirties suddenly women discovered cricket, and they came to the Tests in great numbers. Sir Leo Cussen even had cause to comment on the way ladies' tickets were used with abandon. They were handed about from person to person, and he was convinced that during the Larwood Test there was not a moment of the day when every lady's ticket was not in use. Then the women had an extra advantage—they could get to the cricket early in the morning and pick good seats before the men could get away from the office.

However, the members would have none of it. They were prepared to admit another 1000 members, but they would not surrender any of their ladies' tickets. So there was only one thing to do, the pre-1936 members kept two tickets, and from then on every new member received only one lady's ticket. The new stand was almost, but not quite, finished for the Third Test match at the M.C.G.

The new English captain was G. O. B. Allen, and this was the happiest of tours, no bodyline and no shocking incidents. Furthermore the excitement was tremendous, because both teams went into the final round with two Tests each.

The newspapers were fatter than in the lean years of 1932 and there were pages upon pages of cricket. It was a poor newspaper that did not employ at least three ex-Test cricketers and an all-star cast of English cricket writers travelled with the visiting team. One of them was Neville Cardus of the *Manchester Guardian,* his first trip to Australia.

Australia was thrashed in the first two Tests, so by the Third Test at the M.C.G. the situation had reached the proportions of a national crisis. Len Darling, Fleetwood-Smith and Bill Brown took the places of Chipperfield, Sievers and R. Robinson. Fleetwood-Smith had just taken 7 for 17 against Queensland, so his selection was inevitable. Keith Rigg was another newcomer. He had played against South Africa in 1932, when he made 127, but never since had he been considered for selection. As the *Sun News-Pictorial* said: "It is one of the mysteries of the game why he has escaped selection. He has done everything a batsman could do to deserve it."

On the first day there was a crowd of 78,630, so many that they scrambled over the barriers into the still uncompleted bays of the new stand. The Attorney-General, Mr. R. G. Menzies, was there. His passion for cricket was notorious. The *Herald* reported that Cabinet business conveniently had taken him to Sydney for the Second Test, there were legal aspects of the game he would have to study during the Third Test, and he had announced that he would have to go to Adelaide to discuss a future referendum during the Fourth Test. Naturally there were further legal cricketing matters to be observed during the Fifth Test back in Melbourne.

McCormick injured his hand, Sievers was back in the team after all, and

167

Australia for the first time since 1928 was without an opening fast bowler. The situation was more frightening than ever.

Bradman won the toss and the tension was so great that when Voce bowled the first ball a roar went up, almost is if the umpire had bounced the ball at a football Grand Final. The roar was a little premature; it was a poor day's cricket. Bradman went for 13, and at stumps Australia was 6 down for 181. Then came the rain, and on Saturday morning the crowd had to sit patiently until after lunch. But, of course, Neville Cardus, who was writing for a great number of newspapers, had to keep on writing. He was never finer than on these occasions when there was no cricket at all.

He wrote that after seeing so much rain both in Australia and in Manchester he felt he should publish this advertisement: "Cricket writer in reduced circumstances seeks position in meteorological office, either in Australia or in England; not afraid of hard work. Graduated at Manchester Weather Bureau."

He said:

> The patience of the crowd was exemplary. The women talked profusely and the bars were well supported. So the morning dragged on while the police guarded the pitch as though it were the Crown jewels. There were repeated visits by the captains to the wicket and the crowd counted them out. But there was no need for the reading of the Riot Act. Cricket crowds are well broken in. If they can stand Test matches they can stand anything.
>
> Apparently the captains could not agree, for when they left the scene the umpires had a look and walked around the pitch warily, as though half expecting it to get up and shake itself and wet everybody. Profound consultation went forward. It did not require to elaborate the doctrine of relativity. The problem of establishing objective wetness or dryness of a cricket pitch is as deep and mysterious as all your metaphysics from Descartes to Professor Whitehead. It is a serious business and no mistake; let us be grateful for the cheering quality of Melbourne ale.

When play finally started he wrote:

> "The wicket was beginning to amuse itself and the crowd. The first ball to O'Reilly stood up and stared him in the face; he patted the wicket manfully, and really it deserved all the smacking it got."

Yet at this stage Cardus did not realise actually how much the wicket deserved a spanking. Bradman declared the Australian innings closed at 9 for 200. As one spectator remarked rudely, he could not afford to give Fleetwood-Smith a knock; who knows, he might stay there for a couple of days.

The sun shone and the disobedient pitch became a classic sticky wicket. O'Reilly and Sievers were almost unplayable. Sievers took 5 for 21 and O'Reilly 3 for 28. Allen declared at 9 for 76. This started one of those delightful arguments that are conducted in the newspapers and continued in cricketing memoirs for a decade, all on what might have been. The critics said now if only Allen had been more daring. He had two Tests already to his credit, why then did he not declare at 40 or even 30? He could have had Australia's six best wickets by stumps, then the Test match and the rubber would have been his.

Of course, Allen did not do this. The day was almost over when a new Australian opening pair came to the wicket—O'Reilly and Fleetwood-Smith. O'Reilly went before stumps for 0, and Fleetwood-Smith went the next morning for 0. This was another Test record a zero beginning by the opening partners.

Keith Rigg made 47 runs and solidly held the side together until the wicket improved, then Fingleton and Bradman quietly set about digging England's grave. As Cardus put it, Fingleton was sober and steady. As the number two gravedigger of the cemetery he never lifted his bat higher than his knee. Number one gravedigger, Donald Bradman, also was very correct in his behaviour. In the past he had been accused of being reckless and over-dashing for the benefit of the crowd. This time it was a captain's innings, and even the famous hook shot was not there. He did not cut loose until he passed 200. Fingleton made 136 and Bradman 270. It was yet another record for Bradman—the highest Test score ever made on the M.C.G.

England was left 689 runs down in the grave. It was a fearful, hopeless task. Yet there was fine batting at the finish. Leyland made 111, Robins 61, and Hammond, the world's prettiest batsman, scored 51. His driving was superb, according to Cardus as classic as the Elgin marbles. England's final score was 323, giving Australia the victory by 365 runs. Fleetwood-Smith took 5 for 124.

The match set a series of attendance records that remained unbroken until the 1961 Fifth Test against the West Indies. For six days the total was 350,534 and the receipts £29,168. The best figure was on the Monday with 87,798. It brought Melbourne to a standstill. An example of this was a notice that appeared in the Sun News-Pictorial:

"There will be no rise in bread prices while the Test cricket is on. A meeting of the Master Bakers' Council that was to take place yesterday to consider an increase has been postponed until Thursday afternoon—if the cricket is finished by then. Members of the council were unanimous that watching

Bradman yesterday was more entertaining than risking the wrath of housewives by raising prices."

The Fifth Test was the Diamond Jubilee of Test matches between England and Australia, and after 139 Tests there was only one game the difference, which showed how even the Tests had been. Yet even more important, the new stand was finished at last. One enthusiastic reporter wrote after the first day's play: "The best seats at the M.C.G. yesterday cost 2/2. The giant stand is completed at last and proved the greatest investment ever made by the M.C.C. During the afternoon hundreds of men and women deserted the members' reserve for the breathing space and comfort of the Outer. Gold medallions and lifelong passes of the time-honoured privileges of the club reserve didn't even secure the comfort prepared for the rank and file." To commemorate the Jubilee the President of the M.C.C., Sir Edward Mitchell, unveiled a bronze tablet under the new stand before play began.

Australia won the toss and immediately set about amassing a huge score. Arthur Mailey said he had endured a massacre or two himself on the M.C.G., but never had he seen a team of Test bowlers so completely collared. Bradman made 169, McCabe 112, Badcock 118 and Ross Gregory 80. The total was 604 runs.

There were some interesting examples of the close attention that Australians pay to Test cricket. At Camperdown a gentleman put a tin of tar on the kitchen stove. He went into the next room to listen to the Test cricket. He became enthralled and time passed unnoticed. The tar boiled over, great clouds of smoke poured out of the kitchen, but he went on listening. The newspapers reported that the eight-room weatherboard house caught fire and was badly damaged. But one can't think of everything while one is listening to the activities of Bradman and McCabe.

On the same day thieves broke into Harry Brereton's house at Xavier Avenue, Glenferrie. They ransacked the place from end to end. They chose a good time, for Harry Brereton was secretary of the V.C.A. and naturally he and all his family were at the cricket.

These incidents made many people recall that lovely little piece written by the Australian humourist Len Lower. The Third Test was on at Leeds, when the burglar pushed up the window. The year was 1930, the time 2.30 a.m. Bradman had passed 300 and the family was huddled around the loud speaker of the wireless set. One of the sons was putting down all Bradman's hits on the back of a player roll.

> " 'Who's bowling?' said the burglar excitedly, stepping into the room.
> 'Larwood,' said the whole family, without looking up.
> 'Goodo!' exclaimed the burglar.

Searching the house he packed up the most portable valuables and was looking for more when a loud, harmonious groan came from around the loud speaker.

'Wot's up!' he cried, rushing in. 'Is he out?'

'Clean bowled by that beast Larwood,' sobbed the mother, dabbing her eyes with her handkerchief.

'That's the front door,' said the father. 'Someone answer it.'

No one answered it. 'Tate bowling,' said the announcer.

'I suppose I'll 'ave to go,' grumbled the burglar. A scream came from the room as he opened the door.

'What's wrong here?' said the policeman sternly.

'Richardson's out for one!' murmured the burglar in a hoarse voice.

'My God!' exclaimed the policeman, rushing in.

And at 3.45 a.m., the blear-eyed family dragged itself to bed, the policeman, nervously gazing about for the sergeant, went back to his beat, and the burglar went home, having forgotten his loot.

'Any 'ow,' he muttered, as he climbed wearily into his bed, 'I don't care. Five 'undred and sixty-six is goin' to take some catchin'.' "

And it was much the same in 1937; 604 was goin' to take some catchin'. It was the first time that three Test centuries had been scored in one innings on the M.C.G. Ross Gregory's 80 was particularly interesting—he made it the day before his 21st birthday. Neville Cardus was moved to comment, "Heaven bless us, we have again witnessed strokes in a Test match, gay and handsome and cultured strokes."

It was his second Test match and his last. He was killed while serving with the R.A.A.F. in 1942.

Australia this time had a double-pronged speed attack with Ernie McCormick and Laurie Nash. Then with O'Reilly and Fleetwood-Smith it was a formidable combination. They dismissed England for 239 and again for 208, and so Australia won the Jubilee Test match and the Ashes.

While the Fifth Test was being played cricket news had to compete with the news of the Civil War in Spain. In March 1938 Hitler invaded Austria and there was little cricket left to be played. But the finish of the 1937-38 season was very satisfying for the Melbourne Cricket Club. The first three club elevens reached the finals, and Hans Ebeling led the first eleven to its fourth successive premiership. He equalled Bert Cohen's record of four straight premierships for St. Kilda from 1923-24 to 1926-27.

This was a mighty Melbourne eleven, and when the players were available, it was practically a Test side with Ponsford, Ebeling, the Nagel brothers, Rigg, Darling, Thomas and Fleetwood-Smith. Yet Melbourne was lucky to win at the finish. After going through the season undefeated the club found itself in a sorry position. In the last innings Fitzroy needed only 129 runs to win the premiership. Lisle Nagel took 4 for 48, and at stumps Fitzroy were 9 for 115—one wicket in hand and still 14 runs to get. Incredibly the next Saturday over 1000 people turned out to see the finish of a match which at the most could produce only these 14 runs. Hans Ebeling bowled a maiden, then Lisle Nagel took the final wicket off his first ball. Fitzroy did not add another run and the premiership, plus £50 from the V.C.A., went to Melbourne.

Hugh Trumble, who had been secretary of the M.C.C. for 26 years, died of a heart attack on August 14, 1938. He was 71. Vernon Ransford described him as the greatest bowler Australia ever produced. While he was secretary the new members' stand was built and the vast £100,000 stand in the Outer. He was the elder statesman of cricket in Australia. Whenever the newspapers wanted a comment on cricket they would call Hugh Trumble. If ever they wanted a special article for a Saturday magazine during a Test match, they would ask Hugh Trumble to write it. He was 6 ft. 4 in. tall and a conspicuous man at any time, but his famous hats made him even more conspicuous. Always he wore the same type of hat, a soft grey felt with a lighter band—large crowned. They were imported from the United States specially for him.

As he proved in his newspaper articles, he was a marvellous story teller. The visits of touring cricketers would put him in a yarning mood. Then he would put his feet on the edge of the office table and reminisce, telling his stories with appropriate gestures of those long fingers, which once had such an incredible control over a cricket ball.

One of his favourite stories was about a visit to New Zealand, and a very sad piece of umpiring. On the Sunday morning after the Saturday's play one of the umpires went to church, according to Mr. Trumble, to do penance for his sins. The umpire fell asleep during the sermon and thereby missed a most impressive peroration which had as its climax: "How is it, I say? How is it?"

The sleeping umpire, naturally, at this point woke up, and replied: "NOT OUT."

There were exciting stories, too, and it was strange that one of the most dramatic involved his old team-mate J. J. Kelly, who died on the same day. It was in 1896 at Old Trafford, where the Second Test was being played. England had scored 231 and 305. Australia had made 412 in the first innings and was now seven wickets down in the second with 25 runs still to get. Trumble and Kelly were batting, and the strain was so terrible that Harry Trott, the Australian captain, left the ground and went for a ride in a hansom cab to save himself from a nervous collapse. When he returned he found that Trumble and Kelly had made the necessary runs, giving Australia a three-wicket victory. They had batted for 90 minutes. Trumble scored 17 not out and Kelly 8 not out.

Vernon Ransford became the new secretary of the M.C.C.

That year was centenary year for the Melbourne Cricket Club, only three years after the centenary of Melbourne, and on Saturday night, December 10, 1938, the club celebrated the 100th anniversary of Melbourne's first cricket match—the M.C.C. versus the Military.

The players and the spectators all were dressed in period costume, the women wore crinolines and the men wore tight trousers, cut-away coats, bell-toppers and beards. The members' stand was lit with fairy lights and gay with floral decorations of the three colours of the Melbourne Cricket Club.

The cricket match was the thing to see. The first to arrive was Captain Smyth's team of the 80th Regiment. Then arrived the "Gentlemen Civilians" with the ladies in a Cobb & Co. coach, and another party in a bullock wagon. There was a batch, too, of the first cricket barrackers, aboriginals all dressed for a corroboree. Ladies in bonnets and crinolines nodded and curtsied, and it was reported that Captain Smyth's redcoats made a brave sight as they marched to the wicket. The toss was decided by a draw from the umpire's hat, and the historic match proceeded exactly according to the script.

The 100 years of progress was represented by the presentation of Don Bradman and his 1938 Australian Test team. Bradman introduced each player with a nickname. McCormick was "The Richmond Terror" and Ben Barnett "The Wizard of the Gloves." The President, Sir Edward Mitchell, made an address and the celebration ended with a noisy fire works display.

On December 14 the club held the Centenary Ball in the Members' Pavilion. The ladies wore period dress and they danced everything from the Minuet to the very latest dance of 1938, the Lambeth Walk. It was the first time in the history of the Melbourne Cricket Club that women had been admitted to the Lounge and Dining Room of the members.

Indeed, many felt that this was one of the most remarkable things that had happened in the club's first 100 years.

CHAPTER SIXTEEN

Camp Murphy and Camp Ransford

O N THE night of September 3, 1939, the Prime Minister, Mr. R. G. Menzies, made an announcement in a radio hook-up throughout the nation. He said: "Fellow Australians, it is my melancholy duty to inform you officially that in consequence of the persistence of Germany in her invasion of Poland Great Britain has declared war upon her.

"No harder task can fall to the lot of a democratic leader than to make such an announcement. Great Britain and France, with the co-operation of the British Dominions, have struggled to avoid this tragedy. They have, as I firmly believe, been patient. They have kept the door of negotiations open. They have given no cause for provocation. But in the result their efforts have failed, and we are therefore as a great family of nations involved in a struggle which we must at all times win, and which we believe in our hearts we will win.

"Where Britain stands there stands the people of the entire British world."

The newspapers printed photographs of the British Prime Minister, Mr. Chamberlain, along with his historic words: "This is a sad day for all of us. Everything that I have worked for and believed in has crashed in ruins. I trust that I may be permitted to see the day when Hitlerism has been destroyed."

It was all so different from 1914. There were no "demonstrations of enthusiasm," no displays of patriotic fervour in Collins Street. It was obvious to everyone that this would be a long, heartbreaking struggle. In 1914 the cricket authorities were so confident that it would be a short war they merely postponed their international programme for one year. This time the cricket associations played out the 1939-40 season, then suspended Sheffield Shield cricket and district cricket pennants for the duration of the war.

Cricket went on, but so much depended on the best players getting leave, for State players like Ross Gregory, Lindsay Hassett, Ben Barnett, Ian Johnson, Keith Miller, Frank Sides and Barry Scott soon were in the services. There were patriotic matches, but never were they as successful as the patriotic matches of the First World War, and after Pearl Harbour they attracted almost no interest at all. Only one stands out—Bradman's Eleven versus McCabe's Eleven at the M.C.G. on New Year's Day, 1941. Lieutenant Bradman had gone into a physical training school at Frankston the previous November.

The first day was wonderful cricket before a crowd of 8690. McCabe's Eleven finished with 9 for 449, including 105 from Badcock and 137 from Sid Barnes. Bradman's team made 205, then followed on with 141, but the sad shock was Bradman himself. In the first innings he was bowled first ball, which brought his score that season to three times out for six runs. So when he made only 12 in the second innings many of the critics nodded their heads. It was all too clear that the mighty Bradman at last was finished. The prediction was a little premature.

But it is intriguing now to read the newspaper comments about the young airman, Keith Miller. He had a reputation as a batsman, and that was all. He did not get a bowl in the first innings, nor would he have had a bowl in the second but for the fact that both McCabe and Sievers were injured. The *Argus* said: "With McCabe and Sievers both out of the team another bowler had to be found to open with Ellis in the second innings. Keith Miller was chosen, and, although he seldom bowls, he performed splendidly. He is a right-hander of about medium-pace, and, after beginning with two half-pitchers, he bowled fairly accurately. He was able to make his good length ball stand up a little, and Ridings touched one to give him his first wicket." He took 1 for 24, but it was Bill O'Reilly with 5 for 53 and Grimmett with 4 for 46 who did all the damage.

On December 8, 1941, came the news of the Japanese attack on Pearl Harbour, followed on February 19 by the devastating air raid on Darwin. Now Australia was really at war. It was a strange Christmas. At the height of the Christmas shopping rush the Government brought in the black-out. It was not easy to get used to the darkness, the awful gloom of Bourke and Swanston Streets, the complete absence of Neon signs. In many streets the only colour to be had was the red and green of the traffic lights.

Invasion seemed imminent, and there were hundreds of digging squads tearing up the parks and gardens for hideous air raid shelters. There was air raid drill, and, at the sound of a siren, the 1500 public servants in the State offices had to scurry into the shelters at the Treasury Gardens. The *Age* reported on one occasion that the State offices were cleared in four minutes, except for two departmental heads, who refused to take part.

The Americans arrived in March, and already the Services were desperate for space. Schools, high schools, and all available large buildings were taken over. The Melbourne Cricket Ground was a choice site almost in the city; it was obvious that something had to happen. At first there was a move to use it as a large dump for storing incoming munitions. This would have ruined the arena for years to come and the trustees fought against it. Just in time there was another idea. The Commonwealth decided to use the M.C.G. buildings as a staging camp for military forces. This time there was no quibble either from the trustees or the Melbourne Cricket Club. All agreed that the M.C.G. was needed for the war effort and the Crown took it over on April 7, 1942. The club was left with only the bowling pavilion and its greens.

That Easter the M.C.C. staff, including Vernon Ransford and Albert Cut-triss, worked right through Good Friday, Saturday and Easter Day, stock-taking. They knew it was goodbye to the ground for a long, long time. All the valuable furniture and all the seats had to be stored under stands. The United States Air Force moved into the buildings on the northern side of the ground and airmen pitched tents all around the bitumen concourse inside the boundary fence. The M.C.G. had moved into a new stage of its career. Now it was known as Camp Murphy, and even Vernon Ransford, the club secretary, could not enter unless he had his properly accredited pass from the U.S. Forces.

The Richmond Cricket Club very generously offered the Richmond Ground for the Melbourne Football Club's home matches, and the offer was accepted. The subscription for M.C.C. members was reduced to one guinea, and the 1,226 members in the Services went on the absentee list. They paid nothing.

On May 14, 1942, Squadron-Leader Keith Truscott, D.F.C. and Bar, returned to Melbourne after fighting in the Battle of Britain. He had been a great footballer in the 1939-40 Melbourne premiership teams. Later his welcome was to be overwhelming, but when first he arrived nobody knew, or even believed, that he was in Melbourne, particularly his old coach, Checker Hughes. Ivan Southall in his biography "Bluey Truscott" tells the story of his homecoming. Truscott had been at the Showgrounds reception depot only a few hours when he decided to call Checker. "Hullo," he said, "Do you want a good half-forward for Saturday?"

"No," said Checker. "I don't. I'm not interested in football this season. Can't you read the papers?" Checker Hughes had given up coaching for the duration of the war.

Blue laughed. "Go on," he said. "You can play a good man. There's always room for a good one."

"I am not connected with football," said Checker. "I cannot play you. If

176

you're that good why don't you go through the proper channels? Who did you say you were?"

"Truscott's the name. Bluey Truscott."

"Sure," said Checker. "And I'm King Henry VIII." And he hung up.

The telephone rang again and the voice said, "Would you like a good half-forward for Saturday?"

"No," stormed Checker. "Go and drown yourself!"

"Hey," yelled Blue, "it's me! It's Bluey. What's wrong with you, you old bat?" ·

Checker did not approve of the trick at all. "So you're Bluey Truscott?"

"Of course I am."

"Well, I don't think you are. No. You don't even sound like Bluey Truscott to me."

"Strike me!" said Blue. "Listen, you grab your horse and buggy and come out to the Showgrounds. Ask at the gate for Bluey Truscott. You see what happens."

"I'll think about it," said Checker. "But don't expect me. My time's valuable." And hung up.

According to Ivan Southall, Checker Hughes was still very sceptical, but eventually he did go to the Showgrounds, and there they had their incredible reunion. For hours they talked together in the mess and Bluey Truscott put his big question. He knew he was over-weight, he knew he was sluggish, but he was dying to get his hands on a football again. Could Checker fix it? Checker did fix it. Blue would play for his old team in his old place. Southall wrote later:

Bluey played that afternoon, even in the old sweater he used to wear. They had kept it in mothballs for him. The thousands rose as one to honour him. . . . They rushed him bodily. Hundreds of excited schoolboys and men and women engulfed him. Dyer (the Richmond captain) paraded him into the heart of the Richmond team and towards the great block of Richmond supporters, and the reception was a vast human roar and very nearly overwhelming.

Bluey played his game, but he was an athlete no longer. Before long he was so tired he could hardly drag one foot behind the other. He battled to control the ball, but he couldn't make it. When he kicked the man wasn't there. When he leapt the ball wasn't there. They flashed past him in the field. They left him standing. He stumbled and staggered and they rolled him in the mud. "Let's have a go at the ball," he pleaded. "Slow down. Give me a kick."

The Tigers did slow down, bless them, but if they had slowed any more when the ball was near them they would have stopped, and the thousands thought he was clowning and laughed until they could laugh no more. At last Jack Dyer dropped the ball in the goal-mouth and Blue captured it and put it through. He kicked his goal and the multitude cheered until it was hoarse.

That night Blue was in agony, every muscle seemed to be talking and he learned that it was a long way from the seat of a fighter aircraft to the football field. It was one thing to shoot down 14 German planes, another to kick goals for Melbourne. Yet it made no difference to his reception in Melbourne, and the M.C.C. committee presented him with a tea and coffee service.

Southall recalled that Bluey Truscott met his old teacher, the former Test captain, Bill Woodfull. They almost collided in the street. "Well, Keith, how do you like playing League football again?" Blue replied: "Not for me. Too dangerous."

Truscott went off to Milne Bay with 76 Squadron. On March 28, 1943, he died in a Kittyhawk near the Bay of Rest in Western Australia.

The U.S. Air Force left the Melbourne Cricket Ground after some months and the United States Marines took over. Edward "Joe" Matthews, then the Maintenance Supervisor at the M.C.G., remembered it well. In 1942 he was the maintenance expert at the Royal Melbourne Hospital, which also was taken over by the Americans. They switched him from the hospital to do the maintenance work at the M.C.G., and, but for the uniform, he became virtually a U.S. Marine.

He says that the American Air Force called the M.C.G. "Camp Murphy," but in honour of Vernon Ransford the Marines switched the title to "Camp Ransford." The committee made all the senior officers honorary members of the M.C.C. A skeleton body of the ground staff under Bert Luttrell was kept on to maintain the ground.

This was a fantastic time in Melbourne. The Americans were pouring in for the great push forward, and at one time they reached a peak of 14,000 at the M.C.G. It was one vast dormitory, swarming with Americans, and the Coca Cola consumption was said to be something unbelievable. The Marines at once screened off all the fronts of the grandstands with fibro-plaster sheets. Where five years before the fans had watched Wally Hammond and Don Bradman, now there were thousands of beds with legs short on one side, long on the other, to accommodate the tiers. The engineers put a wooden floor over the road underneath the southern stand to provide space for more beds. "Pneumonia Alley," they called it. Then, for even more beds, they built extra floors up around the concrete stairs. Bay 18 in the Southern Stand was the picture theatre, and here was the ideal arrangement. The Americans could sit where the cricket and football fans sat, and the movie screen was fixed against the fibro-sheeting that now closed off the front of the stand.

The officers, of course, took over the Members' Long Room and the sergeants were on the floor above. The Melbourne Football Club Gymnasium in the old public stand was the medical centre and the number one Outer dressing room was the lock-up. It was divided into wire partitions which served as cells. The little room right at the end under the stairs was the special cell for difficult cases—as safe as Sing Sing.

The No. 1 Outer dressing room is now the umpires' changing room. This could be something for the umpires to think about, particularly after life has been rugged out there in the middle. Then they can ponder the thought that their dressing room does, after all, provide the security of what was once an American gaol.

What else? The changing rooms in the Grey Smith stand, that almost sacred area where the Test cricketers once anxiously watched Larwood in action, was now the American armoury, the storehouse for light machine guns, carbines and rifles. The Grey Smith bar was a canteen and the old members' tearoom was the American PX. In 1942 this was the best shop in Melbourne. An American who would bring one a gift from the PX at the Melbourne Cricket Ground was someone to know. It sold beautiful white towels, superior quality cotton shirts and trousers, watches, tinned foods, bowie knives, chocolate, tinned nuts, boots, shoes, raincoats . . . anything that was hard to get was available at the PX. And best of all, there were Lucky Strikes, Camels and Chesterfields at five shillings a carton.

Joe Matthews remembers that the Americans refused to endure the cold at the M.C.G. They installed hundreds of tent heaters, little fuel stoves that gave off a flood of heat. These they placed around the stands on large slabs of concrete and they fixed elaborate connecting flues to take away the smoke. Furthermore, there were several of these heaters, slabs of concrete and all, in the Long Room.

It was no easy task to cater for so many troops even at the M.C.G. The Americans had to build a series of great kitchens, and this they did in an ingenious way. They built abutments on to the gates of the Southern Stand, which extended 50 feet or more out into the park. Joe Matthews looks back on the food they served with a certain amount of happiness. He says the cooking for the Americans was much better, more imaginative, than anything the Australians ever received. There was always lashings of ham. There was chicken. There was turkey. They would fry whole parsnips in breadcrumbs,

179

and they would fry bananas. There was tinned fruit juice, tinned grapefruit, plenty of cole slaw and a wonderful dish of hot beetroot and sauce that he has never seen since. But the pièce de résistance was frogs' legs, beautiful frogs' legs like the most tender of chicken.

They installed big refrigerators for the storing of food and for the cooling of drinks and large boilers for the hot and cold showers. They looked after their own comfort, but at the same time they were efficient and there was little red tape. Joe says that on one occasion a boiler split, that was needed for the hot showers. He had to get a new one at once. He went to Melbourne's most reputable supplier of such goods and he was told that no boiler was available. But as he was leaving the office he noticed that there was a boiler unit out in the yard, the very thing he needed. He reported this to the Marine Sergeant at the M.C.G., who did not hesitate. He whistled up 10 men, fetched a truck, went straight to the yard and collected the boiler unit. They installed it at Camp Ransford before the firm knew it was gone. However, the Americans paid for it and they paid well.

The newspapers at this time were censored. Rarely indeed was there any mention of Camp Ransford. If one had to depend upon the papers, then it would have been impossible to find out who or what was at the M.C.G. But nobody had to read the paper to find out about the Americans—they were as obvious as the setting of the sun.

The taxi-drivers went to the M.C.G. in a never-ending stream. It was the latest version of the gold rush. Girls were there, too. They waited all around the ground from early in the morning until late at night. The Americans would hang out of the windows high up in the stands. They would wave to the girls and the girls would wave to them. On one or two occasions girls were even smuggled inside up into the grandstands. For the officers it was different. They had a dance every Saturday night in the Long Room.

This was the time when tension began to build between Australian and American servicemen. Some of the finest brawls since the days of the diggings took place outside Young & Jackson's and other city hotels. The American service police and the Australian provosts became a very familiar sight patrolling down Swanston Street. Something had to be done, so on April 14, 1943, the Americans made a gesture of good will, an open house at the M.C.G. There wasn't enough room to cater for everybody, but the invitation went out to all those Australian servicemen who had returned from battle areas.

The souvenir programmes read "U.S. Forces Welcome Australian Forces," and the entertainment was good. There was a famous U.S. band, which had entertained troops all around the Pacific. There was Max Oldaker and Gladys

The library at the M.C.C., a unique
institution.

Left
Sir Albert Chadwick, captain of the
Melbourne Football Club 1924–1927.
President, Melbourne Cricket Club,
1965–1979.

Jim Cardwell, secretary, Melbourne
Football Club, 1951–1975.

The V.F.L. Grand Final, 1960 —
Melbourne v. Collingwood.
From left: Thorogood, Beckworth,
Adams, Dixon, Barassi and Tassie
Johnson.

Hans Ebeling, who played for
Australia in 1934 and was president,
Melbourne Cricket Club, 1979–80.

Sir Bernard Callinan, President,
1980–86.

Moncrieff, who starred so often together in "Maid of the Mountains." Then the girls from the Tivoli revue "Strip for Action" volunteered their services. Between 9 p.m. and 10.30 the show was broadcast over the national stations and sent by short wave to America and Great Britain.

The gates opened at 6.30 p.m., and it was just like old times—there were long queues outside the M.C.G. But there was this difference: all the queuers were men and in uniform. It was a bucks' party, and judging by some of the jokes that were put over it had to be. Out in the centre, on Bert Luttrell's famous Test wicket, the U.S. band was in action, and all around the boundary there were booths which provided beer, hot dogs and hamburgers . . . and it was all free. All night long the troops marched steadily towards the barrels.

On the square leg boundary there was a large stage, and across the front it carried the words in letters three feet high—HI YA, DIGGER. Early there was little mingling between the Australians and the Americans. They watched each other warily. However, as the beer flowed freely they relaxed and, according to the *Argus,* by eight or nine o'clock they were arm in arm together singing *Roll Out the Barrel.*

When they were off the air much of the entertainment was very hearty, hardly suited to the respectable Australian Broadcasting Commission. Nor could the A.B.C. have handled some of the stories that were told in the short story competition. These had to be limited to 150 words. The winner in the Australian section was a sailor, Leading Signalman Laurie Smith. His story was this:

An American and a British sailor were discussing aircraft carriers. The American said, "Say, buddy, you know we have the Saratoga, which can do 38 knots, and the Ranger can do 40 knots?" At this moment he looked out the window and saw H.M.S. *Eagle* lying in the harbour. "Say, fella," said the American, "how many knots can that doggone tub knock up?"

"Oh," replied the British sailor, "we don't worry much about that. As long as our carriers keep up with the aircraft we reckon they're going fast enough."

The winner of the U.S. division was Sgt. Marvin J. Swanson, who told a story about a moose. He strode the length of the stage to show how long were the horns of a moose that decorated his den back home. These horns were so big that they were the envy of all his friends, but never would they believe that he had shot it. He became tired of this, so eventually whenever he was asked how he got the horns he told this story.

"It was like this," he said. "I was out in the woods one day and this big bull moose with those large horns charged me. I had no gun and I couldn't run fast

181

enough to get away from him. The only thing I had was a bottle of turpentine, so jumping aside as he charged I threw that bottle and it burst right on his hindquarters. That turpentine sure must have stung him, because he backed against a tree and rubbed and rubbed and rubbed until all that was left of him were these horns that you see decorating my den. That's how I got them."

The two winners, Leading Signalman Smith and Sgt. Swanson, each was presented with a silver pot full of beer.

On September 19, 1943, the Americans paid a special tribute to Bert Luttrell, the M.C.G. curator. They made him an honorary Master Sergeant in the U.S. forces, with stripes, warrant and all. The *Herald* commented: "He seems even prouder of his new honour than of tributes from Test captains in the past about his world-famous wickets. Although not being used for sport, the M.C.G. arena is being kept in splendid condition by a skeleton ground staff."

These years saw some historic changes in the Melbourne Cricket Club. On May 7, 1941, Sir Edward Mitchell, K.C., died, aged 86. He had been President of the club since 1933, a trustee, and he had been a member for more than 60 years. He was a distinguished barrister and for years he was the leader of the Victorian Bar. He was born in Surrey, England, but he was educated at Melbourne Grammar. He took his B.A. and LL.B. at Cambridge. Few members were ever so closely associated with the M.C.C. as Sir Edward. He joined as a junior member in 1873, and often he walked over for practice from Melbourne Grammar in the evenings. In those days Sam Cosstick was the professional bowler, and, according to Sir Edward, a very fine bowler too, the best purely round-arm bowler Victoria had ever seen. He practised, too, with Mr. G. Gibson, a good wicket-keeper in the days before the daring Jack Blackham abolished long stops. Sir Edward used to tell the story how Gibson concentrated on improving his batting by practising with an axe-handle instead of a bat. Sir Edward and Dr. Ramsay Mailer, perhaps more than anyone, helped to smooth over the bitterness of the 1912 battle with the Board of Control and the V.C.A.

Dr. Ramsay Mailer was the new president, but his time in office was tragically brief. He died on December 28, 1943, at the age of 78. It is not easy to tell the story of Dr. Mailer in a short space, for his name has been perpetuated in so many ways. He studied at Melbourne University and finished his medical training in Edinburgh, then he returned to Melbourne, where he became a Collins Street specialist in nervous diseases.

He could have made a name for himself as a cricketer, but always he refused to play in senior competition. He played for Coburg in the Boyle and

Scott competition, which in those days attracted crowds of up to 10,000 people. He was one of the very few Australians to play for and against Dr. W. G. Grace. He appeared for a combined Victorian team against Grace at the M.C.G., and as a medical student he played under Grace for an English team against a Scottish eleven.

In 1936 he retired from his medical practice so that he could give all his time to slum clearance. He founded the Motive Club in Collingwood, and he was one of the founders of the Opportunity Clubs for Boys and Girls. He said then: "I'm prouder of my boys' club at Collingwood than of anything in my cricket career."

He used to look upon Collins Street as the pretty painted face, which hid the slums behind, and one time he said, "Children are the foundation on which everything for the future must be built. In my dream city there will be no blighted industrial areas, where families grow up in the shadow of factory chimneys, with the street as their playground, and the homes that are the recruiting place of hospitals."

The bulk of his estate he left in trust to continue his life work, and many children now have cause to be grateful to the scholarships given to them by the Ramsay Mailer Opportunity Club. Right until the time of his death he was a powerful force in the Melbourne Cricket Club, and he was one of the leaders in the £100,000 rebuilding scheme that gave the M.C.G. the Southern Stand. The new President was Dr. W. C. McClelland.

When the Americans moved out of the M.C.G. in 1943 the R.A.A.F. moved in, and Camp Ransford became No. 1 Personnel Depot. All those airmen who were moving north, going overseas, or returning from overseas passed through the M.C.G. When they entered the Orderly Room to file their papers they always entered through two doors marked "Members Only."

The Grey Smith stand became the Quartermaster's store. Here many thousands of airmen received their shirts and ties and their boots. Tailors, too, worked there shaping uniforms to fit. The R.A.A.F. took over the ground much as the Americans had left it and under the same conditions. Except that the new lock-up was the old security room, the place where the pass-out tickets were kept and the takings locked away after cricket matches. Nor was the ground quite so comfortable. The cosy tent heaters had gone and Pneumonia Alley was almost true to its name. Many an ex-serviceman can remember the winter cold of the Southern Stand, the nights when one needed at least seven blankets to keep warm. The food, too, was not quite as good as it used to be, and the R.A.A.F. officers certainly did not hold dances every Saturday night in the Long Room.

Furthermore many an old airman can remember the nights of guard duty patrolling the labyrinth of passages. It was then on a moonlight night that one would look out across the arena and wonder when cricket would be played again, and, maybe, think of some of the old names. Hedley Verity had died from wounds after leading an attack in Italy. Ross Gregory was dead. Farnes had died in flying operations in 1941. Bill Bowes was a P.O.W. In July 1944 the *Herald* interviewed some of the airmen at the ground, and one Flight Sergeant was nostalgic. He was wearing a D.F.M. ribbon. "My dad started to bring me here when I was a kid. Dad had the idea that these seats below where those two W.A.A.A.Fs. are sitting were the best. That's where the kids used to get their autographs. I remember the day Bowes clean bowled Bradman first ball. Dad got the sulks and didn't speak for half an hour."

Even to this day it is possible to see faded signs of the occupation. Mostly they are painted on the walls around "Pneumonia Alley" in the Southern Stand. On a door it is possible to read "Out of Bounds for Troops" or on a wall "R.A.A.F. HOT AND COLD SHOWERS"; then high up under the stairs "Room for 8 Men" and the red and black colours of some U.S. regiment. Then outside a men's toilet block don't be startled if you see the still clear notice "W.A.A.A.F. ONLY."

The agitation to get the R.A.A.F. to leave started in 1944. Cr. Nettlefold said it was a great pity that the continued occupation of the M.C.G. prevented its use for national purposes. It was such a waste when the ground could be used for raising thousands of pounds for patriotic funds. The Air Force did not need it, for the ground was only partly occupied.

The R.A.A.F. replied that there were now 3000 airmen at the ground and every building was in full use. The M.C.C. President, Dr. McClelland, said the committee did not intend to take any active steps to regain the ground until it knew it was no longer needed for Australia's war effort. He kept to his word. Neither the M.C.C. nor the V.C.A. nor the Victorian Football League made any approaches to the Government until the war was over.

Then came the end of the war and the world was at peace for the first time since Japan invaded Manchuria in 1931. The *Herald* reported on August 15, 1945:

> Melbourne is boiling over with joy. A quarter of a million people who heard the news just as they started work turned out into the streets as soon as the full truth of it dawned on them.
>
> It took the city a while to realise it was all over. A few who heard the wireless news came to office windows yelling 'Peace' and 'It's finished.' Here and there handfuls of paper scrap were thrown out. Then the whole city stirred. By 9.10 Collins Street was like a snowstorm with paper falling. 'There go all the boss's

engagements for the rest of the year,' said a lass in the Manchester Unity building as she threw all the leaves from his bunch of dates out the window.

Papers falling stuck to the windows of cars moving slowly in the drizzle. Sprinkler alarm bells began to ring and someone hurried up and down pealing an auction bell. By 10.25 Collins Street was packed with an amazing crowd. Someone was "rolling out the barrel" with a vengeance at the Town Hall intersection, where a big oil drum was being kicked and rolled among the crowd. It broke up several crocodiles and sent hundreds scurrying out of the way.

Revellers could be heard thundering *Australia Will Be There*, *Pack Up Your Troubles* and *Bless 'Em All* a quarter of a mile away.

It was quite a morning, and one city barmaid as a patriotic gesture dyed her hair red, white and blue.

Once the war was over the agitation was on again to get the use of the M.C.G. As the war ended in Europe there were even dreams that it might be available for the 1945 Grand Final of the League football. But few people realised just how much work had to be done to reconvert the ground from a military camp back to what it was before the war.

The R.A.A.F. moved out on October 27, 1945, and, at last, once again the Melbourne Cricket Club was in occupation. The U.S. Air Force and the 1st Division of the U.S. Marines, before it won fame at Guadalcanal, had the ground from April 7, 1942, until Cup Day, November 4, 1943. The R.A.A.F. had it from then on. The club could quarrel with nothing they did. The playing arena was never harmed; possibly after the lack of use it was even better than in 1939.

The R.A.A.F. left behind one memento. The former O.C. of the camp, Wing-Commander Bazely, presented the club with a bronze plaque.

The committee placed it just inside the main gates of the members' reserve. It reads: "This tablet records that 200,000 members of the R.A.A.F. passed through this sports arena to and from their battle stations, 1943-45."

It was a big job to renovate the ground. All the sheets of fibro-cement that boarded up the stands had to be torn away. Emergency living quarters under the stairs had to be cleared out. All the seats had to be put back, and everything in sight had to be painted. Nor did the M.C.G. have a high priority for labour and materials, so the operation took nine months.

The first event on the ground was the club football match, Melbourne against Hawthorn, on August 17, 1946. Many people that day remembered the 1940 Grand Final and four of the Melbourne players who took part. There was Syd Anderson, who played on the wing—shot down over New Guinea. There was Harold Ball, the ruck player—lost during the fight for Singapore.

185

There was Bluey Truscott on the half-forward line—died in a crash off the coast of Western Australia. And there was Ron Barassi, the father of Melbourne's former captain. He came on as emergency during the afternoon—killed at Tobruk.

There were two club matches, the finals, then Bert Luttrell was preparing Test wickets once again. He was wearing the same model panama he wore when he rolled wickets for the Test matches of the 'thirties, and the pipe he was chewing looked suspiciously like the one he bit the end off when Jack Ryder hit Larwood for six back in '28.

Not many people remembered that once he had been Honorary Master Sergeant Bert Luttrell of the United States Marines.

CHAPTER SEVENTEEN

Post War

ONCE the war was over there was a desperate urge to get back to big cricket. In some respects it was like bolting down one's dinner to look at television. Everything was rushed a little too quickly. English cricket was not ready for an international tour so soon. The touring side contained far too many of the pre-war veterans and too few of the young men with red corpuscles. However, if winning matches was the most important thing, England should never have contemplated a tour in 1946. But if the playing of the cricket was more important then the time was ideal. Even the Prime Minister, Mr. Chifley, had called for an early resumption of cricket tours.

The similarity to 1919 was astonishing. It was almost like looking at a replay of an old movie. The Services team had provided a crop of new players just as the Services team did in 1919. The 1919 team produced a great all-rounder in Jack Gregory; the 1946 team produced a great all-rounder in Keith Miller. After the First World War there was the devastating opening attack of Gregory and McDonald; now there was a pair equally as good in Lindwall and Miller.

In 1946 Keith Miller was a character. It was as if he had a neurotic hatred of the cricket ball. There had been no one quite like him since George Bonnor. He gave an example of the shape of things to come in the England against the Dominions match at Lord's in 1945. He hit seven sixes, including a majestic six off Hollies high up into the top tier of the pavilion and another that went down a shrapnel hole in the roof of the commentary box. The ball had to be poked up with a stick.

The first glimpse that Melbourne had of this new Miller at full throttle was in the 1946-47 Victoria-N.S.W. match. Miller came in when Victoria was one wicket down for 31. He had made just three runs when Toshack came on at the Richmond end. Miller with a mighty hook sent the third ball over the fine leg fence, the sixth he lifted to a great height over square leg and it carried the distance for another six. The seventh ball he drove with appalling force straight into Toshack's hands and it bounced out again. The crowd by now was roaring, and to celebrate his escape Miller lifted the next ball high over the long-on fence—three sixes in one over.

That day the M.C.G. seemed to shrink in size. It was reported that every time he shaped to Toshack the crowd in the boundary seats ducked. He reached his 50 in 41 minutes, and he had made 153 when he was run out.

The Englishmen arrived at Perth in September 1946. With all the industrial unrest that came after the war this was an uneasy time in Australia. There were tram strikes, railway strikes, strikes in the mines and on the waterfront. Prices were soaring. The Board of Control announced that there would be a 50 per cent. increase in prices for Test matches. Now it would cost 3/3 to get into the Outer and 5/11 for the public stand. Pre-war the charges were 2/2 and 4/-.

Never mind about the prices; after all the years of rationing Australia to the Englishmen looked like heaven. The food in the shops at Perth was almost beyond belief—the pastry, the cream cakes, the steaks, the bananas, the pineapples. Soon it was reported that the ex-airman, Bill Edrich, D.F.C., was suffering from a slight stomach upset.

The Third Test match was the first at the M.C.G. for 10 years, and of the Australians only Bradman had ever played in a Test there before. It had been a long time, and for many this was Test cricket for the first time. Australia had won the first two Tests, so this could be the match to decide the rubber.

On New Year's Eve 1946 the crowds gathered around the Town Hall and Post Office clocks just as they had done in 1939. Yet this time it was different. After singing the New Year in, the young people decided that there was little point in going home. Why not go straight to the M.C.G. and get a good position in the queue for the Third Test? So hundreds of the revellers marched to the ground, where they waited more than seven hours for the gates to open. They filled in the time by singing and playing cards.

When the gates opened at 9 a.m. one queue went all the way to the foot-bridge over the railway line at Jolimont Station, another snaked so far across the park that crowds who stepped off the trains at Richmond station had only to turn the corner and they were in the queue. The first man in the queue was a 70-year-old cricket veteran, Mr. Harry Graham, of North Richmond, who was reading *For the Term of His Natural Life,* the grim novel of early Tasmanian convicts by Marcus Clarke. No doubt Mr. Graham was in a very stern, for-bidding mood when the time came for the toss.

If so, he was in the correct frame of mind, for it was a stern, forbidding Test match, as so many of them were in the 'forties and 'fifties. Lindsay Hassett took nearly an hour to make 12 runs and Sid Barnes scored at the rate of 4

188

runs every 10 minutes. Don Bradman made 79, not the equal of his 187 in Brisbane or his 234 in Sydney, but it was a sound chanceless innings. The only light relief came when Bradman was 65. A young man jumped the fence, and with his shirt tail flapping in the wind, he ran towards the wicket. Incredibly nobody made any attempt to stop him, and soon he was out in the centre with the Englishmen. He shook hands with Fishlock, he chatted to several of the fieldsmen, and he was just making his way towards Bradman when Umpire Scott intervened and tried to persuade him to leave the ground. He then took the man by one arm and by the seat of his pants, and to the accompaniment of yells and boos from the crowd, he ran him towards a group of policemen.

The *Herald* commented: "Nobody present could recall a precedent. It was as if a non-Christian had got in among the lions back in Nero's Rome."

At the end of the day Australia was 6 down for 255, and considering the fine conditions critics felt this was a good effort by England. The day's scores were picked up by the American Associated Press, and it was fascinating to read of the first day of the Third Test in pure baseball parlance.

This was the version that appeared in American newspapers:

> The English bowlers held Australian batsmen to a low 255 score today, fanning six men with a succession of speedy cannon balls and slow drop curves in the opening of the Third Test match in the Cricket World Series. Even Don Bradman, who usually romps home a 100 or more in his turn at the bat, was dismissed with only 79 runs.
>
> Bradman was fooled by Norman Yardley, who immediately followed up the job by fanning Ian Johnson without a run.

Australia went on to make 365. England replied with 351. There is not a great deal to remember from this match, which eventually was drawn, except three things.

The first was over two lbw decisions given against Edrich and Compton by Umpire Scott. For days the cables to England ran hot. At least four of the English pressmen were of the opinion that neither batsman was out. The controversy became so tedious that one morning before the start of play Umpire Scott decided to make a visit to the press box. He wanted to know how men 150 yards away on an angle could get a better view than he did at 22 yards range with his nose near the bowler's stumps.

Leslie Bailey of the *Star* told Scott: "If you are in the slightest doubt about an lbw decision out there, Jack, just look up here and I'll give you a sign."

Umpire Scott's only comment was: "It's even worse than I feared."

The second point worth remembering was the fine performances of two all-rounders. Colin McCool made 104 not out in the first innings and John Wren gave him £1 for every run he scored. Then Ray Lindwall scored a century in the second innings. He made his hundred in 113 minutes, including 13 fours and a six. This was an astonishing performance; he was rather like a boy who was making too much noise in church; he was forgetting the due solemnity of the occasion. How he hit: he showed that no living batsman could drive with such power.

The third point worth remembering was the bowling of Norman Yardley. He took Bradman's wicket in each innings, and this was the third consecutive occasion on which he had taken his wicket. Yet as recently as five weeks before, Norman Yardley was almost unheard of as a bowler. In the second innings he got Bradman for 49. Neville Cardus made this comment: "Yardley fumbled his length, pitched short enough for a novice's stroke. Possibly it popped a little, and Bradman, attempting a hit towards the on, was too precipitate and lobbed the ball, so that Yardley running a few yards down the pitch made a catch, which he is likely to recall with emotion and incredulity while life shall last."

At times it was difficult to know which side was playing for a draw. Australia left England 552 runs to make in 420 minutes. England finished with 7/310, including 112 by Washbrook. The attendance throughout was extraordinarily good and, as at all Test matches, the Lost Property room scored well. At the finish it contained umbrellas, overcoats, hats, caps, a bowler, four front door keys, cushions, a toy train, six autograph books, a woman's shoe, a bunch of carrots, 1 lb. of fruit cake, a thermos and portions of a red wig.

As for property lost to the M.C.G., not only did all the stumps disappear at precisely 6 p.m. with all the speed of a cover drive but the spare stumps went, too. Eight of them vanished during the afternoon from a dressing room.

The Fourth Test was drawn, and Australia won the Fifth Test by five wickets. The series was yet another triumph for Bradman. At 39 he topped the batting averages with 680 at an average of 97.14.

On July 14, 1947, Warwick Armstrong died at his home at Darling Point, Sydney, aged 69. He joined the Club in 1900 after his transfer from South Melbourne. He was elected a life member in 1922 and he served, on the committee until he transferred to Sydney. He played 42 Test matches against England, with tours to England in 1902, 1905, 1909 and 1921. For days the newspapers ran stories about him, but particularly they recalled the triumphant tour of 1921. This was the tour that depicted his huge personality best of all.

In the Fourth Test match at Manchester the Hon. Lionel (later Lord) Tennyson was the English captain. At 5.40 p.m. on the first day Tennyson closed the English innings. It was only 50 minutes to stumps, and by the rule there could not be a closure after 4.50 p.m. Armstrong wasn't having any. The story goes that he went to Tennyson and said: "You can't close, Lionel."

"Be damned," replied the explosive grandson of the famous poet. "We have closed and that's the end of it." But it was not the end of it. Out came the rule book and Armstrong proved his point. He had no intention of letting England take Australian wickets in the failing light.

When Armstrong took his men on to the field he was hooted from all around the ground. The noise was so great that he sat his great frame on the grass until the racket subsided. Meanwhile Tennyson went round the boundary and tried to explain to the barrackers what had happened. He told them Armstrong was perfectly right in what he had done.

And so the game went on, with Armstrong bowling, but nobody in all the excitement noticed that he had also bowled the last over before Tennyson led his men off the field. So Armstrong set one cricket record which is never likely to be taken from him. He bowled two overs in succession in a Test match.

Armstrong was undoubtedly a law unto himself. He had a tremendously dominating personality and this no doubt was one reason for his great success as a captain. He remained unabashed in even the most distinguished company and never hesitated to make his point.

There was the story about his appearance at the Imperial Cricket Conference in 1921. Armstrong suggested that umpires in the Tests should not be appointed until the day of the match. Lord Harris asked, "Why?" and Armstrong replied, "These umpires are paid very little for their services, and one of them might easily be tempted. There is a lot of betting on Tests, and it would be wise to remove the umpires from temptation."

Lord Harris replied: "This is a most serious matter, and I suggest that we hold it over till our next meeting. In the meantime we can make inquiries." The next day he said, "I can find no evidence to support the allegation."

Said Armstrong, "Do you think so, my Lord? You give me £500 and I will get it on for you."

The funeral in Sydney was attended by eight members of his 1921 side— H. L. Collins, Warren Bardsley, C. G. Macartney, T. J. Andrews, J. Taylor, Arthur Mailey, W. A. Oldfield and H. L. Hendry.

The big attraction for the 1947-48 season was the visit of a team from India, the first to visit this country. Except for stars like Mankad, Hazare, Phadkar and Amarnath, the captain, they were not a powerful combination. Australia won the First Test in Brisbane, the Second Test in Sydney was a draw because of bad weather, and the Third Test was at the M.C.G. on New Year's Day. This was one Test series when the newspapers did not employ cricket commentators by the half-dozen. It was no insult to the Indians. The post-war dollar shortage was now at its worst, and on the first day of the Third Test the Government announced new newsprint restrictions. The Melbourne tabloids were down to 12 pages, and newspapers were thinner than at any time since 1942. The match was one-sided but mercifully it was bright. Bradman made 132 in the first innings and 127 not out in the second—the first time he had made a century in each innings of a Test match. One rather wondered why he had never done this before, but maybe this was the reason: often he made so many runs in his first trip to the wicket that a second innings was not necessary. Mankad scored 116 in 182 minutes, and at one stage Miller hit three lovely sixes, two off Phadkar in succession. Ian Johnson had the best bowling figures by taking 4 for 59 in the first innings and 4 for 35 in the second.

The M.C.G. crowd liked the Indians, and particularly they liked Rai Singh. He was the only member of the team who wore a beard and a turban. He was a Sikh and thus he was compelled by his religion to cover his head and not to cut his hair or shave. During the game he appeared in three different-coloured turbans—pink, blue and yellow. No matter what Rai Singh was doing on the field the turbans always looked immaculate. Seeing that they contained eight yards of material, many people wondered how long they took to put on, but Rai Singh said it was no trouble at all. He could fix his turban in less than two minutes.

On January 30, Mahatma Gandhi, the spiritual leader of the Indians, was assassinated. It was a terrible shock to the Indian cricketers. The Fifth Test was due to start in Melbourne the following Friday, and at first it seemed the logical thing to cancel it. Mr. P. Gupta, manager of the team, cabled the Indian Board of Control, but finally they decided to go ahead.

On the Friday the flags at the M.C.G. were half-mast. The Indian cricketers wore black armbands, and as a mark of respect to Gandhi the two teams and the umpires lined up on the arena and observed a minute's silence, while the crowd stood bareheaded.

This was Neil Harvey's Test match. For more than a year the cricket writers had been boosting him as the boy most likely to wear a green cap. As an 18-year-old in the match Victoria against England he had shown himself as a boy with a delicious urge to make runs. He didn't seem to be bound by any of the old conventions. Old players when they approached 50 looked upon it as a frightening hurdle. As they approached this hurdle they slowed to a stop, eyed the awful thing for 20 minutes or so, then ever so gingerly climbed over.

Harvey on this day, full of naive gusto, ran from his early forties to his sixties without hesitation and scored 69 against the best of England.

His attitude was the same as a 19-year-old in the Fifth Test against India. He came into the side for the Fourth Test at Adelaide, where he scored only 13. But for the Fifth Test at the M.C.G. all the Harveys were there—Mr. and Mrs. Harvey plus Neil's five cricketing brothers. Merv, the first of the Harveys to play for Australia, was in the Members' Reserve and, according to the *Herald*, he spent the day mentally playing every stroke.

He did not need to be concerned. Young Neil made 153 runs. There was something fresh and different about his batting. An example of this was the way he got his century. At 95 he pulled Rangachary almost square, then with Ray Lindwall he sprinted up and down the wicket to get five runs. The crowd went mad. What other batsman had ever completed a century by scoring five, all run? Harvey had arrived, and arrived to stay for a long, long time. The next morning one newspaper printed the comment: "Neil Harvey, of course, must be selected for England. He can apply for his passport immediately." Another player who worked very hard for his passport that day was Sam Loxton. He scored 80 runs. The leading issuer of passports, Captain Don Bradman, retired with a torn muscle for 57 runs. Altogether Australia scored 575 runs for eight wickets and went on to a very easy victory, taking four Tests out of five.

The 1948 tour to England was the most successful of all in the record books. Warwick Armstrong in 1921 had three Test wins and two drawn games. Bradman won four out of his five Tests. It was his farewell to cricket, and as soon as the team returned to Australia plans were made for the Bradman testimonial match. There was long discussion as to where and when it should be, but finally the organisers chose the ground where the crowds would be biggest and keenest—the Melbourne Cricket Ground, December 3-7, 1948.

The best 22 cricketers in Australia took part, Bradman captain of one team, Lindsay Hassett the other. Hassett won the toss and decided to bat. One couldn't help but feel that there was an element of divine providence in this. As the newspapermen were quick to point out, now Hassett's men would bat all Friday and inevitably the stage would be set for Don Bradman himself to play before the biggest possible crowd on the Saturday afternoon.

On the Friday Hassett's men scored 383 runs for the loss of nine wickets. Ray Lindwall hit five sixes, scoring 104 in 85 minutes. Then on the Saturday Don Bradman went to the wicket. Everyone hoped and prayed that for this, his last match in big cricket, he would score yet another century. There were 52,960 people waiting to see him do it.

193

As he made his way from the pavilion he received a tremendous reception, which continued until he arrived at the crease. The crowd's cheering died as Hassett's players surrounded Bradman in the centre of the pitch, but as soon as they had given him three cheers the crowd resumed its welcome, and it was some minutes before he could settle down. There was silence when he took his first delivery and cheering when he put it away for a single.

Bradman was now 40. It was not one of his hurricane innings, but at the same time he hit 13 fours, and all the old Bradman cunning and subtlety was there. He thought out his moves like a Russian playing chess. He would find his gaps in the field and score with an easy fluency. Hassett would close off those gaps, but just to prove the futility of it all Bradman would send the ball to the very places from where the fieldsmen had been moved.

The crowd cheered everything, particularly when he turned a ball from Lindwall to the fine leg boundary to reach 70. Oddly enough, this was the first time Bradman had ever faced Lindwall. The next ball was a head-high bumper. There was a murmur of disapproval from the Outer to the Members' Reserve, but Sid Barnes turned it into a lovely situation, full of comedy, by running over to Lindwall and wagging his finger at him. That was the last bumper of the day.

At 97 Bradman gave Colin McCool what looked an easy catch off Bill Johnston. There was a groan of agony, which changed to a roar of happiness when McCool dropped it. There was much speculation and a great deal of head-shaking over this. Did McCool drop it deliberately? Or on the other hand did he try quite as hard as he might have done? It is something we will never know, but the fact remained that Bradman was undefeated, and he went on to make his 117th century in first-class cricket.

After getting his century Bradman felt, apparently, that he had been playing long enough and he made every effort to lose his wicket. He gave another chance at 108 but Lindwall missed the catch. He was 123, and after scoring 15 off one over from Dooland he skied a ball over square leg, and this time Neil Harvey held the catch.

Bradman had to force his way to the dressing room, and the cheering was as prolonged as when he first walked to the wicket. Few cricketers have received anything like it at the M.C.G.

There was a lot of fun and some very good cricket in that match. There were centuries from Ken Meuleman, Arthur Morris, Lindsay Hassett and a marvellous 146 not out from Don Tallon in 123 minutes. Sid Barnes made 89 runs in 59 minutes, including 11 fours and two sixes. There was the occasion after lunch when Ian Johnson went to bowl his first ball and Sid Barnes pulled a toy bat, only 12 inches long, from his pocket. Another time Hamence swopped the cricket ball for a tennis ball, but these were diversions; the cricket was serious enough.

The finish was a thriller. Bradman's team had to make 402 runs in the second innings to win. With 10 minutes to go, 9 wickets were down and 20 runs still needed. Tallon batted brilliantly, and before the last ball was bowled the difference was only two. The bowler ran in. Tallon pushed the ball away for a comfortable two, probably three. The fieldsmen all urged him to give the third a go, but Tallon just looked at them cunningly, grinned and said: "You won't suck me in that way," then promptly walked off the field.

When he reached the dressing room he boasted: "They tried to play me for a sucker out there. Tried to get me to run a third so they could run me out. But I fooled them and played it safe. Don't know what sort of dill they must think I am!"

Whereupon Don Bradman remarked drily: "That extra run would have given us a win. Still, a tie is a good result." "What!" exploded Tallon, "were the scores level fair dinkum?" It took quite some time to convince the by now hapless Tallon that they really were!

Never before had there been a testimonial like it in Australia. Melbourne Cricket Club members gave £728, there was a further donation of £450 from the Club. Then along with the proceeds of the benefit match, and donations from the various State Associations, Bradman ultimately received a cheque for £9342.

Very soon after this the news came through in the New Year Honours. On January 1, 1949, he was knighted by the King to become Sir Donald Bradman. He was in Melbourne at the time for a Board of Control meeting, and when the reporters called him very early he was in bed at the Hotel Windsor. His telephone did not stop ringing all morning.

In these years Test matches came thick and fast to the eternal interruption of District and Sheffield Shield Cricket. For the 1950-51 season F. R. Brown brought a team to Australia. It was astonishing that his last visit to Australia was in 1932-33 with Jardine's team, and now 18 years had gone by. W. G. Grace did the same thing. He came out in 1873-74 and did not return again until 18 years later in 1891-92. Australia was not so confident about the outcome of this series. Bradman, Sid Barnes and Bill Brown all had retired. As far as Bradman was concerned it was like a Hollywood studio trying to find a replacement for Clark Gable. Would the crowds come to see his successor?

Six Victorians were in the team for the First Test—Lindsay Hassett, Ian Johnson, Bill Johnston, Neil Harvey, Sam Loxton and Jack Iverson.

Jack Iverson's selection was the news. He was 35, and when the reporters went around to see him, he confessed that he had never seen a Test match. His rapid rise had been one of the strangest stories in cricket. He said: "Actually I hadn't even thought of cricket at all until 1946. For some reason or other I wandered along to the Brighton Sub-district ground one evening and asked if I could get a game. After that things happened quickly; I got a game with the thirds, and before long I found myself in the first eleven. And all the time I was wondering when they were going to wake up and kick me out of the team. I just never dreamed that I would make Test cricket."

Iverson was a sergeant in Ninth Division, where he served in the Middle East and New Guinea. As a bowler he was a freak. He gained incredible spin by flicking the ball from between his doubled-back middle finger and thumb. He first got the idea from twiddling a table tennis ball while playing miniature cricket in Army huts and tents when he was overseas with the A.I.F. Later, he experimented, spinning a tennis ball and then a cricket ball.

With the Brighton thirds he took 26 wickets at an average of 5. In the next season he took 79 wickets at an average of 10, and not unnaturally Melbourne invited him to play with them for the 1948-49 season. He took his first 38 wickets at an average of 8.9, and he was chiefly responsible for the club winning the premiership that season. In the match against Collingwood he took seven wickets for six runs off 53 balls. He was a freak, but he could put the ball down where he wanted.

He was the mystery bowler for the new Test series, and as a result there was a good deal of scepticism in England. Just before the First Test the *Daily Graphic* sports editor, Stephen Fagan, wrote that wild reports and rumours always circulated to bemuse and bewilder the Englishmen whenever England was playing Australia at cricket.

He said: "The latest is Iverson, whose feats around Melbourne—so they tell us—surpass even the Indian rope trick. It is all part of the Australian nerve war on our youngsters. There is no doubt that Australians pride themselves they can kid us. Now the Australian soothsayers are without a Bradman, we may naturally expect them to turn elsewhere. They seize on Jack Iverson. I don't suppose Captain Freddie Brown feels the least alarmed."

There was perhaps a little truth in this, yet Iverson topped the averages for the Australians with 21 wickets at an average of 15.23. His day of days was in Sydney, when he smashed England's second innings in the Third Test with 6 wickets for 27 runs. His bag included Hutton, Washbrook, Simpson and Freddie Brown. This was the day that Neville Cardus wrote his article which was headed, "I eat my words about Jack Iverson."

Look for a drawcard? Dr Billy Graham, with 130,000 inside the M.C.G. and another 4,000 trying to get in.

Left
Frank Worrell and G. E. Gomez, of the West Indies in a Melbourne 'tickertape' farewell . . . probably the most touching tribute ever paid to a sporting team.

Right
The greatest crowd in Test cricket
history: 90,800 at the M.C.G. on 11
February 1961, the Fifth Test against
the West Indies.

Right
Albert Cuttriss, Assistant Secretary,
1946–1963.

Australia won the First Test at Brisbane by 70 runs. The Second Test was at the M.C.G. There was a great gathering of cricketers and ex-cricketers in Melbourne. Among them was Harold Larwood, now resident in Sydney. It was interesting to note how fortunes changed. The Larwood of 1950 was almost grey, and looked upon with great affection in Australia. He came to Melbourne to write for one of the newspapers, and the reporters took him to the Supreme Court Hotel, where for years his cricket boots had been hanging in the bar, labelled simply, "Harold Larwood's Boots." There were those who were not wholly convinced they were the real thing. Now was the time to prove it.

They were his all right; the very boots he used in the Second Test at Melbourne in 1933. "There's no doubt about it," he said. "They're my boots. I ought to remember them. I dragged the toecap nearly off at a critical stage of the match. Then I borrowed George Duckworth's. They suffered the same fate. They also took all the skin off my toes. I had to grin and bear it. The crowd wasn't exactly on my side at the time."

Hassett, just as he had done in Brisbane, won the toss at Melbourne. Brown called "tails," but his luck was way out. Jack Fingleton went so far as to report that the coin rolled almost flat on its tail, then suddenly it decided to turn the other way. Lindsay Hassett said: "It's no use, Freddie. We have a cross-eyed Chinaman who's taken up permanent residence in our dressing room."

This was a match of tumbling wickets. Australia was expected to make a huge score, but by stumps the side was all out for 191. Lindsay Hassett had been the only man who even looked like a batsman. He made 52. But Alec Bedser was formidable this day. He had a perfect length with a late swing, usually inwards to right-handers and outwards for the left-handers, Morris and Harvey. The old-timers in the Members' Stand were a little like maiden aunts. They asked the question: "Who is he like?" Some felt he was like Maurice Tate. Others preferred to go back nearly 40 years and they said here was another Sid Barnes, which was the greatest compliment an old-timer could make. Bedser took 4 for 37. England was in the best position for 10 years, but next day the side was all out for 197 and Jack Iverson, like Bedser, took 4 for 37. And that was the pattern for the match. In the second innings Australia made 181 and England 150—an Australian victory by 28 runs. If only someone on the English side had decided to cut loose and have a hit then victory surely would have been theirs.

It was proving a very strange series. In two Test matches 74 wickets had fallen for only 979 runs, an average of a little over 13. One newspaper remarked: "Thank goodness! At last something is cheap in Australia—

wickets." Yet what was wrong? A mere 979 runs! Why, in the old days that had been a score for one innings. Had pitches changed? Bill Vanthoff, the M.C.G. Curator, said this was a typical pitch prepared in the old style. Was the bowling better, then? Perhaps, but many of the experts, and the older experts in particular, felt that batting was not as good as it used to be.

By the Fifth Test England was four Tests down and Freddie Brown won the toss only on one occasion and that was in Sydney. A week before the Fifth Test he attended an Empire Society meeting. He was the guest of honour and the president offered him a double-headed penny. Brown looked at it very sadly. "No good." he said, "I always call 'tails.' " He tried his system of calling "tails" once more for the Fifth Test and the coin came down "heads."

At no time was Australia impressive in the Fifth Test. Indeed, many people felt that this match was the turning point for English cricket. Reg Simpson made a glorious 156 not out. He took the control of the game right out of the hands of the bowlers and fieldsmen, something that had not happened before in the series. Alec Bedser took 5 for 46 in the first innings and 5 for 59 in the second innings. He was the destroyer, the man who constantly tied up the Australian batting.

So England won by eight wickets. It is not difficult to imagine the excitement. The date was February 28, 1951, and it was England's first victory in a Test match against Australia since 1938. The *Sun News-Pictorial* reported:

> People streamed from all parts of the ground to the front of the dressing rooms and stood in a tight mass chanting "We want Brown. We want Hassett."
>
> Cheers greeted both captains as they mounted the stairway above the rooms and spoke from the Grey Smith Stand.
>
> The match ended in high comedy. Twice all the stumps were snatched by the eager players before the winning run was scored. The fun began when Hassett took the ball with England only needing four runs to win. After Compton and Hutton took singles from normal deliveries Hassett threw up a tremendous donkey drop. Compton slashed hard, but the ball went only a short distance from the wicket. Compton waved back his partner, Len Hutton, who had already grabbed a stump from the bowler's end.
>
> Hassett tossed up another high slow ball, but again Compton did not connect properly and again Hutton had to throw down a stump which he had snatched as Hassett bowled. The umpires had to recover stumps from fieldsmen and set up wickets again before Hutton hit the next ball from Hassett slowly to leg and trotted the last run. Long before he reached the other end all the stumps were missing and players were scrambling for bails.

All the stump pulling and all the fun were partly due to Hassett and Hutton.

They had plotted together before Hassett came on to bowl the last over, and they agreed to share the spoils.

Compton actually ran the last run waving a stump in the air. Contrary to the rules of the Marylebone Cricket Club, perhaps, but who cared, this was a victory for England at last.

The *Herald* had a poster which said just that: "ENGLAND WINS AT LAST."

Len Hutton dominated the English batting with 553 runs at an average of 88.8. Trevor Bailey topped the bowling with 14 wickets at an average of 14.1 runs, but Alec Bedser was the real star with 30 wickets, average 16.1. In previous tours only Larwood with 33 wickets and Tate with 38 had done better.

Keith Miller headed the Australian batting with 350 runs, average 43.7, and Jack Iverson the bowling, 21 wickets, average 15.23. This was Iverson's only series against England.

The 1950-51 series were among the happiest of all against England, and particularly happy were the pictures of Freddie Brown that appeared on the front pages of the newspapers on the last day. There he was, grinning from ear to ear, that white scarf he always wore around his neck, and he was making the Churchill victory sign.

During the 1951-52 season the West Indian side under John Goddard came to Australia. At times there was a freshness and a gaiety in their cricket as if they were performing at an Annual Picnic. They had, too, the natural ability of born athletes, but so often at critical stages they failed to push through their advantages. One couldn't describe it as "dropping the bundle"; it was an open-handed tossing away of the game. With the iron-fisted attitude of a Bradman or a Jardine behind them they would have won the series instead of just the one Test match.

The best Test match of all was the Fourth Test at the M.C.G. One newspaper described it as "The Test match of the century." This was rather a bold claim. There were some excellent Test matches with the West Indians still to come in the current century, but it had all the ingredients that Hollywood tries to build into its vast Biblical dramas. There was no shedding of blood, you understand, but the drama was there, and hour by hour it worked steadily and surely towards a vast climax.

The preliminaries were excellent, like the 108 by Worrell, Miller's five wickets for 60 runs, Harvey's 83, John Trim's 5 for 34, and then the last day, January 3, 1952. What a day! First one side, then the other, seemed to be on the brink of victory. Australia started the morning needing 192 runs to win.

Wickets fell like autumn leaves. Only Lindsay Hassett, the Australian captain, was able to stay put, and as long as he was there an Australian win seemed possible. He nibbled away steadily and with monumental patience he made 102 runs in 5½ hours; his first Test century on the M.C.G. Then he went also, and the West Indies were on top. Langley's visit to the wicket was just a short walk in the afternoon sunshine, and now came the last partnership, Bill Johnston and Doug Ring.

The score was 222 and Australia still needed 37 runs. What hope was there? The policemen thought there was very little. They moved inside the arena all ready for the crowd that soon would jump the fence.

"I'll stop here," said Johnston. "You have a hit Doug." "O.K., Bill," said Ring.

Goddard had a conference with his bowlers, and meanwhile there was some special cheering from a section of the crowd. No doubt it was lost on the West Indians, because here at the wicket were the two representatives from the Richmond Club, and there were cries, "Come on the Tigers—Eat 'em alive."

Soon the Tigers were in action. They stole cheeky singles. They cared nothing at all for the reputations of the spinners Ramadhin and Valentine, and there was one glorious over when Ring boosted Valentine's average by 13 runs.

The score mounted to 250—9 behind, 10 to win. The tension was hard to bear. It was almost like that day at the Oval on August 29, 1886, when a gentleman in the pavilion severely bit the handle of his umbrella. Goddard called another conference of his bowlers. What plot was he hatching?

There were some terrible moments, for example, when Guillen made an unsuccessful appeal for a caught behind, again when Valentine fell flat on his back after a wild throw at the wicket in an attempt to remove Ring.

Four runs to go and the batsmen had a conference. Said Doug: "If Worrell pitches a rising ball on the off stump give it some curry. It might go for four."

Said Bill: "Oh, let's get them in singles."

And that's what they did. Ring straight-pushed Worrell for a single to tie at 259. There were cries of "Come on the Tigers." Then amid silence Worrell bowled again. Johnston turned him for a single and the cheers swept the ground. The West Indians rushed down the wicket to congratulate the batsmen.

Johnston and Ring walked ahead into the pavilion with the crowd of 30,000 clapping them all the way. They deserved every clap they got.

When Bill reached the dressing room Lindsay Hassett said: "Well done. How do you feel?"

Bill modestly replied that he felt pretty good, whereupon Lindsay said, "How did you feel when you went out to bat? With the whole fate of the side and the series on your shoulders? Were you very nervous?"

"Nervous?" replied an indignant Johnston. "Don't be so damn silly. When I went out I knew we didn't have a chance!"

There was no break from Test matches. Next year there was the visit of Jack Cheetham and his Springboks. When they arrived at Perth, the Australian newspapers at once expressed their sympathy for these poor South Africans. There were few big names—no Dudley Nourse, no Eric Rowan. This was the youngest, most inexperienced touring side ever to come to the country. Nobody questioned their enthusiasm or their courage, but it was well known that South Africans treated their cricket in a light-hearted picnic fashion. Yet these young men intended to pit themselves against the formidable, battle-hardened Australians, who had not lost a Test series since the days of Jardine and Larwood. It would surprise no one if the tour lost £5000 or more.

Never was a tour so underestimated. Before two Tests had gone by they had the selectors sadly rattled, and they all but won the series. The final score was two Tests won, two lost and one drawn.

There was nothing lighthearted about Jack Cheetham. He was like Harry Hopman training young tennis players. Certainly he did not fine them for little misdemeanours, but he did everything else. There were pep talks every morning, training runs, and practice, practice, practice. Even when the weather was too wet for batting he had his men out at fielding practice. Golf was banned for the tour because Jack Cheetham felt that the swing of the golf club might interfere with the swing of the bat.

Furthermore, there were no late nights. After the South Africans won the Second Test a Melbourne newspaper sent a reporter to their hotel to get pictures of the victory celebrations, but there were none. The South Africans were going to bed early to prepare for the next encounter.

The Second and Fifth Test matches were played at the M.C.G., both won by South Africa. Many, many times have English captains criticised Melbourne crowds, but this was a curious situation. For both Tests one would have thought that the entire crowd had been imported from Cape Town. The spectators seemed to be yearning for a South African victory, and on both occasions they were very happy when they got it.

In the Second Test Hugh Tayfield proved that he was one of the world's finest bowlers by taking a total of 13 wickets for 165 runs, but it was the fielding and the catching of the South Africans that made the game so memorable. The big day of catches took place during Australia's first innings.

Hugh Tayfield took the wicket of Arthur Morris with one of the greatest caught and bowled ever seen on the M.C.G. Morris hit the ball with such power that it should have crashed the fence. But Jack Cheetham, who was fielding only eight yards from the bat, put his hand over his head and took the pace off the ball, and it rebounded off his hand towards mid-off. Tayfield, recovering quickly from his bowling, sprinted and caught the ball just inches off the ground. Cheetham in dismissing Harvey brought off a superb one-handed catch at silly point. McDonald fell to a fine catch taken above the fieldsman's head, and then Endean caught Miller high above his head from a ball that appeared to be passing over the fence. It is doubtful if four such outstanding catches have been taken in a single day on the M.C.G.

South Africa won by 82 runs. The Melbourne *Herald's* London correspondent filed a most interesting cable: "Britain's big news is the grin. It is the biggest, most spontaneous, most universal grin of modern times. All England cannot stop grinning because a scratch team of South African cricketers mowed down mighty Australia. The commentators are still gulping for breath. The cartoonists recovering theirs, are running riot with the old gentlemen in the clubs—'Bay gad, sir, because I remember the last time they beat them, it doesn't necessarily follow that I was an intimate of Dr. Grace."

For the Fifth Test Australia lost its opening barrage—both Lindwall and Miller were unfit. Geoff Noblet and Ron Archer took their places. But the colourful name in the eleven was that of 17-year-old Ian Craig. It could almost be said that a wave of popular opinion had forced him into the side. Indeed, if Mr. Menzies, during the then recent elections, had gone to the country on the platform of Craig for the Tests, he would have won even more votes.

Apart from Craig's astonishing ability he seemed to have everything. On all occasions when he was interviewed he was modest, respectful and for a 17-year-old remarkably articulate. Nothing seemed to go to his head. When selected for the Test side he said: "I'm still going to be a chemist—I want some security in life." But his youth, that was the thing. Australians love success in the very young, and there seemed to be something very romantic about a 17-year-old playing in a Test side. The selectors were rebuked for the stodginess when he was merely 12th man for the Fourth Test.

Yet his record showed he was ready for Test matches. Even at the age of 11 he was a batting prodigy. At that time he played for Mosman's D grade team in the Sydney Northern Suburbs competition. Graeme Hole, though four years older, was captain of this team. It was odd that Craig ousted his former captain to win a place in this Fifth Test match. His sudden elevation to fame came when he made 213 not out for New South Wales against the South Africans.

Keith Miller was one of the few to strike a note of warning. He said: "Many critics have said that Craig was better than the Don at the same age. Perhaps they are right. But remembering the almost unbelievable feats performed by Bradman, it immediately puts this unassuming lad from Mosman in an unenviable position of having to rip off massive scores in every innings. Rather than link Craig with Bradman at the moment, let's be fair to him and say he has an extraordinarily bright future, but not impress upon him the fantastic feats of Bradman as a goal."

Australia batted first, and at the end of the first day everything seemed to be most satisfactorily sewn up. The score was 2 wickets for 246 runs. Arthur Morris had been in the horrors for some time, but when he was 99 he made one of the most delightful gestures seen in the game.

Morris was run out by an impetuous call from Neil Harvey, who dashed for a doubtful run after hitting a ball between point and cover. Morris did not respond until Harvey was half-way down the pitch and John Watkins had moved smartly from cover and fielded the ball cleanly. Morris, of course, could have stayed exactly where he was. He was within one run of his 11th Test century at a time when many people were wondering whether all his former greatness as a batsman was behind him.

When he saw that Harvey had no chance of going back he trotted out of his crease and sacrificed his wicket. Harvey hung his head down as Morris turned towards the pavilion. It was a gesture that will be remembered far longer than big scores, yet too much blame should not be placed on Harvey. If Morris had moved the instant that Harvey called, who knows, maybe he would have got home.

Harvey was 25 not out, but here he went on to make 205 in 295 minutes, an aggressive, glorious display of free hitting. Hassett was run out for 40 and Ian Craig was the next man in. He had waited all the day before and now for 35 minutes he had sat there padded up, ready to go. He showed no sign of nerves as he walked quickly to the wicket. As the batsmen passed each other, Hassett said, "Good luck, Ian."

His first scoring shot was a four—a glorious cover drive off the fourth ball he received. Four times in the first half-hour he sent the ball to the fence, and for a while he rivalled Harvey as a quick scorer. He slowed down before he reached his half-century, then at 53 he was out to a catch in the covers.

As the newspapers pointed out, it was a fine debut in big cricket. The young chemist had the right prescription.

Australia made 520, and it was an incredible feat that the South Africans could make 435 and eventually go on to win the Test match. In Australia's second innings only Ian Craig with 47 made a respectable score.

On the last day South Africa made a death or glory bid for victory. When South Africa was tottering, four down for 191, Roy McLean took charge, and he started to hit. The excitement was so great it was reported that four chauffeur-driven cars drew up outside the gates and the occupants RAN into the Members' Stand.

McLean helped himself to fours galore—14 in all—and he scored 76 in 80 minutes to give South Africa victory by six wickets. It was a very happy finish to a remarkable cricket tour. Neil Harvey was the outstanding Australian— 834 runs for an average of 92.7. Hugh Tayfield was the outstanding South African. He took 30 wickets in the five Tests, and his tally of 70 wickets in first-class games was a record by a visiting bowler.

The *Sun News-Pictorial* summed up the tour this way: "The young South African team came to Australia to learn. They will go away at least the peers, if not the masters, of their teachers. More than that, they have given us the very salutary lesson that it takes something besides mere cricket to win Test matches."

The tide had turned, an era in cricket was over. In 1953 Lindsay Hassett took a team to England for a damp season in that country. Four Test matches were drawn and Australia lost the final Test at The Oval. Colin McDonald was the only M.C.C. representative, but he had yet to learn the technique that was to make him such a reliable opening batsman, and something happened to Ian Craig. Perhaps it was the over-powering attention he received from the moment he arrived, the unceasing pressure of the television interviewers, the reporters from the glossy magazines and the cricket writers who observed his every action. He never got going. His confidence went utterly, and he returned with the sad total of 429 runs made at an average of 16.5. He was never quite the same batsman again.

Even as the Tests were being played, planning was under way for the greatest Royal Tour yet, the visit of Queen Elizabeth and Prince Philip in February-March, 1954. The planning for the children's display on the Melbourne Cricket Ground started in July. The experts had to work out plans which would allot a position for each of the 17,000 children who would appear on the ground. For weeks members of the physical education staff were out on the ground with measuring sticks and charts. The Government supplied 70,000 yards of materials for costumes, all of which had to be cut, dyed and sewn for the day.

On February 24 Queen Elizabeth and Prince Philip arrived at Essendon aerodrome, and nearly a million people lined the route from the aerodrome to Government House to welcome the Royal Party. All Victorian school children under 15 received a medal from the State Government and 346,000 were distributed.

The visit did wonderful things for the city. It was cleaned and painted from end to end. Wherever the Queen was to travel the road was made perfect, as if it had always been that way. For fear that the Queen might slip on the steps of Parliament House the Government spent £20,000 to make them as new.

It was like the Centenary, a remarkable time to be in Melbourne. Melbourne is a very loyal city, but with such a young and handsome couple in town, they had to be seen, and some people went to extraordinary lengths to do it. They would sit on the pavement with rugs and thermos flasks all night, and the weather was fine for sitting. Some people reported that they saw the Queen as often as 16 to 20 times. There were some keen competitions there. One woman unashamedly told the newspapers that while she was out looking at the Queen her children went without a bath for a week and they ate cold meat every day.

There were two visits to the Melbourne Cricket Ground. On February 25 there was the gathering of men and women's ex-service organisations. Her Majesty and Prince Philip drove around the arena in a Land Rover, then they walked through a veterans' guard of honour, where they looked at an exhibition by marching girls and a tableau by Junior Legatees.

But the big day was the demonstration by 17,000 children organised by the Education Department. There had been rehearsals beforehand and over 250 transport buses had been used to bring the children to the ground. However, on March 4 the Tramways Board had to lay on every available tram and bus. The official attendance was 92,438, and the *Herald* described the occasion as "The greatest yell in all our history." The parkland outside the M.C.G. looked like a huge secondhand dealer's shop. The ground was covered with little heaps of children's clothing and belongings.

As the Royal cars approached the ground an official said over the loudspeakers, "Children, this is the moment you have waited for for a long time." When the Queen and Duke arrived they saw all the children on the arena. Thousands formed a huge "WELCOME," while thousands more formed a border around the living greeting. They performed to a series of whistle blasts. One moment they lay flat on the ground, then as the whistle screeched they sat up and the "WELCOME" seemed to jump out of the ground.

There was a gymnastic display by senior girls and a maypole dance performed by 1400 10-year-old boys and girls. The Queen laughed when, at a signal, thousands of smiling girls' faces peeped out from between the maypole scarves.

The Queen and the Duke toured the ground in the Land Rover, and at times they were in the centre of a wildly cheering mass. They overstayed their scheduled time at the ground by 25 minutes. As for the proud parents in the grandstands, if they ever imagined that they would be able to pick out Tommy or Mary on the ground they had little chance. The Welcome letters were huge and there were only a few yards to spare at either end. There were 116 children in the letter W alone, standing eight abreast.

It was one of the best organised and easily the most spectacular function during Melbourne's Royal Visit. The Duke had another function that day at the University, which was a little less conventional. He was ragged by the students. Among other things, he was presented with a hand of the Martin Place clock, Sydney. The hand was taken by Sydney University students during the Commencement rag the previous year and had now been replaced with a new one. The co-editor of *Farrago,* Ian Siggins, told the Duke that he made the presentation on behalf of the Faculty of Oxometrical Science—the science of unscrewing the inscrutable.

It was the last full day in Melbourne before the Royal couple left on their tour of Victoria. The Melbourne Cricket Club made Prince Philip an Honorary Life Member. The President, Dr. W. C. McClelland, presented him with the gold Life Member's Badge.

In 1954 the triumphant England team, the holder of the Ashes, came to Australia. Len Hutton was the captain, and it was billed as the best team since the bodyline era. And there were similarities—here was a team that was laced with pace. Bedser apart, there was Statham, Tyson, Loader and Bailey.

The awesome propaganda about Frank Tyson arrived in the early spring. Typhoon Tyson was the fastest bowler in the world. He was a school teacher and, although kindly in the classroom, he was a terror on the cricket field. It was rumoured that he had the longest run-up in cricket, and the cartoonists frequently had depicted him as starting that run from somewhere behind the turnstiles. There was no need to question the fact that he was fast. The Australians saw him at Northampton on the 1953 tour. It was obvious then that he was the coming bowler, and Arthur Morris said that the first two overs that Tyson bowled to him were the fastest he faced on the entire tour.

The English newspapermen relished these nicknames, and it was almost like a return to the eighteen-eighties when we had "The Demon" Spofforth. "Fearsome Freddie" Trueman just escaped selection, but, of course, there was "Typhoon" Tyson and on several occasions Brian Statham was called "Hate-'Em" Statham. The Australian newspapermen valiantly tried to retaliate, but they were at a disadvantage. There was little one could do with names like Ray Lindwall and Keith Miller. Admittedly Lindwall sometimes was called "Killer," but nothing sufficiently euphonious could be devised to fit the occasion.

However, Miller and Lindwall had their own methods for inspiring terror. Lindwall was an expert at this, particularly before he bowled the first ball to Hutton. He would delay matters several minutes just to put the opposition ill at ease. While Hutton waited at the crease, Ray would limber up. He would jog back and forth to loosen his muscles. He would make a trial run up and swing his arm over several times. He made such a thing of his little physical training exercises that one almost expected him to get down on the wicket and do several push ups. With Miller it was more the look of defiance, the swagger, the way he would let his hair fall down on his face and then toss it back over his head. Occasionally a crusty gentleman in the Pavilion would remark: "That fellow would bowl a damned sight better if he had his hair cut."

By the Third Test at the Melbourne Cricket Ground the score was one all, and the strain was on. Len Hutton was tired and nervy, and on the morning of the first day he seemed far from well. He had to face the worst problem of his career—what to do with Alec Bedser? He was 36, he had missed the Sydney Test, his best bowling was behind him, and with the Statham-Tyson attack he was no longer necessary. It wasn't until 40 minutes before the start of play that Hutton was able to make the final decision to leave him out.

According to one English cricketer Bedser did not know that he was to be dropped until Len Hutton pinned the team list on the dressing room door. There was no easing of the pain by explaining the situation beforehand. Yet he must have known that he had little chance, and some of the English newspapermen, who like to put things in dramatic terms, already were predicting his end. One wrote: "It looks like the passing of a great champion. I just cannot see Alec Bedser being chosen for the Third Test. The greatness that was his—oh, such a short time ago—is now associated with memory, not present-day fact." But Alec was very popular with the Australians, and they were sad to see him left out. Many thought he was the best bowler ever to be left out of a cricket team.

207

Australia started superbly by routing England for 191. Ron Archer took 4 for 33, but it was Keith Miller who did the real damage. He had Hutton for 12, Edrich for 4 and Compton for 4. His nine overs before lunch, when he took 3 wickets for 5, were something to see, Keith Miller inspired, turning on everything from high-speed bowling to spinners. It was Colin Cowdrey who saved the situation. He made 102, and it was doubtful if he will ever forget the burden that was on his shoulders this day.

At stumps on the Saturday night Australia was 8 wickets down for 188. Len Maddocks and Ian Johnson were showing several of the star batsmen just how to stand up to the speed of Tyson and Statham. On the Sunday all Australia was perspiring under a heat wave. At Port Augusta in South Australia the temperature was 116 degrees. The worst bushfires for nine years were burning in Victoria's Western District, and 14 houses burned down between Casterton and Bairnsdale. Melbourne had a frightful day. The temperature rose to 105 degrees and there was no let-up even later. The hot day changed into one of those sweltering, writhing nights, and in an attempt to escape the heat thousands slept on the beaches. The temperature at midnight was 96, the hottest night in Melbourne's history. Meanwhile London was in the midst of a freeze. Roy Ulyett did a lovely cartoon for the *Daily Express.* There was snow piled against the window. Inside there was a bescarved shivering couple at the breakfast table. Father was reading the Test scores. Mother said: "Don't bother about the score, read me the bits about the baking sun and temperatures rising to 105 degrees."

Early on Monday morning Ian Johnson, the Australian captain, and Arthur Morris, his deputy, walked out to the wicket to see about the rolling. They looked in amazement. On Saturday evening the wicket had been tired and battle-scarred; already it had been lined with cracks. But now the cracks were healed. It was smooth and clean, like a new wicket. Johnson scraped the pitch with his boot and said: "Arthur, this wicket has been watered. We'd better keep quiet about this." Morris agreed. However, they reported what they had seen to Jack Ledward, Secretary of the V.C.A., and the Board of Control.

However, no one could ever keep this quiet. Soon the Englishmen were out on the ground, standing around this impish creature, the pitch, studying it as closely as if it were a picture of their wives or their girl friends.

All day there were hints and insinuations, then next morning the news broke. One newspaper came out and said definitely, "The Test wicket has been watered." The Melbourne *Sun News-Pictorial* said: "Did something extraordinary happen to the M.C.G. pitch for the Third Test during the weekend? Players of both teams were amazed that cracks in the pitch, which they expected to widen during Sunday's heat, were smaller yesterday than on Saturday. They were surprised to find that the pitch showed distinct signs of dampness and that it was marked by their boot sprigs at the start of play. From the first ball bowled it was apparent that the wicket was much slower than on Saturday."

The cables too were humming. Frank Rostron wrote in the *Daily Express*: "Has anyone been monkeying with the pitch? If so—and rumour suggested it —it is an illegal and horrifying act. We should have one of Test cricket's major scandals on our hands."

Vernon Ransford, Secretary of the M.C.C., said he was confident that neither Mr. Jack House, who had charge of preparation of the wicket, nor anybody else had watered the wicket. From the end of play at 6 p.m. on Saturday until Monday morning the wicket was under surveillance, he said. A night watchman guarded it during the Test, and was on duty on Saturday and Sunday night. Furthermore, on the Sunday there were cleaners working all around the ground. They at once would have seen anyone watering the wicket.

He added: "The honour of the Melbourne Cricket Club is at stake in this. I am bewildered and worried. I intend to confer with Dr. McClelland, the President, about an inquiry."

And there was an inquiry. At one stage the Australian Board of Control considered a suggestion that if Australia won the Test it would offer to replay the match because of the suspicions about the wicket. Everyone at the ground was questioned, and on top of this the curator, Mr. W. Vanthoff, Mr. House and the night watchman swore statutory declarations before Dr. McClelland and Mr. J. A. Seitz, president of the V.C.A., that the pitch had not been watered.

The assistant secretary of the M.C.C., Mr. Albert Cuttriss, made this statement: "After a searching inquiry, the Melbourne Cricket Club and the Victorian Cricket Association emphatically deny that the pitch or any portion of the ground has been watered since the commencement of the Third Test match on December 31."

Nor did it end there. Two leading civil engineers, Mr. G. D. Aitchison, senior research officer, division of soils, of the Commonwealth Scientific and Industrial Research Organisation, and Mr. D. H. Trollope, senior lecturer in civil engineering, Melbourne University, gave an opinion. They believed it was all the result of "sweating" under the covers on Sunday night. They explained that with the hot sun of the Sunday the top of the wicket dried to a hard crust, and the moisture underneath tended naturally to go down to

209

colder, lower regions. "Then early on Monday morning, when the cool change came, a reversal of the temperature conditions occurred, so that vapour movement was from warm subsoil to the cold surface. With the covers over the wicket, moisture loss by evaporation would have been greatly restricted. Thus an accumulation of moisture in the soil surface would result, and the dry crust would disappear. The consequent swelling of the clay and closing of the cracks led to the recovery of the wicket."

In Mildura, the hot border town on the Murray, greenkeepers and bowls players thought it a great joke. They couldn't understand why nobody had realised that dew could have been responsible for the condition of the wicket following the great fall in temperature in Melbourne on Sunday night.

The night playing of bowls in Mildura had taught the greenkeepers that an amazing amount of water came out of the turf when there was a sudden change after a hot period. And the cool change in Melbourne had meant a temperature drop of 30 or 40 degrees.

Earlier it looked like becoming a great scandal, but the irony of it was that a reformed pitch could only favour England. Although Maddocks hung on for 47 runs and Ian Johnson for 33, Australia was all out for 231 runs at 12.53 p.m. Then England had all afternoon on this dead wicket. They made 279, including 91 from Peter May. By the last day the wicket was almost back to its former state, when Australia with an appalling exhibition of batting was crucified.

Typhoon Tyson now richly deserved his awesome title. In 51 devastating balls he took six wickets for 16 runs. His total for the innings was 7 for 27. Australia was all out for 111 and the Test was lost by 128 runs. England was cock-a-hoop. The London newspapers had the headlines: TYSON THE MAGNIFICENT. The *Evening News:* "Not even an auctioneer could have dealt more rapidly with the assorted batting lots than Tyson. The Australian batting was woeful."

The *Evening Standard:* "One of the greatest bowling feats in Test cricket history goes down into the records. This six-footer—harmless-looking, with student mien until he bowls—bowled like one possessed. The much-discussed wicket served us well."

The Star: "Not for years have I seen such a brilliant spell of controlled fast bowling as put up by Tyson. Tyson is England's greatest match-winning bowler since Larwood."

At the finish crowds ran to the centre of the ground and secured precious lumps of the controversial wicket to keep as souvenirs for all time. Then the groundsmen came out, and while the spectators stood all about as if they were paying their last respects at the grave of a dear friend, they turned on the hoses. Soon the centre of the ground was a vast lake, and it could be said by all who saw it that this time the wicket was well and truly watered.

England won the Fourth Test in Adelaide to clinch the series. That evening the players had a marvellous celebration, where with their guests they uncorked at least 60 bottles of champagne. It would have been a party worth attending. This was the rain after a long, weary drought, England's first successful series in Australia since 1932.

CHAPTER EIGHTEEN

Olympic Year

IN THE long history of the Melbourne Cricket Ground the stirring 16 days in November 1956 would be among the most spectacular. For this was Olympic Year, and the M.C.G. was the focal point of it all, a time to be remembered with pleasure and pride.

Yet before the athletes could run out on to the cinder track so much had to happen. There were so many organisations involved, all of whom had different interests and believed strongly in different principles. The Melbourne Cricket Ground was far from being the only choice—there were the Showgrounds, Olympic Park, the Carlton Ground and even Albert Park.

Four years went by before there was a final decision for the M.C.G. in February 1953. Then there was so little time left, but the troubles were not over. A new stand for the Olympics at the M.C.G. had to be built with all possible speed, yet there were repeated strikes, and on one occasion no work was done for a month. In the finish it was agony for all concerned. There were serious doubts as to whether the M.C.G. would be ready in time, and the situation had all the drama of a heavy radio serial. Then there was the president of the International Olympic Committee, the millionaire Mr. Avery Brundage. He was always hovering in the background like a forbidding headmaster with a cane in his hand.

In the worst days it seemed that surely he would take away the Games from Melbourne.

The first approach to the Melbourne Cricket Ground Trustees came in November 1949. Many members were worried about the idea of having the Games at the M.C.G. The Crown Grant said that the land was especially granted *inter alia* "to be at all times maintained and used as and for a place for playing cricket . . . and when not required for cricket for such other purposes not inconsistent with the foregoing . . ." Admittedly for more than 100 years it had been used for every conceivable kind of sport, but this was something different. The ground could be out of use for a year or more and it could be utterly wrecked in the process.

The Olympic Games Organising Committee made it clear that the M.C.G.

Above
The Olympic Parade from high above the Yarra — a fine hour for the Melbourne Cricket Ground.

Left
"Just possibly the finest cricket museum": the cricket museum at the M.C.G.

The old Melbourne Cricket Club office in Jolimont Street, Jolimont.

The Queen Mother and M.C.C. secretary Ian Johnson, and Mrs Johnson, 1958.

would need to be perfectly flat to conform to Olympic requirements. Engineers looked at the arena and they found that there was a fall of 7 feet 6 inches from east to west. This meant virtually that they would have to tear away the whole surface of the ground. There were many other conditions, such as the building of an underground tunnel to the arena, with which it would have been impracticable for the M.C.G. to comply.

So the Trustees sent the letter to the M.C.C. Committee, which in April 1950, said it was sorry but it could not do these things and the M.C.G. Trustees agreed. Yet the ground was not refused altogether. The M.C.G. would be available as it was for any Olympic functions that could be held there.

The M.C.G. was dropped as a site for the Games and no further approach was made for 18 months, but this did not stop the public debate. Some said that the M.C.G. was far too large anyway, it wasn't an Olympic type arena and the spectators would be too far away from the athletes. Others said that if the M.C.G. had been mentioned in the original plan Melbourne would never have got the Games, and there was an incredible charge that this was a ground that had been tainted by professional sport. No amateur athlete would dare set foot there. Yet the amateur sporting bodies were not keen on the Showgrounds plan. It was an unlovely area and they could see such a stadium becoming a dreary post-Olympics white elephant. So the discussion inevitably came back to the M.C.G., and according to a Gallup Poll the public overwhelmingly wanted the Games there.

The Olympic Games organisers wrote in November 1951 and again asked for a regrading of the M.C.G. The negotiations lasted for three months, and the investigations were as thorough as they could be. Engineers gave their opinions, soil experts gave their opinions, grass experts gave their opinions, bores were taken in various sections of the arena to find out what was underneath and a report was made. There were conferences between the Trustees, the Committee, the V.F.L. and the V.C.A. Finally, in February 1952, the Committee of the Club adopted this resolution: "That this Committee considers on the information at its disposal, and having regard to the views expressed by the bodies with whom it has agreements, it would not be in the interests of the Melbourne Cricket Club, the Victorian Football League, the Victorian Cricket Association and the public to carry out the work required to hold the Games on the Melbourne Cricket Ground."

The Premier, Mr. McDonald, said that the Olympic Games would not be held on the M.C.G., and the decision was final. After an hour's talk with the Trustees he was convinced the decision not to make the M.C.G. available had been properly arrived at, and that the public would have to accept it.

213

Cr. E. L. Jones of Brighton wrote to the newspapers and said: "To cut up and practically destroy for many years the M.C.C. ground simply to use it for a few weeks for Olympic Games would be a national calamity. The ground is used by many hundreds of people during the year who derive great pleasure from cricket and football. I say straight out I am entirely opposed to the holding of these Games in Melbourne, because of the using of vast quantities of materials that are so urgently required in the building of homes."

Mr. Kent Hughes, the chairman of the Olympic Games organising committee, was bitter. He said: "Cricket interests have prevented the M.C.G., the finest arena in the Southern Hemisphere, from being used for the greatest sporting fixture known in the modern world. Cricket interests have been placed first by the arch-priests of cricket in Victoria, who apparently do not even know how to play the game."

The manoeuvring went on and on and on. Now St. Kilda Cricket Ground, Olympic Park and the Carlton Cricket Ground were the top contenders for the main stadium. Carlton won and the decision was approved by Olympic officials at the 1952 Games in Helsinki. Melbourne sighed with relief. It was as if a man had stopped talking after a 24-hour filibuster. Now there would be an end to all the arguments. One newspaper commented slyly that this was an interesting situation. After 1956 Melbourne would have two big sporting centres. The Carlton ground would have its bright Olympic Stadium and there was no doubt that with its superior charm many big sporting events would go there.

In December 1952 Mr. McDonald's Government went out and Mr. Cain's Labor Government came in. This little item appeared in one of the newspaper columns: "There's a lot of smoke about and around the question of transferring the Olympic Games back to the M.C.G. We're told to watch for some fire now the Labor Government is installed."

It was all too true. Soon it was obvious that Mr. Cain wanted to use the M.C.G. Mr. A. W. Coles, who was chairman of the Olympic Control Committee, was angry. He said that in 1949 at Rome the International Olympics Committee first approved the Showgrounds site. At Helsinki it approved the change to Carlton. If we tried another change we could virtually kiss the Games goodbye. He said that even Inigo Jones, the long-range weather forecaster, would not dare to forecast what would happen if we changed our plans again.

On January 22, 1953, there was a surprise move. The Premier, Mr. John Cain, had called on the M.C.C. President, Dr. McClelland, and asked him to reconsider the matter, as his Government had neither the desire nor the

214

money to finance another ground. The M.C.C. Committee held a special meeting and passed this resolution: "This Committee resolves to give whole-hearted support to the Government for the use of the Melbourne Cricket Ground for the Olympic Games in 1956 if the Government deems the same to be in the public interest and will prevent wasteful and unnecessary expenditure in staging the Games in 1956. This Committee will co-operate with the Premier in any steps which are deemed necessary to give effect to the above purpose."

One official said: "What has happened to all that expert advice that the M.C.G. was unsuitable for the Olympics? Someone answer me that."

On the surface the change did seem astonishing, but a great deal had happened and much hard work had been done since 1949. The Club was very fortunate in its two Honorary Consulting Engineers, Major-General Clive Steele and Mr. D. J. McClelland. In all they issued three reports. First, the Games Committee told the M.C.C. that the arena would have to be perfectly flat, which entailed such drainage problems that the engineers had to put in an unfavourable report. Eighteen months later, in November 1951, the Games Committee varied the conditions. The Games required a grade of not over 1 in 1000 along the course, and the engineers worked out a plan which met these conditions, and other slight modifications to the original stringent requirements. However, there was too much uncertainty about the time required for regrassing and restoring the ground, and the M.C.C., V.C.A. and V.F.L. all were worried about the long periods that the ground would be out of use. They stuck to their original decision.

But under the third plan, which meant filling in one side, levelling on the other, the Test wickets would be disturbed hardly at all, and by working the programme carefully in three stages only two cricket seasons and one football season would be affected. Furthermore, the Federal and State Governments and the Melbourne City Council agreed to pay the cost of grading the ground and restoring it once again for cricket and football. On top of this the State Government promised to guarantee a loan of £300,000 which the Club would require to borrow to build the new grandstand. In fact, it was necessary to increase this loan commitment first to £450,000 and finally to £500,000. These loans were negotiated by Mr. C. W. Simmonds with the Colonial Mutual Life Assurance Society Ltd.

The situation was still far from settled. There were many, particularly in Melbourne City Council, who felt that the Games should go to Carlton. Mr. Coles was adamant about Carlton. Mr. Lewis Luxton, one of the delegates to I.O.C., said: "I originally didn't care where we held the Games—we could

215

have built a roof on top of Flinders Street Station and held them there for that matter—but now we have decided on a site let us stick to it."

Then there was Mr. Avery Brundage. In a radio-telephone call from the New York Athletic Club he said: "Tell Melbourne to stop talking and get down to work. It is much too late to be changing the site of the main stadium now. If the site is changed, your chances of holding the Games will be not very good."

Yet Melbourne's bookmakers didn't feel that way. After the news that the M.C.G. was available the odds shortened. Before the betting was 2 to 1 on that Melbourne would lose the Games. Now it was 10 to 9.

It was the eleventh hour and something had to be done very quickly. On January 26, 1953, Mr. Cain called a Premier's Conference of all interested parties at the State Offices. There was an all-star cast. The Prime Minister, Mr. Menzies, was there. Also there was the Lord Mayor, Cr. Brens; Mr. Arthur Calwell, Chairman of the M.C.G. Trustees; Mr. Stanley Lewis, Q.C., Secretary of the Trustees; Sir Herbert Hyland; the representatives of the I.O.C., Mr. Lewis Luxton and Mr. Hugh Weir; Cr. Coleman, M.L.C.; Cr. Barry, M.L.A., and others; the Club was represented by Messrs. Simmonds, Chadwick and Ransford.

The discussions went on for days, and even on the last, February 2, there seemed to be less unanimity than when they started. Both Mr. Coles and Mr. Weir made last-minute attempts to prevent the Games from being switched from Carlton. Mr. Weir told the conference that he was convinced that a change of plan would be fatal to the holding of the Games in Melbourne.

It was the Premier, Mr. John Cain, who decided the issue. He told the meeting: "There is not room in Melbourne for two stadiums each with a capacity of 100,000 persons. They would be used for only about 12 days a year except when Test cricket was being played every four years. The income of the M.C.C. from the four football finals is £4700. It is proposed to spend £850,000 on a new stadium. From where will we obtain the interest on that money? Our successors will have to shoulder the burden forever."

Mr. Cain was asked, why then had he voted for the Carlton ground?

He replied: "I did so because the M.C.G. was not available. Then it was a case of 'Carlton or the bush', now it's a case of 'Melbourne or the bush'." And he added: "I do not intend to back and fill. If the Prime Minister and the Lord Mayor wish the Games to go to Carlton the Games can go there, without money from me. I will put the £300,000 into the building of schools and hospitals."

Mr. Menzies pointed out that if the State Government withdrew its support

216

for Carlton that was the end of it. The Committee could never raise the money for a stadium at Carlton.

Mr. Cain finished it with these words: "The Games can be held at Carlton so long as it is distinctly understood that the State Government does not make a contribution. The State Government will contribute for the Games to be held at the M.C.G."

There was no point in arguing further. Mr. Stanley Lewis put the resolution and Sir Herbert Hyland seconded: "That all parties to this conference undertake to give wholehearted support to the approval by the I.O.C. of the Melbourne Cricket Ground as the site for the Olympic Games 1956."

Some were still a little reluctant, but it was carried, and the wrangling of four years was over.

One serious worry remained. What would the headmaster say? There had been repeated warnings during the Premier's Conference that if the Olympic Committee switched to the M.C.G., Mr. Avery Brundage might take the Games from Melbourne. On February 23 there was a story in the newspapers that Mr. Brundage had written to Mr. Luxton and Mr. Weir suggesting that Melbourne should forgo the Games and gracefully bow out of the picture. In a telephone call from Santa Barbara Mr. Brundage denied that he had written such a letter or even issued an ultimatum. He said that Melbourne would not lose the Games if she lived up to her obligations.

There was one strange sidelight. Mr. Brundage received an astonishing number of unofficial letters signed and unsigned. Some people even went to the trouble of expressing their dissatisfaction by cable. One letter said: "No one believes the Games should be held here." Another said: "There's so much trouble . . . why bother with talk any longer about holding the Games in Australia?" There were other letters that talked of intrigue, plotting and internal politics.

Now it was up to the Trustees and the Committee to keep to their side of the bargain. The master plan was to increase the capacity of the ground ultimately to 150,000. The first stage to be carried out before the Olympic Games called for the demolition of the old Public Grandstand. The Northern Stand, much larger and spreading over a new grant of two acres of land, would take its place.

It was hoped that the new building would increase accommodation to nearly 120,000. The stand was designed to accommodate 41,000 compared with 10,000 for the Public Grandstand. It would be a solid concrete structure with an amphitheatre of seats rising from the arena fence similar to the Southern Stand. The internal roadway which the R.A.A.F. called 'Pneumonia

217

Alley' would continue on right through the new building. There would be dressing rooms, bars, tearooms, buffets, toilets and a very handsome dining room. From the open roof deck, 81 feet high, there would be a view right across Melbourne. By the end of 1953 the plans were all ready and the M.C.C. Committee accepted the lowest tender. It came from E. A. Watts Pty. Ltd. for £535,975. The contract said that the building had to be finished by the end of 1955. To help pay for it the Club increased membership from 6200 to 9800.

The final cost of the construction work proved to be nearly £700,000, of which the Olympic Financing Authority contributed £100,000 because of the special requirements which were incorporated in the new buildings. The remainder of the finance was provided by loans raised by the Club and made up from Club funds.

The Club also received £35,000 for the use of the ground and buildings, which were occupied for many months prior to the Games, with a consequent loss of revenue to the Club.

The old Public Grandstand survived until after the Royal visit by Queen Elizabeth and Prince Philip, then the wreckers moved in. The first concrete was poured for the foundations of the new stand on June 20, 1954. When the Englishmen played the Third Test after Christmas all that could be seen was a mess of concrete and scaffolding as if the workmen were preparing a launching pad. As for the ground itself, it seemed strange without the old double-headed Public Grandstand. The M.C.G. looked like a giant that had lost a couple of its teeth.

The time was late 1954, but the after-pains of war were still with Melbourne. It was difficult to put up any large building, or to organise any major undertaking without a go-slow, or a strike. Those who could only see matters in straight shades of black and white put it all down to the work of Communist organisers. There was more to it than that. This was a time of rapid inflation, and even more important, a time of a great unsatisfied demand for labour. If carpenters or builders did not want to work on the new Olympic stand they could go elsewhere and often gain better rates.

The rolling strikes, the black bans, and go-slows started in October 1954. In March 1955 the carpenters went on strike. They asked for 23/- a week above award rates and the contractor, Mr. E. A. Watts, refused to pay it. When the dispute came before the Conciliation Commissioner, Mr. Chambers, he said that he believed the Australian people would rather go without the Olympic Games than submit to industrial blackmail. No threats or waving of battle axes would prevail over law and order, he said. So he refused to arbitrate until the men went back to work.

218

The strike lasted for a month. Nothing was being done at the M.C.G., and day by day the Games drew nearer. Soon there was an air of panic in Melbourne. One newspaper said the contractors should pay the workmen anything, no matter what the cost. The *Sun News-Pictorial* said:

> Unless the strike of carpenters at the M.C.G. is quickly settled there is small hope of the Olympic stadium being completed in time for the 1956 Games.
>
> What is wrong with Melbourne? Whether it is the building of a bridge, a subway or a telephone exchange, the same story of frustration and procrastination has to be told . . . From one official quarter has come an assurance that whether or not the new stands are completed the Games will be held.
>
> This is not good enough.
>
> Is Melbourne to undergo the shame of introducing thousands of overseas visitors to an unfinished stadium? Is the Duke to be asked to declare the Games open from an improvised structure?

The carpenters went back to work on April 6, curiously enough on the very day that Mr. Avery Brundage arrived from the U.S.A. to make his official inspection of progress. The carpenters lifted their claims to 36 shillings a week over the award rate, but ultimately they settled for 4/- a day, which amounted to £1 for an unbroken week's work. Although not obliged to do so under its building contract nor under its agreement with the Olympic authorities, the Club decided to carry this additional cost in order to ensure the completion of the work in the required time.

The carpenters were one problem, Mr. Brundage was another. Melbourne knew all about him. He had a reputation for toughness and he had caused many a stir in other parts of the world before he ever came to Australia. There was a suspicion that his bark was worse than his bite, but just the same he was known as Mr. Slavery Brundage, Mr. Umbrage, or the man with a discus for a heart. He was six feet tall, a man with a big head and bulky body. He looked what he was—a successful American business executive.

At first he started very quietly. He gave only kind encouragement. He seemed to like what he saw. He almost overlooked the strikes at the M.C.G. and he had more confidence than some of the M.C.C. Committee when he said: "This will be finished in six months."

But on April 11, 1955, he called a press conference and for an hour he lashed out. He said: "I am told you are going to do it, but all I know is what has happened in the past six years. A group of pretty smart leading Melbourne citizens attended the Rome meeting six years ago, at which the Games were awarded to Melbourne. I don't know how they did it. There were a dozen other cities after the Games. Some were prepared to spend up to 20 million dollars to stage the Games, but your delegation was successful. For six years we have had nothing but squabbling, changes of management and bickering. Melbourne has a deplorable record in its preparations for the Games— promises and promises. I have seen the plans and places. It can be done, but won't be done unless all the rivalries and bitternesses are submerged, jealousies harmonised and obstructions eliminated. I am putting Melbourne on its honour to do the necessary work in the time remaining."

Asked if the Games had ever been taken away from a city, Mr. Brundage said: "There are still three or four cities that could do the job." Even while he was talking an offer came from Philadelphia to take over the Games at once from Melbourne.

Melbourne was moved by the harangue, but not terribly frightened. All the inefficiencies that he was lambasting had been rectified before he came to Melbourne, and now the Olympic machinery under Lieut.-General Bill Bridgeford was working very smoothly. One American newspaperman commented: "The trouble was you were too kind to Avery Brundage. You should have answered him back like we do."

A committee of soil experts and engineers was formed under the chairmanship of Mr. A. E. Chadwick, who was also a member of the Olympic Construction Committee and carried out all liaison functions for the building operations.

Test plots were established at the Old Scotch College Ground, off Batman Avenue, and the types of soils and grasses used in the reconstruction of the ground were determined by these experiments.

Immediately after the 1955 football Grand Final bulldozers, mechanical shovels and graders moved on to the ground. Oh, the turf! The sacred turf! For all those who watched it, it was a paralysing sight. To see the bulldozers tearing up the green turf, which had been nourished with such care for a century, was hard to bear. Heaven knows what those famous 1862 entrepreneurs, Messrs. Spiers and Pond, would have thought.

Gone was the wicket which was the stage for the magical work of Trumper, W. G. Grace, Armstrong, Hammond, Ponsford. Where Larwood, Lindwall, Miller and Tyson had started their fearsome pounding runs, now something else was starting its equally fearsome run—a diesel-powered grader.

Over 3000 tons of Merri Creek soil was torn away and carefully stored for future use. It was fascinating to see this famous stuff that set so concrete hard, capable of producing an innings of over 1000 runs. What did it look like?—it was hard and black, more than anything like over-cooked plum pudding.

So the regrading went on. The seven-foot fall from one side to the other was rectified. The engineers put in 3000 cubic feet of ash drainage beds and over 5000 feet of drainage pipes, and it was said that this would make the M.C.G. "one of the best all-weather grounds in the world."

The ground and the new stand were both ready for the 1956 football finals. The day of the Grand Final between Melbourne and Collingwood was fantastic. There was a record crowd of 115,902, which has never been bettered for a sporting event in Australia. Officials estimate that at least 2000 more broke their way in and 25,000 were locked out. They were jammed in the aisles, they clambered on to the roofs. Some climbed up into the girders, others sat precariously on the narrow parapet at the top of the new stand with an 80-foot drop behind them. Many who paid 7/6 to get in paid another 5/- for empty Coca-Cola boxes to stand on. Nobody knew precisely just how many the ground could accommodate with its new facilities, so this was a valuable lesson. For the Olympics the organisers were careful not to let many more than 102,000 into the ground. The overall accommodation was reduced to 102,000 by placing seats in areas which were designed for standing room patrons. Anyway, the *New York Times* was impressed by the crowd of 115,902. It ran a story that this was the biggest crowd ever to watch a *soccer* game in Australia. That hurt a little, but the fact remains that no football finals were required to be played off the ground.

With the Grand Final over, the next stage went into action. Once again the power machinery moved on to the ground—this time to lay the special cinder track that had been imported from England.

For the Games the M.C.C. members voted themselves out of their rights. For the duration of the Olympic events the Members' Pavilion and all its club facilities no longer would be theirs. However, there were special concessions to members for the purchase of tickets, and their quick response brought in £125,000. To have this money in early was a big thing, and it contributed in no small measure to the success of the Games.

So much had to be prepared at the M.C.G. It was not only the main stadium, it was the nerve centre. More than 1000 correspondents had to operate from the ground. Facilities for the Press and radio included 800 seats in the members' stand and more than 100 seats in other parts of the ground for broadcasters. In addition, there were numerous individual Press offices, 48 soundproof broadcasting boxes, film-processing laboratories and inter-view rooms. Furthermore there was an Overseas Telecommunications Commission centre in the members' stand with the ability to clear a quarter of a million words a day. News from Melbourne had to go everywhere—

Aberdeen ... Budapest ... Casablanca ... Moscow ... Yokohama ... Zurich.

The crowds began to line up outside the M.C.G. at 3 p.m. on November 21, 1956, 25½ hours before the Duke of Edinburgh was due to open the Games. There were hundreds of them. They arrived with fuel stoves, portable radios, sleeping bags, flasks of tea, chess sets, blankets—and they even had a sing-song.

That night 250,000 people filled the city streets and the police battled with a hopeless tangle of traffic which jammed every intersection from Flinders Street to Lonsdale Street along Swanston, Elizabeth and Russell Streets. Family groups wandered everywhere looking at the decorations. There were no traffic rules; Melbourne was a happy, crazy throng, and a tram was jammed for 40 minutes in Bourke Street before the tram driver was able to appeal to the police for help.

And so the great day, November 22, arrived. The date that had been fixed in so many people's minds as almost a day of doom, a day when nothing would be ready and all would be chaos. Yet on this day all was perfect, and everything went exactly according to plan. A reporter who witnessed the opening from the air said that the M.C.G. was a sight to take one's breath away. The richness and variety of colour was dazzling in the sunshine, and dominating all was the ground itself, as green as a billiard table with its broad red ribbon of running track.

This was a new and different M.C.G., and perhaps even the cricketers and footballers would have admitted that it was the greatest moment of all. At 3.30 p.m. the roar of the crowd of more than 100,000 people began to swell like an organ as the Greek team in navy blue blazers led the teams of 68 nations on to the ground. It was the world on parade.

After the Greeks the teams came in alphabetical order. There was Afghanistan in grey-green, the four-man team from the Bahamas, the Belgians, with a 14-year-old girl holding a toy kangaroo, the Bermudans, the Brazilians, the Bulgarians and the Ceylonese. And so it went on: the Danes, the French, the Indonesians in their black tarbooshes, the Japanese, the Rumanians, the Turks, United Kingdom, the great party from the U.S.S.R., and finally the Australians, the hosts, in the green and gold, worn by many a Test international since the turn of the century.

After the march the climax came quite suddenly. The Duke of Edinburgh said simply: "I declare open the Olympic Games of Melbourne, celebrating the XVI Olympiad of the modern era."

There was a fanfare of trumpets, the five-ringed Olympic flag broke out from the masthead, a 21-gun salute boomed out and the air was filled with 4000 pigeons. A white bird, which looked surprisingly like the dove of peace, circled the ground several times, looking at the incredible scene. It rose higher and higher, above the stands, until finally it disappeared.

Then there was a spark of light among the stands. It was Ron Clarke, the 18-year-old junior athlete, bearing the Olympic torch, that had been passed from hand to hand over 2000 miles all the way from Cairns. The name of the man who was to bear the torch into the M.C.G. had been a well-kept secret. Even Clarke himself did not know until nine days before, and when it was all over that day he went from Richmond back home in a crowded train—unidentified.

The *Age* reported the arrival of the torch in this report:

> The diminutive figure of Ron Clarke appeared, his Olympic torch flaring brilliantly and showering the green turf with sparks. As he ran down the back stretch the military discipline of the opening relaxed. Athletes of all nations swarmed across the track to cheer him on or take photographs of him. He disappeared with his little torch, then he was up on the roof setting a light to the bronze brazier.
>
> This was the great moment of the ceremony. There were speeches and anthems.
>
> We stood for the Hallelujah Chorus and the National Anthem, sat to watch John Landy taking the Olympic oath, finally wavered irresolutely thinking of crowded trams, but anxious to watch the teams file off the ground, the Russians tossing little red flags to the crowd.
>
> Before they left, the ranks of the U.S.A. and the U.S.S.R., drawn up side by side, had merged and mingled. That was a good omen.
>
> It had been a wonderful show. The sun shone dully, went behind cloud, and finally appeared again for the crowning moments of the ceremony. An old Anson and a helicopter buzzed overhead—it would not have been complete without them.

It is not the purpose of this book to give an account of the track events at the Olympic Games. These events have been well recorded elsewhere. Nobody who was in Melbourne that week is ever likely to forget Vladimir Kuts of the U.S.S.R. winning the 5,000 and the 10,000 metres, Betty Cuthbert of Australia winning the women's 100 and 200 metres, Ron Delany taking Ireland's first gold medal in 24 years by winning the 1500 metres, and Charlie Dumas in his long struggle right into the evening to gain his mastery of Australia's Chilla Porter in the high jump.

On the last day, December 8, it was a quiet, sad crowd that gathered at the M.C.G. It went to see the flame go out on the most glorious 16 days in Australia's sporting history, and at the finish to sing the very moving song *Will ye no come back again?* The arena looked so different, white running track lines, the long jump pits, the throwing circles were all gone. The 68 national flags around the stands were starting to become tattered.

On the scoreboard there was this sign:

THE 1956 OLYMPIC RACE IS RUN.

MAY ALL WHO HAVE BEEN PRESENT GO FORTH

TO THEIR HOMELANDS AND

MAY THE OLYMPIC SPIRIT GO WITH THEM.

And what of the awesome headmaster, Mr. Avery Brundage, the man who had thundered and threatened for nearly six months? He couldn't have been more happy. He said such kind things that Melbourne began to look upon the man they called "Slavery Umbrage" as almost a dear, personal friend.

After the opening he said: "It was the best Olympic Games opening ever—it was MAGNIFICENT! We have never had a better Games opening. Everyone is deserving of high praise for the wonderful organisation behind Melbourne's effort."

Then there was the occasion of the Lord Mayor's dinner, when he tossed out praise with abandon. He announced that he had a secret gift for the Lord Mayor. With a big smile he said: "I'm going to recommend that all future Games be held in Melbourne."

This set Melburnians dreaming and hoping. Would it take another 100 years to get the Games back in Melbourne. Never had the city known such a happy time as those glorious days in 1956.

CHAPTER NINETEEN

May Day

VERNON RANSFORD was a Neil Harvey who came 40 years earlier. He was a left-hander. Not one of those stubborn, unyielding left-handers, but a man with an impatient streak of brilliance, one who could let loose in a gale of run-getting. The old-timers, when they wanted to pay a particularly gracious compliment, would say: "That boy can drive like Vernon Ransford." Ransford's batting was the measuring stick, the ultimate test. Again like Neil Harvey he was a baseballer, and again like Neil Harvey it was a pleasure to watch him in the outfield. It was suicide to take risks when Ransford was running for the ball. He could pick it up and throw it, all in one perfect movement, and that ball came low and hard to the top of the wicket.

He was part of the tradition of great M.C.C. cricketing secretaries: Ben Wardill, Hugh Trumble and then Vernon Ransford. When the position became vacant in 1939 he and Don Bradman were the leading contenders. Bradman was so much in the public eye it seemed certain that he would get the job. But how could the Committee overlook Vernon Ransford? He had so much more experience. He had been on the M.C.C. committee for 25 years, and he had been a life member since 1931. Cricket ability alone could not decide a job like that.

He first played for Victoria when he was 18, and in 1909 he scored a faultless 143 against England at Lord's. He averaged 38.82 in his 20 Test matches. He was embroiled in the famous 1912 controversy, and he was sadly disappointed when he missed this opportunity to tour at the very height of his career, yet he never regretted his decision to stand down.

As secretary he was a worthy successor to Hugh Trumble and no one could say more than that. He was not an easy man to lead into cricket controversies, but he would say this much, that Joe Darling's 1902 team was the greatest of all. "Look at the batting order," he would say. "Trumper, Duff, Hill, Noble; then Syd Gregory or Darling ... why, Warwick Armstrong had to go in seventh! And the bowling ... express Ernie Jones, a perfect physical specimen; Hugh Trumble, one of the greatest bowlers cricket has known; Noble, Armstrong and left-hander Saunders, with Hopkins as all-rounder and J. J.

Kelly as wicket-keeper. What cricket names!" The most difficult bowler he ever faced, he said, was the great English spinner Sid Barnes.

Vernon Ransford retired in April 1957 because of ill-health. He died a year later. He was 73.

There were 45 applicants for the job as new secretary, and it was won by the South Melbourne player Ian Johnson. He had a colourful and fascinating record. For some time, he, Ray Lindwall and Tony Lock were the only cricketers who have played Test cricket in every cricketing country in the world, and he had performed the remarkable Test double of taking 100 wickets and scoring 1000 runs. He captained Australia against England in Australia in 1954-55 and in England in 1956. He also had the unique honour of captaining the first Australian teams to tour West Indies in 1955, Pakistan 1956 and India 1956. For his services in the West Indies he was awarded the M.B.E. During the Second World War he was a Beaufighter pilot in the R.A.A.F. Indeed, he never quite lost his love of flying aeroplanes. Keith Miller also was a wartime pilot, and when on tour, flying from one match to another, they loved to get at the controls of the aeroplane, much to the horror of their team-mates. In 1955 Ian flew the aeroplane from Trinidad to Tobago in the West Indies. Immediately after this the Board of Control found a new clause for the players' contracts. It was forbidden for any player to take over the controls of an aeroplane in which the team was travelling.

There were many points about Ian Johnson which must have impressed the M.C.C. committee. As a captain he had been diplomatic and an excellent mixer. He was a strong personality and he had shown this in his remarkable comeback to big cricket. He was dropped from the Test team in 1952 and he missed selection for the 1953 tour to England. At this stage it would have been natural had he retired. Instead he worked at his game. Already something of a fanatic for physical fitness, he tried even harder. That season he led Victoria into second place in the Sheffield Shield and he took 37 wickets at an average of 16.37 runs. It was a performance nobody could overlook. He was the best spinner in the country. So the reject returned to become Australian captain.

He was also a footballer of note and played centre for the Victorian Amateur team in interstate football.

Although he played for South Melbourne he had had a long association with the Melbourne Cricket Club. He came to the M.C.C. as an exhibitioner from Wesley College in 1935 and became a Junior Member in 1937. Yet there was one intriguing situation. After he returned from England in 1956 he retired from Test cricket, but he was keen to go on playing for South Melbourne. He actually gained permission from the committee to captain South

Melbourne while he was secretary of the M.C.C. However, an injury stopped it from ever coming about. Yet sometimes he must have had some wry thoughts about the job. He claimed that he made more ducks on the M.C.G. than on any other ground in the world.

At this time there was also a change in Club Presidents. Dr. W. C. McClelland, who had been associated with the Club since the eighteen nineties, died on May 30, 1957. He was President of the Victorian Football League for 30 years and President of the M.C.C. for 14 years. When he took over from Dr. Ramsay Mailer there were those who asked whether a top man in football should also be the top man in cricket. This was strange reasoning. Perhaps they felt cricket should be opposed to football as summer is opposed to winter. But Dr. McClelland brought distinction to the Club as he had done to the V.F.L.

He joined the Melbourne Football Club in 1897, where he quickly won fame as a brilliant centre half-back. He played in the Club's first premiership side in 1900 and he was captain from 1901 to 1904. Then while working at the Ballarat Hospital he played with Ballarat in 1905 and 1906.

The new President was Mr. C. W. Simmonds. Mr. Hans Ebeling became Senior Vice-president and Mr. A. E. Chadwick the new Vice-president. On the day of his appointment Mr. Simmonds fascinated the reporters. He was 83, yet here he was, off for a round of golf. He was in training, he said, to get his handicap down. They felt he was the youngest 83-year-old they had ever seen. He gave this recipe for the youthful look: "Take care of your health, play a lot of sport, work as long as you are physically and mentally able, and do physical jerks every day." He took up golf when he was 47. He worked his handicap down to 5 and now it was 20. Three times since becoming President he had attained the ultimate in golf, by beating his age off the stick. All three occasions were on his club course, Metropolitan.

Charles Simmonds' top sport was always baseball, and he played with Australia against the U.S.A. in the early nineteen-hundreds. Also he was an enthusiastic boxer, he captained the Corowa football team in 1899 and, he says, he was a "mediocre" cricketer. He joined the M.C.C. Committee in 1920 and he was made an honorary life member in 1940.

In 1957 the old in Australian cricket was giving place to the new. Miller, Johnson, Langley and Burke retired from the international scene, and Ron Archer was forced out of the game with a knee injury.

Ian Craig was made captain of the team to tour South Africa and had much to do with moulding a new side. He led the team splendidly and surprised many by winning the series. Then, soon after returning to Australia, he contracted hepatitis and it quickly became obvious that he would miss the 1958-59 season, which meant the English visit.

There had to be another new captain. Neil Harvey was the odds-on favourite with, perhaps, Colin McDonald 4 to 1 against. The Board of Control made what was then a surprise choice in Richie Benaud, and it proved a good choice, for his side went on to win four Tests with one drawn.

Australia won the first in Brisbane by eight wickets and the Second Test was on the M.C.G. Enthusiasm for cricket was coming back, just like the nineteen-thirties. Even the P.M.G.'s Department was taking notice. Other countries might have a Dial-a-Prayer service, Dial-a-Recipe, or Dial for Tourist Information, but the P.M.G. introduced the Dial-a-Cricket Score service. By ringing 6006 the caller could get the progressive total, the scores of batsmen at the wicket, and the score and details of dismissal of the last batsman out. The idea was a mighty money-spinner for the Government. The calls came in by the thousand.

Peter May won the toss for the second time and batted. The start was a sensation. England's first three wickets fell for seven runs. In one of the most hostile overs ever seen at the M.C.G. Alan Davidson sent back Peter Richardson, Willie Watson and Tom Graveney. He had three wickets for four runs off 14 deliveries.

It was Trevor Bailey and Peter May who stopped the rout. In any Test match there are always heroes and villains. The arch-villain of the England team was Bailey. For Australia it was Ken Mackay, and there was a curious similarity between the two. Both were all-rounders, both were blissfully impervious to the hottest criticism from the crowd, both could make the actual scoring of a run seem like a vast occasion, and both were the darlings of the chewing gum manufacturers. They chewed constantly. Yet whatever the spectators thought of them, they were valued highly by their captains. When they were most badly needed always they were there, frustrating the moves of the opposition. By the time he came to Melbourne Bailey already had enhanced his ominous reputation. In Brisbane there was the occasion when he didn't score for 48 minutes and a barracker commented: "Look, he's got a bonzer bat worth about seven quid. Ain't it a shame he doesn't use it." However, he used that bonzer bat to make 68 runs . . . in 7 hours 38 minutes. The Australian players called him "The Boil"—mighty prolonged and mighty irritating. Even so he had their grudging respect.

As opening bat in the Second Test he was more aggressive. He made 48 in 151 minutes. He was badly needed, for England was in trouble. May came in to bat on his 29th birthday and, as Sir Leonard Hutton said: "Unless you have

Right
Bob Crockett, umpire from 1887 to 1926.

Below
Fifth Test match: Australia v. England, 1937.

Right
Keith Truscott, D.F.C. and Bar.

Below
Harry Hopman, Davis Cup player,
1928–1932, and Captain of Davis Cup
teams, 1939–1967.

Below right
Bert Luttrell, 1902–1946. He designed
those granite hard wickets of the
'scoring twenties'.

heard it, it is difficult to appreciate the loudness of the roar that greets the downfall of an English batsman. It sounds loudest for the next man in."

For a time he was like a man hanging on a precipice. Meckiff should have got him several times. Benaud dropped the simplest of catches off his own bowling when he was 20. Then May settled down and for five hours he worked his way towards a painful century. He made 113, and couldn't have asked for a more valuable birthday present. It was the first Test century by an English captain in Australia since the days of Archie McLaren in the 1901-02 tour.

There were some fine performances: Alan Davidson's 6 for 64, Brian Statham's 7 for 57 and Neil Harvey's chanceless innings of 167, perhaps the soundest innings he ever played. Then this was Norman O'Neill's first Test match on the M.C.G. He had made a brilliant 71 in Brisbane, and this time he made 37, but how impressive he was. Even in his defensive strokes he seemed to be chastising the ball. He was as solid as a wrestler with muscles as big as tins of peaches. His head sat close down on his shoulders and he wore fine big trousers that came high on his chest towards his armpits. One always needed to be careful of a man who wore his trousers like that.

It was Ian Meckiff who polished off England's second innings ahead of time and cost the touring side thousands in gate money. England was all out for 87 in 177 minutes on a perfect wicket. The *Sun News-Pictorial* estimated that the batting flop cost £50,000 in gate receipts, for the match surely should have gone another two days. It said: "The direct loss to the Marylebone Cricket Club can be reckoned at about £1000 for each of the 10 wickets so meekly surrendered for 87 runs in less than three hours."

There had been a great deal of discussion in the press box about Ian Meckiff. Statham and Lindwall moved to the wicket like beautifully controlled machinery, all smoothness and action. Meckiff looked untidy as if he needed a drop of oil somewhere. One former Test captain remarked: "I'll tell you how he gets his wickets. He's so appallingly inaccurate you don't know where the ball's coming from next. Then after several overs there's one right on the wicket. The batsman, completely overcome with astonishment, suddenly is bowled."

Nobody could accuse him of inaccuracy on this day. It was the greatest performance of his career. He took six wickets for 38 runs off 15.2 overs. He took the wickets of Richardson, Bailey, Graveney, May, Cowdrey and Loader. But this was the start of the flood of criticism from the English newspapermen which was to do such damage to his game.

He was an inspired bowler, and all the time that he was wrecking England he had no idea what was going on in the Press Box. The typewriters were almost steaming, and the message boys were running off with cable stories which accused Meckiff bluntly of being nothing more than a chucker. Some of the stories must have been on the streets before he got his last wicket. Even if Meckiff had known what was going on he could not have realised the significance of it all. This was a controversy that was to last for a year and very nearly wreck his cricket career.

That night he shared the front page of the Melbourne *Herald* with the Soviet attempt to fire a rocket to the moon. Not all the stories on that page gave him pleasure. One with the by-line of Johnny Wardle said: "Peter May would be well within his rights to ask for a slow-motion camera shot of Meckiff. I am not squealing because England are getting beaten. I am sure no Australian would be happy about victory if he found England were being thrown out. Almost every man on the ground agrees that Meckiff throws. So why isn't something done about it?"

E. M. Wellings, of the London *Evening News,* wrote: "Meckiff is only one of numerous alleged bowlers who throw in Australia today. Queensland is the only State side without a thrower. New South Wales has Rorke, who is the fastest of all, and Burke; South Australia has Trethewey and Hitchcox; Western Australia has Slater, and Victoria's chucker is Meckiff."

Richie Benaud said he was completely satisfied that Meckiff's action was fair and legitimate. He had studied his action from every position in the field and he was absolutely certain that it conformed with the laws of the Marylebone Club. To the great credit of the sportsmanship of Peter May and the manager, F. R. Brown, neither made any complaint about Ian Meckiff's bowling that day.

Australia won the Second Test by eight wickets, the Third Test in Sydney was a draw and Australia won in Adelaide to retake the Ashes. The Fifth Test was due to start in Melbourne on Friday the 13th February or May Day, as some people called it, the old R.A.A.F. emergency or bailing out signal, and nobody was in a greater emergency than Peter May.

Richie Benaud had lost the toss four times in succession. He pinned all his faith on an English 1887 four-shilling piece, and always he called "tails". At 11 p.m. in his room at the Pier Hotel in Adelaide he had tossing practice on the eve of the Fourth Test. There were terrible thwacks on the carpet as this great piece of metal hit the floor. It came down tails seven times in succession.

However, there was a nice piece of irony about it. Benaud didn't have to win the toss at all. May sent the Australians in to bat. The score was 1 for 200 at stumps and McDonald went on to make 170. But at last when Benaud finally won the toss at the Fifth Test, what did he do?—he sent England in to bat.

Sir Leonard Hutton, a little startled, commented: "Is Richie Benaud trying to do the impossible? Is he trying to rub the bitterest of salt into English wounds? It is not far short of 50 years since a captain successfully put the other side in to bat in an England-Australia Test match. In the First Test of the 1954-55 tour I put Australia in to bat having won the toss. We lost. In the Second Test Arthur Morris tried the same gambit. He lost. On this tour in Adelaide in the Fourth Test Peter May tried this challenge to the gods. The same fate befell him. Yet now Benaud, knowing the history of such attempts, has dared the fates . . . never has anyone looked more like succeeding."

The Fifth Test was something of a sentimental occasion. Ray Lindwall, the old killer, was back. He had made a desperate attempt to return to Test cricket. He had been performing well as captain of Queensland, but some critics said that at 37 he was too old. His guile was there but not the sting. Ray had worked on an exhausting physical fitness campaign. He went for training runs and he had a machine in his back garden for strengthening his legs.

He missed the first three Tests and he came into the side at Adelaide. By the Fifth Test he was one wicket short of Clarrie Grimmett's record of 216 Test wickets, the best ever for an Australian. To us he looked the same old Ray Lindwall. His psychological warfare was still in very good shape. First Davidson had an over, then Benaud tossed the ball to Ray.

There was a cheer all around the ground. The crowd had come especially for this. Lindwall went through all the old antics just like we remembered. He rubbed the ball vigorously on his thigh—he paced out his run, he tossed a few contemptuous looks at the poor batsman, then he did a few physical jerks and everyone looked on in awe.

He hitched up his trousers, rolled his shoulders like Carnera, and finally came moving in with that lovely rhythmical stride. There was a sensation. Bailey snicked this first ball and Davidson took it in the slips. Lindwall in his old style swung round, leapt six feet, both arms high in the air. His appeal must have been heard in Collins Street. It was his 216th wicket and he was tied with Clarrie Grimmett. England was all out for 205, and but for a merry partnership of 63 between Freddie Trueman and John Mortimore, Friday the 13th would have been even worse than they feared.

The Australian crowds loved Freddie Trueman. They liked his rebellious attitude, his impudence before authority. When he was fielding by the boundary one crowd showed him a mug of beer. "Would you like one, Freddie?"

He nodded back vigorously. He too could put on a show when he was bowling. He would take a long walk back, slowly, as if he were trying to hitch a ride. Then as he reached almost half-way to the boundary, suddenly he would turn round, as if he had forgotten something. Then he would bolt towards the wicket, gathering pace like a North of England express. Finally he would hurl the ball at the batsman. After that there would be another delay while he put his hands on his hips, and standing there, black hair falling over his forehead, he would glare at the batsman.

He took the wickets of Harvey and O'Neill with successive balls, and so it was up to McDonald and Mackay to stand firm. Mackay was very much Mackay this day. The drawbridge was up, everything was locked and barred. In two hours he made only one stroke that could be described as more than a gentle tap. A historian dug out the information that Piper Ken Mackay of the 79th Cameron Highlanders in 1815 was the saviour of the side at Waterloo. He coolly kept on piping during the repeated charges of the French cavalry.

Batsman Ken Mackay was no doubt thinking of his worthy ancestor. His jaw was set and he shaped up to the repeated charges of the British cavalry-men—cavalrymen Trueman, Tyson and Bailey. Mackay was out for 23, but Colin McDonald, a most dependable opener, made 133, Richie Benaud 64 and Grout 74, to bring the total to 351.

The Tuesday was Ray Lindwall's day. In 11 racing deliveries, full of his old-time pace and swing, he clean-bowled Trevor Bailey and he had Peter May caught in slips. The record was his. The other players rushed to con-gratulate him. And as Lindwall walked back to bowl again he waved the ball towards the M.C.G. reserve. His wave was answered by his wife Peggy. She had waited four days for just that moment.

It was big news in Brisbane. The suburb of Mt. Gravatt already had named Lindwall Street in his honour. That night somebody decorated the street sign with streamers.

His bowling figures at the end of the innings were 3 wickets for 37 runs and he finished with 219 Test wickets. Keith Miller, his old partner, commented: "There was never any question in the minds of those people who played with or against Ray of his place among the bowlers in the history of the game. Now it is in the record books for everyone to see. I expect a lot of people will point out that Lindwall has played in many more Tests than Clarrie Grimmett. But Ray got the Australian record in fewer overs and I'll wager that many more of his victims have been among the top half of the batting order, because he's a new ball bowler."

There was great interest, too, in Gordon Rorke, the 20-year-old fast bowler from Sydney. He was the heaviest bowler since Warwick Armstrong, 6 ft. 4 in. and 15 stone. He trained on honey, raw eggs and fruit juice. There was much talk of "International Rorketty" and it was said that his approach to the wicket wasn't so much a run up as a count down. He proved himself very fast indeed and he took 3 for 41.

Graveney top-scored with 54, but Colin Cowdrey was the man to see. He hit seven glorious fours and it was a tragedy when he was run out for 46. The decision was close and it cut short one of the best innings of the whole series. England was all out for 214, and on the final day Australia made the necessary 70 runs for the loss of one wicket. Colin McDonald, as he so richly deserved, made the winning hit. Just then one of the English pressmen said sadly: "Here endeth the fifth lesson."

What a season it had been for McDonald, the M.C.C. and Victorian captain. He headed the batting averages in the Tests with 520 runs, average 65, and he scored two centuries. He stood up to the fast attack with a courage that reminded one of Woodfull.

It was a great triumph for Richie Benaud. He had led the revival in Australian cricket against England. In the final Test he took the risk of taking the field with four fast bowlers and only one spinner, and after winning the toss he put his opponents in to bat. His decision turned out right.

The series had a notable effect on local cricket. Out in Collingwood some small boys were seen playing cricket with a telegraph pole for stumps. Only the bowler was in front of the wicket. The others were all behind the telegraph pole in a perfect umbrella field. It was reported, too, that the captain after winning the toss had sent his opposition in to bat.

In over 100 years many have been the uses for the Melbourne Cricket Ground. It has been the scene for balloon ascents, fireworks displays, professional bicycle races, receptions for Royalty, Highland Games, one of the early aeroplane flights and, of course, the Olympic Games. One began to wonder if anything else could take place at the M.C.G. But there was something: on March 15, 1959, it became a church for a day—the rallying point for the final meeting of the Billy Graham Crusade. It was interesting that it was not a football final, a Test match or the Olympic Games that created the all-time record at the M.C.G., but an American evangelist. Dr. Billy Graham drew approximately 130,000 people. Another 4000 people were unable to get inside and they listened to the meeting over loudspeakers.

Dr. Graham said it was the largest attendance at any of his crusades in any part of the world. The next largest attendance figure was 120,000 at his Greater London crusade meetings.

People began to arrive at 8.30 a.m., and an hour before the meeting began at 3 p.m. all the stands were packed and 10,000 more spilled out on to the ground itself. It was one of the rare occasions when women were allowed into the members' stand. The stand was filled to capacity. The Governor, Sir Dallas Brooks, and Lady Brooks were on the platform.

Dr. Billy Graham told the meeting: "I could not stand here and see this vast crowd without being deeply moved. This is a great historic moment in the life of Australia—it is the Lord's doing. It is also typical of the warm-hearted reception we have had in Melbourne. It is indicative too of the spiritual hunger of the people in this State. I believe this is a sovereign move of God, I believe this great meeting today will be an encouragement to people throughout the world in the midst of despair and discouragement. This Melbourne crusade has brought thousands of people to a knowledge of Christ."

When the meeting closed the huge audience sang, *God Be With You Till We Meet Again*. Billy Graham said: "I feel very humble. It was the Lord's doing and I am only His messenger."

The great crowd should have caused all kinds of traffic jams, but they melted away with ease. Ian Johnson said the crowd was remarkably well behaved. They left about as much mess as a football crowd of 20,000, and it was pleasing to note, there were practically no bottles.

CHAPTER TWENTY

Brown Magic

THE 1960-61 tour by Frank Worrell and his men was one of the great tours that remains unforgotten—like the visits of W. G. Grace. When they first arrived at Perth we wrote them down as a happy-go-lucky bunch. Admittedly there were one or two brilliant fellows among them, but they treated cricket as if it were a game. Always they played just for fun. When the pressure was on they would collapse all too easily before the unyielding tactics of the battle-hardened Australians.

The West Indians did not change. Right to the end they treated cricket as a game. They always played just for fun, but they didn't collapse, not at any stage, and they provided the most exciting series ever seen in Australia. Frank Worrell and Richie Benaud adopted the same policy—the scoring of runs was more important than anything. This was winning cricket and by the time the final Test had been played the incredible had happened. After 99 years of International cricket the West Indies had replaced England as the team Australians most wanted to see. Three out of the five Tests were fought to the last minute in an agonising crescendo of excitement.

Frank Worrell described it as the tour of tours, the tour to end all tours. The only pity was there had to be a decision in the end. Everybody agreed with him when he said, "I don't think Australia deserved to beat us . . . and I don't think we deserved to beat Australia."

Once upon a time cricket was a most restful occupation like fishing. It was wrong to expect from it the thrills of ice hockey or prizefighting. Furthermore there were great subtleties to the game. One never scored at the beginning because one was digging in. One never scored before drinks or after drinks, before lunch or after lunch, before tea or after tea, or before and after reaching one's 50, and certainly one never dared to score in the last half-hour before stumps. Most times one didn't score.

But these West Indians ignored all time-honoured subtleties. It was a mistake for a man even to blink, in case he missed three fours or an amazing piece of fielding. The team was filled with personality cricketers. There was Garfield Sobers, a cricketer who could turn on a variety of bowling like Keith

235

Miller then bat like Bradman. Then like his namesake Sir Garfield Barwick he always looked immaculate, his sleeves rolled down, not a button out of place. Whereas other batsmen took cheeky singles, he took cheeky fours. How could anyone forget his innings in the First Test? He rushed to his 100 intemperately in 125 minutes, then he seemed to let loose even more steam. He belted several tremendous fours off Kline. There was one shot off Davidson which he picked up outside his off stump, then pulled round to leg so that it went like a bullet straight to the fence.

The critics were full of wonder. They said there hadn't been a shot like it played in Test cricket since the Stone Age.

Then there was Wesley Hall; whether he was bowling or batting he kept the game erupting. Was there ever so much flailing movement in a man? One could only describe him as being like a speeded-up character in a silent movie. It was said that even before the start of the first Test he had broken up three pairs of boots, and Rohan Kanhai penned a calypso song on the subject.

> I tell you the story of fast bowler Hall,
> The fastest fast bowler who ever threw ball.
> He busts up the wicket with terrible shoots,
> But never as badly as he busts his boots.

It was a good calypso, but considering the delicate situation in international cricket the part about throwing could have been better phrased.

When in full cry he could be very frightening indeed, and openers like Colin McDonald soon found that a stay at the wicket was almost unendurable without rubber padding. He wore a gold cross around his neck which would bounce everywhere as he charged to the wicket. The Test umpire, Col Hoy, recalls that several times it popped into his mouth. He recalls too that when a batsman snicked one of his thunderbolts over the heads of slips Wes would raise his arms to the sky and moan, "The good Lord's gone and left us."

Col Hoy was something of a character himself. Right back to the pre-Grace era it has been the duty of umpires to act as clothes pegs. They have tied innumerable sweaters around their middle, catered for all the players' caps. Col Hoy introduced an innovation for this series. He brought out a large plastic bag which he used as a carry-all. One wondered whether the Board of Control should have provided him with something like a bookmaker's bag, green and gold of course, and embossed with the Australian coat of arms.

The First Test was the unbelievable tie at Brisbane, the Second Test was won by Australia in Melbourne, the West Indies won the Third Test in Sydney, and the Adelaide Test was a draw when Lindsay Kline and Ken Mackay made their two-hour last-ditch stand. So the stage was all set. It was only the fourth time that an Australian rubber had reached a Melbourne Fifth Test with the winning honours even. Certainly it was the first of such occasions that Australia's opponent had not been an England team.

Furthermore, so that there would not be another draw an extra day was added. This was to be a six-day Test. Could one stand the strain? Will Rogers, the American humorist, would have had a word for the occasion. Once he went to a Test match at Lord's. The Prince of Wales asked him if the game could ever take in the U.S. "It might, but with one improvement," said Will. "Before the game starts I'd line the teams up and say, 'Now listen, fellas, no food till you're through'."

Ian Johnson said that interest in the Test was greater than for a V.F.L. grand final. Inquiries for seats were the heaviest on record. Two fans were flying out from India for the match. Other inquiries had come from New Zealand and all the Australian States.

Once again Richie Benaud dared the fates. After winning the toss he sent the West Indies in to bat. His move was not so successful as on Friday the 13th against the Englishmen, but it did have a psychological effect. For the first time they seemed a little overawed by the occasion. They scored only like ordinary Test mortals, and they failed to get their usual 300 runs in a day. The score for the innings was 292, and Frank Misson was Australia's most successful bowler with 4 for 58. Misson, blond and 6 ft. 3 in., was another physical fitness enthusiast. It was reported that he lived on fruit, glucose and cereals. The players called him "Strepto", short for Strepto-"Misson", the wonder drug. The wonder drug on this occasion took the wickets of Smith, Alexander, Gibbs and Hall. He took a reasonable run, 15 paces. He wasn't dynamically fast, but he was forever, almost unbearably, energetic. As he ran he became red in the face and his shoulders tossed from side to side. He got up a wobble like an old Bondi tram.

Much of the fun came from Wesley Hall. He batted late in the evening when the TV cameras were in action, and like an astute politician it seemed that he was conscious of his TV rating. He fancied himself as a batsman, and every so often he would give dry-run exhibitions of the fine strokes he could play. He was nearly run out several times and he tumbled over little Joe Solomon in the middle of the pitch. He was even impetuous enough to sneak a single in the last over. Obviously Wesley wanted to he the first to take strike to the bowling on the Saturday. Then there was more fun in the morning. When Wes hit the ball he clouted it. One time he broke his bat. Actually he more than broke it; the bat gloriously disintegrated. Even veteran cricket writers like Tom Goodman of the *Sydney Morning Herald,* who had been on the circuit

237

for many a year, could not remember the like. Of course, Wes made the most of the situation. He made a gesture of mock indignation, then went to shape up to Davidson just holding the handle.

The atmosphere was different from the First Test. So much had happened. Then everyone was saying, "Wouldn't it be awfully good for cricket if the West Indies gave us a jolly good hiding." Now that situation was too close for comfort, and the title of "world champions" was slipping out of Australia's hands.

The date, February 11, 1961, was one to remember. The greatest crowd gathered in cricket history—90,800. It was the ultimate proof of the revival of cricket. The oohs and aahs welled up like thunder claps. Mobs of brave people climbed up through the barbed wire and sat on the top of the concrete stanchions.

Then there were the stoics who sat right behind the concrete pillars. They could see nothing, but they had the satisfaction of being able to report afterwards that they were present on the historic day at the M.C.G. when cricket came back. The crowd was so thick it was impossible to wriggle out for a beer. Once one had found a seat then one had to stay put.

All this had its effect on the cricket. It made the players more tense, more tentative in their actions. Even in a Saturday afternoon game at the local park it is embarrassing when a player drops a catch, but imagine how much more so in the centre of the M.C.G. before 181,600 staring eyes.

Simpson made 75, McDonald made 91. When Colin McDonald went lbw to Sobers the M.C.G. really came alive. At first there was an astonished silence. It was hard to believe this had happened so close to his century. Then the great sound welled up and up and up and they cheered him all the way to the gate. Someone let loose a pile of confetti from one of the upper tiers. It sparkled in the sun and rained down like ticker tape.

The next great moment was when Ken Mackay came in. He was the hero, one of the two who helped save the Adelaide Test. After years and years of tribulation "Slasher" at last had won the heart of the M.C.G. The applause thundered as slowly he chewed his way to the wicket. It was a most satisfactory moment for him. Both Simpson and O'Neill had gone in the space of two balls and Slasher, at the hideous stage of 3/181, was coming in to save the side. He made 19 runs in 95 minutes.

Yet because of the agility of the West Indians no runs were easy, and the man who deserved special commendation was the wicketkeeper, Gerry Alexander. The wonderful fieldsmen, Cammie Smith, Kanhai, Conrad Hunte and Co., always hurled the ball at the stumps, as if they were going for the king hit at a bowling alley. Alexander, the great wicketkeeper and the most reliable batsman, was the rock of the side. The West Indians should erect a statue outside his home in Jamaica and label it "Alexander the Great".

All in all, it was an amazing day . . . amazing that 90,800 people could pass the day in one spot in such peace and harmony . . . amazing that they could get in and out with such little difficulty. Maybe this was a tribute to the police and officials at the M.C.G. Then there was another amazing thing, the number of girls on that hot summer day who went there bare-footed in thongs. It takes a special kind of courage to wear thongs when there are 181,600 feet about.

Australia made 356 to gain a lead of 64 runs, and the West Indies replied with 321. Gerry Alexander top-scored with 73. Melbourne could talk of nothing else. It was impossible to predict who would win and very little work was being done in the city. One department of the Commonwealth Bank put its staff on a three-hourly roster system. Every three hours another group went off to the cricket, and half the firms in town had the same idea. Then there was the farmer who drove to the M.C.G. in a grey utility truck with a South Australian number-plate. He parked near the entrance to the members' reserve. He had baby-sitting troubles. Tethered in the back of the utility was a large ram. While Simpson was batting inside, the ram was baa-ing dolefully outside.

There was nothing doleful about Simpson. The crowd settled down for a restful start to Australia's second innings and Simpson hit 18 off Hall's first over. Rarely had there been a start to an innings like this. Simpson went berserk. He was batting like a man who was frightened he would miss his dinner. At the end of two overs he had 27 on the board-

This was the tally for the first over: 4,2,4,0 (bumper),4,0 (another bumper),4,0.

Garfield Sobers then bowled a maiden over to Colin McDonald. Hall bowled again to Simpson, and this time: 2,4,0,0,0,3,0,0. Some critics had said that Simpson was frightened of Hall. If so, Simpson had his answer this day. Hall was forced out of the attack after three overs, from which 31 runs were scored.

The barrackers in the outer were quite up to the situation. In Hall's second over there was a rare occasion when Simpson played a straight bat. Someone called out: "Wot's up with yer, Simpson? Losin' yer punch? 'Ave a go."

Australia went into the last day with a score of 1 for 57 and 201 runs were needed to win. Richie Benaud said: "I am happy with the situation. If we can't score 201 more runs we don't deserve to win." But it wasn't as easy as all that. Davidson, Grout, O'Neill and Harvey all were suffering from injuries. Grout

239

was in the worst position. He kept wicket all the day before despite severe pain from a chipped bone in his right wrist.

Work was not easy either. Countless members of office staffs did their jobs with one ear on the radio descriptions. D24, the police radio station, kept police car crews up to date with the scores all day. Fortunately there was very little crime. There was no time for villainy when the whole series hung in the balance. Even in the sombre atmosphere of the Supreme Court building the learned gentlemen were taking note of proceedings at another place. Barristers, jury panels, court officials and judges were keeping in touch with the press rooms for the scores.

Simpson made 92, O'Neill 48, Burge 53, until finally there were only three wickets to fall and four runs to get. Alf Valentine was bowling to Wally Grout. Grout back-cut the ball, which went past Alexander and Worrell at slip. Mackay called and the batsmen ran two. But Alexander was there gesturing, the palms of his gloves upturned, appealing for all the world to look. One of the bails was lying on the ground. Umpire Egar at the bowler's end hesitated for seconds which seemed like hours. Then while the crowd of 41,000 murmured he walked over to Umpire Hoy at square leg and asked him what he had seen. Hoy told all he could; Grout's bat had not touched the wicket nor had the wicketkeeper's gloves. Umpire Egar's view had been obstructed by the bowler, so what could he do? He called that Grout was not out.

Alexander clutched his head with his gloves. Lashley and Solomon threw themselves on the ground in disgust. Worrell and Alexander immediately beckoned to them to get up, but the West Indians were unhappy over it. Many of the newspaper critics felt Egar should have dismissed Grout. If neither Grout nor Alexander had touched the wicket, then it was a simple matter of logic—Grout must have glanced the ball on to his wicket.

Now there were only two runs to go. Grout skied a ball off Valentine and he was out. Eight wickets down and still two runs to go. Those last minutes were unendurable. The bars were deserted. The crowd everywhere was standing on top of the seats. At least 400 youths were spread around the field, crouched ready to sprint for the centre.

Martin skied one, the batsmen ran a single, and the youths sprinted towards the centre with the police after them. One tall fellow with his shirt undone almost reached the pitch. He had a transistor radio over his shoulder and no doubt he heard a fine description of his dash from the radio commentators. The police tried vainly to clear the ground, but it was a hopeless task. They might just as easily have tried to move the Grey Smith stand.

One to go. One to go. Ken Mackay was cheered and heckled at every ball.

One barracker called out perhaps the best comment of the series: "You'll never die by a stroke, Mackay."

And he didn't die by a stroke. The end was an anti-climax, two byes. On all sides the crowd sprinted to the centre and the players, as if they were trying to escape from a lynching, dashed to the dressing room. The umpires, too, were quick. The old souveniring game had been banned, and now it was up to the umpires to return the cricket material to the dressing room. Umpire Egar, who looked like a Stawell Gift candidate, was first home. Umpire Hoy was caught for a moment, but then he made a brilliant run and fought his way through. However, a boy scooted off with the ball. At first it seemed lost forever, but Wesley Hall went after him.

The boy reported later: "I had just hopped over the fence when Wesley Hall tapped me on the shoulder and said, 'Mr. Frank Worrell would like that ball'. He looked so big I didn't like to argue; I handed the ball over."

The crowd did not want to go home. Fifteen thousand or more gathered on the arena in front of the Grey Smith stand dressing rooms and they chanted: WE WANT WORRELL. WE WANT WORRELL. An announcer came out and said that Mr. Worrell was taking a shower. Half an hour went past and Worrell seemed to take an unconscionable time over his shower, but the crowd would not be put off.

At last he did come and he took part in the presentation of the Frank Worrell trophy to Richie Benaud. This was a perpetual trophy which had been announced as a surprise by the Chairman of the Board of Control, Sir Donald Bradman, only a week before. The trophy had the emblems of the palm tree on one side, a kangaroo on the other, and mounted on the top was one of the balls used in the famous tie of the First Test.

Worrell was so hoarse he could barely talk, and the crowd, which had every right to be hoarse too, pushed closer to hear him. He announced that he had his own presentation to make to Richie Benaud. He handed over his cap, that represented his scalp; his tie, that was his neck; and his blazer, that was his body. But he wouldn't give Richie his legs. Those legs weren't what they used to be; they wouldn't stand him in very good stead.

It was spontaneous. Before long everybody in front of the stand began to sing *For He's a Jolly Good Fellow*. The Southern Command Band followed it with *Will Ye No Come Back Again?* As Richie Benaud had said before, it was a sad moment, the end of the greatest Test series any of us had known, and we knew we might never see Frank Worrell again.

It was a series that created a special type of devotion. The next morning the newspapers reported a beautiful example of this. On the Monday three professional fishermen, with their own boats, were fishing out of Stanley, Tasmania, listening by radio to the cricket. Suddenly they came to a decision. They had 60 dozen crayfish, the cricket was too good to miss, why not give it away now and sail across Bass Strait to Melbourne? So Ernie Walter, George French and Bill Dart did just that. They sold their crays in Melbourne and arrived just in time for the excitement at the M.C.G.

Like everyone else they did not go home disappointed.

There was just one thing more. On February 17 there was a "ticker tape" farewell through Melbourne to the West Indies team. Streamers, confetti, rice, balloons and torn paper fluttered down from office buildings as the team rode around the city in a procession of ten open cars. The farewell procession began outside the Hotel Australia in Collins Street at 9.50 a.m. When they came out there was a crowd of 20,000 waiting to cheer them. Girls, who were waiting in the windows of offices opposite, threw maroon and white streamers—the team colours. The crowd hemmed in so closely that the cars could not move faster than three miles an hour for the whole journey. Every player was slapped on the back. They shook hands with the crowd constantly.

The trams in Elizabeth, Flinders and Bourke Streets all were stopped, and at the corner of Collins and Elizabeth office girls shouted and threw kisses. Some sang *For They are Jolly Good Fellows*, others said "God bless you all. Come back again soon . . . we love you." It all wound up with a civic reception at the Town Hall.

The next day Frank Worrell wrote in the Melbourne *Herald:* "I'm completely stuck for words. It was easily the most touching tribute ever paid to a sporting team anywhere in the world. I can't tell you how overwhelmed the boys and I were. I can tell you tears came easily to me in that extraordinary procession—and I couldn't be bothered wiping them away—and I wasn't the only one. It was incredible.

"I won't say goodbye, because I'd love to come back to Australia—the sooner the better, in any capacity connected with cricket. I will say from us all, a heartfelt 'Thank you, Australia'."

The West Indies team was a boon to cricket the world over. From now on this was the standard that had to be followed. Richie Benaud did his best to provide brighter cricket during the 1961 series in England. He was like the professional wrestler who was prepared to put on a spectacular show at every performance, and in the County matches he made a series of spectacular early closures that were almost guaranteed to provide an exciting finish. His team retained the Ashes, winning two games, losing one, with two drawn. The tour produced a brilliant new opener in Bill Lawry.

Centenaries can be a trifle awkward. The centenary of international cricket should have been celebrated with a fine match on the Melbourne Cricket Ground on New Year's Day 1962, culminating with a spectacular balloon ascent. Regrettably 1961-62 was a quiet almost non-season with no hope of a joyous occasion until the arrival of Ted Dexter's M.C.C. team the following November.

The logical plan was to have the celebration before the start of the Second Test match, the only Test for the series on the M.C.G. Mr. Percy Page of the Melbourne Cricket Club played a similar role as organiser-promoter to Sir Asher Joel at the opening of the Sydney Opera House. Originally the celebration of the Centenary of International Cricket was to be a vast affair. There was to have been a great parade of period vehicles through the streets with the teams arriving at the ground in Cobb & Co. coaches. Mr. Page also looked at the possibility of repeating Mr. and Mrs. Brown's famous balloon ascent, but alas, all this did not win great enthusiasm from the Cricket Board of Control.

Sir Donald Bradman did not want the Second Test match upstaged with the possibility that the centenary players might even outshine Ted Dexter and his men.

So the centenary replay became an all-important event. Early the Melbourne Cricket Club announced that Harold Larwood would lead the All England XI and Bill Ponsford would lead the Melbourne and Districts XVIII. The prospect of Harold Larwood bowling under-arm had all the makings of a never-to-be-forgotten event. However, Larwood turned down the invitation. He could not get away from his mixed-business shop in Sydney and Frank Tyson took his place. Furthermore Bill Ponsford thought the days were past when he could return to the cricket field.

The position was desperate with only three days to go. Who could possibly take Ponsford's place? Then the club had a brilliant idea; why not the sport-loving, extrovert Premier of Victoria, Henry Bolte? After all, as a young man he did play country cricket.

Mr. Bolte (later Sir Henry) took over the role of George Marshall, publican at the Cricketer's Arms and skipper of the Melbourne and Districts XVIII. Frank Tyson played the part of Mr. H. H. Stephenson, captain of Surrey and captain of the first touring side.

Mr. Bolte entered into the game with a gusto that was almost above and beyond the call of duty. He wore the correct buff-coloured shirt with huge red spots, white trousers tucked into puce socks, and black shoes. With this spotted shirt he committed the sin of wearing a vividly striped tie. He wore grey

243

mutton-chop whiskers without a moustache. Then on the middle of his back, almost incredibly, he had a proper driver's L plate fixed with safety pins.

According to the script Mr. "George Marshall" Bolte was supposed to go for a duck. But he was not pleased about this, so he pushed on regardless turning his "blob" into a star performance. This is how he handled the situation. When he made a fine stroke he refrained from running. Two of the finer strokes were overhead smashes through the covers from lofted Jack Iverson under-arms. The nature of his final dismissal is unclear but there was a strange run around with Mr. Bolte hitting the ball soccer fashion around the arena and finally running off. So much for the Centenary Carnival. The more serious matter was the clash with the power of the M.C.C. Captain Ted Dexter had to prove himself beside the brilliance of the preceding West Indies tour. But the series was like a book which was missing the final chapter as each side won a Test and three were drawn.

Of course there were great moments. Colin Cowdrey made 307 against South Australia, the highest score ever in Australia by an Englishman. Then there were some great deeds at the M.C.G., the first of which was Ted Dexter's century against the Australian XI captained by Neil Harvey. Admittedly the Australian XI attack was not overstrong—Colin Guest, Frank Misson, Johnny Martin and Tom Veivers—and Dexter made the most of the situation. He hit a dazzling 102 in 110 minutes.

He looked like Keith Miller in the days of Miller greatness. When one is tall and straight every shot looks perfect, and Dexter this day had action written all over him. He couldn't wait. He patted the bat on the ground like a drum stick as the bowler made his dozen paces to the wicket. His beautiful confidence and mastery were shown when he hit balls from Tom Veivers for sizzling sixes straight over the sight screen.

This wasn't all. Cowdrey made 88, Ken Barrington 219 not out and England declared at 7 for 633. In reply Simpson made 130, Shepherd 114, total 451 and after such scores the match could only be a draw.

Sir Donald Bradman need not have worried about the Second Test match being overshadowed. It was historic for a number of reasons.

A social historian would remember it as the first beer-can test. Beer cans had only recently come on the Australian market and for the first time we heard that most representative M.C.G. noise, a can gently cascading from concrete step down to concrete step in the Southern Stand. Furthermore the vociferous cricket enthusiasts in the Outer discovered a new method of expressing their displeasure at slow play—the slow clap done with a beer can in each hand.

But the cricket lover would remember other things; for example, the two ageing but great fast bowlers. Alan Davidson was now a greying thirty-three years and clearly this was his last Test on the M.C.G. He showed all his great control, pace and swing and took 6 for 75 off England's first innings.

Fred Trueman was thirty-one, reportedly suffering from back trouble, and sometimes did look a trifle elderly. Yet he was the same Ferocious Fred, quite bandy-legged, and when he walked back to bowl he swayed as if he had six guns on either hip. After delivering the ball he would stand and glare at the batsman with his hands on his hips and hair all over his eyes like a cocker spaniel. His best performance was in the second innings when he ripped through the Australian middle order batsmen with 5 for 62.

There were some great innings as on the day when Cowdrey made 113 and Ted Dexter 93. It was a fascinating struggle between the two captains, Dexter and Richie Benaud.

Dexter set out immediately to slaughter Benaud. His loveliest shot was purely aggressive as he took the shortest distance between two points, and straight drove along the wicket to the fence. But later when Benaud started to pitch the ball high Dexter played some awkward strokes.

Twice Benaud beat him, then Dexter played an infinitesimal fraction of a second too late to a well-flighted ball and he snicked it to Simpson in slips. Benaud portrayed such glee that the old athletics trainer Percy Cerutty could not have done better had Herb Elliott run a three minute mile. Yet nobody wanted to see Dexter go. It was like shooting Nellie Melba at the height of her performance.

The Reverend David Sheppard had a fascination for Australian crowds; somehow they adored the idea of a reverend gentleman at the wicket.

Whereas Richie Benaud's shirt flapped in the breeze and his chest was bare to the waist, Sheppard was immaculate—not a hair, button or crease out of place, and always wearing a singlet. Unkindly the crowd kept calling him "Your Reverend." When a fast one from Davidson painfully hit him on the thigh, the cry was "What did you say, Your Reverend?" Mrs. Sheppard watched the game from the ladies' section of the members' reserve. When the Australians were all out she decided there might just be time to feed her nine-months old baby, Jenny. At 12.40 p.m., she left the stand. She was away for less than ten minutes, but alas, when she returned her husband had gone too —off Davidson's fourth ball. He gave Mrs. Sheppard better entertainment in the second innings when he scored 113.

It was a bad Test for Norman O'Neill. He made 19 in the first innings and in the second innings Freddie Trueman bowled him for a duck. The *Sun News-*

Pictorial recalled that years before Trueman took O'Neill for a duck, caught by Colin Cowdrey, in the Fifth Test at the M.C.G. Here we were again, same ground, same batsman, same end of ground, same bowler, same fieldsman to do the catching and same type of ball. Again it was the first ball he bowled to O'Neill and again he went for a duck.

The optimism of the English swelled after this match. Dexter's men dictated the style of play from beginning to end and won by seven wickets. Had this style of aggression continued they would have won the series but it wasn't to be.

The 1963-64 season brought the fourth South African tour to Australia. We were just a little patronising; we had no inkling of the mighty South African cricketers who were just reaching what the mining industry would describe as the growth stage. Most cricket writers thought Australia would win five nil.

Also this was the season for the ultimate testing of Ian Meckiff. Since the great day in 1958 when he took 6 wickets for 38 against Peter May's team on the M.C.G. he had suffered the accusations of being "Chucker" Meckiff. He had tried to alter his action to give an impeccable style, but he wasn't quite the same; like the boozy artist who reforms, something was gone. But now Meckiff was making his come-back. Sir Donald Bradman and Mr. Bill Dowling of the Australian Board of Control had flown to London to sit at a conference to define the rules of throwing. So at the start of this season instructions to umpires were stern, and Meckiff's come-back was tragically brief.

He played against Trevor Goddard's team in the First Test at Brisbane. Umpire Col Egar no-balled him four times in his first over and his captain, Richie Benaud, did not bowl him again. Yet there is nothing an Australian crowd loves more than an underdog, particularly someone who has been injured by authority. At the end of the match the Brisbane crowd chaired him off the ground as if he had taken 15 wickets.

So the Second Test match was particularly interesting. Meckiff, of course, could not be played. Richie Benaud made a spectacular decision. He announced himself unavailable for the tour to England, because of newspaper contracts, so he stood down as captain. Yet he announced he could continue to play in this series as a common private, so to speak. Bobby Simpson took over as captain.

Keith Miller wrote: "Spare a thought for him as he takes the field against Trevor Goddard's South Africans at the M.C.G. today. He has been handed the hottest potato given a skipper since the war. He takes over from the all conquering Benaud with the weakest team put in the field for donkey's years.'

246

Yet the nostalgia for Meckiff was still there, the feeling for what might have been. There were anonymous threats against Umpire Egar's life. A man rang the South Melbourne police and said: "Egar will get the Kennedy treatment today". So police drove him to and from the M.C.G. Police also guarded the players and umpires' dressing rooms during the match.

It was a dismal day for the Justice-for-Meckiff parade. They tried to erect a WE WANT MECKIFF banner in the Outer without success. They tried again to erect it in the scoreboard stand but instantly two constables made them take it down. There was something familiar about this banner. It was at least 20 feet long and the letters were stitched in cotton, showing all the skill of the football fans. This deduction was correct. The police said that on the back of the banner was the message CARN THE BOMBERS, which seemed to indicate where Essendon supporters go in the summer time—they become Egar roasters.

God was kind to the new Australian captain. Many thought Simpson was courageous to the point of foolhardiness when on his maiden voyage he sent South Africa in to bat. Eddie Barlow made 109 but then McKenzie took 4 for 82 and Wally Grout made three catches, two of them magnificent one-handed dives, and South Africa was all out for 274.

Peter Pollock, billed as the most exciting new-ball bowler in the world, got Simpson for a duck off his fifth ball, but it was not so easy to shift the stubborn Bill Lawry, who scored 157. Lawry was in one of those splendid incidents which are good for 100,000 words of cabled copy. He hadn't added to his overnight score of four when he hooked a bumper from Joe Partridge. While everyone was following the flight of the ball to the fence he fell on all fours and knocked over his wicket. Excitedly the South Africans pointed to the broken wicket while Lawry was still on the ground.

Umpire Rowan deliberated and gave what to many was a shock decision "not out". Rowan concluded that Lawry had completed his stroke, but many cricket writers thought otherwise.

Lawry's big score, plus his newsworthy controversy, sadly left little news space for a great newcomer, Ian Redpath, aged twenty-two, who, with 97 runs, very nearly made a century in his first Test. The Australian total was 447 and with such a vast margin to chase, South Africa never got back into this Test match. The series ended with one match each and three draws. So many draws, was it ever possible to have a conclusive Test series?

The winter was deeply stirring for M.C.C. members, because 1964 was the end of a beautiful era for the Melbourne Football Club. The Demons won their twelfth pennant and it was to be the last for many years. It was an incredible and brilliant Grand Final. It all seemed over when the Collingwood captain Ray Gabelich, a vast mountain of a man, made a daring and undefended seventy-yard dash for goal. He bounced the ball as he went and everyone thought he would lose it with each wobbly bounce, but he scored.

In the last seconds Hassa Mann missed a point-blank shot for goal for the Demons and Demon supports were shattered. Yet just then, Neil Crompton, a back pocket player, dashed out of position, grabbed the ball as it fell from the pack and snapped a seemingly blind shot over the heads of the threatening opposition to score and win the game for Melbourne.

It was the football club's greatest hour, the sixth flag for coach Norm Smith and a career triumph for the Melbourne captain, Ron Barassi, now acknowledged as one of the greatest ruck-rovers the game had seen. The Melbourne committee appointed him assistant coach, and there was no question that here was Norm Smith's successor.

But the big shock had yet to come. On December 10 Carlton Football Club offered Barassi $18,000 on a three year contract to become playing coach of Carlton. The whole idea seemed too shocking, too non-Melbourne, and there was an audible sigh of relief from Melbourne supporters when he rejected it. Melbourne made a counter offer, and Norm Smith even offered to stand down, so that Barassi could take over as coach.

Yet Carlton kept pushing, offering all kinds of side benefits, until finally, almost on Christmas Eve, Ron Barassi accepted. The shock was profound. One must remember Barassi was the symbol of Melbourne, the ultimate Demon in the blue and red guernsey. His father, the late Ron Barassi, had been a famous Demon. Then when he was killed in the Second World War Norm Smith had taken over. Young Ron virtually became Norm Smith's adopted son, so he was born to be a Demon.

There was a very genuine grief among supporters, and at first they refused to believe it. This was a typical letter to the newspapers:

> A staunch Demon supporter, I cried when I learned of Ron Barassi's appointment to Carlton. If Barassi feels that he is too good for Melbourne then why go to a lower club? The victories won't be as frequent nor will the praise and sympathy from his supporters, Carlton and Melbourne alike.
> —Demons Supporter, Melbourne.

There were even pathetic letters from women who kept budgerigars. One lady said she had trained her bird to say "Come on the Demons—Kick a goal Barassi". What would she do now?

Presumably she had to strangle the bird.

There was much debate over the clearance. Many critics said Barassi had given long and great service to Melbourne, therefore he deserved to be cleared. And cleared he was. Furthermore he went with the best wishes of the Club. It is doubtful whether ever again such "valuable football property" will get such an easy and cash free clearance.

If the Melbourne Football Club lost Ron Barassi at least it gained Richmond. Originally the Richmond Football Club decided it would have to move because of a scheduled widening of Punt Road. They could see this artery, due to be a ring road, taking a great slice of their treasured ground. The Melbourne-Richmond marriage was splendid, a financial boon to both clubs. Football goers always preferred the M.C.G. and in the second year of the union, a season when Melbourne finished second last and Richmond fifth, between them, they drew 27½ per cent of all League football attendances.

During this season Mr. Charles W. Simmonds decided to stand down as President of the Melbourne Cricket Club. It was hard to believe that he was ninety-one years old, yet here was a man who could remember Trumper and Noble as close friends, a man who had represented Australia at baseball before the First World War. The M.C.C. News Letter recorded: "During the 127 years of the Club's existence there have been some who served the club magnificently and far beyond the normal expectancy. These men have won the club its present pre-eminent position in sport. A few have gone beyond even the outstanding services of these gentlemen. Mr. C. W. Simmonds is one of the select few." He died aged ninety-five on July 22, 1969.

The new President was Mr. A. E. (Bert) Chadwick. He was a top businessman and chairman of the Overseas Telecommunications Commission (Aust.). But there was a break in tradition; at last there was a footballer as club president. Admittedly he had played with the club XI as a wicketkeeper but he had made his name as one of the greatest ruckmen the Melbourne Football Club ever had. In the first Brownlow Medal voting in 1924 he was second to Geelong's Cargie Greeves by only one vote.

He played 142 games and he was captain and coach when the club won the flag in 1926. That was a deeply moving occasion, remembered even in the club song. It was the first Melbourne premiership since 1900. Bert Chadwick for many years was also captain and coach of Victoria. Mr. Chadwick became Sir Albert Chadwick in the 1974 New Year's honours.

The Englishmen arrived again in the spring of 1965, for a somewhat tortuous tour. The hunt for brighter cricket was evident, but excessive caution and fear of losing produced the old pattern—one Test win each and three draws. Mike Smith was the English captain, and he was the most popular for

249

many years. Walter Hammond was often away from the team during tour, Freddie Brown did not appear to get on with some of his men, and Len Hutton was a master of technique but lacked tolerance for players with less skill than he. Ted Dexter was self-centred and imperious. But Mike Smith was a democrat, he got on with everyone.

The M.C.G. was fortunate to have the State match and two Tests. Victoria actually beat England for the first time in forty-one years. The match had some fascinating aspects. Keith Stackpole tied up the Englishmen with his spin and took 4 for 64 on the Saturday. Even his devoted Collingwood supporters do not think he is a great bowler. His club mates say his bowling average measured in runs per wicket is invariably higher than his batting average. In Sheffield Shield games his wickets had cost 41.4 each. But he had some lovely scalps in this match—Eric Russell, Ken Barrington, John Edrich and John Murray.

The Second Test was hardly an affair to be remembered for ever, yet there are memories of an exquisitely put together 104 by Colin Cowdrey. At times he looked so relaxed one wondered whether he was awake. Even when Connolly buzzed bumpers straight at his head he beamed back a bland smile as if he were saying, "Yes, thank-you, I like milk and two lumps of sugar please." He was so relaxed that he went from 90 to his century in five minutes. This was in defiance of the rules. It was generally accepted that all batsmen should wallow in the Nervous Nineties for at least forty minutes.

Then Doug Walters, aged twenty, scored 115 in his second Test match. He scored 155 in Brisbane, so those indefatigable gentlemen who keep the records were able to say he was the first Australian batsman in forty-one years to hit a century in both his first and second Test matches against England. Then there was another statistic, this was the eleventh draw in seventeen England-Australia Tests.

For the Fifth Test everything was superbly poised, just as promoters would have wanted it. The opposing teams were one Test all, England had won in Sydney, Australia in Adelaide. This time they appeared to have the big chance. On the second day Mike Smith was able to declare at 9 down for 485. Ken Barrington, often described as hard to watch, demolished his reputation with 115 runs scored off 153 balls. Then there was 85 from Edrich and 79 from Cowdrey.

So the Australians batted late on Saturday, an event eagerly awaited by the crowd of 68,476. David Brown clean-bowled Simpson very quickly. There was no sense of tragedy in this for nobody was looking forward to another Simpson-Lawry stiff-upper-lip partnership.

Now for the last hour Bill Lawry and Bob Cowper fought to contain the

English beachhead. It was dour but Cowper at least was making some strokes. The Englishmen by this time were becoming very weary of Lawry. He took four and a half hours to score his 88 in the Second Test and by the time this Test started they had bowled against him for 21 hours 46 minutes.

He was the Lawry of old. At the wicket he didn't smile, he didn't frown, he didn't show emotion in any way. One time Barry Knight made an appeal so confidently that Lawry should have shrunk in fear. He did not even look up. He had the unmoved, unknowing expression on his face of a husband reading the paper at breakfast. Maybe he shifted his wad of chewing gum from one side of his face to the other. Not the least of his achievements was this capacity for chewing the same wad of gum for two hours.

Lawry went on to score 108 runs in 369 minutes. Ian Woolridge of London's *Daily Mail* commented: "The prize that Mike Smith rated as a miserable urn continues here to have crown jewel status. And when William Morris Lawry decides to defend them as such it is time to look up the plane times back to the Northern Hemisphere. As long as Lawry survives anything but a draw is unlikely." Doug Ring, a famous spinner himself, asked Fred Titmus what he thought of the M.C.G. wicket. Solemnly he replied that he would use it as a base for building flats.

But there was worse to come. Play was washed out on the Tuesday and Bob Cowper, who was 159 not out on Monday, went on to score a mammoth 307, the type of come-back a player has only in his Walter Mitty dreams.

Cowper had been dropped to twelfth man for the Fourth Test. When he took his score past 270 he heard clapping and cheering but could not understand why. Later he discovered he had broken Sir Donald Bradman's record of 270 runs for the highest score by an Australian in Australia against England. Then when he reached 300 he had passed Sir Donald's record of 299, the highest score by a batsman in Test cricket in Australia.

Yet perhaps Cowper was getting even with the selectors, because even when he took over, the match was already suffering from rigor mortis. His first 100 runs took five hours ten minutes. His second hundred took 3¾ hours and altogether for his 307 runs he batted seven minutes over 12 hours.

Australia declared at 8 for 543, but where could they go from here? There was no time left. At stumps England was 3 for 69, all wickets falling to Graham McKenzie. It was an unsatisfactory result to a series. How could this ultra defensive attitude be changed? There may be other grave crimes like blackmail, armed robbery, rape and murder but the ultimate crime as far as Englishmen and Australians were concerned seemed to be failure in a Test cricket match.

If cricket was failing to brighten up, Melbourne was improving miraculously. No longer was it a sin to have licensed restaurants and in February 1966 hotels were at last permitted to remain open until 10 p.m. Six o'clock closing had begun on October 25, 1916, as a temporary measure to help defeat the Kaiser. Whether it did have this effect is open to doubt but it took just on half a century to get rid of the idea. Furthermore experiments were being made with Sunday cricket for Sheffield matches. Pre-war, cricket on a Sunday would have seemed beyond belief. Now there was a curious lack of opposition. It was agreed that Sunday cricket would be all right as long as matches did not start before noon. This way cricket would not become a temptation to distract one from morning service.

The year 1966 was significant and challenging for the old Paddock, which seemed like an old maestro looking across at the birth of an infant prodigy. The Victorian Football League, after deciding it wanted its own ground with its own membership entirely devoted to football, turned the first sod at Waverley on January 5. This was to be the super stadium, the first arena ever excusively for Australian Rules football with an eventual capacity of 160,000.

Many thought the construction of the new stadium would bring to a sudden stop all future expansion plans for the M.C.G. This did not happen for immediately after the 1966 Grand Final the wreckers moved in to make way for the building of the new Western stand which would increase accommodation to over 120,000.

Scot Palmer wrote in the *Sun News-Pictorial:*

> The MCG is playing the game with all the courage and pride you would expect from such a body. For yesterday it faced up gamely to perhaps the toughest sporting decision the club has made in its 128 years as manager of Melbourne's greatest sporting arena. It committed itself to a total debt of $3,700,000 for buildings with full knowledge of what the VFL one day might decide to do to Waverley.

The old Grey Smith stand, born in 1906, plus the scoreboard stand, had to go to make way for the new building. Whelan the Wrecker started his methodical work and the speed with which the vintage masonry began to disappear was frightening. Crunch went the old changing rooms—visitors to the right, home team on the left. One thought of the great men they had housed, Hobbs, Rhodes, Hendren, Trumper, Hammond, Kippax, W. W. Armstrong, Bradman, McCabe . . . Some tried to hide their grief by speculating on how Neville Cardus would have covered the event. He would have been impressed by the handling of the steel ball by Mr. Whelan. He would have noted the beauty of the back swing, the glorious authority of the follow through, and the evenness of the scoring rate.

The next to come down was the Snake Pit. Now the Snake Pit was the bar just beside the changing rooms and one could say many a good Test match was watched from here. The sophisticated drinker would have a subtle ear for crowd noises and as soon as the roar reached heroic proportions he would rush outside to see what triumph or disaster had been perpetrated.

Without the Grey Smith stand the big arena looked like a fat doughnut from which someone had taken a huge bite. For more than half a century it had been nigh impossible to hit a ball out of the M.C.G. Now it could be done with relative ease and the *Sun News-Pictorial* offered $50 to any batsman who would do so during a Shield or pennant match. Nobody did.

The builders had a lovely time during this period of construction. First they had the opportunity to watch football, then cricket. They even had the opportunity to see a Test match, Australia versus India. The Indians under the Nawab of Pataudi came and lost all four Test matches. During the Second Test at the M.C.G. Graham McKenzie caused a rout—he took 7 wickets for 66. But for a stubborn knock of 75 by Pataudi with an injured leg it would have been an almost total disaster. The Indians were all out for 173.

Then Australia came in to amass 529. This was a time when Bill Lawry could be depended upon to produce a century with all the reliability of the milkman delivering the morning bottle. Paul Sheahan scored 100 and Ian Chappell made his first Test century with 151. The Indians did better in their second innings but by that time it was too late. They failed against the all-powerful Australian cricket machine but they won all votes for the gusto and attractiveness of their play.

The new Western stand progressed rapidly. Prince Philip, Duke of Edinburgh laid the foundation stone and the *Guardian* in London expressed astonishment that these remarkable improvements were being done to a *cricket* ground. It said: "This is all part of a scheme to increase capacity to 123,000. Cricket rises triumphant from the ashes of boredom, you think. Actually the whole plan is to meet the gladiatorial demands of the American football they play there in the winter. What price Lord's for bingo." The unfortunate editor reported that after this monstrous error he was besieged by twenty-five thousand irate citizens of Kangaroo Valley, Earl's Court.

The stand had its first use for the Melbourne-Footscray match on Saturday, August 10, 1968. The Lieutenant-Governor, Sir Edmund Herring, a fifty-year member of the club, opened it officially on Friday, August 9. The Western stand, a very handsome three-tier affair, was built to house nineteen thousand spectators, two-thirds being open to the general public. Club members rose from 9800 to 12,800. The architects were Tompkins, Shaw and Evans with engineers Milton Johnson and Associates. The building committee of the club was B. J. Callinan (chairman), A. E. Chadwick (club president), H. I. Ebeling and D. P. Cordner.

The changes were dramatic. For a start the scoreboard was way aloft, re-assembled above the stand so that now it was 155 feet above street level or the height of a ten-storey building. A self-contained unit, it had its own showers and lavatories for the scoreboard workers.

The seats were meticulously designed to give comfort to all sizes and shapes. Furthermore, the architect, Stan Evans, said his men put them through the most rigorous tests. It was decided that the seats would be good enough if they could withstand six large men jumping on them while another six pushed from the rear. The architect had to allow 18 inches for each seat, instead of 15 inches as in the old stand. The affluent Melbourne behind had become more ample.

The back room comforts of the new stand were something to see. The new members' bar had black vinyl club-like armchairs, wall-to-wall carpet with the M.C.C. insignia, panelled walls and ceiling. The dining room and ladies bar were equally splendid. There were closed-circuit television screens so that one could keep track of the score at all times.

The players' rooms were air conditioned and they had a parquet floor just like the very best banks. Stan Evans paced out the distance from the dressing rooms to the batting crease and now it was further than ever, as far as from Flinders Street station to the G.P.O., a very long walk after scoring, say, a duck, with ninety-thousand pairs of eyes looking and not a handclap.

The Grand Final between Carlton and Essendon did not produce quite the crowd that was expected—116,828—but it was a record just the same.

The spring of 1968 brought the West Indies back to Australia under the leadership of Gary Sobers. Everyone expected a marvellous, zestful series like the "Brown Magic" of 1961, but the old dash was not there. Desperately they needed the Wes Hall and the Charlie Griffith of old; instead their bowling was often miserably thin.

They won the toss in Brisbane, batted well, then proceeded to carve up Australia with spin on a crumbling wicket. Yet the tale was very different when they came to Melbourne for the Second Test, starting on a frigid Boxing Day. Captain Bill Lawry, who had been defeated by an innings in Brisbane, was now as determined and as ruthless as an Israeli general. He badly wanted to even the score and he did. Many were startled when after winning the toss he sent the West Indies in to bat.

254

Sobers' men were unfortunate that they struck Graham McKenzie at the height of his energy and skill, with accuracy instilled in him by a season with the Lancashire League. There were no stray balls; it was machine tool precision and he finished that innings with eight wickets for 71. The West Indies were all out for 200.

Then the West Indies had to contend with the awesome power of Bill Lawry and Ian Chappell. Gary Sobers must have been wondering when Chappell was going to stop. In five completed innings against them already he had scored 814 runs with the terrifying average of 162. He did not have the scrupulous style of Paul Sheahan or the straightbacked magnificence of Sobers himself, but he had the power. He loved the pulls, the cross-bat blast to the boundary and the huge off-drive.

An even more significant fact was that Bill Lawry was a changed man. Bob Simpson commented that he hadn't seen Lawry display such a range of shots except in a picnic match. He had discovered the square cut and at one stage he sent a six straight over the sightboard, an unheard-of thing from Lawry. Lawry said he could only recall having hit one other six on the M.C.G. Simpson wrote in the *Sun News-Pictorial:* "It was one of the finest Test innings I have seen Lawry play. If he had shown the same dash over the years as he did in this innings he would have gained more runs and earned more plaudits." Lawry made his 205 runs in 461 minutes and 165 in 310 minutes.

There was a new fashion among the young—the excursion out to the middle of the oval—and they did it four times on the Saturday. They believed that, upon each batsman reaching his half century or century, it was their right to rush out and offer their personal congratulations. As the appropriate time drew near they infiltrated to the fence like invading Viet Cong, some even climbed it and sat on the boundary line. Then, as soon as Lawry or Chappell hit the triumphant run, they charged.

It was harrowing for the umpires. A set of bails disappeared during one invasion. In another a youth tried to wrest a stump from Umpire Col Egar. A flying tackle by a policeman stopped another young man from getting away with a middle stump. In all sixteen minutes were lost because of these infiltrations.

At first the administration at the M.C.G. was a little sympathetic to these personal middle-of-the-ground congratulations. After all, it is wise to encourage the young, but the behaviour became irresponsible, and it was upsetting the concentration of the players.

Australia was all out for 510, yet Bill Lawry still was not happy. He had hoped that Australia would reach 600. Now the West Indies had to face the Australian attack again and they did only marginally better. This time the

255

Australian destroyer was Johnny Gleeson. He pushed the ball through faster than one would expect from a spin bowler, and his run was almost as long as that of Alan Connolly. He was bandy, round-shouldered and he had the craggy, almost unbelievably Australian face, so adored by the painter, Albert Tucker. Frank Tyson commented in the *Age* that the number of bad balls he sent down could be counted on the fingers of one hand—excluding his bent spinning finger. Gleeson's 5 wickets for 61 was his best Test performance so far.

Graham McKenzie took his 200th Test wicket and perhaps it was the most important wicket of the match. It was a ball that pitched just outside the line of the off stump, whipped back fast and slightly slow, beating Gary Sobers' bat. He was out lbw for 67. He defeated Sobers with almost exactly the same ball in the first innings when he got him for 19.

The West Indies was all out for 280 and Australia won by an innings and 30 runs. Bill Lawry, not one given to over extravagant statements, said; "It was a good result."

From then on play from the West Indies was like a fireworks display—brilliant in flashes. They lost the Third Test match, drew the Fourth, and Australia won the Fifth by 382 runs. No, the fun had gone and there was no parade of honour through the streets of Melbourne this time.

But if the M.C.G. now looked newer and more modern, the tradition was still growing. On November 14, 1969 there was a reception in the club to launch the museum. The club president, Mr Bert Chadwick, was superbly discreet about it. He would never suggest that an antipodean museum was better than the famous museum at Lord's. That would be a piece of sacrilege like saying you had something holier than the Holy Grail. Yet there were some people present who suggested that just possibly this was the finest sporting exhibition anywhere and it was beautifully housed in a special room which was a former dining room in the members' pavilion.

The museum came to the M.C.G. through a remarkable piece of generosity and good fortune. Tony Baer, thirty-one, was a rich young Englishman with an interest in the stock market. He was never much good at cricket. He was captain of his school 4th XI until he was dropped. His top score was 28.

At fifteen he bought his first piece of "cricket-ana," a mug for five shillings. After that he bought up lavishly. He bought every item with a cricket motif that he could find—pictures, cartoons, scorecards, silver, porcelain, glassware, oil paintings, snuff boxes, wood carvings. In the early 'sixties he visited the M.C.G. and there was something about Australians and the atmosphere of the place that he liked for he willed his collection to the club.

But then things began to get difficult in his London flat. Every available square inch was covered or filled with "cricket-ana." Even the toilet-seat cover was nicely decorated with a famous Australian cricketer. He was just about to start decorating the ceilings when he made a decision. Why wait until he died? Give it to the Melbourne Cricket Club now—and he did.

The decision was not entirely well received in England. Many thought it was so valuable it should never have been allowed out of England. For example there was Walter Hammond's personal collection of silver trophies. There was the silver cigarette box presented to Sir Pelham Warner at the end of the famous 1932-33 tour to Australia. The top of the silver box had the famous names etched upon it, Douglas Jardine, Bill Voce, Harold Larwood, Bill Bowes . . . It was like having the bullet that killed Nelson residing in a French museum. Then there was an exquisite bowl depicting a 1730 cricket scene, a piece of English porcelain so rare the Victoria and Albert Museum pleaded with Tony Baer to give it to them. But no, he was determined to keep the collection together.

So it all came to Melbourne and the collection is huge. Some pieces are so famous it is hard to believe one is looking at the original. There is the magnificent painting by Sir Martin Archer Shee R.A., painted in 1841, which depicts "The Godson Brothers" playing cricket at Eton. Beautiful they are, in black velvet and Eton collars.

The old "villain," Dr. W. G. Grace, features many times. There are linen handkerchiefs and scarves which illustrate his imposing countenance and every run he has made. He is on plates, he is commemorated in china and in silver. There are letters he has written, books he has autographed, and there is even a pipe carved in the shape of W.G.'s head. A very strong smoke, one would imagine. There is a framed menu of a dinner given to him by His Grace the Duke of Beaufort, at the Clifton Club on February 5, 1896.

They started with sandwiches, then savoured thick turtle soup, boiled salmon and sweetbreads. After that they moved into the roast fillet of beef, then wild duck. There was Bavaroise à la Marguerite to follow, herring roe, and Italian ice-cream with dessert to finish. There was wine to go with every dish, including a 25-year-old German hock, a 15-year-old Perrier Jouet champagne, 25-year-old French claret and port which was fifty-six years old.

There is much, much more in the museum, even a little porcelain statuette depicting Freddie Trueman about to bowl. One suspects that Freddie Trueman never dreamed that he would be perpetuated in china at the Melbourne Cricket Club.

On April 5, 1970 some very interesting signatures appeared in the visitors' book. One above the other down the page they read:

Elizabeth R.

Philip.

Charles.

Anne.

Her Majesty the Queen, Prince Philip, the Prince of Wales and Princess Anne came to the M.C.G. to see the third quarter of the football match between Richmond and Fitzroy. The match was historic in many ways. Never before had the Royal Family seen an Australian Rules match, and to fit it into the tight royal schedule the Victorian Football League set the game for a Sunday afternoon.

Many times have football writers and individual clubs suggested Sunday League football, but always the opposition has been strong. So the royal match was a royal first. All the bars were closed and locked. The only refreshments available were canned lemonade, chocolate and pies. Long before the Royal Party arrived there was an air of tension about the ground. Halfway through the first quarter one member actually dropped a pie wrapping, and Mr. Ian Johnson, secretary of the M.C.C., hurried down and picked it up.

At half time there was a message over the loud speakers advising that when the Royal Family arrived everyone should stand for the national anthem. They made their appearance right on time. VFL officials led them straight down to a dais in front of the Members Stand and it was obvious that some advice had been given. The Queen was in pale apricot and Princess Ann in moon blue—nothing that could be described as partisan colours.

Then came the national anthem and it was in the Grand Final tradition. A few distinguishable bars with the rest drowned by enthusiastic cheering.

Both teams lined up for the presentation. Rarely, particularly at half time on the M.C.G., had we seen such beautiful, well-scrubbed footballers. They had been told to shower and turn out in completely fresh gear. Also their instructions were to stand to attention, not speak until spoken to, pull their socks up and have their teeth in. As football is such a hazardous occupation it is fairly normal for players to appear without teeth.

The Royal Family made a grand tour of the ground in Land Rovers. They received a mighty reception in the best cheer squad tradition—crackers, whistles, plus the plaintive cry of a bugle, an instrument that is always brought out at the M.C.G. at times of deep emotion. From the top of the stand they also were honoured with a spray of at least four cut-up books. The Richmond cheer squad waved their floggers up and down, and it was interesting to note that in the midst of all the flying paper, they produced one large, splendid Union Jack.

The Queen, Prince Philip, Prince Charles and Princess Anne saw the best football of the day when Fitzroy scored five goals in a little over seven minutes. Did they like the game?

They were there hardly long enough to judge that, scarcely twenty-five minutes. Their next move was on to Albert Park to look at basketball and table-tennis. According to the schedule their stay there was actually ten minutes longer than at the M.C.G. As one commentator put it, a little unkindly, this was a ten minute victory for actual ping-pong over aerial ping-pong.

The Grand Final for the football that season broke all records with Carlton beating Collingwood before a crowd of 121,696. The four finals produced a lovely parade of customers, 104,239, 112,838, 108,215 and then the bumper 121,696. The M.C.C. News Letter recorded that the total crowd for the season at the M.C.G. was 1,108,189 and it said: "The enormity of these attendances is better appreciated when it is realised that the Eiffel Tower in Paris, one of the great tourist attractions of the world, has only 1,500,000 visitors each full year."

The coming summer was early anticipated for the Englishmen were on their way to Australia again. This time there were to be six Test matches and Perth was to hold its first ever. When the series was all over the two captains, Ray Illingworth and Ian Chappell, both said that the Ashes should be scrapped and buried. Maybe it would have been better had they done this early in December 1970 for the tour was far from happy. Only two Tests were finished out of the seven—the Fourth and the *Seventh,* both in Sydney, and both won by England.

The Third Test at the M.C.G. was historic because not a ball was bowled. Forty-six points of rain fell on the first day and the downpour continued on through the second with awesome prospects for a miserable week-end. Typical headlines were:

BIG TEST SINKS IN THE M.C.G. MUD

TEST FIZZLES IN THE DRIZZLE

But the historic feature was this, members of the Australian Cricket Board of Control and representatives of the Marylebone Cricket Club met on the third day and decided to abandon the Test match. It still had to be called the Third Test because the captains had tossed and therefore it had actually started.

It was important to appreciate the depth of the tragedy. Melbourne with its M.C.G. can draw a bigger cricket crowd in one day than most other places can attract for an entire Test match. Now this match was cancelled, the one and only Test. It was Sydney's turn to get two Test matches. However the Summit meeting of cricket officials was both brave and inspired. They dropped an England-Victoria Country XI match which was due to start on January 20, and replaced it with an extra Test, to become the Fifth Test.

Sir Donald Bradman, chairman of the Board of Control, was praised as if the old days of the 1930s had returned. E. M. Wellings of London's *Evening News* was one of the few to hand out a rebuke: "This high-handed action of officials cannot be too strongly deplored. Without authority to do so they have ridden roughshod over captains and umpires."

Yet for some the sodden, unstarted Third Test was an irreparable loss. One felt particularly for the members of England's Cricket Society. To celebrate their 25th anniversary forty-two members flew to Australia with the object of seeing the Third and Fourth Test matches. All they saw in Melbourne was rain. A particularly touching case was Albert Willars of Leicestershire. Fifty years had gone by since he had seen the Australians play. This was by design for it had taken him fifty years to forgive them. He explained to a reporter in Melbourne:

> It happened during the 1921 series. I was twenty-five and I rode my bicycle twenty-five miles to see the Second Test at Nottingham. I think admission was two shillings and I had sixpence to spend. Australia had made about a thousand and England was in a hopeless position. Gregory bowling to Tyldesley cracked him a terrible one and smashed his jaw. The ball dropped down the wicket. What did the Australians do? Every one of them immediately appealed. I didn't wait. I smartly got on my bicycle and rode home. I haven't been to a Test match since.

Mr Willars did manage to see the Fourth Test in Sydney but he had no hope of returning for the next Test in Melbourne as the Cricket Society schedule was too tight. They had to play a match in Hong Kong on the way home.

Newspapers and firms provided all sorts of inducements for high speed scoring. The Melbourne Cricket Club offered $2000 to anyone who could smash the clock on the members' stand at the M.C.G. This would have been a prodigious feat. Jack Ryder is the only man to ever come remotely near it, when he gave the clock on the Smokers stand a fright in that historic 1107 Victorian innings against N.S.W. during the Christmas of 1926. The Fifth Test of January 1970 did not inspire such behaviour. As one inn-keeper put it: "They didn't even look like breaking the umpires' watches."

Australia opened the symphony with a long and very slow movement.

Above
Premier of Victoria, John Cain, Prime Minister R. J. Hawke and Ray Hornsby, Manager Westpac, at the opening of the Australian Gallery of Sport.

Left
Dr Donald Cordner, President M.C.C. since 1985.

Right
Bruce Church, Vice President 1987,
M.C.C. committee since 1978.

Below
John Mitchell, Vice President
since 1986.

Below right
Mr Justice Alec Southwell, M.C.C.
committee 1979, Vice President
since 1988.

Keith Stackpole took nine minutes more than two hours to make his 30 before being bowled by d'Oliveira. Bill Lawry retired hurt at 38 after 2 hours 45 minutes. Australia toiled until late on the second day when Lawry declared at 9 wickets for 493. The tale would have been different had England held its catches.

How one felt for Cowdrey. Normally there wouldn't be a safer pair of hands in all England, but he seemed to have lost confidence. There were eight catches grassed in that innings and he dropped four of them.

The new game of invade-the-wicket was on once more. When Ian Chappell reached his century more than a thousand people made the grand dash. Both Chappell and Cowdrey lost their caps. One end of the wicket was damaged and a stump stolen. The players were even pummelled and Ian Chappell told the *Age* later: "I was petrified I would fall and be trampled under all those feet."

Ian Johnson, secretary of the Melbourne Cricket Club, said he was distressed at what happened: "It was a disgraceful performance," he said. "The adults were either sheer exhibitionists or drunken louts."

Yet what could be done about it? There were all sorts of suggestions. Some recalled the Macapagal ground in Brazil where there was a moat right around the ground to dampen the ardour of over-enthusiastic spectators. Ian Johnson even mentioned the possibility of installing barbed wire and he winced at the thought of such a fate for a cricket ground.

All sorts of appeals asking the public to refrain from swarming the wicket went out over loudspeakers at the ground, on radio and through the press. The big test came on the Sunday before 65,860 spectators when the England opener, Brian Luckhurst, was making his gallant stand. If ever a player deserved personal congratulations it was he. He broke the little finger of his left hand early in the innings, but bravely battled on for five and a half hours. When he was 97 four mounted troopers came to the gates. As he drove Stackpole for four to reach his century uniformed police moved all around the ground. They could never have checked a real rush, but fortunately nobody tried. The battle of the middle was over. A delighted Ian Johnson said very briefly over the loudspeakers: "Announcement—Thank-you." This was greeted with loud applause.

England scored 392, including 117 from Basil d'Oliveira. From then it became the "ho-hum" Test. One cricket writer went further. His mind must have been far away at some sunny surf beach for he described the match as "the corpse which needed the kiss of life."

On the fourth day both sides made only 204 runs in a full day's play.

261

England perhaps could be excused for Illingworth's men were fighting to avoid defeat. Australia on the other hand wasn't trying to win. Stackpole, usually the extrovert hitter, took ninety minutes to make 18 and Lawry 135 to make 39. Ian Chappell was there for forty-four minutes before stumps to make four runs. So on the fifth day the whole affair expired into a draw.

The Sixth Test in Adelaide was yet another draw. Then came the shock, the selectors not only sacked Bill Lawry as captain but they dropped him from the team. It was the first time an Australian Test captain had been dropped from a side during a series.

There were some American spacemen on tour to the moon, but hardly anyone seemed to notice. The talk of all Melbourne was of the home town boy, Bill Lawry, often called the Phantom, who had been dropped. At the time it seemed like the greatest sacking since President Truman fired General MacArthur. At the sportsmen's haven, Lou Richards' Phoenix Hotel, the Phantom's caricature was sadly and ceremoniously hung upside down, as one writer said, like a distressed warship's ensign. Ian Chappell took over as the new captain, but he had to wait until later for his successes, for England won the Seventh Test and the Ashes in Sydney. The margin for that match was 62 runs.

If the tour by the Englishmen had all the long drawn out movement of a Chinese opera the South African tour in the summer of 1971-72 seemed to offer everything. Here was the greatest team in the world, an all-star cast composed of Eddie Barlow, the Pollock brothers, the world's greatest batsman Barry Richards, the paceman Mike Proctor, just to mention a few. So when this tour never took place the sense of disappointment was sharp.

Politics entered cricket. The all-white Springbok rugby tour of Australia had been an agonising time with demonstration after demonstration. On June 23 protestors daubed anti-apartheid slogans in letters two-feet high outside the M.C.G. There were maybe fifty different signs at the M.C.G. and Olympic Park. One read:

SMASH APARTHEID—
NO RUGBY OR CRICKET TOURS BY RASCISTS.

It was interesting that the protestors did not know how to spell. The controversy made front-page news for five months. The States were divided on the issue. Premiers Mr Tonkin of Western Australia and Mr Dunstan of South Australia both later said the South Africans would receive nothing from them —no receptions and no hospitality. Sir Henry Bolte of Victoria and Mr. Bjelke-Petersen of Queensland said they would be delighted to see this all-white South African team.

A Gallup poll taken in September showed that 63 per cent approved of the tour, 23 per cent disapproved and 14 per cent were undecided. Yet, as most newspapers pointed out, the tour was doomed. It is possible for a large force of policemen to ensure that a football match will take place, but how do you look after a thirty-hour five-day Test match. You can't stop spectators from flashing mirrors in the eyes of batsmen, you can't prevent demonstrators from setting off crackers and smoke bombs. And how can you forever stop them from damaging the wicket? So Sir Donald Bradman announced with great regret the cancellation of the tour and to take its place invitations went to a Rest of the World side under the leadership of Gary Sobers.

Richie Benaud wrote "Sobers can make the tour a sizzler" and he did have a remarkable collection of hot coals to provide the sizzle—Tony Greig, Peter and Graeme Pollock, Clive Lloyd, Farook Engineer, Rohan Kanhai, Sunil Gavaskar, Intikhab Alam, Hylton Ackerman, Bishan Bedi, Zahir Abbas, Bob Cunis, Richard Hutton and Norman Gifford.

Like many a star-studded team often they seemed to sizzle a little too much in opposite directions. The first international match was washed out by the Brisbane rain. The second saw the arrival of a new Australian star, Dennis Lillee. He had such a pretty name the cricket writers at first did not know what to call him, but they settled for Lethal Lillee. He took 8 wickets for 29 in the first innings and 4 for 63 in the second, making the match a financial disaster for it was all over in two days and ninety minutes.

The Rest of the World had an equally disastrous match against South Australia and the situation did not look over-exciting for the third international match at the M.C.G. Percy Beames wrote in the *Age:* "The World XI tour of Australia is fast becoming the biggest blunder in recent years. Top money— $200 a week—is being paid to the World XI players, and on what they have produced they are grossly overpaid."

To make matters even worse the sizzlers were beset with injuries, a casualty list that ran to twenty different injuries even before Christmas. After reading the newspaper accounts day after day it seemed almost possible to graduate in medicine. The worst was Clive Lloyd who injured his spine in a fall and was out for the rest of the tour.

The best news was the advent of the Pollock brothers from South Africa. They had been delayed because of home town commitments and they were injected into the so-called Third unofficial Test only twelve hours after flying into Melbourne.

But Lillee was the star again. A visitor from Mars could have been startled by one news poster LILLEE WRECKS THE WORLD. He took 5 wickets for 48

263

off 16.3 overs. He bowled Graeme Pollock and Gary Sobers with successive balls and only a shower of rain and the unflappable Tony Greig prevented him from getting a hat trick. Kevin Hogan, the veteran cricket writer of the *Sun News-Pictorial* thought the long downward delivery sweep of Lillee's bowling arm was reminiscent of Ernie McCormick. Actually McCormick was present this day and like Kevin Hogan he was very impressed.

The World was all out for 184. Australia replied with 285, including 115 not out from Greg Chappell, but the historic event, the innings which will and should be remembered forever at the M.C.G., came when Gary Sobers returned to the wicket for the second time. Curiously, Sobers had never shone in Melbourne, the M.C.G. to him was nothing but an omen of bad luck.

His innings started at 2.04 p.m. on the Monday and he was dismissed at 2.20 p.m. on the Tuesday for 254. Here are the cold statistics. He made 50 in sixty-nine minutes with 8 fours, 100 in 135 minutes, 16 fours; 150 in 261 minutes, 21 fours; 200 in 330 minutes, 24 fours; 250 in 373 minutes. That doesn't include two towering sixes over the fence off successive balls from spinner Kerry O'Keeffe.

The M.C.C. secretary, Mr. Ian Johnson said: "It was the best innings I've seen. You would have to go back to the Bradman of the early thirties to see its equal." Doug Ring was asked for his comment and he said: "Words escape me."

The English fast bowler, John Snow, who was watching from the grandstand, had the best words to describe Sobers:

> Bowling to Sobers is a gamble. He gives you a chance to get him out when he flails at balls outside the off stump. But if his eye is in and he connects he is merciless and gathers confidence every time he sees the ball rattle the pickets. He is like a runaway train . . . the buffers are no good . . . and you just have to wait for him to run out of steam or crash.

The Rest of the World finished with 514, and Sobers, aided by 86 from Abbas, very nearly won the match on his own. Yet the game was not over. On the fifth day, faced with an impossible task, Doug Walters created another piece of history when he became the first man in first-class cricket at the M.C.G. to score a century before lunch. While his colleagues marched in and out he hit 102 runs in the pre-lunch session. He dawdled at first and his fifty could be described as pleasant two-star entertainment. Then suddenly he took off. Bob Massie was his foil at the other end and he proceeded to spread fours all around the wicket. He scored his next 50 in thirty-six minutes and finally he was out for 127.

Australia lost the match by 96 runs, but that was a very unimportant fact and one did not remember the tiresome details. It had been a cricket match that had everything. Colin McDonald commented: "This was a game that made me proud to talk about cricket again."

The "World" gathered pace after this match. The fourth international match in Sydney was a draw after a winning chance for Australia was spoiled by the weather, and the Fifth Test in Adelaide gave Sobers his second win. So after all the dire knocking predictions, the Rest of the World won the series.

The summer of '73 brought an interesting variety of events. Sometimes one thinks that there should be a better name for the great arena in Richmond Park than the Melbourne Cricket Ground. In its time it has absorbed all Melbourne's history, not only its cricket, its football and athletics. It has had one of the city's first balloon ascents, one of the first aeroplane flights; it has been converted into a military camp; it has absorbed an Olympic Games.

In February 1973 it took over yet another role, it became a great open-air cathedral, the scene for the 40th International Eucharistic Congress. Ian Johnson, secretary of the Melbourne Cricket Club, recalled one unforgettable sight—the day when the Members Stand was filled with priests and nuns, the priests all in black on one side, the nuns all in white on the other.

The congress had five great religious serves at the M.C.G.—a combined migrant mass, a mass for schools, an ecumenical service, a Byzantine rite ceremony and a grand closing ceremony on February 25. Those of us who had sat in the concrete stands on hot summer afternoons and witnessed beer cans cascading down the steps like waterfalls, were startled at the transformation. The "holy" end of the ground was close to Bay 13 and Bay 14. Early in February workmen began building a podium 124 feet by 100 feet for the throne of the Papal Legate, Cardinal Lawrence Sheehan, plus an altar. Around that altar and podium were to sit 200 cardinals and bishops from all over the world.

The *Australian* commented:

> Any event that can attract a greater crowd to the Melbourne Cricket Ground than an Australian Rules Grand Final is noteworthy. When it is a gathering of Christians in an age that has proclaimed a lingering death for the Church, it is remarkable.

It would be a mistake to say that there were record crowds at the M.C.G. but the Eucharistic Congress certainly outpaced the 1973 football finals. At the Children's Mass on February 23 there were 100,000 children. They came in 86 special trains, 92 trams and 229 buses. The Papal Legate, Cardinal

265

Sheehan, and the Archbishop of Melbourne, Cardinal-designate Knox, drove on to the ground in a purple Rolls-Royce convertible and 25 mounted police escorted them in a lap of the ground. So for three hours the M.C.G. was a church and as four hundred priests went among the crowd administering the sacrament, the voices of fourteen choirs could be heard over the trees in East Melbourne.

The biggest crowd, 120,000, was on the night of February 25 for the closing ceremony "Statio Orbis"—station of the world. The crowd, or should it be called congregation, spilled over the boundary line on to the grass, which was a rich enough scene, without the formality in the centre of the cardinals, bishops, priests, choirs and bands in their dazzling robes.

When the cantor made his chants and when the 120,000 in the grandstands made their response, there was an enormous, orchestral mega-voice boom that one gets only on very big occasions in the M.C.G. Ian Johnson said it reminded him of the final day of the 1956 Olympic Games. He said: "This is the most impressive show I've seen here with that exception and I rate it equal with that."

After Communion and the concluding rite of Light, Faith and Mission, heralded by trumpets, the crowd exploded in joy. They clapped and stamped and cheered and whistled. Then the 120,000 began singing "Waltzing Matilda." They broke the barricades and sang the choruses over and over as the Papal Legate and the Archbishop of Melbourne circled the arena. It was all over.

The other big event for the summer of '73 was the Pakistani tour. The Pakistani team arrived under the leadership of Intikhab Alam for a three Test series. A Test win in Australia was being described as "the impossible dream" for Pakistan had beaten Australia only once and that was in Karachi in 1956. Never had there been a win on Australian soil. Yet Intikhab was confident. He had just frightened the Englishmen in England and even when the name Lillee was mentioned he showed no concern at all.

"I doubt whether Australia's new fast bowling find, Dennis Lillee, will be our bugbear this season," he said. "Our batsmen are used to facing fast bowlers." But the same batsmen had an unhappy time. Western Australia crushed them in their first match and the demon Lillee took 6 wickets for 40 runs. Pakistan lost the First Test in Adelaide by an innings and 114 runs. The soothsayers said Lillee would not be dangerous on this dead, dusty patch, but he still managed 4 wickets for 49 in the first innings. In the second Ashley Mallett on his home ground had the extraordinary figures 8 for 49.

The Second Test match was at the M.C.G. and there was a new fast bowler in the Australian line up—the Melbourne Cricket Club player, Max Walker, six feet three inches tall, a first-eighteen football ruckman. Because of his ungainly bowling action he had the nickname "Tanglefoot." Nor was he over-fast, but he could move the ball late and he was capable of almost radar-like accuracy. Would he frighten the Pakistanis as much as Dennis Lillee? Perhaps not with his speed, but he was awe-inspiring in appearance. He had long untidy hair and a splendid Zapata moustache which drooped with all the trendy menace of a television villain.

The New Year Second Test was ideal for those who revel in statistics. In the first two days only four batsmen were actually dismissed by bowlers and 726 runs went up on the board. Then two of those batsmen only left the crease because they gorged themselves with runs. That was one statistic. Another choice figure was the triumph of Sadiq, who became the fourth of the Muhammed brothers to score a Test century.

Australia batted first—Ian Redpath 135, Ian Chappell 66, Greg Chappell 116 not out and Paul Sheahan run out for 23. Ian Chappell declared at 5 wickets for 441, but the remorseless run getting went on. By the end of the second day Sadiq was not out 125, Saeed retired hurt 18, Abbas run out 51, Khan not out 92. The runs flowed at the rate of 8 and often 10 an over. Those with a streak of sadism who like a steady procession back to the pavilion had to endure a very lean Saturday. All they had to cling to was the run out of Abbas due to a brilliant throw by Lillee. The ejection of a batsman was a rare event, equivalent perhaps to the Relief of Mafeking or to Stanley finding Livingstone in Africa. Rodney Marsh, the Australian wicket-keeper, was so excited that he ran the length of the pitch to give Lillee a heart-felt hug. That was another record that could have gone down in the statistics. Tough old cricketers in the nineteen-thirties never hugged each other.

Barrie Bretland of the *Sun News-Pictorial* wrote:

> The track is so dead it would test the endurance and patience of a seasoned swaggie. But the MCG's international production of "How To Hit Runs Without Really Trying" currently playing to packed houses is likely to continue unchanged for another three days.

It certainly did on the third day. Intikhab declared at 8 wickets for 574, which included 158 from Mushtaq. Now Mr. Bretland wrote: "There is just a remote chance that this Test can still be won—and only the Pakistanis can win it." But interesting things were yet to happen. In Australia's second innings Richie Benaud's young brother John, played the innings of his career with a ferocious 142 in 211 minutes. Paul Sheahan, elegant and a little more sedate, put together a beautiful 127.

267

Intikhab needed only 293 runs for victory on the last day and the swagman's hard old track was as solid as ever, but Pakistan crumpled under pressure and was all out for 200. Top destroyer was the new boy, Max Walker, who took 3 wickets for 39. A bitterly disappointed Intikhab said: "We had a chance to win and we muffed it."

The Third Test in Sydney was a clean sweep. Australia won by 52 runs and Max Walker took 6 for 15 off 16 overs. As a Test bowler it was a debut to dream about, enough to make him twirl that Zapata moustache. In two Tests he had taken 12 wickets at a cost of only 19.19 runs apiece.

CHAPTER TWENTY-ONE

The Other Paddock

THE year 1974 was the time of crisis for the old Paddock. It had continued to improve. The administration had moved out of the old offices in Jolimont Terrace into new air-conditioned offices with a view across the bowling-green to the city skyline.

Then the passages and corridors of the club had been converted into an historic gallery, a collection of a thousand cricket, football and other sporting photographs. All this started two years earlier. The club records state that the Vice-President, Hans Ebeling, was nosing his way around various remote corners of the Pavilion when he spotted a trap-door that intrigued him. He investigated. There were cobwebs and there was dust, but there were also piles upon piles of pictures. Apparently they had been stored in the old attic after the Pavilion was built in 1926. He returned next morning in his gardening clothes and later emerged from the attic rather worse in appearance, but triumphantly bearing samples of incredible treasure—photographs of cricket teams dating back to Stephenson's day, old shots of the Austral Wheel Race, royal visits long forgotten and even a picture of the crash of the ill-fated little Bleriot aeroplane that hit the scoreboard. This collection was quite apart from the museum and when restored surely comprised one of the finest collections of sporting pictures anywhere.

The crisis however was this. Were football finals at the Melbourne Cricket Ground coming to an end? Now there was another "paddock"—Waverley—a potentially luxurious football stadium fifteen miles out of Melbourne, and it was reaching true rival proportions. Could Melbourne support two stadiums of this size?

Long before Waverley opened there were many people who were prepared to say that the great Melbourne Cricket Ground was doomed to become a white elephant, used for playing cricket before sparse crowds in the summer, lonely and empty during the winter. In 1966, a Liberal member of the State Parliament, Mr Jona M.L.A., said in the House that club football might not be played on the M.C.G. after 1968 and finals would possibly not be held there after 1971.

Dr. Don Duffy, Chairman of the Melbourne Football Club, was outraged. "Leave the ground?" he said. "Never. As long as Melbourne is a football club we will use the M.C.G. as a home ground. I believe home and away games will continue on the M.C.G. as long as Melbourne and Richmond occupy it."

It was natural that the Victorian Football League should want its own ground, its own headquarters, exclusive for football. But there were some interesting ironies in this. It was the Melbourne Cricket Club which invented their game. The club was looking for a way to keep its cricketers fit during the winter. They designed Australian Rules because Rugby was too dangerous on the sun-baked rock-hard grounds. Indeed, Mr Ian Johnson, Secretary of the Melbourne Cricket Club, as he took part in tough negotiations with the Victorian Football League, could ponder the thought that it was one of his predecessors, T. W. Wills, club secretary 1857-58, who was the prime inventor.

Admittedly the club believed then that football was only a diversion from the main game, cricket. The Melbourne Cricket Club would not have the game played on the main oval. This was considered a preposterous suggestion—imagine what football players would do to the beautiful turf. The match was between Melbourne and Carlton, and it drew a crowd between eight and ten thousand, with gate receipts of $200. What club cricket match could ever equal that?

The *Australian* cricket writer commented:

> This pretty clearly demonstrates that football is the most popular of our outdoor sports. Whoever heard of such an attendance at a cricket match? Who wouldn't have a cricket ground and let it after this? Impecunious cricket clubs take heart of grace, and let your ground for this purpose say in the month of June, when the damage to the turf signifies but little.

And so they did. Soon the football clubs were playing on all the cricket grounds for the whole winter season, and how the turf would recover and be ready for cricket only weeks after the end of football was looked upon as an antipodean miracle. Yet as cricket had arrived first it was inevitable that it should control all the venues.

Naturally the offspring constantly grumbled about the terms, particularly when the Melbourne Circket Ground Trustees still retained some controls over the sale of tickets for the Grand Final series. So the Victorian Football League decided to build a ground of its own.

Some sporting writers insisted that it all began through the Olympic Games. V.F.L. Park, Waverley, was conceived in the mind of Sir Kenneth Luke, the League President in the year 1958. Sir Kenneth was still smarting at the change of venue of the 1956 Olympic Games from his club, Carlton, to the Melbourne Cricket Ground. The Carlton committee had hoped that its ground would be transformed into a "dream" stadium, but the Games organizers ran out of time and ran out of patience over costs. They returned to the Melbourne Cricket Club, the club which had rejected the original scheme as impractical.

So Sir Kenneth, president of the V.F.L. from 1956 until his death in 1971, became the prime mover behind the establishment of Waverley. As a great businessman he was always impatient with the League system of twelve delegates and divided control.

His ally through this period was the V.F.L. administrative director, Mr. Eric McCutchan. In September 1962 the two men bought 212 acres of grazing and market-garden land at Waverley, fifteen miles from the city, for $500,000. They were just in time for within eighteen months this became the prime area for hungry land developers and who knows how much it would cost then. The M.C.G. itself owned land at Waverley, but when the V.F.L. moved in, it decided to sell.

Their idea was to build the first ground ever designed purely for Australian Rules football and one of the world's great football stadiums, an area that would never be stained by cricket. Cricket grounds recover quickly from a football season, but the reverse is not true. After several generations of thick black Merri Creek soil have been applied to the centre for the making of Test wickets, strange things happen. This soil is the almost mystic material described in hundreds of thousands of words by such eloquent people as Neville Cardus, but it is black glue after a week of rain and creates misery for the ruckman.

Sir Kenneth and Mr. McCutchan planned virtually a perfect grandstand-to-grandstand carpet and certainly the biggest ground in Australia. There was 30 feet between the boundary line and the fence. Eric McCutchan said they planned this for two reasons. Firstly, even if you are sitting close to the fence you get a better view of the player. And secondly, it is extremely difficult for a sprinting player to injure himself against the fence. There is another reason he did not mention. The players also are a long way from the devoted attentions of the spectators. It is a long way to throw a bottle.

Yet it had not been easy for the V.F.L. Sometimes the critics had been around in squadrons, battalions and regiments. These have been the typical complaints.

Too big. Difficult for spectators to see from one side to the other. Players finish each quarter "dropping with exhaustion".

271

The costs are astronomical. It is bleeding the clubs white to the detriment of the still squalid other grounds.

It will never in a hundred years have the drawing power of the M.C.G.

It is too far out. No public transport. Traffic problems are quite disastrous.

Mr. McCutchan of the V.F.L. was used to answering all these criticisms and he did it well. He said the size of the playing area is an optical illusion. Waverley was 58.217 metres from the centre to the goal. The M.C.G. was 53.590 metres.

The strain of paying off the new ground had led to a near revolt. Richmond, which shared the M.C.G. with the Melbourne club, threatened to form a breakaway from the Victorian Football League with disenchanted clubs possibly including Richmond, Melbourne, Collingwood, and Fitzroy as a starting nucleus.

In 1973 the V.F.L. owed $7.3 million on Waverley and the Fitzroy President, Mr. E. Joseph, claimed that the V.F.L. was endangering the future of football with its extravagant expenditure. It was repaying its loans over eight years whereas if it borrowed sensibly it could do it over twenty-five years and put the money into club grounds which were losing spectators because of their poor facilities. Mr. McCutchan replied that if they did this they would have to pay a far higher rate of interest. And he claimed that V.F.L. Park was a huge future money-maker for the League. He said:

> At V.F.L. Park we get all the broadcasting and television money. We have all the catering rights. We take all the parking proceeds and we receive money from everybody who comes through the turnstiles. Everyone at V.F.L. Park, including members is a daily payer.

The M.C.C. knew all about huge interest debts and had endured them for more than a century. The bigger the ground the more they multiply. A spectator may be worth more money at Waverley, but the M.C.G. was still sure to gather bigger crowds. For example, until the 1974 season Richmond had played Collingwood twice at the M.C.G. and twice at Waverley. At Waverley the crowds were 29,939 and 53,827. At the M.C.G. they were 82,191 and 72,659. Take the same figures Richmond against St. Kilda—33,489 and 41,502 at Waverley; 38,149 and 44,348 at the M.C.G. Or take Melbourne against St. Kilda—22,570 and 22,507 at Waverley and 39,830 and 44,348 at the M.C.G.

The Melbourne Cricket Ground had an extraordinary advantage in that probably no sporting ground in the world was so superbly situated, being on open parkland on the very edge of the city's centre with two railway stations, trams and buses within minutes walk. Ian Johnson claimed the ground could be emptied of 120,000 people in eleven minutes and all dispersed within half an hour. In 1965, for example, the final siren went at one minute to five and at 5.30 p.m. the Victorian Railways reported that their job was done. They had cleared 35,000 passengers. The Melbourne and Metropolitan Tramways Board reported all clear at 5.40 p.m. They had cleared 16,000.

These were the official figures for the 1973 Grand Final. The crowd was 116,956 and the game finished at 5.05 p.m. The Railways reported that the first spectators reached their gates at 5.10 p.m. The platforms were clear by 5.45 p.m. and more than 40,000 of these spectators had gone by train from Jolimont and Richmond stations in that 35 minutes. The Tramways Board estimated that from 15,000 to 20,000 spectators caught trams from the M.C.G. in the hour from 5.05 p.m. The Victoria Police Force reported all cars dispersed by 6.15 p.m.

In 1972 and 1973 two finals were played at Waverley and four at the M.C.G. The second semi-final of 1973—Carlton versus Collingwood—drew 60,072, Waverley's record. For the 60,072 people there were 20,000 cars. How else could one get there? The only way was car or bus. The result was a classic traffic jam. The *Sun News-Pictorial* said the real game started when the footy was over: "the great new driving home game, a game that required skill and patience". It took 1½ hours along "the crawlway". According to the *Sun* many just stayed there and had picnics or sat in their cars reading magazines and newspapers.

One woman reported that she went to the St. Kilda-Richmond semi-final at the M.C.G., left ten minutes before the siren and was home at Springvale, twelve miles away, in half an hour. Her husband went to the Carlton-Colling-wood match at Waverley and did not get home to Springvale, 1½ miles away until 6.46 p.m. . . . . it took him 1½ hours.

Mr McCutchan replied to this. He said:

> We printed charts. We had them in the newspapers. If only motorists had studied these they would all have been out of the car park, no fuss, no bother. The trouble was they all fought to get to the same exists. We had a new freeway opened only temporarily for the occasion. By next year the arteries will have been widened and everything will be much better.

His faith in the future was undaunted.

> Look, for sheer beauty you can't beat Waverley. This is where the popu-

lation is going to be. We have only done what the retailers are doing. The trend is away from the city. If we were starting all over again and that land were still available we would still go out there and build Waverley.

The truth is that no city anywhere is so fanatically devoted to sport as Melbourne. At racing, football, tennis and cricket the greatest crowds per head of population are always in Melbourne. Neither, Sydney, Adelaide, Brisbane, London nor New York display such enthusiasm. There is room for two great stadia and football will always need its mother ground, the M.C.G.

In 1974 the M.C.G. was not the world's biggest sporting ground, but it was within the first five biggest and financed entirely by its membership of nineteen thousand with another forty-eight thousand on the waiting list. Few clubs in the world had so many on the waiting list and few were so democratic. The members came from every trade and profession, from those who were on unemployment relief to the Chairman of Broken Hill Pty Ltd. Unless a candidate had been a member of an M.C.G. first-grade team for six years there were no short cuts. Some of the most distinguished men in the country had many years ahead of them on the waiting list.

Although the M.C.G. was now vast, it had an intangible quality that could only be described as atmosphere. Sometimes you could feel the ghosts of 120 years of teams that had played there with the triumphs and excitements. The heart of it all was the large and beautiful Long Room in the Members' Stand. There were others in Melbourne which were just as impressive, such as Queen's Hall in Parliament House, the Legislative Council chamber, the ballroom at Government House, but there was something different about the Long Room. The past speaks back, and with its plate-glass windows, its leather chairs and its dining room, it was a superbly comfortable place from which to watch cricket and football. When young members first entered they sensed this. They wondered if they dared sit on this seat or that seat; what great sporting personality of the past might they be edging to one side?

Those great cricket personalities were all around in more ways than one. The walls were decorated with paintings of club presidents and secretaries and old players like Tommy Wills and bearded John McCarthy Blackham behind the stumps.

In the autumn of 1974 the Long Room was being redecorated with a new carpet on the floor and a servery for sandwiches, and some of the precious relics were removed from the museum. But one remembered the glass cases that were filled with cricket bats of every description. Some dated back to the mid-eighteenth century—massive things weighing five pounds and as solid as a shillelagh. Then there were others more modern and very famous, like the bat with which Bill Ponsford made 3,000 runs, including his record 437. There was Clem Hill's bat, Colin McDonald's bat and Don Bradman's bat. There were the trousers, shirt and boots of Warwick Armstrong, all of immense size. The shirt was spread across the back of the cabinet and was so large that one could imagine two or three people living in it like a tent. The boots were of indeterminable size but surely beyond the range of manufacturers' numerals.

Only one other person had worn them and that was Governor of Victoria, Sir Dallas Brooks, once a first-class cricketer himself. When he visited the ground for a social match Ian Johnson searched the place for a suitable pair of boots but found none that were large enough. The situation was becoming desperate when he thought of teh famous boots of W. W. Armstrong. They fitted perfectly. It is not recorded whether or not Sir Dallas actually played like the big man that day.

Close by the boots there was Hugh Trumble's famous Stetson-type American hat and the bent-stemmed Peterson pipe presented to him during the 1902 tour. It looked almost as heavy as the 1750 cricket bats. Yet perhaps the most valuable item of all was the framed original agreement drawn up by five gentlemen on November 15, 1838, with the object of forming the "Melbourne Cricket Club'. You could read where originally they planned to make the subscription 10s 6d, then decided to be bold and crossed it out and made it one guinea. After 136 years the ink had barely dimmed.

CHAPTER TWENTY-TWO

A Century of Tests

THE year 1974 had its triumphs and tragedies. January floods inundated Brisbane and left thousands homeless. A Christmas cyclone flattened Darwin and destroyed a city. The dollar devalued 12 cents and Gough Whitlam appointed Sir John Kerr to be his Governor-General, a decision he had cause to regret. The Melbourne Football Club had moved securely into the long term horrors. The Demons finished bottom of the ladder in 1973 and a miserable tenth in 1974. The faithful gentlemen who looked on from the Members' Stand were to continue in glumness for at least another 15 years.

In 1973 they had mixed feelings. The Demons as usual put their red and blue guernseys back into mothballs by late August but then wistfully they watched their club brother Richmond. The Tigers had shared the Melbourne Cricket Ground for home matches since 1965. Richmond beat Carlton in the 1973 Grand Final before a crowd of 116,950. Not only did they win the Grand Final, they took four Premierships, the Firsts, the Reserves, the Under 19s and the Under 17s. Richmond went on to win the Premiership again the next year. Melbourne changed its coach. Bobby Skilton took over from Ian Ridley and in 1974 Melbourne's best first-year player was an 18-year-old named Robert Flower.

The stock market was down, the weather violent, but it was a beautiful sublime era for Australian cricket, no splits, no controversies. There was a certain feeling of confidence about the power of the Australian game. How could it be otherwise? The opening bowling combination was Lillee and Thomson, backed by Max Walker and Ashley Mallett. The batting line up included Ian Redpath, the brothers Chappell, Ian and Greg, plus Doug Walters. To say nothing of Rodney Marsh behind the stumps.

There were just faint signs of the commercialism that was to come. The Melbourne Cricket Club accepted fence advertising for the first time. So that beautiful cliché "with a full-blooded drive he rattled the pickets" disappeared for ever. Now if Mr. Ian Chappell or Mr. Redpath made a full-blooded drive he was more likely to rattle Toyota, Four 'n' Twenty Pies, the State Bank, Foster's or Rothmans. Some members were shocked. In the days of W.G. and

Left
When the M.C.G. was under siege —
the building of the light towers.

Below
A packed M.C.G. in 1987.

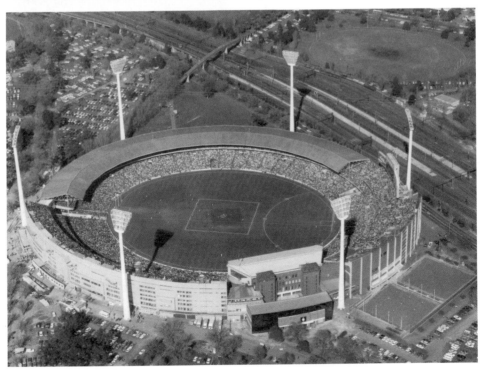

Below

Dr Davis McCaughey, Governor of Victoria, at the Melbourne Cricket Club 150th Anniversary Dinner, 3 February 1988.

Right

Detail from working drawing for the creation of a panel for the bronze doors at the entrance to the Club (created by Robert Ingpen). Sports shown are rifle-shooting, tennis, hockey, squash, lacrosse, baseball and bowls.

Hugh Trumble, there were no such horrors. One looked across to shady trees.

The club newsletter quietened mutinous thoughts with the words: "It is of some sentimental interest that even the illustrious Lord's Ground in England has for long been ringed by signs. Some have opined that Thomas Lord, the founder, would turn in his grave at the thought. But no, he was a practical man and would have appreciated that any objections are far outweighed by the benefits."

The picket fence was sold by the square foot and the areas which were likely to pick up the TV cameras received the heaviest loading. The club would not allow actual cigarette brand names. The return for the first year was $32,000.

Actually the old Paddock was superbly capable of handling almost any eventuality. On March 10, 1974 they leased the ground for David Cassidy, the idol of the teeny-boppers. The organisers set up a stage, complete with changing rooms in the centre of the ground, right beside the sacred turf. M.C.C. secretary Ian Johnson estimated the crowd between 25,000 and 30,000. Price of entry was $3.20. Cassidy wore pale blue pants, pale blue waistcoat and he did not stay still for more than a thousandth of a second.

When the club moved its offices from the lovely old two-storey Victorian villa in Jolimont Terrace, Ian Johnson in his upstairs lair could look straight across the road into Richmond Park where early games of Australian football were played. The new offices, much brighter, roomier and more efficient were right in the Melbourne Cricket Ground, the entrance by the bowling green and the practice wicket. There were renovations everywhere. A new bar went into the north-west corner of the Long Room. The carpet runners which had been there since Vernon Ransford was a boy, were out and now plush red went wall-to-wall. One could pick up one's glass of beer, wander across to the window and sip while wondering whether Redpath and Wally Edwards could survive to lunch. Bert Chadwick, the Club President, became a knight bachelor in the New Year's honours and was now Sir Albert Chadwick.

It was a formidable season for England in Australia. Mike Denness' men came to play six Tests. They lost four, drew one and had one brilliant final victory. Their happiest time, unquestionably, was at the Melbourne Cricket Ground where they scored a draw in the Third Test and a win in the Sixth. It was bad enough having to cope with Lillee but in the summer of 1974-75 Jeff Thomson was awesome. The English pressmen could not believe his extraordinary style. They were used to fast bowlers sprinting in almost from the

277

boundary. Jeff Thomson seemed to have just a few strides and with his beach boy shoulders hurl the ball with the muzzle velocity of a rifle. Then there was the other fear. There was no pin-point accuracy with Jeff Thomson; there was always an awesome feeling of not knowing what was to happen next. The ball could whizz down anywhere between your ankle or your ears.

There were growls from the English press camp about the potency of the Australian attack. E. W. Swanton, of London's *Daily Telegraph*, the elder statesman of English cricket, was shocked by Dennis Lillee. He reported Lillee's remarks on television, regarding the theory and practice of bouncers. "I aim to hit him somewhere between the stomach and the rib cage" adding that he didn't want to injure him in any way, just soften him up a bit.

But Mr. Swanton was impressed with the Boxing Day crowd at the M.C.G., 77,165, more people than he had ever seen at a cricket match. Ian Johnson, usually a wily predictor of crowds, admitted he had expected only 50,000 to 55,000. The caterers ran out of pies, cigarettes and soft drinks but the beer lasted until 5.30 p.m.

It was not a great Test match. There is a law which often applies: the greater the crowd, the slower the cricket. Jeff Thomson took a total of 8 wickets for 143 runs, but maybe Titmus and Underwood really saved the match for England. They had the accuracy of a dentist operating with a jet drill, working on a bicuspid, not a millimetre out of place. In Australia's second innings they bowled seven overs to Marsh and Walker for seven runs. Perhaps this is what inspired one character in Bay 13 to wear a T-shirt with the message TITMUS IS A RODENT. But Australia ran out of time and at stumps was still eight runs short of its target with two wickets in hand. In the Sixth and final Test one heard many kindly patronising thoughts: "Wouldn't it be nice if the Poms took this one. It would be good for cricket." However when it comes to the crunch, when the gentlemen in green and gold are going down in flames, Australians really detest losing and are not always over nice about it. Australia was all out for 152. There was some beautiful tight, accurate bowling from Peter Lever. He took 6 for 52. Then England replied with 529 and as they piled on the runs the Australian crowd became quieter and quieter. The Members' Stand was so solemn and respectful you would have thought the Archbishop was conducting mass. The hero this time was Mike Denness who made a confident, unworried 189 runs. At last somebody up there appeared to like him, because he had suffered an awful tour. He even dropped himself for the Fourth Test, his form was so bad. So the quixotic English press at last loved him again. The only real happiness for Australia was a triumphant Max Walker, who on his own ground took 8 for 143.

England won by an innings and four runs. In the end the crowd in the Outer could not bear it. They booed whenever an English fieldsman tried to cut off a four. Greg Chappell was finally bowled by Lever for 102 and it was all over. Many of the crowd with beer cans still welded to their right hands invaded the ground to inspect the wicket. Some dug out chunks to take home as souvenirs. Why they wanted pieces of that pitch is a mystery.

It was a nervous period for the club. Sir Albert Chadwick gave warning that costs were going up and revenue was falling. V.F.L. Park was now an obvious success, a good football ground. Melbourne and Richmond played many of their first round matches there. It was home too for interstate matches and for the first time the V.F.L. staged the Preliminary Final at V.F.L. Park rather than the M.C.G. The crowd there was 71,130 with $216,091 receipts. For the Grand Final at the M.C.G. the crowd was 110,551 with record receipts of $308,172. North Melbourne 19.8 beat Hawthorn 9.13. This was yet another event to make the members wistful. Not only was it the first North Melbourne Premiership in history, but the Kangaroos were coached by Melbourne old boy, Ron Barassi.

So for a time there was an amiable peace with the V.F.L. There was an agreement that for the next three years there would be two semi-finals and the Grand Final at the M.C.G. The Club would receive a flat payment of $120,000 a match and a $5000 television fee, all subject to the consumer price index. But times were changing. The old feeling that the Club was always as open as your home was starting to disappear. The notice went out for the 1975 Grand Final. There would be a 'Finals' charge for ladies tickets: one dollar for ladies and boys and girls under 14. If you wanted to attend all three finals please send your cheque for $3.

The West Indies, captained by Clive Lloyd, came to Australia in the summer of 1975-76 and Greg Chappell's men beat them five to one. There were two Tests, the Third and the Sixth at the M.C.G. Boxing Day at the M.C.G. all seemed a repeat of that incredible day in 1961 when a world record crowd of 90,800 turned out for the battle against the warriors of Frank Worrell. There was much talk that the 1961 record was ripe to be broken. We did not get there. The final count on December 26, 1975 was 85,596. The weather was 32 degrees Celsius. "The weather cost us 10,000 to 15,000," said Ian Johnson. "It was just a little too hot for comfort—especially for those people who waited to see what it was like before deciding where to go." Presumably the missing 10,000 went to the beach, but the second greatest cricket crowd in history was not over-disappointing.

At least the temperature was sufficient to inspire the streakers. This was a curious phenomenon of the mid-1970s. Maybe it was a reaction against the deep wowserdom of the 1960s, a novel way of showing defiance for authority, or perhaps just a desperate desire of the insignificant to be noticed, but there were three of them this day, all long-haired youths. They rushed to the centre and tried to shake hands with Lillee and Rod Marsh. Both treated them with contempt. Cricketers hate this interruption to their concentration. All three streakers were arrested. One finished his sprint in the ladies' section of the Members' Stand. Many thought that was an interesting move in International Women's Year.

This was the Test that saw the full flowering of the chanting to the fast bowler. As soon as Jeff Thomson started his run there was this moan of Thomm-oooooh ... Thomm-ooooh! But the most memorable cry was for Dennis Lillee. Coming from a crowd of over 80,000 it was an awesome, terrifying cry of battle, a cry for blood. From then on we heard it every time Lillee picked up the ball. Lill-eeee ... Lilleeee ... Lill-eee. One only hopes someone has preserved that chant in the national archives. Somehow it symbolised the cry of an entire generation. Often it worked. I am sure it unnerved the West Indians in the first innings.

Lillee took seven wickets for the match and Thomson took six. Then there was the extraordinary leaping acrobatic Rod Marsh who took three catches in the first innings and five in the second. Ian Redpath made a stolid 102 and Gary Cosier, 22, playing in his first Test match made 109. It was interesting to observe the contrast between these two. Redpath looked so under-nourished he might have been suffering from anorexia nervosa. Cosier was large, red-headed and you would have had no doubt whatsoever that he enjoyed an excellent Christmas dinner. Australia won by eight wickets.

The Sixth Test at the M.C.G. was an even bigger Australian triumph. We won by 162 runs. One remembers it particularly because of Lance Gibbs. It was his last before he retired. Thin, small, wiry, this West Indian was always thinking, always worrying. You could imagine him in a very serious occupation, like an accountant or undertaker. He was very good at disposing of batsmen. In this Test he passed Freddie Trueman's world record of 307 wickets and when Ian Redpath ill-fatedly tried to hit him out of the ground he moved his score to 309.

Retirements were in the air. Redpath, who made 101 in the first innings and 70 in the second, deservedly man of the match, announced his retirement. So too did Ian Chappell, only 32 years old. The *Sun News-Pictorial* commented: "It's monstrous that the man of the match in the Sixth Test, the ballast, the anchor of the Australian Test side, should be allowed to walk out ahead of time. This has become a regular thing in Victoria. Look at the young stars we have looking on. Ian Redpath is 34. Paul Sheahan only 29 is teaching at Geelong Grammar. Bob Cowper, the sort of man likely to make a triple century, is lost to us but only 35 and how about Keith Stackpole, also 35, now retired to District cricket, but unquestionably the most entertaining opening batsman of all time." Clearly the rewards were insufficient and the way was being opened for Kerry Packer.

The Pakistanis came to Australia in the summer of 1976-77 amidst all sorts of agonies. There had been a near strike over terms and conditions of the tour. The Pakistan Board of Control sacked the captain Mushtaq Mohammad whereupon half the players withdrew. The Prime Minister, Mr. Bhutto, then did a strong man act, ordered that players' allowances be increased and Mushtaq was re-instated as captain. The players, tense and uneasy, drew the First Test, lost the Second and won the Third.

The Second Test was a triumph for Australia and one of Dennis Lillee's greatest. Australia opened with an imposing total of 517. Gary Cosier was the home town boy returning from South Australia. He suffered jeers from the crowd for some tortuous slow batting in the First Test. Suddenly something snapped. He used his hefty frame to slaughter everything and scored 168 off 206 deliveries. Greg Chappell showed his usual elegant style, that wonderful straight-backed grace, and scored 121. Dennis Lillee however was not happy. The wicket was dull and slow. No bouncer could possibly rise more than waist high. His mate Jeff Thomson was not there. He was the victim of a collision, a virtual head-on with Alan Turner in the First Test and was out for the season. So he opened with Gary Gilmour and was clearly nervous at what he had to achieve. He tried bowling several bumpers to the Pakistani opener Sadiq Mohammad and received a warning from the umpire. He was furious. First he pretended that he would bowl underarm. Then he found a balloon floating round the ground. He grabbed it and ran up to the wicket as if he were about to use it for his next ball. Greg Chappell came in to cool him down. In his book My Life in Cricket, Lillee commented: "At the end of it all I had a fairly interesting exchange with some of the 'gentlemen' sitting on their fat backsides in front of the Members' Stand."

But obviously it does no harm to make Dennis Lillee angry. Now he had something to prove. He took six wickets in the first innings and four in the second to make a total 10 for 135. He was named man-of-the-match. Frank Tyson wrote: "Seldom have I witnessed a fast bowling performance of such impressive proportions on a wicket which was so exasperatingly slow."

However for anyone who was alive and well the summer of 1977 was enchanting. Greg Chappell came back from the Test tour in New Zealand at the beginning of March. Melbourne was consumed by cricket fever and he walked into the foyer of the Melbourne Hilton. He was amazed. Almost every legendary cricket figure from the past was there.

It was almost the eve of the great Centenary Test. The idea for the Centenary Test came from Hans Ebeling, Vice-President of the Melbourne Cricket Club. His Test record was not huge. He played in one Test match at the Oval in England in 1934 and took 3 for 89. But he adored cricket and he adored the M.C.G. Almost always he was there, looking, helping, organising. In 1973 he reminded the M.C.G. Committee that 1977 would be the centenary of Test matches between England and Australia. He suggested, "Wouldn't it be a great idea if an England team could come to Australia and play a Centenary Test Match." He went even further . . . and it seemed a wild idea at the time . . . why not invite every living Test player from either country to be there. Surely they could find sponsors. He suggested too that Australia Post could issue a commemorative stamp.

So started a long process of negotiations. First he had to sell the idea to the Victorian Cricket Association, so he went to the President of the V.C.A., Mr. W. J. Dowling. Then it had to be sold to the Australian Cricket Board and ultimately the English Test and County Cricket Board. Getting things organised with the English Board was not all that easy. An English tour to South Africa was on the schedule but they cancelled this and substituted an Indian tour. So the agreement was an England team would come to Australia from India, play a warm-up match in Perth, then the Centenary Test in Melbourne.

The Australian Board appointed the Victorian delegates Ray Steele, Bob Parish and Len Maddocks as a sub-committee with V.C.A. secretary David Richards as secretary. Sir John Holland represented the State Government and Hans Ebeling the M.C.C.

The wild idea of bringing players from all over now did not seem so outrageous. Qantas agreed to fly out English old players, TAA offered to fly the Australian players to Melbourne and Benson & Hedges sponsored the match. There were 244 players who were eligible to come and 218 actually made it. "Tiger" Smith, 91, Frank Woolley, 89, and Herbert Sutcliffe, 82, could not get here, but Percy Fender at 84 managed the trip. He was almost blind and he brought his grandson, Nicholas, to describe the match for him. Jack Ryder, 87, one of the greatest batsmen to grace the M.C.G., was the senior Australian player. Sadly he died less than a month after the Centenary Test was over.

It was difficult to believe the faces one saw: Harold Larwood, Bill Voce,

Dennis Compton, Keith Miller, Sir Len Hutton, Ray Lindwall, Cyril Washbrook, Trevor Bailey, Peter May, John Edrich, Colin Cowdrey, Freddie
Brown, Alec Bedser, Alan Davidson, Gubby Allen . . . all it needed was a fat
doctor with a dark bushy beard to make things complete.

There were numerous receptions and parties. The Melbourne Cricket Centenary Test Match Dinner took place at the M.C.G. on March 16. It did
honour to the two great cricket clubs, the Marylebone Cricket Club and the
Melbourne Cricket Club. The two presidents both had a chance to speak; Sir
Albert Chadwick spoke for the younger M.C.C. and Mr W. H. Webster for the
elder.

Mr Webster had done his homework on the Melbourne Cricket Club very
thoroughly. He was aware that the club's first president F. W. Powlett had a
duel with a merchant named Hogue and even sent a bullet through Hogue's
clothing.

Judge Ian Gray gave the toast to cricket and one of the miracles of the
evening was the special edition of the club newsletter. A photographer took
pictures of the guests during the pre-dinner drinks. Before they had time to
drink the club port and eat the Moe Camembert, there was the newsletter, all
published with the very pictures taken that evening. Sir Albert Chadwick and
Mr W. H. Webster were on the cover shaking hands, and inside were instant
shots of all the celebrities, Harold Larwood, Trevor Bailey, Bill Lawry, Ken
Meulemen, Jack Ikin, Bill O'Reilly, Keith Rigg, Donald Bradman, Cyril Washbrook, Mike Denness, L. Fishlock and many more. Nobody wanted to go
home. Frank Tyson records that Trevor Bailey could still find time to speak to
Ray Lindwall in spite of being his hundredth victim in England-Australia
games.

But for those with stamina there was also the Australian Cricket Board
dinner at the Melbourne Hilton.

Sir Donald Bradman has made many great speeches and this night he gave
one of his greatest. First he gave a fascinating resumé of the 100 Test years,
recalling remarkable players and their triumphs. What a pleasure it was, he
said, to greet Percy Fender . . . "For the benefit of our younger listeners may I
remind you that Fender's century in 35 minutes made well over 50 years ago,
is still the fastest ever recorded in first-class cricket." He was very modest
about his own achievements: "A young chap named Bradman played at the
First Test at Brisbane in 1928. I remember it well, because I saw my first sticky
wicket. We lost by the biggest margin in history, 675 runs and I was promptly
dropped from the side." He made a special point of praising bowlers. He
spoke of the lovable, whimsical Arthur Mailey, of the speed skills of Ray

Lindwall and of the greatest English medium-pacers, Maurice Tate and Alec Bedser.

The others to receive mention were Clarrie Grimmett, 85, "probably the best leg spinner the world has known" and "Bill O'Reilly, the greatest bowler I ever faced". There was Bob Massie "who without the aid of lipstick, vaseline or anything else to aid his swing, took more wickets than anyone has ever done in his first Test—16 wickets at Lord's" and finally Jim Laker: "The man, who in 1956, put up the greatest bowling performance in history by taking nine Australian wickets in one innings and ten in the other—a feat which I don't think will ever be equalled."

But Sir Donald said he did not believe individual skill had varied a great deal over the century. You had to remember changes in rules and conditions. "For instance," said he, "Greg Chappell throughout his career has had to defend a set of stumps one inch higher and 12½ per cent. wider than the stumps Trumper had to guard. He has had to bat against a smaller ball and cope with a more difficult lbw rule. On the other hand, Trumper had to bat on uncovered wickets. How can anyone possibly equate those differences?"

The Chairman of the Australian Cricket Board, Mr. Bob Parish, opened the ceremony before the start of play on Saturday, March 12. He introduced former captains Bob Wyatt, Gubby Allen, Don Bradman, Norman Yardley, Lindsay Hassett, Freddie Brown, Ian Johnson, Len Hutton, Richie Benaud, right through to Mike Denness and Ian Chappell. The two captains, Greg Chappell and Tony Greig, walked out on to the oval. Greg Chappell tossed a specially minted gold medallion. Tony called correctly and many an old critic in the grandstand could not believe it when he said to Greg Chappell: "O.K. You can have a hit."

It seemed that Tony Greig had made an inspired decision. The Australians were all out for a miserable 138 with three of the players dismissed going for the hook. The disaster was opening batsman Rick McCosker. He tried to hook a bumper from Bob Willis and deflected the ball on to his face. He went to hospital and later the news came through that he had a broken jaw and it had to be wired. The Englishmen did no better. They were all out for 95 runs. They were 8/86 at lunch on the second day. Then it was not long after their chicken and salad had settled that they were all out for 95. It was difficult to believe such miserable batting by both sides. The weather was that sublime balmy stuff Melbourne always gets in early autumn. The wicket was beautifully prepared with no hidden terrors. There was one possible explanation, the occasion was just too awesome, too overwhelming. Everyone was just so desperate to do well in front of such an august audience, strokes became too nervous and tentative.

Then, of course, there was nothing tentative about the bowling. Dennis Lillee scored his best figures in Test cricket, 6/26. Because of this some were inclined not to notice the efforts of Max Walker, but he too was splendid. Bowling with his strange contortionist action, a jigsaw of knees and elbows, he managed a flawless length and the great Alec Bedser himself must have admired the way he moved the ball off the seam. He took 4/54.

Australia's second innings had its moments. When Gary Cosier tried yet another hook Australia was 3 down for 53, but Ian Davis scored 68, Doug Walters 66, and there was a remarkable innings from the 21-year-old David Hookes. He batted as if he was frightened of missing his dinner. He hit five successive fours off Tony Greig in one over before Underwood got him for 56.

Even better was to come from Rodney Marsh. Already he had eclipsed Wally Grout's record for the most dismissals in Tests. He moved the score on to 353 and looked in danger of running out of partners. When Lillee was caught in the covers by Underwood off Old there were eight wickets down and the crowd expected to see Max Walker. But, no, incredibly, in came Rick McCosker, the number one casualty, his face encircled by bandages. Kerry O'Keeffe was his runner. Dennis Lillee recorded later that his eyes welled with tears as he watched McCosker walk on. He thought it one of the most courageous acts he ever saw. Marsh scored 110 not out, McCosker was caught Greig, bowled Old for 25 and Chappell declared at 9 for 419. Now Tony Greig had to ponder the awful problem of getting 463 in 590 minutes for victory, something which had never been achieved in Test cricket. Yet the Englishmen did not give in. Mike Brearley scored 43, Amiss 64, Greig 41 and Knott 42. However the day and almost the match belonged to Derek Randall. It was almost as if he had an uncontrollable itch or the film was in fast motion; he never stopped moving, gesturing, taking walks up the wicket, and rarely did he ever stop talking. He would talk to anyone who would listen to him; the bowler, the fieldsmen, the umpire. He accepted all Dennis Lillee's glares and histrionics, he was not disturbed by Bay 13 chanting Lillee-eee and howling for blood. He took one Lillee bouncer on the head, paused a little while, then went on, all aggression, his small frame miraculously, again and again, delivering the ball to the fence.

When Randall was 161 he snicked a medium pacer from Greg Chappell and, to almost everyone, it appeared to go straight into the gloves of Rodney

Marsh. Umpire Brooks raised his finger and he was out. But then Marsh signalled that the ball had hit the ground before he took it. Chappell called Randall to come back and resume playing. It was a fine act of sportsmanship by Marsh and symbolised the spirit in which the two teams played the Centenary Test. Randall did not last much longer. He was out for 174, caught Cosier, bowled O'Keeffe.

The Englishmen failed by 45 runs to reach their target, which was exactly the margin by which Australia won the very first Test 100 years earlier. It was one of the truly great memorable cricket matches, almost as if it had been scripted by God. Derek Randall was the man of the match and Dennis Lillee won the Herald & Weekly Times trophy for the best bowler. He finished with 11 wickets for 165.

Queen Elizabeth and Prince Philip visited the ground during the lunch break on the final day and met all the players. England with Derek Randall was in full cry while she was there, but then collapsed after she had gone. One of the Australian players allegedly remarked, you could almost swear it was Doug Walters: "We were just being courteous, letting the Poms appear to be in control while SHE was there."

CHAPTER TWENTY-THREE

A Packer Affair

B OB WILLIS, the English fast bowler, complained that come the mid-1970s, nothing was ever the same again. There was a new ruthlessness in Test cricket. Winning the game was paramount, above any charming old-fashioned niceties. Gamesmanship was the thing, and there was an entirely new term "sledging," which meant it was customary to abuse a batsman at the wicket, to unnerve him, to get him on edge.

It was gamesmanship also to slow down a game, to make an eternity out of an over, so that one could concentrate power in the hands of the fast bowlers. If appeals to the umpire had been dramatic in the 1960s it was nothing to what they were now. They were accompanied by leaps, shrieks, and diabolic glares at the umpire. Often it mattered little whether the batsman was out or not, it was part of the intimidation process.

Then came the great split and the most divisive period the game has ever known. It lasted through the years 1977 and 1978 and the ripples it caused, both good and bad, are still being felt. Briefly Kerry Packer, son of the famous newspaper magnate Frank Packer, wanted television rights for cricket on his Channel 9 television network. It was not to be. The Australian Cricket Board of Control already had granted them to the Australian Broadcasting Commission.

Australia had dominated cricket since 1972. The nation was cricket mad and cricket was just right for television. So Packer decided to run the game himself. He contracted fifteen Australians, fifteen from the Rest of the World and then a third team of West Indians. By the end of the Centenary Test in Melbourne already he had signed ten Australians plus the England captain, Tony Greig. Official Australian cricket now was decimated, it meant virtually playing Test matches with a second eleven.

Oddly enough all this did not have a vast effect on the Melbourne Cricket Club. There was a drop in attendances at the M.C.G., but then the club depends more on member subscriptions than on cash through the turnstiles. Very early Ian Johnson had a feeling that something strange was happening. As early as September 1976 the Club received a letter from the general manager of GTV9 making application for the use of the ground for a series of cricket matches during December, January and February 1977-78. After consultation with the committee Ian Johnson wrote back and asked whether these matches had been approved by the Victorian Cricket Association and the Cricket Board.

The club committee agreed to keep its options open regarding the matches and to work at all times with the Board and the V.C.A. They did not hear again from the Packer group and never at any time was there an application to play Packer cricket on the M.C.G. Obviously they thought this would be akin to asking for a Baptist church service at the Vatican. However it was a different story in Sydney. The Sydney Cricket Ground was owned and operated by Trustees appointed by the New South Wales Parliament. The M.C.G., too, was owned by Trustees appointed by the Victorian Government, but there was a difference. The M.C.G. was operated by the Melbourne Cricket Club, the very home of traditional cricket, whereas the S.C.G. was owned and operated by the Trustees. Packer cricket was ultimately played on the S.C.G. but never on the M.C.G.

The committee minutes only rarely refer to the Packer game and then using the term "The Packer Circus." The club agreed that players connected with the circus could use the Melbourne Cricket Club if they were members, but only as members.

There were misgivings about Max Walker, who immediately signed as a Packer player. Max Walker was deeply associated with the club. He was a past Melbourne footballer. He was a Melbourne Demon cricketer who had come up through the District ranks to play Test cricket for his country. Sir Bernard Callinan, then Vice-President and later President of the Melbourne Cricket Club, said it was tough having to ban Max from the Melbourne team, because he was such a good club man, always willing to help the younger players.

The 1977-78 season was a time of change in more ways than one. Joe Kinnear, the famous character in the scoreboard, retired. So too did Bill Watt, the curator, who had been with the club for more than 20 years.

Joe Kinnear did not realise it at the time, but at the very moment of his retirement in 1977 Ian Johnson was touring the United States looking at the latest Matrix electronic scoreboards. Yet Joe was proud of his old board. It recorded more information than any other cricket scoreboard on earth. It gave the toss winner, the fall of wickets, how a batsman was dismissed, and by whom, the number of overs bowled and even the number bowled in the previous hour. Then there were the little lights that shone beside a player's name after he had fielded the ball.

288

Joe was with the club for 45 years. In his younger days he was a left-arm bowler, he played for the club and represented Victoria. He was also in the Melbourne Football Club first eighteen.

Up there in the scoreboard Joe's box was a narrow chasm four metres deep and 12 metres high, full of platforms, steep ladders and little cranks with bicycle chains to work the numbers.

The players' names were on black cloth which had to be tacked to three-metre boards. Joe had preserved famous names right back to the 1910 England tourists. Bradman, Hutton, Sutcliffe and Edrich were all still there. Then in the scorebox Joe had his own picture gallery—shots of Bradman cutting; Verity; Simpson catching; Kippax, Ponsford and O'Reilly with King George V and Queen Mary at Windsor Castle. There was also a framed picture of the world record score from Christmas 1926 when Victoria gave N.S.W. 1107 to chase . . . Woodfull 133, Ponsford 352, Hendry 100, Ryder 295 and the unfortunate Arthur Mailey, 4/362. Joe retired after the Centenary Test.

Bill Watt had the nickname "Grassy," which was appropriate because he spent much of his life worrying about the unpredictable behaviour of couch grass in black soil. Bill worked at the Sydney Cricket Ground for 23 years and for the M.C.G. for 20. Bill found being a ground curator a little like being a weather forecaster, nobody was ever satisfied.

The batsmen would complain that he had prepared the wicket for the exclusive delight of the fast bowlers, so that they could be lambs for the slaughter. The bowlers would complain he had prepared wickets as dead as the Birdsville Track, so that there would be no hope whatever of dismissing the batsmen twice.

Bill would just nod his head and say nothing. But it was always so. Even back in the 1950s he suffered criticism from batsmen who complained that he doctored up the Sydney wicket just for the benefit of Lindwall and Miller.

Bill claimed it was normal to be called out at midnight to handle emergencies, real or imaginary. When they were real they could be awful. He remembers the eve of the Second Test between Australia and the West Indies back in 1960-61. He received the call at his Jolimont flat at 1 a.m. There was a burst water main almost right next to the sacred turf. He said: "There was a hole in the ground big enough to put a man in. We worked and worked and when the gates opened at 9 a.m., you wouldn't have known anything was wrong."

Bill Watt came into an entirely new world of fungicides, weedicides, new grasses, heat treatments for speeding growth and the problems of finding soil.

In the old days Merri Creek soil was always there, but it became scarcer and scarcer. He would pull out Department of Agriculture maps and every season he would head into the country to inspect some new soil. Not many people realised that the oft-maligned Merri wickets were not always Merri.

Jack Lyons, the new curator, took over in March 1978.

India came to Australia in the summer of 1977-78, the affair which the cynics referred to caustically as the second-rate fight between second-rate teams. However it was better than that. Bob Simpson, after being in retirement for 10 years, came back at 41 to lead a band of very young Australians. In that team there were names like Yallop, Dyson, Hughes, Cosier and Jeff Thomson who remained true to the Board. Thomson, very early, looked as if he would waver, but he was under contract, being sponsored by a Brisbane radio station.

Australia won the series three Tests to two but our batsmen never quite learned to handle the wiles of Bedi, Chandra, Prasanna and co. and we just got there in the first two Tests. The Third Test was at the M.C.G. and we lost by 222 runs. We were rather expecting another miracle by Bobby Simpson. In Perth he had been the wondrous born-again hero; he made 176 in the first innings and was run out for 39 in the second. Alas at the M.C.G. Chandra got him for 2 and 4.

The near immortal Sunil Gavaskar scored his third century of the series with 113, but the man of the match was Bhagwat Subramaniam Chandrasekhar who returned nearly the best figures in India's Test history with 12/104. It was very tidy, 6/52 in each innings. Naturally Chandra was the man of the match. The Indians chaired him off the ground. You might say they even went partially berserk. It was India's first Test win on Australian soil.

The Melbourne Cricket Ground was steadily being improved. Just before the football finals the club spent $122,000 putting in 5085 seats under cover. This meant less standing area in front of the Southern Stand and nigh on 3000 less people could squeeze into the ground. But we were moving into an era when people were yearning for comfort not records.

There was also corporate comfort. The club installed 33 boxes in the standing room underneath the Northern Stand. There were 27 eight-seater boxes which cost $1500 a year and a number of six-seater boxes for $1200. Among the first customers were the National Bank, Wills, Rothmans, and Henderson Springs.

Hawthorn won the 1978 final over North Melbourne, who appeared in their sixth consecutive Grand Final. These events were now becoming spectacular all round entertainment. One of the star performers was Keith Michell who sang "The Impossible Dream."

Part of our impossible dream was to take on Mike Brearley's Englishmen during the summer of 1978-79. The new captain Graham Yallop boldly predicted that his men would beat the "Poms" six-nil. He had his figures slightly wrong. As it turned out England won 5-1. The only Test Australia won was at the M.C.G.

It was a very busy summer; there was also a team tour by Pakistan. The Pakistanis led by Mushtaq Mohammad had all eight of their World Series players. Australia had none of its eighteen players who had signed with Packer. There were two Tests; Australia lost the Test at the M.C.G. by 71 runs and won in Perth by seven wickets.

The First Test began at Moomba time, March 10 and by now we were feeling the effects of a long summer and the rival series. The Packer Circus was playing cricket at V.F.L. Park on pre-prepared wickets in concrete dishes, carried in like TV dinners. So crowds were not over impressive at either establishment.

The total crowd for the M.C.G. Test against Pakistan was 37,495, the sort of figures one might expect for Brisbane. One remembers it for three reasons, Allan Border scored 105, his first Test century, and Sarfraz Narwaz in Australia's second innings turned in the unbelievable figures of 9/86. He dismissed four Australian batsmen without scoring and in one spell he had the figures of seven wickets for one run.

The Pakistanis were not only on edge for political reasons, there was some angry feeling against the Australians. There was the spectacular incident between Rodney Hogg and Javed Miandad. Hogg touched his bat behind the crease and did the usual wander up the wicket to do a little prod to see whether it was still alive. He had not checked to see whether the ball had actually come to rest. Javed in gully ran him out. Umpire Clarence Harvey, elder brother of Neil Harvey, gave him out. Hogg in a fury bashed down the wickets with his bat.

Statisticians who are never at a loss on such an occasion recalled that nothing like this had happened since Dr. W. G. Grace ran out the Australian, Samuel Percy Jones, during the "Ashes" Test at the Oval in 1882. This was the incident which inspired "Demon" Spofforth to take his seven wickets in the second innings.

Meanwhile, Barry Flynn, the Melbourne Football Club's promotions officer, came up with an ingenious fund-raising idea. Why not "sell" off the

291

sacred turf in the centre of the M.C.G. The idea was to offer 70 square feet in the centre at $50 a square, and plots in front of the goals at $10 a square. Out on the wings one could purchase bargain pieces for $5. Advertisements in the newspapers offered readers the chance to have a "certificate describing one square foot of the hallowed M.C.G. turf inscribed with your name." Also buyers received a presentation bottle of M.C.G. turf.

It came with a message stressing its importance; W. G. Grace played there, the first football match under lights was there, the highest first-class cricket score was made there, and one of Victoria's first aircraft flights, followed very quickly by the State's first aircraft crash, took place there. There was no shortage of buyers and sales went very well indeed, but there was a fine footnote to the contract: "Certificates do not constitute or imply any legal ownership or tenure and are not to be taken as legal documents as such."

The same wicket caused so much trouble in subsequent years not everyone would have wanted a legal claim to the sacred turf.

In February 1979 Sir Albert Chadwick retired as President of the Melbourne Cricket Club. He had been President for 16 years and a committeeman for 40 years. He had an extraordinary career with the Club, both in sport and as an administrator. Since he first went to the ground in 1920, carrying his football togs, he did all things. He was the star centre half-back for the Melbourne Firsts. He was captain and coach of Melbourne, President of the Melbourne Football Club, Vice-President of the M.C.G., the M.C.C. construction co-ordinator for the 1956 Olympic Games and then Club President.

His father was a chemist in the Victorian town of Tungamah near Yarrawonga. Bert was a good scholar and won a scholarship to University High School. When he left school he became apprenticed to an electrical engineering firm so that he could take up engineering. But at the outbreak of World War I he put up his age from 17 to 18 and joined the A.I.F. as a member of the Light Horse. As Sergeant Chadwick he later transferred to the Australian Flying Corps.

He played football in the Middle East and became captain of his squadron's team, which included the famous aviator Sir Ross Smith. He also became an A.I.F. boxing champion. On one occasion he fought before an audience of 100,000 troops at the holding base of Kantara.

After the war he spent 10 years with Shell, then moved to the Victorian Gas & Fuel Corporation where he became general manager and chairman.

Ian Johnson remembers him as a good President, charming but quite ruthless. Maurie Gibb, the Assistant Secretary, once said, there was one thing you

Grant Lawry, M.C.C. committee
since 1985, Treasurer since 1987.

Dr John Lill, Secretary since 1983.

Pope John Paul II turned the M.C.G. into a cathedral on 27 and 28 November 1986.

Clive Fairbairn, M.C.C. committee
since 1978

Every wondrous method is used in the production of the perfect wicket.
Here is the wicket under flood lamps.

wouldn't do with Bert Chadwick and that was take the first mark over him. After that you would be a marked man. He had extraordinary energy with a tremendous drive to win.

Some thought that at 81 he remained President too long, leaving insufficient time for those who followed.

The new President was Hans Ebeling, curiously, the first President in the history of the Club, who had actually played cricket for Australia. He did have his brief Test career with the side that toured England in 1934, but his part in Club cricket was huge. He started with the Melbourne first eleven in 1922, and from then he was almost as important a fixture as the scoreboard. He played for 17 seasons, and according to the statistics he bowled 2366 overs, took 450 wickets at 15.5 runs apiece and in 96 innings with 24 not outs he totalled 1174 runs at 16.3. He captained the club to its four premierships from 1934 to 1938 and led Victoria to victory in the Sheffield Shield.

He reminded one a little of a St. Bernard, large, forever amiable, but utterly dependable. Hans Ebeling was always there. It was Hans who restored the amazing picture collection to be seen around the club. Even though he did not play bowls, he ran the bowls section of the club. That is how keen he was.

It was committeeman Tom Trumble who first noted that 1977 would be the centenary year for England-Australia Test cricket, but it was Hans who suggested the idea of a centenary Test match and inspired the various authorities into action.

Sir Bernard Callinan said: "At his very first meeting as President he said how he wanted the club to be run. He had his own clear ideas as to what committees and sub-committees should do and we are still using his ideas. But it was tragic. Almost as soon as he became President he was hit by cancer. I think he actually chaired only one meeting."

He died on January 12, 1980 and Sir Bernard, the senior Vice-President, became the new President.

There were other changes; Maurie Gibb, another large amiable man, retired. Maurie, the assistant secretary, the Mr. Fixit, was an institution. In 1934 when two members of the office staff, Bill Ponsford and Len Darling, were selected to tour England, in came Maurie as a temporary clerk to fill in for six months. He was 20, and a football recruit from Rosedale. His temporary job lasted 45 years and he saw membership grow in that time from 6200 to 28,000.

He was a very good footballer, a member of two successive Melbourne premiership sides in 1939 and 1940, but he was also an unflappable organiser, with the right skills and charm to calm any infuriated arrival at the front desk. Ian Johnson says hours meant nothing to him, his loyalty to the club was tremendous.

Ian Johnson always liked to tell one story about Maurie Gibb: "It was just after a Grand Final and I was talking to one large League ruckman who was renowned for his toughness. We were outside the glass doors going into the pavilion. Oh Gawd, there was a fight, a couple of men getting stuck into a bloke. I rushed across, jumped in between them, held them apart, held my foot up against the third bloke, looking up hoping to see this burly ruckman running to give me a hand. No, he had his back turned and was taking no interest in the proceedings. I was starting to get a bit worried when Maurie Gibb came along, right into the middle of it. I had absolutely no worries at all. He handled matters very smartly, but I never thought that League ruckman was very tough from then on."

The new club assistant secretary was Bryce Thomas. He had been a systems analyst and programmer with Jas Miller and later chief industrial engineer. Bryce won his colours in football, cricket and athletics at Melbourne Grammar, represented Victoria in amateur football and in 1956 he was the number four hurdler in Australia and only narrowly missed selection for the Olympic Games.

Not only was it a time for changes in big names for the club, it was a time of change for the club itself. One of Sir Albert Chadwick's last acts as President was to make an agreement to play three finals, including the Grand Final, at the M.C.G. through until 1983. In return the Victorian Football League demanded a much better financial return. The terms of the agreement were, the Melbourne Cricket Club would get 10 per cent. of the gross receipts from the M.C.G. finals, 10 per cent. of the television rights and a half share of income from the catering rights and fence advertising.

Sir Albert Chadwick broke the bad news in the club newsletter that members would have to pay $5 at the gate to see each of the three finals. He told an *Age* reporter: "It will now cost a member and his wife $30 to see the finals on their own premises. This is on top of an annual subscription of $42, which is soon to go up. If we are going to meet the VFL's demands we have no choice but to do this."

The shock was profound. Many complained having to pay to get into your own club was like paying an entry fee into your own living room or bedroom. On February 14, 1979 there was a special meeting and 850 members attended. Sir Albert Chadwick proposed the motion to alter the rule to permit payment by members for football finals. Dr. Don Cordner seconded.

The meeting was hostile. Some members accused the committee of trying to bulldoze them into accepting the new charge, but much of the hostility was directed against football and one member called the V.F.L. a bunch of vultures. The meeting rejected the motion 10 votes to one.

However there was sufficient power at the meeting to call for a postal vote. Some members jeered at this decision and accused the committee of being bad losers. The postal vote cost the club $5000 and Ian Johnson commented. "The rowdy nature of the special meeting did not give the committee the opportunity to explain the full story."

Of course, he was right. There was a total formal vote of 7375 members and 57 per cent. agreed to pay the new charge. Only a simple majority was necessary to enforce the proposal. In 1980 the charge went up from $5 to $5.50. However it was not a bad deal for members. Price of admission for adults to the Grand Final of 1979 was $13. John Farnham sang "Waltzing Matilda" before a crowd of 112,845 and they saw Carlton beat Collingwood by five points.

So there was a temporary truce between the Melbourne Cricket Club and the Victorian Football League. There was also a truce in May 1979 between Kerry Packer's company PBL Sports Pty. Ltd. and the Australian Cricket Board. It was inevitable something had to happen. In 1975-76 the A.C.B. made a huge profit from a revenue of $1.9 million. During the two years of W.S.C. the A.C.B. lost $810,000. As for Kerry Packer, when it was all over, the W.S.C. players presented him with a bat which they had all signed. According to John Benaud he would pat it affectionately and call it "my six million dollar bat." In the end PBL Sports received exclusive promotion rights to all matches arranged by the Board including sub-letting rights to Channel Nine. The agreement was for 10 years and the Board was to be in sole control henceforward of the conduct of the game in Australia.

CHAPTER TWENTY·FOUR

The Cruel Pitch

W E CALLED the 1880s "The Roaring Eighties," because it was such a time of optimism and turbulent expansion. They were no less turbulent 100 years later. Once upon a time the M.C.C. Trustees met only when asked for a decision by the Club Committee. Sometimes in the 1980s it seemed the Trustees were rarely out of their chairs.

Always there was something happening and nearly always it was controversial. The pitch was forever under debate. Often it was talked about as if it were a living breathing thing, something which was in intensive care and only clever surgery could save it. This was true; it received every kind of treatment save possibly a quadruple bypass. The Club put in lights for night cricket and football, but it was not easy. Almost unwittingly the M.C.C. found itself out there in no·man's land in the crossfire of bullets between the Government and the unions. There were fears for the M.C.G. itself in the continuing struggle for the Grand Final, was it to be at Waverley or would the Paddock lose it for ever. The World Series cricketers all returned with the message that "all was forgiven" and they were free to play in Test, Sheffield Shield and club sides. It was not easy. There was a feeling of distrust between Packer and Establishment players that never quite went away. What's more the W.S.C. players brought much with them, and the greatest thing of all was the revolution of one·day cricket which they had made so popular. Ian Johnson made the point that there was absolutely nothing new about one·day cricket. It started in England in the early 1960s and immediately became so popular amongst the county teams it had to be recognised by the Marylebone club.

Ian Johnson like many an old club cricketer commented that he didn't like the way it split the game, so that you had one·day specialist teams and five·day Test teams. "I dislike it intensely. I can't be bothered watching it. I find it boring and most unsatisfactory." But he did say it had brought in vast numbers of people who never before had been interested in cricket.

Nor did he have any doubts about its future. He said that in 1977 while talking to Gubby Allen and Sir Donald Bradman, he made the prediction: "Very soon you will come to an arrangement with Packer. Then within 20 to

25 years you will find that Test matches, as we know them, will not be played. In their place we will have a Test series which will comprise five matches with each match like an American baseball series. That is, a match will consist of five one-day games." Ian still thinks that could happen.

The one-day matches may have been born in England, but they had an astonishing rebirth under Packer. It was Packer cricket that invented the idea of the white ball. It was Packer cricket that got players out of pristine white into designer colours that made them look like Elizabethan court jesters. It was Packer cricket that invented circles on the ground and imposed field restrictions. If the old hands like Bill O'Reilly shuddered at the very mention of limited-over cricket it just kept growing in popularity. According to a Gallup Poll published in March 1986 58 per cent. of Australians preferred one-day contests and only 25 per cent. went for Test matches. In the 16- to 24-year-old age group the difference was even more marked: 61 per cent. for one-day and 22 per cent. for Test cricket.

The Club President during this tumultuous period was Sir Bernard Callinan. He was the perfect example of "find a busy man if you want a job done." Bernard Callinan seemed to be running everything. He was a Councillor of the University of Melbourne, a member of the Pontifical Commission of Justice and Peace, headquartered in Rome. He was chairman of the Canberra Parliament House Construction Authority, a commissioner of the Atomic Energy Commission, a commissioner of the Australian Broadcasting Commission, a commissioner of the State Electricity Commission, deputy chairman of the West Gate Bridge Authority . . . one could go on.

He graduated from Melbourne University in engineering, had a few years in the field then went into the Army soon after the outbreak of the Second World War. He was with the Independent Company which was left behind in Timor following the Japanese occupation. He was company commander and later commander of the force that performed such lengendary feats. He won the Military Cross and later the Distinguished Service Order.

He makes no claim to sporting skills, but Sir Albert Chadwick asked him to come on the committee in 1966. "They had a few doctors, solicitors, and international cricketers. I guess they felt they needed an engineer," said Sir Bernard. "I became chairman of the building committee. Nothing much had been done since the war. So we started repairing. Every month we came along with a recommendation to spend $15,000 or $20,000; none of the other committees were getting any money at all."

Sir Bernard became a Vice-President in 1978 and President in 1980.

He had much to handle right from the beginning. Both the West Indies and

England came to Australia for the 1979-80 season. In the World Series Cup one-day matches Australia failed to make the finals. West Indies triumphed over England. The old faces were back in the Australian team; Greg Chappell, Dennis Lillee, and Rod Marsh. However if they could not win at the one-day game, in Tests at least they beat England three-nil.

The Third Test was at the M.C.G. and Australia won by eight wickets. It was lovely, like old times. Greg Chappell made 114 in the first innings and 40 not out in the second. He seemed indestructible. Lillee, too, was the same power-house. He took 6/60 for the first innings and 5/78 in the second.

The story was very different against the West Indies. The First Test was drawn, and Australia lost the next two, the Second Test in Melbourne by 10 wickets and the Third in Adelaide by 408 runs.

The most vivid memory of the Melbourne Test was the ferocious 96 by Viv Richards. Already he had made 140 in Brisbane. Dennis Lillee in his auto-biography *My Life in Cricket* wrote: "By the end of the tour I'd seen just about enough of Richards' brilliant strokeplay." In Tests he made 386 runs at the average of 96.5.

Through all this cricket the M.C.G. wicket was a commentators' kygmy. The kygmy was a creature created by the American cartoonist Al Capp. A kygmy was a little fellow with a large, inviting posterior. The desire to kick a kygmy was irresistible and the actual sensation of delivering the kick was always helpful to the kicker. The M.C.G. pitch has been exactly like that. Not a sporting columnist, not a visiting captain, passed by without delivering his well-aimed boot.

Part of the problem, of course, was the climate. The Grand Final would finish at the end of September and within a month the M.C.G. curator was expected to have performed his miracle, having turned a sticky black Merri Creek swamp into a glorious couch-grassed, even-bounced multi-run wicket. The Club's newsletter, somewhat sadly, tried to point out the problem: "It is not often appreciated that the growth of couch in Melbourne is much slower than in other mainland capitals. This is due to the different climatic conditions that prevail. Melbourne has lower spring temperatures than any other capital apart from Canberra, and has fewer hours of spring sunshine than all of them. Even Hobart has more hours of sunshine."

And it was true. The wicket needed rest and tender loving care. It was perfect for the Centenary Test Match, which was in March 1977. Ian Johnson remembers the tale of the wicket very well indeed. He said: "Back before World War II it was a good wicket, a bit lively before lunch. It was always thought if you lost a couple of wickets in the first session you were doing fairly well. Then it eased and it was fine for runs. It was always at its best on the second day.

"After the war, it was bad. No doubt about that. There was no grass on it, they got rid of all the couch, which made it drummy, the ball keeping low. By the last day it was hopeless. What happened was, they got rid of all the couch grass and tried to use a winter grass. That was a mistake, it didn't work. When Bill Watt arrived we tried to get couch back again, but it wouldn't grow until December. Then by chance I was talking to Don Bradman, who said, 'Of course, you always had water couch before the war, so that got us thinking. Water couch, thick root, and old Bert Luttrell used to scythe the thing."

The complaints about the wicket came every summer, as regular as the screech of the cicadas. In 1979 it was Graham Yallop who called it dangerous and unpredictable. In 1980 Greg Chappell described it as the worst wicket he had seen. He described it as "marginally behind the wicket at Faisalabad." Considering what Australian Test players thought of wickets in Pakistan that was faint praise indeed.

In March, 1980, the club had the entire wicket rotary hoed, relaid and planted with Derby rye, then in the spring, thousands of plugs of Santa Ana couch. That spring was awful; it never stopped raining. It had been hoped to make the wicket exactly level in time for the Test season, but this proved impossible. Greg Chappell, claiming he had the support of the Indian and New Zealand Test teams wrote a letter of protest to the Australian Cricket Board. He said all matches should be transferred to other venues.

In 1981 the situation was even worse. Greg Chappell maintained a continuing running battle. He called the wicket "a disgrace" and "an embarrassment." He said the wicket was not as uneven as the previous season, but it was even slower and he said the First Test against the West Indies, scheduled for the M.C.G. on Boxing Day, should be shifted elsewhere. He talked of the St. Kilda ground or Princes Park, Carlton. At one stage the barrage of criticism was so overpowering, Jack Lyons, the curator, told the *Age*: "I thought I wouldn't get here today. I thought I would be in an asylum."

Of course, moving a Test match away from the M.C.G. would be like running the Melbourne Cup at Cranbourne. It was unthinkable. Ian Johnson said: "One day I was looking at the wicket. I put my nailfile down a crack and I found it was soft about an inch beneath the soil."

A whole range of experts were called. There was Dr. Don McIntyre, a soils physicist from C.S.I.R.O. in Canberra; Peter McMaugh, a consultant agronomist, and John Maley, then curator at the West Australian Cricket Association ground. The press called Peter McMaugh the Red Adair of cricket pitches.

(Red Adair was the hugely paid American who was always called in when blazing oil wells ran amok.)

Ian Johnson said: "Don McIntyre did some tests and found that the soil underneath was saturated to a depth of 36 inches and the couch runners would not go into that wet soil. They were running sideways under the surface forming a thick two inch crust. This was what was making the pitch drummy and that was why chips were coming out of it."

The M.C.G., already under threat from the Australian Cricket Board to have all matches removed from the ground, decided in December to dig up and replace the entire wicket, starting on January 26, 1982.

Ian Johnson said: "The V.C.A. wanted us to do it all in one year, but that was impossible. We compromised, half one year and half the next. We were lucky to have Ted Ajani on the Committee, who was with the Board of Works. He got us a deposit of soil from Merri Creek, now in very short supply. We had been getting our soil from Templestowe. Ted did a wonderful job. The stuff was hand-picked and sieved to get rid of all the pebbles."

So the wicket was remade, half one year, half the next, and it became as comfortable as the most up-to-date double bed, electrically warmed. Florawarm Pty Ltd supplied electric cables installed eight inches under the surface. There were sensors which gave a read-out of the temperature and there was individual control for each wicket.

Peter Semos, a highly-trained expert trouble-shooter with the Canberra Horticultural Services Unit received the responsibility of building the wickets. According to Ian Johnson the right varieties of couch were planted and it all worked. There was an immediate improvement in the wicket, but to complete the full programme they needed five years.

Both India and New Zealand sent touring sides to Australia in 1980-81 and there were times when it was obvious that cricket was anything but a balm to international relations. It was a wonder that New Zealand did not pull out of the Anzus pact, regardless of coming difficulties with the U.S.A.

Australia beat the Kiwis two-nil and had a 1-1 tie with India. We won the First Test in Brisbane against India by an innings and four runs, had a draw in Adelaide and lost at the M.C.G. Indeed Australia's loss in the Third Test could almost be described as a miraculous achievement and once again there was wailing and gnashing of teeth over the infamous pitch.

Australia made 419 in the first innings, a sweet comfortable advantage of 182 runs. Border made 124, his sixth Test century, and Doug Walters backed him with 78. But tempers were crumbling as well as the pitch. In the second innings India's captain, Sunil Gavaskar, and Chethan Chauhan turned on an

300

opening partnership of 165. What with the wicket already showing signs of decay it was a fightback akin to the siege of Tobruk. Finally Lillee got Gavaskar lbw, but the Indian was outraged. He pointed dramatically to the umpire, indicating to him, the crowd and all humanity that the ball had gone from bat to pad. Lillee, never bashful, waved at the umpire and suggested to Gavaskar that the best thing he could do was start his little hike to the pavilion.

Gavaskar was furious. He already felt his team had suffered from bad umpiring in Adelaide. He spoke to Chauhan: it was time to leave. If this was the state of affairs the match was over.

The crowd was small, 4503; even so not a sound was coming from the grandstands. Everyone realised something dangerous was happening. It was lucky that the Indian team manager, Shahid Durrani, had not gone for a cup of tea or taken a nap. He was there at the fence and waiting. He told Gavaskar to come off and Chauhan to return to the wicket. Had Chauhan taken one further step, technically he would have left the playing area and Greg Chappell would have been entitled to victory on a forfeit.

Obviously when he went back Chauhan could think of little but the agony of the moment. Minutes later Lillee gave him a ball he could well have left alone, he slashed at it and Bruce Yardley took a catch.

That wicket took Lillee past Richie Benaud's record of 248, the highest number of Test wickets for an Australian. It was a pity it came in such circumstances and with so few people to see it. Lillee turned round and waved to Richie Benaud who was in the Channel Nine broadcast box. The message was through that he was the new number one. In the final innings Australia needed only 142 runs, half a day's work, but the wicket had other ideas. Now it was perishing in a hurry. Not one player got as far as 20. There had been much talk about Kapil Dev's injury. He had a torn thigh muscle that had been nursed with ice and soothed with ultrasound. He took 5 for 28 and Australia was all out for 83.

However the ultimate sensation came at the Melbourne Cricket Ground on Sunday, February 1, 1981. Between the Second and Third Tests against India, Australia met New Zealand in the final series of the Benson & Hedges one-day competition. Australia lost the first match in Sydney, won the next encounter in Melbourne and now the scene was set beautifully for a big battle at the M.C.G. There was an incident in the first innings which started a chill in relations. Greg Chappell was scoring lustily when at 58 he skied a ball towards the boundary. Martin Snedden, who was in a nigh impossible position, sprinted like an Olympic quarter-miler and threw himself full length to take the catch. The haughty Chappell stood his ground while the two umpires agreed the ball was not taken cleanly. There was re-play after re-play on the television and many a commentator agreed the Kiwis had been poorly treated. Chappell went on to make 90 of Australia's total of 4/235.

It was tense. The New Zealanders in their innings tumbled to 8/225. Edgar and McKechnie just needed 11 runs off the last over to win. They scored five off the first five balls and with the last ball to come, it wasn't all over. A six would do it.

It was then that Greg Chappell told his brother Trevor to bowl the last ball underarm. Trevor pitched the perfect grubber thus making a score of any kind impossible. McKechnie blocked the ball and hurled his bat in disgust. The startled crowd of 52,900 hooted its disapproval. That uproar lasted for days. Two Prime Ministers entered the fray. The Australian Prime Minister, Mr. Fraser, described it as "a very serious mistake" and the word came through that he had telephoned the Australian Cricket Board to express his disapproval.

New Zealand's Prime Minister, Mr. Muldoon, said Chappell's order was "an act of cowardice." "I thought it was most appropriate," he said, "that the Australian team was dressed in yellow. It was the most disgusting effort I can recall in the history of cricket, a game which used to be played by gentlemen."

Four former captains—Bob Simpson, Ian Johnson, Bill Lawry and Richie Benaud—all expressed their disapproval. Phil Ridings, chairman of the Australian Cricket Board, gave a formal rebuke to Chappell, saying that the underarm delivery was "totally contrary to the spirit of cricket." Chappell almost apologised. He said: "The decision was made when I was under pressure and in the heat of the moment. I regret the decision. It is something I would not do again."

Assistance for Chappell came from an unexpected quarter. Cricket journalist Murray Hedgecock, writing in London, said: "What a load of hypocritical rubbish. Doesn't anyone in Australia understand that this showbiz abortion known as one-day cricket is governed by the idea that you stop the opposition scoring runs. If you want to restrict your best cricketers to the simplistic game of limited overs instead of encouraging them to reveal their full range of skills in real cricket then you have to accept the whole style of a different game."

Greg Chappell had the final say. He top scored for Australia with 87 to beat New Zealand in the final match of the series in Sydney on February 3. Furthermore he was named Man of the Series. Yet one eloquent banner at the Sydney Cricket Ground did say:

GREG . . . YOUR UNDERARM STINKS.

Both Pakistan and the West Indies toured Australia in the summer of 1981-82. Australia beat Pakistan 2-1 and the West Indies squared the series 1-1. For the M.C.G. there was the odd situation where the breaking of records seemed more important than the cricket. For two Test matches the world seemed focused on one man, Dennis Lillee. Already he had broken the Australian all-comers record, now he was on the verge of becoming the greatest collector of Test wickets of all time. It so happened that the Third Test against Pakistan and the First Test against the West Indies followed one another. Lillee was rushing towards his target, nine wickets in Brisbane and at one stage he had 5/18 in Perth.

It seemed certain Lance Gibbs' record of 310 would go in that Third Test against Pakistan at the M.C.G. Channel 9 was so confident that the network made a grand gesture. It discovered that Lance Gibbs was now living in Florida and it flew him to Melbourne for the match.

You can apply a little too much pressure. Pakistan won by an innings and 92 runs and the frustrated Lillee did not take a wicket. Even more frustrated was Mr. Gibbs. He filled in a week watching Dennis not bowling very well and said so. He could not wait until December 26 for the First Test against the West Indies so he returned to Florida.

The record was the talk of the cricket world. Every time he passed near a microphone someone would ask if today or tomorrow was the day. Lillee was feeling the strain; he must have had a faint idea what it would be like being a Jimmy Carter or a Ronald Reagan facing a summit meeting with the Russians.

The old adage about big crowds meaning dull cricket did not work this Boxing Day; it went down as one of the most memorable in Test history. Australia won the toss and batted and there was nothing sleep-making about the artillery power of Michael Holding and Andy Roberts. There was an immediate collapse. Greg Chappell, who was enduring the horrors, was out first ball. The one man who stood there like a knight of old hurling back all attacks was Kim Hughes. When the ninth wicket went down at 155 the situation looked hopeless. Hughes was on 71 and only Terry Alderman was left. Yet Alderman was no rabbit. He closed off one end long enough for Hughes to get his century. Those who were there still rank it is as the finest innings in Hughes' distinguished career. Finally Australia was all out for 198 with 40 minutes remaining for play before stumps.

These were 40 minutes when Dennis Lillee literally set the Melbourne Cricket Ground on fire. As soon as Lillee took the ball the Outer crowd started their baying chant. If their battle cry "Lill-eeee . . . Lill-eeee . . ." had been awesome before, now it was something else. Imagine the hot still evening air, shadows across the ground and these high stands which entirely encircle, creating a sound well, a huge organ pipe. So the Lill-eeee chant rose in pitch . . . louder . . . louder as he made his long run towards the wicket. Had he been a charging lion and eating Christians for the pleasure of Caesar the situation could not have been more menacing. Lillee took three wickets for one run off 12 deliveries . . . Haynes, Bacchus and Viv Richards.

The crowd was in a frenzy lusting for blood; there is no other way to describe it. And Lillee was inspired. He admitted later it was the backing of that crowd in Bay 13 that pushed him on. At stumps the West Indies were 4/10, three wickets to Lillee and one to Terry Alderman. Lillee looked up at the board, read his bowling figures 3/6 and could hardly believe what was happening.

Lillee still needed two wickets for his record and he had no success in the morning. He wondered even whether he would get there and this time he bowled with the crowd strangely silent. The breakthrough came in the afternoon. Dujon went for the hook and was caught by Kim Hughes. Then at precisely 2.55 p.m. Larry Gomes let his bat stray carelessly outside the off stump. He caught an edge and Greg Chappell took the catch.

Dennis Lillee stood in the centre and for the first time he was a bit nonplussed, hardly knowing what to do next. Rodney Marsh sprinted across and gave him a hug of such proportions, you would have thought it was a lost and found situation and he had been hunting for his mate for 20 years. "Well done mate," he said. "Well deserved." He made a vain attempt to try and lift Lillee on to his shoulders. After all, Marsh had been personal assistant in 83 of Lillee's 310 dismissals. Lillee finished with 10 wickets for the match and Australia won by 58 runs.

They were now in the era when there was almost cricket overload. There was also the Benson & Hedges one-day series in which the West Indies beat Australia in the final 3-1. On January 10 there was a final crowd of 78,142, a one-day world record.

Those internationals were the last scores recorded by the old scoreboard. It had been there since 1901. Some members looked on aghast as the wreckers moved in. It was almost as if they were desecrating the shrine of the old greats: Trumble, Trumper, Ryder, Armstrong and Mailey. Ian Johnson even apologised to the press. "The decision to replace the scoreboard has been taken with a lot of sentimental regret. We did not do it happily."

But, of course, it had to be. Investigations on going electronic began in 1977. Ian Johnson first saw a dot matrix type screen that year at the Aloha

Stadium in Hawaii. "It had sepia toning," he said, "and I was very impressed with it. It actually gave an impression of colour. I went on, saw some more on the mainland, and reported back to the Committee."

The Club almost settled for a black and white screen, but then the Melbourne City Council installed its great video in the City Square. Nobody liked it, the Club decided to wait and the V.F.L. went in first with a big black and white video at Waverley. For a moment it looked as if this was a V.F.L. triumph. Relations were particularly sensitive regarding one stadium scoring anything the other did not have. But then came colour. A brochure arrived from the Mitsubishi Electric Company telling of the giant Diamond Vision colour television screen. One had been installed at the Dodgers Stadium in Los Angeles and another in the Kourakuen Stadium in Tokyo.

The Committee thought Ian Johnson had better inspect first hand. "I chose Tokyo," said Ian. "I had already been to L.A. So Lal and I went to Japan. We saw a baseball match at the Kourakuen Stadium and the electronic board was fantastic."

It so happened Sir Bernard Callinan was there just two weeks later and the Mitsubishi people took him to the same stadium. "At first," said Sir Bernard, "I wasn't impressed at all. They would show you colour, then suddenly it would go all grey. It seemed to be breaking down all the time. Then a gentleman from Mitsubishi explained what was happening. 'The man who owns the ground and the lights also owns the team. When his team is batting it is in colour. When the opposition bats it goes grey.' Imagine what would happen if we did this in a game Melbourne versus Collingwood."

Sir Bernard pointed out that the V.F.L. was now committed to a black and white scoreboard and there was no turning back, whereas the M.C.C. committee was delighted it had waited for colour. "Dr. Allen Aylett (President of the V.F.L.) several times raised the point at Trustee meetings that there had been no discussion about the scoreboard. We have to get permission for any major works. We did get permission after we had it all decided, but he thought we should have told the Trustees months before."

Sir Bernard explained, seeing Dr. Aylett wore two hats, as Trustee and a V.F.L. chief, one needed to be a little careful on these matters.

Of course, the M.C.C. was on a good deal. Mitsubishi installed it free of charge and paid for the running costs. In return they received the revenue from all the advertising. However they had to pay the club compensation for losses in fence advertising and this increased yearly to counter inflation. By 1993 ownership would revert to the M.C.G. along with the running costs.

The Japanese with marvellous efficiency installed the Diamond Vision board in nine weeks, just in time for the first football match on Saturday, March 27, 1982. The famous old board, dismantled very carefully, went to the Manuka Oval in Canberra and now brings back memories when the Prime Minister's Eleven plays touring sides.

The giant television screen was splendid. It was 10.85 by 7.235 metres, composed of 38,500 pixels. Each pixel was a small cathode ray tube. There were three trivision screens which perpetually revolved and they gave messages from the first major sponsors: Westpac, Australian Guarantee Corporation, Mitsubishi Motors, A.W.A. Thorn, Coca-Cola, Four 'n' Twenty Pies and the Seiko Watch Co. There was nothing it could not do. It could provide scores, replays, race results, T.A.B. Dividends, interviews, live crosses to other events like tennis, golf or football at other grounds. Once the world title fight between Larry Holmes and Jerry Cooney was shown live at half time during a football match. The cross to the fight coincided with a ferocious blow to the groin of one of the boxers. The roar from the 38,000 football fans could not have been louder had there been a goal for the Demons.

The board had huge memory. It could entertain the crowd with famous feats from the past, show Don Bradman playing his famous shots back in 1934. It could give Niagaras of colour, explode with effusions of joy at a cricketer's century or for a footballer's goal-kicking record. Batsmen could endure the misery of witnessing their own dismissals or learn something from faults in their style. Often players were mesmerised by the screen as much as the spectators. More than one football coach tore strips off his players for paying too much attention to the screen.

Brian Finch from FM-TV Productions ran the board exactly like a mini-television station. He had a carpeted control room with 16 screens.

The big question arose immediately. What about incidents, brawls on the football ground, doubtful decisions, deadly close cricket run-outs, dropped catches, snicks that were never snicked? The Committee agreed there would be no replays to the embarrassment of umpires. Such inflammatory stuff would be left to the TV stations.

England led by Bob Willis came to Australia and most cricket lovers saw their new board for the first time on Boxing Day 1982. It was fascinating how it made everything bigger, larger, closer. Geoff Lawson, like most fast bowlers, suffered from foot trouble. He held up play on one occasion for five minutes. The big screen gave us sensitive close-up stuff of Lawson taking off his boot, his sock and once there was a shot of his bare foot which filled the entire screen. The crowd appreciated such intimate details.

But one felt for failed batsmen. There was the Greg Chappell duck, caught Lamb, bowled Cowans. Not only did he have to endure perhaps the longest walk in the world back to the pavilion, but the playbacks, the sight of Gregory Chappell being dismissed all over again. The new board gave birth to an even more evil trick. It would follow the batsmen in with the image of a little Donald Duck.

This new passion for graphics also had an effect on the crowd. One noted that in the 1980s the old style of clever barracking and vocal wit had all but disappeared. The trend now was to get one's wit noted on television, or even better, picked up by the cameras of the electronic scoreboard.

The M.C.G. became an effusion of banners and flags. It was important to have a flag, particularly during the one-day internationals. On some days there were more flags at the M.C.G. than at the Battle of Agincourt or a Remembrance Day march. Some said simply TOP SHOT, WOW or even OUCH. Some were downright offensive: WHICH IS THE REAL PIG—BOTH'EM. Or almost obscene: WE LIKE BOTHAM'S BALLS. Botham was a perpetual target. He was not having a very good season and was a little overweight. So naturally there had to be a poster: BOTHAM BOWLS WITH GUTS. Kepler Wessels had admitted to praying for divine guidance when scoring his great century during the First Test, so there was a great banner advertising THE REVEREND WESSELS STAND.

The *Sun News-Pictorial* ran a competition encouraging all this. They found their winner when New Zealand lost the final of the one-day competition: THE KIWIS HAVE LOST THEIR POLISH.

There was a big promotion campaign to push cricket with the slogan "The Hottest Cricket in a Hundred Summers." It was certainly hot for Bob Willis' men. They lost in Brisbane, Adelaide and Sydney, but it was a different story in Melbourne. The Fourth Test at the M.C.G. was one of the closest in the history of the game. There were no huge scores, no centuries, but it was a match always evenly poised. England made 284, Australia replied with 287. England made 294, then Australia was left with 292 to get in two days.

In the final innings there were a few reliables, David Hookes 68, Kim Hughes 48, but Britain's new fast bowler, Norman Cowans tore through the side with six wickets. In gloomy weather the ground looked like the Witches scene from *Macbeth* with Australia very dismal, 9/218 and victory 72 runs away. It looked hopeless.

The remaining batsmen were Allan Border and Jeff Thomson. Border hardly filled one with confidence. He had made two in the first innings and he had suffered an awful season, 83 in six expeditions to the crease. Jeff was a muscle man, usually good for a spectacular five minutes.

Incredibly they both stayed there. Jeff, far from being a slash-and-bash artist, looked as sound as an opener. He became so confident he did not worry about the single which would give him blessed security at the other end; he would run doubles instead of singles.

There was a rain delay and at stumps, Border and Thomson were still there with 37 runs to go. But then not many people had real faith. The M.C.G. officials did not believe it was worth their while to pay staff to man the gates on the last day. Little did they realise they had cooked up the best last day crisis in 21 years. Like a bushfire the word spread around Melbourne and 18,000 people came through the turnstiles without having to pay.

What with a night's rest, fast bowlers full of fire in the morning, many presumed Thommo would last one over. But no, it was like the previous afternoon. They were just within three runs of victory and Bob Willis was becoming very worried indeed. Botham, an expert at cleaning up tail-enders, had the ball. Thomson sent a perfect down-the-throat catch to Chris Tavare at slip. The ball bounced clean out of his hands and he could have hung his head as the prize bunny of the tour. But miraculously Chris Miller dived forward and caught it on the rebound. So Australia just failed to make it by three runs, Border was 62 not out and Thomson 21. As Frank Tyson commented, no-one collapsed and died or chewed through the handle of an umbrella as they reputedly did at the Oval in 1882, but repetition of such events would have surprised no-one.

The hottest summer continued unrelenting and it was clear that one-day cricket was becoming a national obsession. Australia played England on Sunday, January 24, 1983 and there was a world record one-day crowd of 84,153. Had it not been for early rain it would have beaten that remarkable day in 1961 when 90,800 turned up for the second day of the Fifth Test against the West Indies. The 84,153 received good value. Dyson, Border and Hookes all scored fifties to murder an English attack and to win by three runs with 12 balls to spare.

Australia then went on to beat New Zealand in the finals. The last match was on Sunday, February 13 and those with long memories found it hard to believe that 71,393 came to the M.C.G. to see a match against the Kiwis. It was a sign of an era, a sign before long that was to prove particularly ominous. Australia set a one-day record of 302; Graeme Wood 91 and Steve Smith 117.

Douglas Heywood, M.C.C. committee
since 1988.

David Jones, M.C.C. committee
since 1987.

Presentation to Robert Flower, Melbourne Football Club's Captain,
on his retirement after the 1987 season.

Robert Lloyd, M.C.C. committee since 1987.

David Meiklejohn, M.C.C. committee since 1987.

M.C.C. meets M.C.C. — John Warr, President of the Marylebone Cricket Club at the 150th Anniversary Dinner.

New Zealand made only 153, but that is not the full story. Just when every-one thought they would have to move off and find an afternoon movie, the Kiwi with the axeman's arms, Lance Cairns, took off as if he had to catch the six o'clock plane. Cairns hit six sixes, the first two off Ken McLeay, the next two off Rodney Hogg in consecutive balls and then two off Dennis Lillee. Early enthusiasm for N.Z. achievements came only from isolated cells of Kiwi spectators, but now one of the world's most insular, most chauvinistic crowds, actually started to show warmth for a foreigner.

So what a summer it was. Since it started on November 12, 1,090,266 people parted with more than $4 million to see Australia regain the Ashes then win the Benson & Hedges Cup.

On the last day of the Cup Final the fancy scoreboard had a significant message. It pointed out that after 26 years this was the last day for Ian John-son as Secretary of the Melbourne Cricket Ground and Melbourne Cricket Club. It wished him happiness in retirement and a well-deserved cheer went around the ground. There was a grand farewell to Ian Johnson in the Long Room. In the old days they had a term for outstanding performers. John Blackham, for example, was the Prince of Wicketkeepers. Ian Johnson was a Prince of Secretaries.

There was much speculation on who would be the new man. After all, there had been only five of them in nigh on a century and the tradition was, he had to be not only a sound administrator but an outstanding sportsman. The newspapers rolled out various names: the outstanding Melbourne wingman and former Victorian politician, Brian Dixon, former Test cricketers Paul Sheahan, Colin McDonald, Ross Edwards, and another footballer was on their list, former Melbourne player, Ian Thorogood. However on September 23, 1982 the Club announced it had chosen Dr. John Lill, a chemical engineer, a Ph.D. who had served ICI for 25 years. As an opening batsman from 1955 to 1964 he made 4067 runs for South Australia at an average of 37.84. He made eight Sheffield Shield centuries and in one match at the M.C.G. in 1960 he tortured Victorian bowlers like Connolly and Meckiff with a score of 176.

His cricket career was actually dominated by ICI which meant he played in three States. He played for the Melbourne Cricket Club First Eleven from 1969 to 1973, then he went to Perth and played for Claremont. He returned to Melbourne and captained the Club's seconds and thirds and only gave up the game because of pressure of work. That was in 1983 when he became secre-tary of the M.C.C. He was also a talented footballer. He played 78 games for Norwood in Adelaide, mostly at centre half-forward.

A different character to Ian Johnson: Ian had the qualities of an attacking bowler, very direct and often controversial in his statements; John Lill was more the opening bat, a brilliant defender, with no dramatics. He was quietly spoken, utterly unflappable, the diplomat and an excellent behind-the-scenes organiser. He took over in February 1983.

CHAPTER TWENTY-FIVE

The Feminine Touch

IT WAS just as well that John Lill was not a nervous man, but calm and unflappable. He was ducking and weaving those bumpers almost immediately upon taking office. Three of them rose very sharply indeed. There was the continuing saga of which ground would get the football Grand Final, but now it was working towards a climax. There was the proposition that women should become full members and the Melbourne Cricket Club through no fault of its own was caught in a political/union battle over lights for the M.C.G.

There had been a temporary truce with the V.F.L., a five-year agreement to keep on playing the Grand Final at the M.C.G. It was a very tender truce, as shaky as a truce in Ireland or Lebanon. Right back to the days of Sir Kenneth Luke the V.F.L. had never hidden its aims: V.F.L. Park, Waverley, was its headquarters and as soon as it was big enough it would be the home for the Grand Final. The target year was 1984. As far as the Melbourne Cricket Club was concerned the date definitely had a touch of George Orwell and there was more than one threatening Big Brother.

V.F.L. Park was always lower, more saucer-like than the M.C.G. The grand plan was to use this for extra tiers, to make a stadium that would seat 150,000. In 1981 the League decided to spend $20 million on extensions to raise accommodation from a comfortable 75,000 to 104,000. In June 1982, the Victorian Government's Minister for Planning and Environment, Evan Walker, refused to grant a building permit.

The M.C.G. was flanked on either side by trams and trains. V.F.L. Park had neither. On big match days congestion was so bad cars were taking up to two hours to get clear of the ground. Mr. Walker made it clear to the V.F.L. there would be no permit for Waverley until new roads were built to ease the traffic.

Dr. Allen Aylett was angry. He described the Government's actions as undemocratic. If necessary the V.F.L. would spend $3 million to $4 million on upgrading the roads around V.F.L. Park. There was no permit forthcoming, but permit or no permit, they wanted the Grand Final at V.F.L. Park. They would have it there even without the improvements. Dr. Aylett insisted that even with a crowd of 80,000 V.F.L. Park still was a better financial deal for them than the M.C.G. At Waverley the V.F.L. owned all the catering and advertising rights.

Which stadium was the more popular? A Gallup Poll in July 1982 sampled 547 Victorians and found 42 per cent. supported the V.F.L.'s plan for 1984, 39 per cent. were against and 19 per cent. had no opinion. The M.C.C. conducted independent polls at both grounds during the finals and 70 per cent. of football followers preferred the M.C.G. As for the players, the *Herald* newspaper conducted a poll among 28 players from 11 clubs and four out of five thought the M.C.G. the better ground.

There were many sentimental articles about the 1983 Grand Final. Most papers treated the M.C.G. as if it were in the intensive care ward and close to death. This was the last Grand Final ever at the old ground. Flowers and obsequies were appropriate.

On the morning of the big day, September 24, Mike Coward wrote in the *Age*: "Thousands of people will file through Yarra Park from early this morning. Many will have heavy hearts. Many will walk as they would to a graveside. Each will be filled with special thoughts, special recollections, special reminiscences. For each of us has a special feeling for the M.C.G. on Grand Final day. If the game is taken away from the ground, each of us will lose a little of ourselves. And this afternoon, when the final siren screams to be heard, tears will be shed not only in victory and in defeat, but in the possible passing of a great event at a great arena."

The Grand Final was between Hawthorn and Essendon, the first time these two had met in the big event. Hawthorn was the winner by 83 points, a V.F.L. record. But there was a shock in store for Dr. Aylett. When HSV7's general manager introduced him to the crowd as President of the Victorian Football League they hooted and jeered. In his book *My Game. A Life in Football*, Aylett commented: "I'm told the boos were loud and long in the M.C.G. Long Room and Committee Room." But in fact the booing was universal. The V.F.L. was locked into a corner. Its subscriptions were almost three times more costly than those of M.C.C. members. They were paying $120 a year on the promise they would get the V.F.L. Grand Final at Waverley. Public opinion was building steadily in favour of the M.C.G. The Premier, Mr. Cain, made it clear that the M.C.G. was his preferred ground and John Elliott, chairman of Elders IXL, the League's biggest sponsor and also President of Carlton, commented that taking the Grand Final away from the M.C.G. would be like taking the Melbourne Cup away from Flemington. The V.F.L. then made the concession that they would use the M.C.G. subject to certain conditions. The V.F.L. would play the 1984 Grand Final at the M.C.G. if it could lease the entire ground. V.F.L. members would occupy the M.C.C. Members' reserve. M.C.C. would have no rights there but they would have priority in purchasing tickets. The V.F.L. went further. Dr. Aylett suggested to the Premier that the V.F.L. should occupy the M.C.G. for six months and the Melbourne Cricket Club take the other half. Sir Bernard Callinan thought the V.F.L.'s plan to control the M.C.G. for six months so dangerous he put it as a postal vote to all members.

The President's letter to members also included a counter proposal to the V.F.L. If the V.F.L. gave a commitment to play the Grand Final at the M.C.G. for the next 20 years the M.C.C. would rebuild the Southern Stand and boost accommodation to 106,000 seats. It would provide special improved facilities for 27,600 V.F.L. members in the Southern Stand. There would be a special rental of $250,000 a year for this service or payment by the V.F.L. of the equivalent amount a head as M.C.C. members pay to go to the Grand Final.

Of course, the result was a foregone conclusion. It was like inviting strangers home to look at television with them occupying the best lounge room chairs while you stood out in the street. The vote was a simple Yes or No to the V.F.L. proposal. There were 10,896 Nos and only 3717 said Yes.

Mr. Cain, commenting on the vote, said: "Frankly, I am sick and tired of this cat and mouse approach to these negotiations." He said that he would ask the M.C.G. Trustees to direct the M.C.C. to accept the V.F.L.'s offer to lease the M.C.G. on Grand Final day, including the Members' reserve for use by V.F.L. members.

All this disregarded the M.C.C. vote. Sir Bernard Callinan was very disturbed. He felt the very future of the Melbourne Cricket Club was in jeopardy. If the Trustees directed the Club to lease the ground then it was virtually the end of the M.C.C. He said: "If the Government is determined to act there's nothing we can do to stop it. We have been here for 125 years and all the facilities have been paid for primarily by Members' subscriptions. The M.C.C. would be prepared to fight the Government on grounds of equity if the Members' reserve is taken away from M.C.C. Members."

V.F.L. officials were delighted with the Premier's intervention. The V.F.L. general manager, Jack Hamilton, said: "The Premier's offer is in exact agreement with the resolution of the V.F.L. Board of DIrectors on October 26: the Grand Final would be played at the M.C.G. in the event of the League leasing the entire ground, including the Members' reserve."

Sir Bernard Callinan recalling these days said: "It became obvious to me after a while that the League had an 'in' with the Premier. At first I thought it was Allen Aylett, but clearly it was the general manager, Jack Hamilton. We would be called up for discussion with the Government only to be told Mr. Cain had virtually come to a decision. It all came out eventually. The V.F.L.'s reason for wanting the Grand Final was simple, unless they got it they would lose a large part of their membership. Many members had paid their sub-scriptions entirely on the belief that the final would be played at Waverley. They knew there was little chance of getting into the Melbourne Cricket Club because of the awful waiting list. The club took no pleasure in that."

The crisis came to a head when the Trustees under the chairmanship of Sir Henry Bolte met at the Premier's office, Number One Treasury Place, at 11.30 a.m. on December 7, 1983. Sir Bernard said: "The meeting was sup-posed to last only for the morning, but the Premier had to send out for sandwiches and it went on into the afternoon. My problem was that the Club was fighting its battle from a position of weakness. The ground is controlled by the Trustees. This dated back to 1933 when the Government brought down the Melbourne Cricket Club Act. The Club until then thought it was all powerful, but the act stated the M.C.C. could have occupancy of the ground so long as it never deliberately offended or refused anything the Trustees ordered and so long as it owed money. In other words the Club could not give it away."

Sir Bernard explained the Government could do anything it liked and the truth was the Melbourne Cricket Club was in a position little better than a committee of management such as you would find with provincial grounds all around Australia.

Mr. Cain made all this very clear at the Treasury Place meeting. He handed round an opinion from the Solicitor-General. The opinion in effect said that the Trustees were all-powerful and could direct the M.C.C. Committee to do anything it wished.

Mr. Cain said it was the wish of the Government that he ask the Trustees to direct the Melbourne Cricket Club to accept the V.F.L.'s offer to take a lease for Grand Final day and take over the M.C.G. It was in the public interest that the big game should remain at the M.C.G. The Trustees in the opinion of the Solicitor-General had the power to do this. They could decide it by regula-tion.

Sir Bernard did not agree. He had legal opinion to the contrary. They could not do it by regulation because regulation was contrary to the act. However this was more of a delaying factor than anything else. "We might have won

314

the battle at this stage," said Sir Bernard, "but we would have lost the war. All the Government had to do was go ahead and change the act."

The Trustees were not happy with the Government direction. Sir Rupert Hamer said whatever happened the V.F.L. should not be permanently dis-advantaged, but ultimately the solution came from another former Premier, Lindsay Thompson. He suggested that both M.C.C. members and V.F.L. members should share an enlarged members' reserve on Grand Final day. At last this was a basis for discussion. The M.C.C. felt that as its members already had undertaken to pay full price for the match it would be only fair that V.F.L. members should pay also.

After the meeting was over Mr. Cain said the State Government would legislate to keep the Grand Final at the M.C.G. for 10 years if the V.F.L. and the M.C.C. could not get together and solve their problems.

Some saw a fascinating parallel between John Cain, Premier of Victoria before the Melbourne Olympics of 1956, and his son, John Cain, Premier of Victoria in 1983. In 1951 the Melbourne Cricket Club was reluctant to use the M.C.G. for the Olympic Games for fear of what it would do to the ground and the future of cricket. Sir Kenneth Luke immediately called in architects and started preparations to make Princes Park at Carlton the main Olympic stadium. John Cain senior intervened and said the main stadium had to be the M.C.G. and this was the only place where the Government would spend money. The M.C.C. Committee reversed its previous decision and Princes Park lost its great opportunity. This was something Kenneth Luke never for-got and undoubtedly inspired his enormous desire to build V.F.L. Park at Waverley.

A meeting of V.F.L. directors on December 14 refused to budge from the hard line that the M.C.G. should be leased to the V.F.L. and any agreement made with the M.C.C. would be for 1984 only.

Sir Bernard Callinan remembers deep feeling among Members in 1983. Some would stop him in the street and say, " 'Why don't you give it away. The M.C.G. can live without V.F.L. football.' However, I wasn't prepared to give it away," he said. "My argument all through was that the Grand Final needed the M.C.G. more than the M.C.G. needed the Grand Final. Yes, I believed in the Grand Final, but if there was a risk of the Government changing the act or changing the Club's hold on the ground in any way, I would have let it go."

The V.F.L. and the M.C.C. did get together in February 1984. Their agree-ment was on three points:

1. V.F.L. Park members would be admitted free to an enlarged members'

315

area. The V.F.L. would pay into the gate their admission as the M.C.C. did for its members.

2. The M.C.C. would instal 4000 extra public seats.

3. There would be no financial disadvantage to the V.F.L. on the basis of what they could have earned at V.F.L. Park.

Item 3 was the tricky one. The M.C.C. and the V.F.L. employed Arthur Anderson and Co. accountants to do a comparison on the money the V.F.L. would earn from a Grand Final at the M.C.G. as opposed to a Grand Final at Waverley. The Club undertook to underwrite any difference.

In the first year this did not work out well for the Melbourne Cricket Club. Only 92,685 people turned out to see Essendon defeat Hawthorn, the lowest Grand Final crowd for 29 years. Members disliked the new arrangement. John Lill, M.C.C. secretary, said: "We kept a block of seats for Members in the top of the Northern Stand, which was practically empty. Members just didn't turn up and when we did our sums afterwards we had to pay the League $150,000, so the ground got practically nothing out of the Grand Final. However it has worked out better in recent years. The V.F.L. has received what it felt it should get and the formula has worked happily for us."

But sharing the Members' reserve with the V.F.L. was not the only social upheaval that came about in 1983-84. In terms of real history, something more important took place, women came into the Long Room.

Dr. Don Cordner was the first to raise the idea. He remembers: "It all began at the end of a Committee meeting in 1967. I didn't even know the wives of the other Committeemen. On Grand Final day or the first few days of a Test match, you brought along your wife and she was banished to the ladies' dining room and you picked her up at the end of the match. At this meeting during general business I suggested, 'I think it would be a good idea at Christmas time if we had a little dinner party in the committee room and asked our wives at our own expense.' There was a stunned, deafening silence. Tom Trumble said, 'What's the matter, son—are you in trouble?' The minutes read: 'Dr. Cordner suggested dinner should be held with wives. After discussion it was decided no action should be taken.' It didn't even get a seconder."

Donald Cordner said he did not get a seconder until 1974 when he received the backing of Colin Spargo. The next move came in 1981. That was not easy either. The plan was to connect the Committee dining room and the ladies' room with a door. Judge Alec Southwell seconded the proposal and it became known as the Cordner-Southwell door. The next historic occasion was in 1983. It was the football match Melbourne versus Geelong and they were

316

celebrating 125 years to the day of the very first Scotch-Melbourne Grammar football match. The headmasters of Scotch and Melbourne Grammar were guests. "We had been inviting the women into the Committee dining room. They would come in late in the day after all the visitors had left. This day the ladies' lunch was set in the ladies' room, the men's in the men's room and we thought we would decide whether we would let the ladies in or not. The answer after some debate was 'Yes'. Sir Bernard Callinan was away in Queensland, but it was OK; the die was cast. We dined with the ladies from then on. However my view all along was that the admission of women was inevitable and we should do it while we had time to make our own rules."

However it was the Premier John Cain who gave the final push. He attended a V.F.L. lunch. Mr. Cain was in one room and Mrs. Cain was in another. They did not like it and both left unfed. The earliest official moves began with the Hamer Liberal Government which brought down an Equal Opportunity Act, but it had one exemption. It did not apply to sporting clubs. The Cain Government removed that exemption. Clubs which occupied Crown land had to give equal rights.

There was a special meeting of club members on May 24, 1983 to discuss a committee recommendation that women should become provisional members. Only 271 or 1.35 per cent. of the membership attended. Sir Bernard Callinan declared the motion passed on a show of hands, but dissenters asked for a division. The final count was 178 for the motion, 93 against. Sir Bernard declared the motion lost. It had failed to gain the necessary two-thirds majority.

The next move was to put the motion to a postal vote of all 19,963 eligible members. One voter, the Premier, made an ominous comment to the *Age*: "I am hopeful that the M.C.C. will put its own house in order but should the postal vote be lost, the Government guarantees to achieve membership for women in some way."

The postal vote went through very quickly and on June 27 Dr. Lill announced the Melbourne Cricket Club had voted by a majority of more than two to one to admit women as provisional members. There were obvious technical difficulties and the biggest of all was the huge male waiting list. "Most women wouldn't live long enough to get in," said Dr. Lill, "so we devised this idea that if we did something with ladies' tickets we wouldn't alter the number of Grand Final Day entries into the ground on which our membership is based and we wouldn't disadvantage anyone on the waiting list. We have 20,000 members with 21,000 ladies' tickets. That's 41,000 potential entries into the ground. We know from experience about 55 per cent. come

317

on Grand Final Day, that's 24,000, the capacity of the Members' stand and that's how we fixed membership numbers. We thought if we took 21,000 ladies' tickets and changed them to a form of membership, we hadn't altered the number of people who come into the ground and we hadn't delayed anyone on the waiting list.

"So we said, 'OK we've changed the rules, women can nominate to be members, they can go on the waiting list and in 30 years they will be voting members of the club. In the mean time we are going to create a new category of membership called provisional membership, which is non-transferable but doesn't have any voting rights, but if you are a provisional member and your husband dies, you retain membership in your own right.' That was the first step. We had 4000 women in that category, but it was open to one sex only and in terms of the Equal Opportunity Act, it was illegal."

Dr. Lill explained the Government had one undeniable weapon, the Liquor Control Commission. If a club failed to live up to its requirements it could apply pressure by refusing to renew its liquor licence. The Club was happy to get rid of provisional membership and realistically it had to give women the chance to stand for the Committee. The next procedure was to offer provisional members the opportunity to become full members with voting rights, provided they were prepared to pay the full entry and membership fee. By 1987 there were 3500 in this category. Women first appeared in the Long Room as provisional members on July 2, 1983. Jane Sullivan reported in the *Age*: "We waited for the portraits of past Melbourne Cricket Club secretaries to grow pale, for the 18th century cricket bats to rattle in their mountings, or for the ghost of W. G. Grace to strike down the sacrilegious female with an extra fast ball. But nothing happened. Saturday's invasion of one of the last male strongholds in Melbourne was one of the quietest on record.

"The most the women had to endure were a few muted comments, some heavy-handed but good-natured jokes and a lot of curious stares—particularly in the direction of a young woman with a daring slit at the back of her skirt. 'Bloody disgrace—there's four or five of them in there already,' muttered one member outside the pavilion a couple of hours before the start of the match between Richmond and North Melbourne. But his reaction was scarcely typical."

There was the minor problem of what to do about dress. After all, if males were required to wear jackets and ties in the Long Room, what was correct for women? Could they get away with anything? The club decided definitely against tight jeans, sandals, shorts and long bare legs. Then on hot days out in the sunshine attendants would suggest that women did not expose too much bare chest and shoulder. After all, old-fashioned males did have to concentrate on their cricket.

Dr. Lill remembers on that first day there was a woman in the Members' bar and clearly she was a sensation. She was tall, glamorous with long hair that hung right down her back. The hair was enhanced by a gorgeous ankle-length mink coat. First he noticed her from behind, but then she turned round and it was clear that she was wearing the tightest pair of jeans he could ever remember. Was she infringing the new rules on dress? For once John Lill decided that this was a time when a rule had been broken, only slightly.

The ladies were fortunate. They won membership in a season that was ablaze with cricket. Australia beat Pakistan 2-nil with three drawn matches. The Fourth Test at the M.C.G. was one of those drawn games but Melburnians had the intense pleasure of seeing Graham Yallop make 268 runs in a 12-hour stand. Only Bradman, Simpson and Cowper had achieved higher Test scores. He shared a record third-wicket partnership with Kim Hughes of 203. Hughes made 94. Then he had another partnership of 185 with Greg Matthews who made 75. Yallop passed his 4000 runs in Test cricket and it was a personal triumph becuase it was his first Test century on his home ground. But as far as crowd enthusiasm is concerned it has to be confessed the Benson and Hedges one-day series between Australia, Paskistan and the West Indies was superior box office. The match between Australia and the West Indies on January 22, 1984 scored yet another world one-day crowd, 86,133. Australia actually was defeated by one man, Isaac Vivian Alexander Richards. There was even a sign up on the Southern Stand: VIV IS GOD. When other batsmen were at the crease they could not penetrate the field—it was snappy little singles. Mr. Richards had no trouble finding the gaps. He made them look as wide as the Simpson Desert. He faced only 96 deliveries in scoring 106 with 12 boundaries and an effortless six off Carl Rackemann, straight into the Members' stand. A member in a red hat caught him beautifully.

The astonishing climax came at the M.C.G. The first final was in Sydney and the West Indies beat Australia by nine wickets. The second final was at the M.C.G. on February 11, 1984 before 42,000 people. The West Indies made 5/222 and Australia replied with 9/222, the first tie in international cricket for 23 years. Then an extraordinary thing happened; the officials did not know what to do next. A tie in this situation was unprecedented. Would there be another match or would there not? For two and a half hours Cricket Board members studied the rule books. But the crowd wanted to know what was going to happen and 40,000 people refused to go home. The electronic scoreboard did its best. Once it even put up the message: DO I WORK

319

TOMORROW OR CAN I GO TO THE BEACH? A group of characters in Bay 13 showing intense patriotism held up the Australian flag for nearly an hour, waiting, waiting for the decision whether there would be a game on the Sunday. The decision did not come through until 9 p.m. Yes, there would be a replay the next day.

Clive Lloyd and his West Indians were not pleased. They thought there was no need for the extra match. They lost only five wickets for their 222 runs, the Australians lost nine.

Neither Viv Richards nor Clive Lloyd played the next day. The word was that both were injured. It should have been the crowd draw of the year but only 19,210 attended. The decision to play the match came far too late, 9 p.m. the previous evening. Somehow, too, it was an anticlimax. Many people felt that morally the West Indies already had won the series.

The West Indies, even without two stars, won easily by five wickets. Joel Garner took 5/31. Perhaps the most important, and certainly the most emotional feature of this match, was the departure of Rodney Marsh. Dennis Lillee and Greg Chappell made their final appearances in the Fifth Test against Pakistan at the Sydney Cricket Ground. Greg Chappell began his Test career with a century and ended it the same way, with a glorious 182. Rod Marsh left his retirement until the end of the one-day matches. At least two-thirds of the banners around the M.C.G. were devoted to Rodney. One enormous, carefully-penned banner said:

ROD MARSH HAS DONE FOR
CRICKET WHAT LEE MARVIN
HAS DONE FOR FISHING.
BOTH HAVE CAUGHT
THE BIG ONES.

CHAPTER TWENTY·SIX

The M.C.G. Sees the Light

FEBRUARY 1985 was the month that the Melbourne Cricket Club saw the light, but in Biblical terms it was not done in a flash. The Club unwittingly was caught in a struggle for power, union against union and union against Government.

Ever since the Packer circus dazzled crowds with night cricket at the Sydney Cricket Ground and V.F.L. Park it was obvious the Melbourne Cricket Club would have to provide lighting for night sport. The decision was made to stage a World Chamionship of Cricket with the final in Melbourne to celebrate Victoria's 150th birthday. It was essential that light should be available for these matches. Every year costs were escalating. The quote for the M.C.G. was $3.5 million. There were immediate protests from local residents. They objected to the prospect of traffic congestion in East Melbourne at night and they had the idea that the lights somehow would be like another sun disturbing their night peace. They formed the East Melbourne Group and started fund-raising to block the whole project.

The Melbourne City Council also objected, prompted by the East Melbourne residents and there was a further objection that the lights would be built on public parkland.

This was true. Dr. John Lill said: "We had to have extra land. In Sydney they fitted their light towers between the stands but we had no room for that. Also we had to go outside the ground so that we could get the angles right to avoid shadows. We also needed the land to upgrade toilet facilities and improve the entrances. In 1983 at the Test match we had long, long queues and we were criticised by everyone. The Government changed the act to give us this land." The extra space granted for light towers, new entry gates and toilets, was a 20-metre ring around the ground.

The East Melbourne Group took their complaints to the Planning Appeals Board but on December 30, 1983 the Government bypassed all the normal planning procedures. The Premier, John Cain, announced that the building of six light towers at the M.C.G. was a matter of State importance. He would not put up with "a charade around the planning process." He would use the law to control the use of Crown land at the M.C.G. He said: "I believe that this city has, over the years, established itself as the principal sporting city in Australia. We are the leaders in sport and we have got the best ground in Australia and we want to keep it that way."

The East Melbourne Group asked for help and got it. The Builders Labourers' Federation immediately announced they would not work on the lights.

The B.L.F. was a very potent force. Already it had been deregistered for contempt of the system between 1970 and 1974. It was denied the national wage increase in September 1977 because of dealings outside wage fixing principles. It had been investigated for corruption by the Winneke Royal Commission in 1981. Its secretary Norm Gallagher went to jail for two months for contempt of the Federal Court in May 1982. It was disaffiliated from the Victorian Trades Hall Council in December 1982 and it waged war on all employers who did not toe the line. At its head was Norm Gallagher, large of stomach, invariably dressed in open-necked shirt, vintage button-up cardigan, pudding basin haircut, ridiculed daily by cartoonists, constantly lacerated by newspaper leading articles and something of a folk hero. *Business Review Weekly* on June 30, 1984 commented: "Underestimate Norm Gallagher at your peril. He is as pugnacious as Alan Bond and as slow-speaking and deliberate as Robert Holmes à Court. He has Rupert Murdoch's flair for media events and John Elliott's native cunning."

There was much more to the problem than the disturbance of the peace of Jolimont residents. Nobody wanted to use the B.L.F. The very words spelt harassment, difficulty and the use of union muscle. Tenders were called and the job went to Prentice Bros and Minson Pty Ltd who did not employ B.L.F. members.

John Lill remembers: "I had a very interesting meeting. I sat in my office with Don Wilkinson, a construction engineer who was working for us, and John Cummins, senior organiser for the B.L.F.

"He said, 'Are you going to use us or aren't you?'

"I said, 'No, we are not. We are going to use the A.W.U. and the F.I.A.'

" 'Why are you doing that?' said Cummins.

" 'They are the unions that have the coverage,' I said.

" 'Does the Government support that?'—'Yes.'

" 'Well, you are going to have all sorts of trouble, aren't you?' replied Mr. Cummins."

Mr. Cummins was true to his word. The battle between the unions proceeded from that day. It was a demarcation dispute which went to the

Arbitration Commission and ultimately to the High Court. The B.L.F. lost all along the line. Commissioner Bob Merriman of the Arbitration Commission ruled that the Australian Workers Union and the Federated Ironworkers Association had the right to build the towers, not the B.L.F. Angrily the B.L.F. accused Commissioner Merriman of bias. It claimed there was a conflict of interest because Merriman was an executive member of the Victorian Cricket Association.

Now the stage was set for a showdown. The B.L.F. put bans on all State Government projects: a hospital at Geelong a bus depot at Northcote, the Police Academy at Glen Waverley, the TAFE College at Knox, primary schools at Hoppers Crossing and Yarraville West and the Queen Victoria Hospital.

The Cain Government was determined the lights would be built and there would be no victory for Norm Gallagher. The workers at the M.C.G., there-fore, would have police protection. So there were two camps at the M.C.G., one occupied by the B.L.F. and one by the police. The police had a command centre in the office of Bryce Thomas, the assistant secretary, plus two cara-vans immediately across the path from the B.L.F. which also had a caravan.

There were mounted police, four horses on the job all the time. John Lill remembers one extraordinary day when about 400 police were at the M.C.G.

Many and various have been the tasks at the M.C.G. in more than a hundred years; now it was back to the days of the nineteenth century, with indoor stables to cater for the horses. Cleaning out the by-product to keep the M.C.G. pure for the patrons was a task in itself. One was reminded of the labour of Hercules when he was ordered to clean the stables of King Augeus.

Meals for the police had to be provided by O'Brien Catering and at the weekend hot meals came down from the Police Commissary. It was winter and cold, vigils had to be conducted daily, around the clock. Senior Sergeant Denis Cairns said that in all his time in the police force he could not remember a place quite so cold. The worst time he said was at 6.30 a.m. That was when they changed the guard, and the police seemed most miserable. The B.L.F. men had an extra way of making them suffer. They had a barbecue; where they cooked steak, chops and sausages. The smell wafting across under police noses was nigh unbearable.

The B.L.F. caravan proudly flew Eureka flags and the B.L.F. battlecry "Dare to Struggle, Dare to Win" was daubed on walls. It seemed extra-ordinary to ordinary citizens that the B.L.F. should be permitted, no questions

323

asked, no fees paid, to be allowed to occupy a caravan in a public park. Had anyone else tried to do it that caravan smartly would have been towed away.

John Lill said: "The police took the view that while they were there they could watch them. They knew what they were up to and could predict events before they happened. There were regular scuffles with police and attempts to prevent the arrival of vehicles. B.L.F. members would shout 'scab' and abuse at the other workers, but at other levels they would communicate. They came to us one day and said: 'Look, we have to walk from our camp right up to the Jolimont station to go to the toilet. Can we use the ones in the ground?' "

John Lill said he was not keen on the idea, but, "the police felt it would do no harm to make this concession. So an agreement was made, they came in one at a time, it was known they were there, and there was to be no snooping around.

"One day Don Wilkinson and I were walking around the internal roadway and one of the builders' labourers was coming in for the toilet. He made a remark to us about scabs. I didn't say anything but said to Don, 'Do you know who he is?' He said, 'Yes.' We passed the message on to the builders' labourers that in future he could use the toilet in Jolimont. We didn't have any more trouble."

The B.L.F. was not only doing its best to stop construction of the light towers but it had bans on other work at the M.C.G. worth $4 million. This included new public lavatories all around the Southern Stand; new entry and exit facilities, 14 luxury executive-style viewing boxes; new dining and viewing rooms in the Northern Stand; improved catering services and new indoor practice wickets.

The B.L.F. gave public notice to steel erectors and riggers that all steel works fabricated by Newsteel Pty Ltd, manufacturers of the towers, were banned. The ban was so effective Newsteel could not get material out of its Clayton factory, also picketed by the B.L.F. May Transport, the company providing the trucks for the construction, also was on a black ban everywhere.

The M.C.G. was under siege. There was a high wire fence around the ground to protect the workers from the B.L.F. pickets. This fence had to come down during weekends to cater for football crowds.

There were fights and scuffles. B.L.F. workers were arrested and charged on June 5 and June 19. John Lill said: "I don't think there was any bitterness

Right
Peter Mitchell, M.C.C. committee
since 1985.

Below
Douglas Patrick, M.C.C. committee
since 1982.

Below right
Paul Sheahan, M.C.C. committee
since 1987.

Right
Tony Street, M.C.C. committee
since 1979.

Below
Reg Geary, M.C.C. committee
since 1973, retired May 1988.

Below right
Geoffrey Collie, M.C.C. committee
since 1977, retired January 1988.

towards us. The bitterness was all directed union to union. It was just a day-to-day fight to keep the job going. The crane drivers would not work or the transport union would not deliver the concrete. We never knew for sure on any one day whether the concrete would arrive or would not. One day a B.L.F. official pulled the gate at the back of a truck and wet concrete was spilt all over Brunton Avenue.

"Once, we needed a very specialised crane. Nobody would provide it for us. In order to beat the B.L.F. we had to bring it a long way, all the way from Karratha in West Australia. When we got it here there were only two people who could drive it. They were happy to do it one day, but when the time came they weren't going to do it. Pressures were so intense.

"Nobody knows the full story. I heard rumours of cars being run off the road, late phone calls, pets being poisoned, nothing can be proved. Pressures were quite intense."

On July 5 an engineer for Gutteridge, Haskins and Davey, which had been doing design work on the towers, was assaulted when visiting D.H. Corrosion Pty Ltd at Dandenong where one of the towers had gone for final sand-blasting and painting. Any plant which was doing work for the M.C.G. received the picket treatment and the pickets there told him he could enter the plant but not leave. The engineer claimed that when he did attempt to leave he was punched and kicked by union workers. Norm Gallagher denied the incident. He told reporters it was just an attempt at provocation by the M.C.C. and the V.C.A. because they were paying the workers at the ground a special site allowance of $83 a week.

It was a great advantage that the steel towers were built away from the site. Newsteel Pty Ltd at Clayton South were working two shifts, 16 hours a day to have them ready in time.

Mr. Noel May of May Transport delivered the first of the 78-metre, 120-tonne light towers to the M.C.G. on August 9. From then, they came at regular intervals until the last delivery arrived under a heavy police escort on October 4. Mr. May said the union had put a ban on his vehicles at all building sites. He said to a *Herald* reporter: "Mr. Gallagher's ban has cost me thousands of dollars. I've lost a lot of clients and only the loyal ones have remained." Worst of all it had cost him vast sums for repairs to damaged trucks and vehicles. "Sand has been poured into our semi-trailer engines and tyres have been slashed," he added.

The B.L.F. actually lifted its bans on August 13 in response to a request by the Arbitration Commission. The Full Bench had refused to hear an appeal by the B.L.F. unless it lifted its bans. The B.L.F. was appealing against Commissioner Merriman's decision as to which unions were to do the work at the M.C.G.

There were still two lonely B.L.F. men observing at the ground almost until Christmas, but there was no more trouble. The triumphant moment came at 9.30 p.m. on December 3, 1984. The Premier, Mr. Cain, the President of the M.C.C., Sir Bernard Callinan, M.C.C Committee, Trustees and all invited guests were there. The Premier threw the switch, the glow became brighter and brighter and it took seven minutes until the ground was completely converted from night into day. There were cheers from the crowd in the Long Room and some deeply felt feelings of relief. There were times back in early August when many had doubts whether the lights would ever be completed in 1984 or even in 1985.

The lights were wonderful indeed. When switched on during a match there was an imperceptible merging of day and night. There were 844 lights in the six towers, the equivalent of more than 30,000 60 watt bulbs, enough power to illuminate a small country town. The light was all computer-directed, designed to disturb neither motorists in Brunton Avenue nor sportsmen on the ground. The light had to be perfectly even for the six TV cameras around the ground. There were few better lit grounds anywhere in the world.

But the cost had been heavy. The original target was $3.5 million. When completed the figure was $4.9 million. Police operations at the M.C.G. during May and June alone cost $1,041,600. Victory for the Government over the B.L.F. was politically important. The improvements at the M.C.G., the lights, the Grand Final, all of these things were politically important.

Furthermore the Government had been prepared to help financially. Sir Bernard Callinan said: "There was a public servant who had the idea we should have some murals around the concourse underneath the stands to make the toilets more attractive. With no reference to us they put $1.5 million into the State Budget for toilets and murals at the M.C.G. I objected. I pointed out to the committee how important it was not to accept the money. No Government has ever spent money on the M.C.G., with one exception. That was £150,000, a contribution to the Northern Stand during the Olympic Games and that came from the Olympic Committee. Eventually I persuaded Mr. Cain to put the money into the Gallery of Sport. We had a Minister who visited the ground a few years ago. He said: 'Yes, we built this ground.' My reply was, 'You bloody well didn't. Your financial contribution was minuscule.' "

Sir Bernard even regretted the money that came from the Olympic Committee. He believed that for its survival the Melbourne Cricket Club should always remain independent. If changes were being made to the M.C.G. they were necessary. Back in the distant 1950s there used to be off-seasons, relaxing times for rebuilding when there was no visit from an international team and State sides could concentrate on Sheffield Shield matches. During the season of 1984-85 there was an orgy of cricket. There was the Australia v West Indies Test series. There was the Benson and Hedges World Series Cup, which involved Australia, West Indies and Sri Lanka. There was the Benson and Hedges World Championship of Cricket between Australia, England, New Zealand, West Indies, India, Pakistan and Sri Lanka. Then, of course, there was the McDonald's Cup and the Sheffield Shield. Cricketers had good cause to complain of overwork and strained backs. Australia lost the First Test in Perth by an innings and 112 runs, the Second test in Brisbane by eight wickets. Kim Hughes was in such a state of despair he resigned as captain. Allan Border took over but did no better. The West Indies won by 191 runs in Adelaide. Yet there were signs of improvement in the traditional Christmas Test at the M.C.G. Andrew Hilditch made 70 and 113 and there was a new fast bowler, Craig McDermott from Queensland, who took three wickets in both innings. But again it was Viv Richards who created his usual slaughter. He dominated proceedings with an innings of 208 runs.

Andrew Hilditch replied with 70 and Kepler Wessels made 90, but even so the West Indies should have won handsomely. However, God was merciful with rain, the West Indians over-cautiously amassed an unnecessary mountain of runs and the match ended in a draw.

When the Series was lost utterly, Australia won the final Test in Sydney by an innings and 55 runs. Bob Holland took 10 wickets and Murray Bennett captured five in a beautiful renaissance of spin bowling. The nation indulged in a short-lived orgy of euphoria. In the season that never seemed to end there was then the World Series Cup. Australia went down yet again to the West Indies in the final, 2-1.

However the all-important match for the Melbourne Cricket Club was on February 17, the first match with lights at the M.C.G. since the fatal day, August 12, 1879, when the club borrowed a light of 7000 candlepower from the Gippsland Railway workshops. It was a football match between Carlton and Melbourne, an event so dim the players lost each other in the gloom. So it took 106 years to repeat the experiment.

The V.C.A. very wisely chose the match, Australia versus England, and no matter whether it is a Test or a one-day affair there is a certain extra mother-child love-hate spice in the age-old encounter. It was the opening match for the World Championship between the eight nations, yet 82,494 turned out for the historic occasion.

The Prime Minister Mr. Hawke officially opened the Championship and introduced the players. As day turned into night the lights came on so gradually it was fascinating. The crowd hardly noticed the lights because the illumination was better than sunlight and there were no shadows. Television viewers watching from interstate had the best view. There were some extraordinary shots taken from a helicopter showing the M.C.G. illuminated, a wondrous circle of blazing light in all the blackness, the Yarra a ribbon of gold snaking towards the fading sunset. What's more, it was one of those rare Australian triumphs for the season. Kerr made 87, Dean Jones 78 and Australia won by seven wickets.

From then on Australia failed even to make the semi-finals. To Australians this seemed unbelievable, the ultimate match at the M.C.G. with not an Australian player on the ground. The excuse was the Australian team was tired, done, suffering from cricket overload. But so too were the other players. The final was between India and Pakistan and the crowd was 35,296, the biggest ever for a match when Australians were not involved. It was a good crowd, considering the number of matches there had been at the M.C.G. during 1984-85 and maybe it proved Melburnians were not so fanatically chauvinistic as their critics claimed.

India won by eight wickets. Imran Khan did everything possible to smash the India batting line-up, but it was too strong. Ravi Shastri, 63 not out, and Krishnamachari Srikkanth, 67, were as solid as the Taj Mahal.

The lights did have some side effects. In deference to the citizens of Jolimont and East Melbourne the Government limited the use of the M.C.G. to 10 nights a year. But some nights could be available for football.

The North Melbourne president Bob Ansett and the general manager Ron Joseph had been looking for a first-class home ground. They had been to Carlton and they had been to Collingwood; now in 1985 they saw a new opportunity. If they could spread their home games on days other than Saturday, there could be room for them to make the M.C.G. their home ground. And so North Melbourne became yet another team which looked upon the M.C.G. as home; it joined the Melbourne and Richmond football clubs. There had been approaches from both North Melbourne and Fitzroy to come to the M.C.G. Ian Johnson said there was always the problem of ground over-kill. It was not so much the big matches that caused the ground to suffer. It was training. There were 50 to 60 players on the training list and on training nights they could do much more damage than in a match. So the club looked for grounds for training. They tried to come to an arrangement with Old Xavierians and Old Scotch Collegians without success. In 1985 the club took a lease on the St. Kilda Cricket Ground, first just for the winter then the whole year. This made it possible for the Melbourne Football Club to train at St. Kilda and for North Melbourne to use the M.C.G. as its home ground. The first match was on a Friday night, March 29, North Melbourne versus Collingwood and it attracted 65,628. The atmosphere was almost like a Grand Final.

Night activities were popular. There was a soccer double-header at the M.C.G. on the night of March 29 between Brazil's Vasco da Gama and Italy's Udinese and Australia versus Tottenham Hotspurs of England, that drew 20,231.

But of particular grief to the football clubs was the Government refusal to allow V.F.L. football on the M.C.G. on Sundays. The Government excuse was this: it was necessary to protect the Victorian Football Association which played its games on Sunday. It drove the V.F.L. to fury. Dr. Allen Aylett, the V.F.L. President, pointed out the best cricket, tennis and motor racing was available on Sundays, why not the best football? If they were running a brothel instead of football on a Sunday he could understand the Government's anxiety. Actually the Liberal Government with Lindsay Thompson as Premier, did allow two Sunday trial matches in 1981, but the experiment was not repeated in 1982. South Melbourne moved to Sydney to become the Sydney Swans. Its home matches on the Sydney Cricket Ground were played on Sundays so that Melburnians could watch the matches on their television. No doubt they received an appropriate sense of sin. The Victorian Government, however, gave the V.F.L. permission to play three Friday night matches and three Sunday matches during the 1986 season.

There were changes on the M.C.C. Committee. Ted Ajani, a Committeeman since 1981, died of a heart attack at 49. His heart gave out in the final stages of the Big M Marathon from Frankston to Melbourne. He was a civil engineer with the Melbourne Board of Works, a former mayor of Doncaster and Templestowe and he had been a top-line cricketer and baseballer with Melbourne.

Sir Ernest Coates retired after serving as a Committeeman for 14 years, four of them as Vice-President. He was a former head of the State Treasury during the days when Sir Henry Bolte was Premier. He had been a great asset in decision-making at the Club.

Sir Bernard Callinan retired after five years as President, and few Presidents in the 147-year history of the club had been called to handle so many tough, controversial issues. But, he, too, had the toughness and ability to handle them. He retired at 72 and it was interesting that it was at his instigation that the Committee introduced the compulsory retiring age. The new President was Dr. Donald Cordner. It was inevitable as the coming of summer that Donald Cordner would rise to the top position. He had been a member for 49 years. He had been on the Committee for 21 years. He had been Chairman of the tennis and squash sections, he originated the Club Ball Pentathlon, he was the M.C.C. representative on the Football Club Committee, he had been on the building sub-committee with the three previous Presidents and there was the whole extraordinary Cordner tradition. The club had recently printed a photograph of the four Cordner brothers, Denis, John, Donald and Edward, all of whom had been great footballers for Melbourne and what seems particularly remarkable in 1988, they played as amateurs. Indeed, seven Cordners had contributed 420 V.F.L. games for the club. As for Donald he played 166 games, won the Brownlow Medal in 1946 and captained the Premiership side in 1948. He also played Club Eleven cricket from 1964 until 1970 and is still an active member of the XXIX Club.

CHAPTER TWENTY·SEVEN

The 150th Year

COME 1985 the Melbourne Cricket Club entered an era that could almost be described as peace; no union strife, no pickets, no charges and counter-charges from the V.F.L. and work proceeded at last on the Club's development programme, estimated to cost $20 million.

There was some disagreement over the exact location of the proposed Gallery of Sport; should it be part of the Members' Pavilion close to the cricket museum, or should it be separate outside the Ground. Then in April the Club signed an agreement with 10 building unions. There was some comment and eyebrows raised; the agreement included an $84 a week site allowance and two tickets for every worker to one of the V.F.L. finals, but not the Grand Final. One of the signatories was the famed, but perhaps a little quietened, secretary of the Builders' Labourers Federation, Norm Gallagher.

But if the agreement did seem a little cosy, work went ahead at a good pace. Sir Henry Bolte, chairman of the Trustees, opened the new Olympic dining rooms in the Northern Stand. The Northern Stand was built for the 1956 Olympics, so it was right that they should be named after three Olympic stars, Shirley Strickland, Betty Cuthbert and John Landy.

There were improved toilets and entries to the Southern Stand. The M.C.G. had provided the daily newspapers with some stories about queues outside toilets, long queues waiting to get into the ground for night and day matches. At last splendid new facilities stopped all this. There were 22 additional sponsor boxes. There were electronic strip scoreboards installed on the parapets of both the Ponsford and Southern stands. In the old days if you could not see the main board then there were gentlemen down below at the fence, who had numbers which they hung on a nail. Nothing primitive like that any more, the whole ground was electronic.

Then the move began for $4 million worth of seats. No more sore backs, these were plastic, shaped to the body with swing backs. The first batch, brilliant red, were for the Southern Stand's top deck. Blue and brown were to follow. There were 26 home football matches on the ground, Melbourne nine, Richmond nine, and North Melbourne eight. The Melbourne Cricket

Ground was very big business. Total revenue for 1985-86 was $7.1 million. The 1985-86 cricket season was advertised as "Double Trouble." Unquestionably it was double trouble for the Australians. The visitors were New Zealand and India. We went down 2-1 to New Zealand and there were three drawn matches against India. Richie Benaud pointed out that five times the opposition knocked up scores of over 500 against Australia. Never before had visiting sides gained such a plethora of runs, and at one stage a down-hearted Allan Border offered to resign as captain.

There was just one Test at the M.C.G., the traditional Boxing Day or New Year Test. There had been 19 days of rain in December and the new M.C.G. wicket was beautifully grass-topped, perfect for the canny spin of Shastri, Yadav and Shivarama. India won the toss and Australia was all out for 262.

The hero was the N.S.W. off-spinner and part-time batsman, Greg Matthews. He had suffered a battle getting anyone to take him seriously. He dressed like a rocker, he had a punk haircut, he talked too much, his antics on the field were constantly embarrassing. He would shout out: "Hey Mum, look at me." But his enthusiasm was undeniable and constantly he was urging his team-mates into action. He made 54 runs on the first day then came back to make his century. He hit nine fours and two sixes. As Trevor Grant of the *Age* put it, he worked the ball around the field as if he had it on a string.

Describing Matthews' joy at his 100 Grant wrote: "Matthews, before he had completed the second run, was jumping in the air. When he made the crease he tore down towards Bay 13 and held his bat to the crowd. A thank-you for their support. Then he kissed the bat and his gloves, shook hands with the most prolific of all Test century-makers, Sunil Gavaskar, and finally kissed the coat of arms on his cap."

There was a beautiful banner up in the stands, highly professional graphics, complete with bat and stumps, which read: THE GREG MATHEWS STAND. One noticed the Matthews adoration did not go as far as learning how to spell his name.

He scored three Test centuries that summer and the ultimate accolade came from the 80-year-old Bill O'Reilly who wrote: "I am completely converted. I admit without the slightest reservation that I am prepared to field beside him all day long without seeking the friendly help of an ear plug. I am on his side. I congratulate all those kids who beat me so smartly to the point."

But the Indians went on to make 445 including 86 from Srikkanth and 75 from Vengsarkar. Allan Border once again came to the rescue with 169, but it was a good solid Melburnian fall of rain that saved the local side. As Bill

O'Reilly put it: "Our boss upstairs came to the party and took the most compassionate course."

The one rosy spot for Australia during the season was its win in the Benson and Hedges World Series Cup. Border's men beat India in the final at the M.C.G. by seven wickets. The season had been so miserable they carried on like a St. Kilda or even a Collingwood winning the Grand Final. They did a lap of honour of the M.C.G. and chaired their skipper, Allan Border, who top-scored with 65 not out. The crowd once again proved that nothing succeeds like one-day cricket, 72,192 were there to see, at last, an Australian triumph.

There were big events to come in 1986. On November 22, the Prime Minister opened the Australian Gallery of Sport. It was a year late. It should have been opened in 1985 as one of the grand events to celebrate Victoria's 150th birthday. When Norm Gallagher placed his black ban on all M.C.C. building projects this became impossible.

However there were other problems. The original idea was to build the Gallery, three storeys, right on to the front of the Members' Stand. This would have given a direct connection with the Cricket Museum. There were complaints from the National Trust. The Members' Stand was a classified building. In romantic terms the Trust described the Members' Stand as "stylish pseudo-Romanesque . . . alive with references to the Lombardy Plains."

The idea for the gallery came originally from Stan Evans, club member, and senior partner of Tompkins, Shaw and Evans, architects. Stan Evans had been on a world tour. He had seen other sporting galleries and halls of fame. He felt that a country as sport crazy as Australia should have the best in the world.

Committee members had mixed feelings about it. They saw it as a constant running drain on Club funds, but Sir Bernard Callinan was keen, so too was Donald Cordner and they pushed it through. The Federal Government supplied $1 million, the Victorian Government gave $1.3 million, both as Sesquicentenary gifts and the Melbourne Cricket Club supplied the rest, nigh on $1.5 million.

There had to be a compromise in the construction. In order that those "Lombardy Plains" be not upset Tompkins Shaw and Evans designed a building which stood 20 metres out from the Members' Stand with an overhead walkway through to the club. The building was a clever mixture of the old and the new, the brick to match the 1927 club coupled with a spread of glass to reflect the Yarra Park elms.

333

The opening exhibition was called "The Olympic Spirit" and it was timed to coincide with the thirtieth anniversary of the 1956 Olympic Games. There was a 900-guest Olympians' dinner on the ground and many famous Olympians were present, Murray Rose, Ron Delany, Fanny Blankers-Koen, Milton Campbell who won the decathalon. In 1956 young Ron Clarke carried the torch into the stadium and kindled the Olympic flame. On this night, as a prelude to the dinner, his son Marcus carried in a torch, kindled a flame and relived the occasion.

A special guest was John Ian Wing. In 1956 Wing was just a teenager. He made the suggestion that when the Games finished the athletes should not march under their national banners. They should intermingle, all mix in together. And so they did and the 1956 Games won the title "The Friendly Games."

Thirty years later a researcher in the National Archives dug up the original letter that Wing wrote to the Olympic Committee. So a hunt was made to find Wing. Journalist Harry Gordon wrote an article asking: "Where is Wing now?" Mark Day took it further on television. First they found Wing's sister, then Wing himself. He left Australia 20 years ago and now had a building business in London. The end of the happy story was that Qantas flew Wing to Australia and he was a guest of honour at the Olympians' dinner.

The Olympics had to be the theme for the first exhibition at the Gallery of Sport. As patrons entered the building they found no stairs. Instead there was a long winding ramp and pictures depicting the Olympics, but that was not all. As the visitor walked by, electric eyes triggered off sound effects from hidden microphones. One heard the pounding of feet, the panting of the athletes, the crescendo of applause from the crowd, and upon entering the main hall, on came the national anthem from 30 years ago, the opening of the Olympics.

The ideas man behind this was the director, Tom McCullough, ebullient, energetic. Born in Belfast, Northern Ireland, he was a professional museum director. Tom pointed out that he did not want a stiff, crusty museum where the visitors were awed into submission. He wanted nostalgia, humour, the whole culture of sport. So the range of material was remarkable. One could press a button and listen to the earliest Edna Everage record, Barry Humphries playing the Melbourne hostess at the 1956 Olympics, inviting all the little darlings and possums to come and stay with her at Moonee Ponds. There was a vintage 1956 AWA Radiola TV set and a massive 1956 TV camera.

There were the running shoes Marjorie Jackson wore when she won the

100 metres at Helsinki, the spikes worn by John Landy when he ran his first sub-four-minute mile, the swimsuit worn by Lily Beaurepaire when she won a silver medal in 1920.

Of course, the Gallery of Sport is not just Olympics. It covers 20 different sports. There are all sorts of fascinating relics. There is the bat that Walter Hammond used to make 203 runs for England on the M.C.G. back in 1932. The bat is more precious because it has on the back a cartoon by that great leg spinner Arthur Mailey. The cartoon is a self-portrait and he has written: "I hate signing bats. They have been my bugbear all my cricket life."

Sir Hubert Opperman presented the bicycle on which he created the 24-hour unpaced world record at the Velodrome in 1924. He also presented his cycling shoes. They are painted in green luminous paint and the idea was that the shoes would flash spectacularly at night.

Perhaps the most fascinating feature of the Gallery is the Hall of Fame. Originally one feared it might be like one of the American halls of fame with a line of busts of departed heroes. Actually the Hall is a computer. Press the appropriate buttons and everything one needs to know about the appropriate hero or heroine comes up on the screen.

On December 10 the Hall of Fame was instituted and 56 famous living athletes were inducted. Candidates could be alive or dead but they had to be retired from their respective sport for at least five years. The greats included Margaret Court, Betty Cuthbert, Marjorie Jackson, Ron Clarke, Henry Herbert, "Dally" Messenger, Sir Donald Bradman, Herb Elliott, Heather McKay, Murray Rose, Haydn Bunton, Shane Gould, Glyn de Villiers Bosisto, Dawn Fraser, Walter Lindrum, Evonne Cawley, Les Darcy, Sir Hubert Opperman, Shirley Strickland, Rod Laver and Bobby Skilton. Eight M.C.C. members were among the 56 famous athletes who attended the induction in the Long Room. They were Bill Ponsford, Percy Pavey, Jock Sturrock, Frank Sedgman, Bob Skilton, Peter Thompson, John Landy and Malcolm Milne.

The Gallery has continued to grow ever since, as contributions have flowed in. Tom McCullough likes the story about Bruce Doull's sweat band. Bruce Doull, bald and long of hair, a Carlton football veteran, retired after the 1986 Grand Final.

"It didn't come from Bruce Doull, a chap donated it," said Tom, "and we announced we had it. Doull himself was most embarrassed. He said he would have given us one if, for a moment, he thought we wanted it. The chap who gave it to us paid $310 for it at a charity auction. He wasn't well-heeled, just an ordinary guy from somewhere in Dandenong and his wife gave him hell.

Every time that sweat band turned up it caused a row. But he wanted to make sure his idol was in the Gallery of Sport." And so it is. It became one of Tom McCullough's most sacred relics.

The club's passion for history has grown steadily with the years. A unique feature during the 1980s was the steady growth of the club library which is developing very nearly into the best sporting library in Australia. The man behind this has been Rex Harcourt, a man with a passion for history, particularly the early history of Melbourne. He was director of research for the Department of Civil Aviation and when he retired in 1979, he became the Club librarian. Initially the library was a single room, but in 1980 the Club architect, Stan Evans, developed much larger and better equipped quarters near to and on the same level as the Long Room, extended in 1986.

By 1988 the library not only had a first-class historic collection of cricket books but it covered a total of 71 different sports. There were almost complete collections of the *Australasian*, *Melbourne Punch*, the *Leader*, a complete facsimile set of Melbourne's earliest newspapers like the *Port Phillip Gazette*, plus some very rare books. One of the oldest is "A Dictionary of French and English Tongues" compiled by Randle Cotgrave in 1611. It contains one of the earliest known printed references to cricket. It has the French words "crocer" or "crosser," meaning to play at cricket. "Now," says Rex Harcourt, "if these words were to get into a dictionary cricket must have been played both in England and France at least in the middle fifteen hundreds."

The fascination with the club's history has meant the unearthing of many important documents and the best finder has been Bill Gray. Before he moved full time into the Melbourne Cricket Ground Bill Gray was the welding supervisor at the Commonwealth Aircraft Corporation. Just before he retired in 1976 he was having lunch with Hans Ebeling, who told how he needed help with Club records and photographs. Bill said: "I'm retiring at the end of the year, I'll give you a hand."

He did that and when Ebeling died in January 1980 Bill Gray took over as curator of the Club Museum. He set out on a great hunt looking through store rooms, in almost forgotten rooms under grandstands, up in attics. One day he was going through an old tin trunk and he found what appeared to be rules for Australian Rules Football. "I think the trunk might have belonged to Major Wardill or Hugh Trumble," he said. "Ian Johnson was just walking by, so I said to him, 'Ian, you might be interested in this.'

" 'Oh yes,' he said, almost off-handedly, 'rules for football.' 'Yes,' I replied, 'but look at the date.' It was May 1859. I thought he was going to fall on the floor. 'Look after these,' he said, 'they had better go in the safe.' "

336

It was a find indeed. It proved that Australian Rules as an organised public sport with a code of proper rules pre-dated Rugby and soccer. English football although played since the fourteenth century was disorganised and varied from place to place.

The rules Bill Gray found were these:

Rules of the Melbourne
Football Club,
May 1859
Rules of Play

1. The distance between the goals and the goal posts shall be decided upon by the captains of the sides playing.
2. The captains on each side shall toss for choice of goal. The side losing the toss has the kick-off from the centre-point between the goals.
3. A goal must be kicked fairly between the posts without touching either of them or a portion of the person of any player of either side.
4. The game shall be played within the space of not more than 200 yards wide, the same to be measured equally upon each side of the line drawn through the centre of the two goals and two posts to be called the kickoff posts shall be erected at a distance of 20 yards on each side of the goal posts at both ends and any straight line with them.
5. In case the ball is kicked behind the goals, anyone on the side behind whose goal it is kicked, may bring it 20 yards in front of any portion of the space between the kick-off posts and shall kick it as nearly as possible in the line of the opposite goal.
6. Any player catching the ball directly from the boot may call "mark." He then has a free kick. No players from the opposite side being allowed to come into the spot marked.
7. Tripping and pushing are both allowed but no hacking when any player is in rapid motion or in possession of the ball except for the case provided by rule 6.
8. The ball may be taken in hand only when caught from the foot or on the hop. In no case shall it be lifted from the ground.
9. When a ball goes out of bounds (the same being indicated by a row of posts) it shall be brought back to the point where it crossed the boundary line and thrown in at right angles with that line.
10. The ball while in play may under no circumstances be thrown.

The signatories were T. W. Wills, T. Smith, W. Hammersley, A. Bruce, J. Sewell and J. B. Thompson.

Come the cricket season of 1986-87 the Committee decided to re-name the

Western Stand. The naming of grandstands at the M.C.G. had been long out of fashion. The feeling was, once one named a stand, it was there for ever. If they named after players, Club presidents, sponsors, benefactors, history quickly made dim those names—the idea was fraught with disaster. The last grandstands to receive names were the Harrison Stand built in 1908 and the Wardill Stand built in 1912. But now was the time to change the policy, the club had a special case. On December 6, 1986 there was a ceremony to ren-ame the Western Stand the W. H. Ponsford Stand and to honour Bill Pons-ford. Of all the great batsmen who played for the club nobody was quite his equal. In all first class matches from 1920 to 1934 he scored 13,819 runs, including 47 centuries. His average was 65.18. In 29 Tests he made 2122 runs and seven centuries with a 48.22 average. He is the only player to have made two scores of more than 400 in first class cricket. He retired in 1934 after that astonishing Australian tour of England in 1934. There were two never-to-be-forgotten Bradman-Ponsford partnerships. In the fourth Test at Leeds they had a partnership of 388, Bradman 304 and Ponsford 181. For the Fifth Test at the Oval they created the world record second wicket partnership, 451 in 315 minutes, Ponsford 266 and Bradman 244.

For a man who achieved so much he was astonishingly shy. Aged 86 he attended the ceremony, but he stuck to his old rule, no speeches, no public appearance, no press interviews. The M.C.C. President, Dr. Don Cordner, made a video-recorded tribute which was played on the scoreboard during lunch break of the match, Victoria against England.

There were no limits to the events the scoreboard could cover or to the versatility of the M.C.G. On November 27 and 28, 1986, His Holiness Pope John Paul II visited Melbourne. There were two services at the M.C.G. and a papal stage with altar was erected out on the turf. On the first night the Pope arrived at Melbourne airport just before 7 p.m. then drove to St. Paul's Angli-can Cathedral in the city where he was greeted by the Anglican Archbishop, Dr. David Penman. It was only the third time in 400 years that a Pope had been inside an Anglican cathedral. From there he drove to the M.C.G. and these events were all portrayed on the video scoreboard for the waiting crowd to see.

The crowd or congregation spilled out on to the ground and all the M.C.G. was available for the historic service, except for the centre where the wickets were being made ready for the big summer cricket. This was too sacred even for the Pope. The press billed the crowd at over 100,000, a count a little too enthusiastic. It was more like 60,000. On the second night there was a Mass in Polish, in the Pontiff's native tongue, and the congregation was 15,000.

It was an event that did not go unnoticed by the fans. When the very serious stuff started against the touring English side up went a large sign in the Outer: LAND ONE IN THE POPE'S FOOTMARKS.

In the heady optimism that one gets around November England performed disastrously in the lead up matches and there were joyous hopes that this would be Australia's year. There were suggestions that this was one of the worst teams ever to leave England. But all that ended with the First Test in Brisbane and Mike Gatting's men had a triumphant season. They retained the Ashes 2-1 and won the Benson and Hedges World Series Cup.

The Fourth Test at the M.C.G. was the ultimate humiliation. It lasted only three days. According to the statisticians, not since 1901 in the First Test at the Sydney Cricket Ground had the Australians been despatched in such a hurry. But then in 1901 they made amends by winning the next four Tests.

The English had lost Dilley through injury. Botham was bowling at only half pace because of cartilage injury and Gladstone Small was in the team, playing his first Test of the series. Yet Small and Botham took five wickets each and Australia was all out for 141. England replied with 349, including a superb 112 from Chris Broad, the international cricketer of the year. Australia was dismissed again for 194 to lose by an innings and 14 runs. The defeat cost an estimated half million dollars in gate money and London's newspapers were in high glee. Rupert Murdoch's *Sun* carried a gloating editorial headed "Up Yours Cobber." As for the crowds at the M.C.G., banners which before had called for the assistance of the Pope declined to: BRING BACK BRADMAN.

Trevor Grant in the *Age* made the sad comment on the 1987 match: "Anyone who witnessed the pitiful submission yesterday would not be game to predict that this team could win even one Test in the foreseeable future." It was one of those comments that inevitably get one into trouble for Australia, thanks to the inspired selection of spinner Peter Taylor, defeated England by 15 runs in the Fifth Test. Taylor took eight wickets.

In the World Series Cup final on February 8, 1987 England defeated Australia by six wickets before a crowd of 51,589. Dean Jones scored 67 but Ian Botham was back to something of his old glory with a devastating 71, a six and 11 fours off 52 balls. England then won the second final by 8 runs in Sydney on February 11. The Crowd was 33,655.

There was one fine consolation about the 1986-87 season; there were no complaints about the notorious M.C.G. wicket. Even though Australian batsmen did not perform up to expectations during the Fourth Test and narrowly failed to carry off the one-day series the wicket at all times performed beautifully and the long agony seemed to be over. It was a good time for Jack Lyons; he could retire happy at the end of the season. He had been a member of the ground staff for 30 years and curator for eight years.

Jack was craggy of features, he wore a hearing aid, formal lace-up black shoes, and one had an instinctive feeling about him, that he knew weather, grass, compost and how a ball would turn come the final day. His parents were dairy and potato farmers near Ballarat. There were 10 children in the family. Naturally the time came when he had to look for something else. One morning back in 1955 he was standing outside Young and Jackson's Hotel in Flinders Street. He said to a bystander: "Mate, do you know where I could get a job?" The bystander replied: "You might get something at the M.C.G., I hear they're preparing it for the Olympic Games." Jack caught a tram up Flinders Street and a very useful ride it proved to be. He got a job first with Roche Bros, which was preparing the tracks for the Games, then with the Melbourne Cricket Club and there he remained until he retired. He learned by trial and error by watching Bill Watt. He was Bill's understudy for 17 years.

Jack Lyons never quite got used to the idea of covering the wickets. He made the comment: "As soon as a spot of rain falls out go those covers. There's too much money in the game now and they're spoilt. I wouldn't cover them at all. Covering 'em's a tragedy. A lot of cricketers don't know what it's like to play on a sticky wicket. Remember that saying 'I got you on a sticky wicket'? Nobody knows what it means any more. I reckon spin bowling is the greatest joy of cricket. Remember Fleetwood-Smith? Remember Jack Iverson? The contest was marvellous. Go upstairs and look at the old pictures . . . Ponsford, McCabe . . . there's some good 'uns up there."

Even though Jack Lyons did not approve of covering the wickets he helped turn it into an art form. Jack said: "When it starts to rain a bit and the umpires walk forward to consult each other in the middle, you know instinctively what the decision is going to be. You have the covers in a roll on the truck. If you put them on wheels and push them out, that's too slow. So you have the gate open, the engine running and as soon as the umpires give the signal out you go. I remember one time when Bill Watt was here, we dashed out. And we heard later that the committee had put a watch on us. We put those covers down in precisely one minute. I wouldn't have believed we were so quick."

The new man, with title of Arenas Manager, was Peter Semos, 37, a specialist in turf management. Before accepting the M.C.C. job he worked as a senior officer with the Department of Territories' horticultural unit in Canberra. The M.C.G. wicket was not new to him. In 1982 and 1983 he supervised the

View of the bronze doors created by Robert Ingpen.

The celebrations on 15 November 1988.

installation of heating cables and the reconstruction of the centre square. That centre square was like a play which had suffered humiliating reviews from every critic in town. So Peter Semos could have been excused for feeling a little unnerved when the New Zealanders came to Melbourne to play the traditional Boxing Day Test. Australia led one to nil and depended on victory to wrap up the series.

Semos had little cause to worry. He received praise from the *Herald*. Martin Blake wrote: "The cricket public has a gentleman named Peter Semos to thank for the enthralling contest we are witnessing at the M.C.G. . . . Here is a pitch with a tinge of green, a strip where the ball comes on to the bat; where any bowler worth his salt can make the ball deviate off the seam. It even provided some spin. This is a wicket that makes a contest possible and what a marvellous contest we have."

It was indeed a marvellous contest. Cinderella never had a better deal than Tony Dodemaide. Dodemaide, the young Victorian all-rounder, came to the team merely on stand-by. The West Australian fast bowler, Bruce Reid, had a back injury. Merv Hughes, the Victorian fast bowler, withdrew because of a hamstring injury and Dodemaide was told he was in the team only 40 minutes before the start of play.

His performance was astonishing; in Australia's first innings when the side was desperate for runs he made a half century. Then in New Zealand's second innings, he took 6 for 58 and set the statisticians hunting for precedents. Finally they claimed it was the best all-round debut performance since the Victorian Albert Trott took 8 for 43 and made 72 in the second innings in 1894-95 against England in Adelaide.

However it was a game of remarkable performances. Martin Crowe of New Zealand made 82 in the first innings and 79 in the second, thus passing 4000 runs in the season, putting him up in the legend class.

But Test matches, like a symphony by Beethoven, have a way of building themselves from slow movement to allegro until finally a majestic climax. On the last day New Zealand set Australia 278 runs to win.

At one stage victory looked close, the score was 5 for 209 with 70 runs to go. But in the space of five deliveries Peter Sleep, Mike Valetta and Greg Dyer fell to Hadlee and Bracewell. Australia now was 8 for 216.

Tony Dodemaide survived the new ball for 26 deliveries then was trapped lbw by Hadlee. Now it was 9 for 227 with the improbable pair Michael Whitney and Craig McDermott left to survive against the best bowler in the world, Richard Hadlee. For 30 deliveries the M.C.G. filled with heavy sighs and deep breathing. One could almost hear the community heartbeats. But

341

survive they did. They missed victory by 17 runs, but they proved for ever that even draws make enthralling Test matches and they gave Allan Border his first series win after seven unproductive tries.

Australia continued its Lazarus-like season to win the triangular one-day World Series Cup against Sri Lanka and New Zealand. The Bicentennial Test Match in Sydney was a draw but there was a very convincing win in the one-day match against England at the M.C.G. on February 4. Everyone from coach Bobby Simpson, to Allan Border, through to the super-critical cricket writers was being super-cautious, terrified of irritating any curious saint or god who controlled the very curious fortunes of cricket, but it did seem at last Australia had a tough, mature professional cricket team which would be hard to beat anywhere on the world scene.

There was also a triumph of sorts at the M.C.G. The summer crowd in Bay 13 always has been hard to tame. In 1971 John Snow wrote bitterly that the Melbourne crowd was like piranha fish. "When you are a gladiator at that colosseum—and the villain of the piece—you can almost feel the jaws of the Melbourne mob snapping at you." Dennis Lillee on the other hand claimed it was this very enthusiastic Bay 13 crowd which inspired him to his greatest achievements.

But always it was obvious that the rate of drunkenness was in direct proportion to the shadows moving over the ground. The amount of beer consumed sometimes outshone even a Munich beer festival. In the 1970s the club introduced dry areas, so that those who wanted peace and calm could escape from the chanting rowdies. In 1982 there was a stronger move, a total ban against the carrying of alcohol into the ground. If one wanted beer it could be bought only at the bars, with a two-can limit.

At the one-day match against New Zealand on January 7 the heat rose to 40 degrees. It was a match under lights and the Outer crowd was in its wildest mood. There were 120 arrests and three policemen were injured.

"Drunken hooligans are making wowsers of us all," wrote Peter Smark in the *Herald*. "I'm tempted to write that hundreds of drunken males acted like apes. But the R.S.P.C.A. would rightly object to such calumny."

The Police Minister, Mr. Crabb, was shocked at the crowd behaviour and the Liquor Control Commission banned full strength alcohol from all public areas at the M.C.G. until the end of the season. The rule did not apply to the Members' nor the private boxes, but the public bars sold only light beer with 2.1 per cent or less alcohol content.

After the first "Light" match on January 14 Andrew Stephens reported in the *Age*: "The results were astonishing. Arrests for drunken behaviour dropped to fewer than a dozen and sales of beer plummeted. To the tune of 'Auld Lang Syne' some adventurous Bay Thirteeners sang, 'Real beer, real beer, we want real beer.' The police down at Bay 11 were feeling mighty pleased with the turn of events. 'It's the best I have ever seen it,' said Senior Sergeant Bill Peart."

So the 1987-88 season came to an end in an era of optimism for Australian cricket and a genuine feeling of pride and achievement for the 150th anniversary of the Melbourne Cricket Club. Women had been absorbed as full members with surprisingly little difficulty. Relations with the Victorian Football League were closer than they had ever been. Three V.F.L. clubs would use the ground through the season and there was no question that the Grand Final would remain at the M.C.G. Every year saw new comforts, better seating, more adequate lavatories and better entry and exit facilities.

But what about the size? Would the Paddock That Grew keep on growing and growing. In the 1970s there were dreams that the Melbourne Cricket Ground could gain a third tier and seat more than 150,000.

"It just won't happen," predicted the President, Dr. Donald Cordner. "The Southern Stand originally cost £110,000. Now you can't even talk to an architect for that money. We are actually spending half a million to a million dollars a year just to maintain it. If we did not do that it would fall down in 10 years. It would be extraordinarily expensive to build over that stand for accommodation that would be used only five or six times a year, perhaps only once. It costs roughly $1000 a seat, an extra 10,000, that's a million. Just to pay the interest you need to fill that seat six times a year and that's not even paying it back.

"I think accommodation at the M.C.G. will remain around 100,000. Should we not consider upgrading the standard of our accommodation rather than striving for the few extra thousand? It is the trend around the world. You use television to reach as many people as you can and charge more for people coming into the ground. The capacity now is 102,000. I think eventually the Health Department will say there is no such thing as standing room. It takes two standing room places to provide one seat. We used to have standing room for 20,000, now for only 7000. It is coming down and down."

So who uses the Club? The M.C.G. now is so big, so much a small city in its own right, that it needs a crowd of at least 10,000 to make it worthwhile turning the turnstiles. Only cricket, football, or maybe the visit of a Pope or a Billy Graham, could achieve such crowds. When the V.F.L. decided to play the Preliminary Final at V.F.L. Park Don remembers discussing the problem with the V.F.L. president, Sir Maurice Nathan. "Are we free to get another function on that day?" asked Don. "Yes, if you like," said Sir Maurice, "but there isn't one is there?" He was correct. Not even a Victorian Football Association final could provide an adequate crowd.

The Melbourne Cricket Club's finances also were healthy. In March 1987 the club sent off the last cheque to pay off the Southern Stand. The club took out a $100,000 loan in 1937 for 50 years at an interest rate of four and a half per cent. The club would be delighted to call on the State Bank to arrange a similar loan today.

The club on its 1980s building programme received Government guarantees for a loan up to $14 million, but borrowed only $10 million and paid back $1 million ahead of time.

A 150th birthday celebration dinner was held at the club on February 3, 1988 in the presence of the Governor of Victoria, Dr. McCaughey, and the Prime Minister, Mr. R. J. Hawke. It was probably the greatest non-sporting club function ever held on the ground. There were 350 guests, including great former players like Colin Cowdrey, Greg Chappell, Alan Davidson, Ted Dexter, Peter May, Ian Johnson, Rod Marsh, Keith Miller, Bob Simpson, Keith Stackpole, Alec Bedser, Keith Rigg, Richie Benaud. As well, there were famous sportsmen from all fields, Frank Sedgman, John Konrads, John Landy, Percy Beames, and Ralph Doubell.

Donald Cordner presented a silver sculpture depicting penguins rising out of the sea to John Warr, president of the Marylebone Cricket Club. The sculpture was by Flynn Bros of Kyneton, whose work has been a favourite for official gifts to visiting Royalty, Pope John Paul II and heads of state. The sculpture carried the emblems of two MCCs. The Marylebone Cricket Club 1787-1987, its 200th anniversary and the Melbourne Cricket Club, 1838-1988, its 150th anniversary. Mr. Warr in return presented to Dr. Cordner a silver cigarette case. Only 50 years separated the two clubs; a memento from one club that was still thriving after 150 years to another whose history dated back 200 years. Both Presidents felt they could be proud of their clubs' achievements.

However, the full-scale celebrations began on 27 October 1988, the beginning of the 150th Anniversary Fortnight. On that day Sir Bernard Callinan opened "From the Paddock" an exhibition at the Australian Gallery of Sport. There was a 19th century model, exquisitely dressed in the correct period cricket costume to welcome visitors to the Gallery, and a replica of the grand old 1857 M.C.C. Pavilion.

Everything was there, from the M.C.G.'s prehistory and how it looked to the Aboriginals, through to the present day. There were portraits and tales of great cricketing figures, like Frederick Spofforth, George Bonnor "The Colonial Hercules", and Jack Blackham "The Prince of Wicketkeepers." There was even a history of that most mysterious of all sciences, turf care and pitch preparation, with a display of tools and analytical equipment.

There for the occasion were two of F. R. Spofforth's eight grandchildren, Derrick Spofforth, 66, and his sister Pamela Spofforth, 64. "The Demon" Spofforth married an Englishwoman, and moved to England in 1888, where he had a successful career in the tea business. So Derrick and Pamela, raised in England, flew out to discover the Demon still had a huge reputation in Australia. They brought with them priceless gifts for the Gallery of Sport. These included a stump that the great bowler shattered while playing for New South Wales against Victoria in Sydney in 1876; two cups commemorating historic performances in international matches and the passport Spofforth used on his last visit to Australia in 1924.

The club was Open House to the general public for more than a fortnight. The whole ground was a wonderful museum. There were displays in the Library, the Buffet Bar, the Long Room and along all the corridors. The displays were put together by a dedicated team of members, co-ordinated by a former committeeman, Dr Ian McDonald. Bill Gray, keeper of the Museum, also put together special stories on the five founders of the Club, F. A. Powlett, R. Russell, Arthur Mundy, C. F. Mundy, and George B. Smyth. Then there were stories on other great figures, like T.W. Wills, cricket captain and originator of Australian Rules Football; his cohort, H.C.A. Harrison, the extraordinary, club secretary; team manager, Major Ben Wardill; then interesting presidents like C. W. Simmonds, Sir Albert Chadwick and Hans Ebeling. One could go everywhere, inspect the wickets, both indoor and outdoor, or maybe even wonder at the famous super boxes.

On 2 November the Governor-General, Sir Ninian Stephen, dedicated the bronze doors at the entrance to the Pavilion. The Club commissioned these doors, and they are the permanent memento of the sesqui-centenary. They replaced the old green doors at the entrance to the Club, and surely the Club never acquired finer pieces of art. The work of the artist Robert Ingpen, they tell the story of many great events on the ground during the 150 years . . . the Austral Wheel race, Betty Cuthbert winning her gold medal at the Olympic Games, Tom Wills and early footballers, the time when the M.C.G. became a camp for the U.S. Marine Corps, the Ashes urn, cricketers like Hugh Trumble, Bill Ponsford and Ray Lindwall, and Melbourne football captain, Robert Flower taking a cloud-scraper mark.

345

But the big occasion, the 150th party of parties, was on the actual birthday, 15 November 1988. The President, Dr Donald Cordner, wanted it with no restrictions — all members could come. So the Club erected a huge tent, marquee, canvas pavilion, whatever you like to call it. It had to be a master-piece of catering, nearly 2200 people sat down to dinner, at more than 200 tables of ten out on the turf where all the greats from Wills to Dean Jones had played. There was a video projected on a great screen, and the members were able to view great and extraordinary events from the past like Alex Jesaulenko indulging in his gravity-defying marking skills, the Chappell under-arm incident and the visit of the Pope.

The honour of proposing the toast to the Club on its 150th birthday went to Club member Campbell McComas, an ingenious public speaker who has created more than 900 original characters for state occasions, conventions and dinners. This time he was Robert Russell, and we were asked to dream that a time capsule had been discovered, dated 15 November 1838, and addressed to the members of the Club in 1988.

Russell gave an amusing picture of Melbourne life in 1838, but then he rose to great eloquence. He told us: "Decades from now, a writer yet unborn — and for the sake of the argument, let us call him Neville Cardus — will take up his quill and inscribe these words: 'A game is exactly what is made of it by the character of the people playing it.'

"Hear, hear. Just as Melbourne is more than a place, just as cricket is more than a game, so the Melbourne Cricket Ground is more — much more — than an historic patch of turf bounded by a set of rules. The Club has no life but in those who belong to it; no spirit but in those who bestir it; no future but those who believe in it.

"The 4th Lord Harris — whoever he was, or is, or will be — speaks as much of a club as he does of cricket when he says: 'You do well to love it, for it is more free of anything sordid, anything dishonourable, than any game in the world. To play it keenly, honourably, generously, self sacrificingly, is a moral lesson in itself, and the classroom is God's air and sunshine.' "The little candle on my table grows dim. Oh for some electricity — or even gas — and a few million pounds for an adequate system of illumination. I can no longer see so clearly, and shall have to close. I trust that this letter finds you in excellent health . . . I remain, Sirs, ever your most humble and devote predecessor,

Robert Russell, Esquire
(Membership No. F00002)"

Dr Donald Cordner, the President of the Melbourne Cricket Club re-sponded. He welcomed the occupants of the top table, the Premier, Mr Cain;

the Leader of the Opposition, Mr Kennett; the chairman of the M.C.C. Trustees, Mr Lindsay Thompson, and also three Honorary Life Members present, Sir Bernard Callinan, Ian Johnson and Keith Rigg. He also read messages from two other Life Members, the Duke of Edinburgh and the Prince of Wales.

What a tremendous year it had been, full of scope and complexity, but above all, at last there had been agreement, and virtually marriage with the Victorian Football League.

The agreement with the League, which took place only 10 days before, was historic, and the end of a very long struggle, sometimes full of acrimony. The agreement ensured that the football Grand Final and the preliminary final would be at the M.C.G. for the next 30 years. The Southern Stand, 51 years old, would be replaced by a new four-tier stand, at a cost of $100 million. This would boost the capacity of the ground to 115,000. The re-development plan would be funded by the M.C.C. V.F.L. Park members would have their own area in the new Southern Stand and they would be admitted free to 22 games during the season.

The new declaration of peace brought much comment in the press. Some looked back with nostalgia upon the end of Bay 13. Peter McFarline said in the *Age* that: "it ended a 34-year-old war between the V.F.L. and the M.C.C., a war that was never declared but was nevertheless at times as vicious and as intense as any conflict in Australian sport. But Donald Cordner and Mr Russ Oakley, whatever else they achieve in their respective roles as M.C.C. and V.F.L. leaders, can rest content that they were signatories to the treaty that finally recognised what most football fans have known since they were forced to watch their favorite team out in the mulga at Mulgrave, that the M.C.G. is football's real home."

As a result of this Dr Cordner spoke with some pride on this 150th birthday. He said it was difficult to forecast the future of this Club or any other institution. Fifty years from now there would be many differences and only a few there tonight would be present at the bi-centenary dinner.

"I foresee," he continued, "a great future for the Club, despite possible difficulties as corporate take-overs and big money deals continue to increase. However, I am confident that with continuing cordial relations with the controlling bodies of cricket and football, with the continuing policy of maintaining the arena and stands to the best possible standard, this Club can face the next 50 years with confidence that it will retain its pre-eminent position in the sporting circles of this country."

He summed up the entire 150 years with some verse of his own:

347

Tonight we celebrate this great occasion
And to our forebears make acknowledgements.
First sporting club throughout this very nation
Let's now remember our great past events.

First, cricket here we started and expounded,
Then football too, and e'en drew up the laws.
Then tennis, baseball, lacrosse, quickly founded,
Of bowls and shooting we espoused the cause.

Test matches then were also our invention.
The V.F.L. we helped get off the ground.
The Cricket Museum I should also mention
And Library where sporting books abound.

Of tattoos, pop groups, royalty, we boasted,
Olympic Games we managed in our stride.
The Pope and Bill Graham we have hosted
And added squash and hockey on the side.

And these are only some of all our winners,
Our Twenty-Niners we should also list,
Pentathlons, Club Elevens and Section dinners,
and Hans Ebeling Awards should not be missed.

Then recently new wickets and their heating,
The Electronic Scoreboard and the Lights,
The AGOS* then and all that plastic seating
New Members' Dining Room and Women's Rights.

The Outer Stand now faces liquidation,
The Ingpen doors attract unstinting praise.
Our treasures now have drawn much admiration
Since we revealed them to the public gaze.

All that and more tonight we do remember.
Of sporting institutions we're the hub
And each tonight so proud to be a member
Of this the marvellous Melbourne Cricket Club.

*Australian Gallery of Sport

APPENDIX I

M.C.C. Club Cricket

IT IS A mistake to think of the Melbourne Cricket Club as merely a convenient organisation for handling the sport of champions. Ever since the Club began there has been a strong tradition of club cricket. It dates from the time when the civilians played the military, when the bearded played the non-bearded and smokers played the non-smokers, and despite the influence of this dangerous habit, often the smokers would have a fine win. However it was never easy to pin down exactly who was a smoker and who was not. There was an occasion when one of the leading non-smokers infamously walked out to bat smoking a cigar.

Then came the happy tradition when the M.C.G. was in use every afternoon. The professional bowlers and batsmen were on the job. There were William Caffyn and the volatile and irrepressible Sam Cosstick. William Caffyn, the England international, was hired by the Club to bowl to members at the impressive fee of £300 a year. Later he wrote of the 'sixties: "I never saw such painstaking cricketers as the Australians were in those days, and it was most interesting work teaching them when one would see the way they improved. I did a good deal of bowling at club members and soon succeeded in improving the play of many of them. The system I worked on was never to try and make all bat alike. If a man was a hitter I tried to make him hit with as great safety as possible; if, on the other hand, another player was naturally a 'stonewaller', I encouraged him in this style of play."

There were professional bowlers at the Club right up to the Second World War. The system was always the same. They would take lunch between 2 p.m. and 4 p.m., when they would go into their headquarters, the visiting team's changing room, and there they would play poker. Then, from 4 p.m. until after 7 p.m., they would bowl. There were eight nets, each member allowed 10 minutes batting against the professionals and other members. After bowling all the week and attending to other duties on the ground they would umpire the club matches on Saturdays.

Among the pro. bowlers there were Herbie Fry, Charlie Over, Alf Woods, Doug Courtney, Snowy Davidson, Bill Vanthoff, Gordon Ogden and Tarzan

Glass. As a coach Herb Fry was a master, and both Jack Ryder and Keith Rigg had cause to be grateful to him.

It was said that he could teach anybody. There was the case of a doctor who more than anything else wanted his son to be a batsman. He was prepared to pay Fry in the hope that he could achieve a Professor Higgins-like change. It was obvious that it would have to be an incredible change, for the boy was near hopeless. Herbie Fry solemnly announced that within 12 weeks the doctor's son would make a century for Melbourne Grammar. Day after day he put him in the nets during the 2 to 4 poker-playing lunch break. Herbie Fry was true to his word. The boy did make a century for Melbourne Grammar.

After the turn of the century the early club captains were Charlie Robertson, Archie Strachan and A. P. Propsting. Then, of course, there was Sue Aitken, who captained many touring teams on country trips, and Hector Donahoo. Hec Donahoo had a playing record of over 50 years with the M.C.C. He was an outstanding schoolboy bowler with Wesley College, and he came to the Club as an exhibitioner in 1892. From then on he played regularly with club elevens until 1941 and controlled mid-week elevens for many years. He was elected to the General Committee in 1926 and made an Honorary Life Member in 1945. He died in 1947. He is remembered by the Hector Donahoo Memorial Trophy, for which the club elevens now compete.

Always on Hec Donahoo's fixture list there was the match against the Combined Hunt Club eleven. He liked to field a strong team against the visitors, and one year he had the famous Australian left-hander, Clem Hill, the last match Hill played. Mr. G. A. Watkins, of the big firm of butchers and a racehorse owner, was called in to bowl to Hill.

Mr. Watkins through his entire cricket career experimented with the same ball, a left-handed, well-directed, under-arm grubber, a ball that didn't rise an inch from the ground. To everybody's amazement Mr. Watkins got Hill with his first ball, out to a simple catch. This was awful—Hill, the mighty Clem, out to a grubber. Hill appealed to the umpire: "Nobody told me he bowled left-handed grubbers."

And there were comments from the team, for Clem Hill was V.A.T.C. handicapper at the time.

"Watty, your horse'll get top weight after this."

Hill tried to browbeat the umpire, but he wouldn't be browbeaten, and so grinning Hill left the field. The next man in was Laurie Chapman, the State Under-Secretary. Mr. Watkins gave him exactly the same ball as he gave Clem Hill. Chapman tried to drive the ball hard, Watkins got his hand to it, and in all the excitement he fell and broke his kneecap in three places. The players carried him from the ground and they used one of Clem Hill's pads as a splint. On the pad they wrote:

"This pad was used as a splint for the world's worst bowler, who captured the wicket of the world's best left-hander."

Mr. Watkins was in hospital for several months.

It was after the First World War that the famous A, B, C and D club elevens were formed. Because the elevens had alphabetical letters it did not mean they were graded that way. The initials came from the names of the captains. The captain of the A team was Sue Aitken, of the B Bricky Woodhouse, of the C Andy Crighton, and of the D Hec Donahoo. They used to play each other about three times a season.

The term A, B, C, D, etc., teams still applies today, and amongst the skippers over the years are many well-known M.C.C. cricketers, such as Wally Cattlin (who later became Assistant Secretary, M.C.C.), Bob Walters, Ivor Warne Smith, Bill and Mel Stokes, Arthur Dickins, Ray Baxter, Frank Mercovich, Roger Moss, Tom Leather, Eddie Wilson, Colin McCutcheon, Cliff James, Crofty Rhoden and others.

Then later came the E team. This was captained by Leo Streiff. They would play anybody, anywhere, and Leo was always looking for players. Anybody who could not get a game with the other teams, or was not eligible for our Senior XIs, he snapped up smartly.

Finally came the F team, the team for the M.C.C. footballers. Mr. Bert Chadwick was the first captain, and the object was to keep the footballers fit and slim during the summer. So the wheel had taken the full turn. The game of Australian Rules came into being to stop cricketers from going to fat in the winter, and now footballers were discovering cricket to stop from going to fat in the summer. There was a mixture of talent, most of them were brilliant in the field, and just occasionally they had a player who was very good indeed. Ivor Warne Smith, who succeeded Bert Chadwick and Charlie Lilley as captain, was one of these. He performed the rare double in public schools cricket of taking a hat-trick and scoring a century in the one match.

In the club elevens of the 'twenties and 'thirties there were all types. There were the older players who had retired from senior cricket and the young players who were still hoping to make the grade. So there was a fine blending of youth and experience. There were some characters. There was Jack Thomson who didn't like cricket boots, so he always wore plain brown rubber-soled boots. There was Norm Vale, a very fine bat, who it is said never had a button on his shirt. He kept it fixed with a pin. Then there was Andy

351

Crighton, captain of the C team. He didn't believe in taking block or adopting the conventional batsman's stance. He held his bat in a position that . . . well, you couldn't describe it as a baseballer's stance . . . it was more like the start of a golfer's swing. He said what was the point of standing with your bat down. You had to lift it anyway, and this saved time.

Nor was there any age limit. Some of the players went on for ever. In 1926 Peter Forman was still playing at the age of 70, batting well and opening the bowling.

The standard was high. Players like Carl Schneider and Stuart King, who played in their early years, went on to play Sheffield Shield cricket. The play was serious without ever being earnest. That is, the club elevens played cricket for fun. For example, in the 'thirties it was often noted that the umpires tended to ease the clock on a little as the time moved towards 6 p.m., a very difficult period in Victoria, for, after all, the hotels closed at six.

There were some incidents worth remembering. Like the time . . . was it 1934? . . . when the C team had only to draw with Leo Streiff's Es to be the club eleven champions. However, the Es were very obstinate. On the first Saturday they made 303 runs. The situation looked frightening and Colin Keon-Cohen practised hard all the week. He practised at one thing—not hitting the ball.

The next Saturday came and disaster hit at once—one of the openers went for a duck. Yet Colin Keon-Cohen was master of the situation. He had trained well and he brilliantly hit nothing for two hours. Between 2 p.m. and tea he scored only two runs. If only Trevor Bailey had been there, how he would have envied his style. By four o'clock a draw was assured, then they started to hit out. Colin hit a century in 75 minutes, Norman Vale got his century, Maurie Starr got 52 and Eddie Wilson 33 not out. At stumps they were 3 for 333.

At Christmas and Easter the club elevens would combine and they would go to such places as Yarrawonga, Hamilton, Bendigo. These teams were the forerunner to the XXIX Club, which is now the Club's social side. In the late 'twenties Bob Walters took a team to Corowa. A last minute addition was a desperately keen young player called "The Baron." They got to Corowa about 10.30 p.m., and the players decided to have a few drinks before they went to bed. "The Baron" promptly started to drink creme de menthe. Bob Walters warned him: "I hope you know what you're doing; that stuff can catch up with you awfully quick."

"The Baron" said: "It's all right, I'm switching to beer soon!" Later B. F. "Flops" Phillips, a famous St. Kilda footballer and a member of the team, came running. "Come quickly, 'The Baron's' dead." He was lying flat on the floor in his room. Bob Walters took his wrist and found that he could just get a pulse. They tucked him into bed and left him to sleep it off.

Next morning he looked far from well, and when play started Bob Walters parked him at mid-off. He was safe there until the batsman skied a ball high in "The Baron's" direction. He moved towards the ball in slow motion, but somehow his hands did not respond. The ball hit him on the side of the head and ricochetted to the boundary. The players rushed to his aid: "How do you feel?" they said.

"Oh, much better now, thank you," said "The Baron." He was perfectly well after that.

It is the little incidents that are remembered long after the big scores are forgotten. Eddie Wilson remembers a match that was played on the narrow University Oval, which is now a cinder track. The leg boundary was so close that a six called for little more than a stretching of the muscles. Leo Streiff, the E captain, decided kindly to give Ivan Tait a bowl at 20 minutes before stumps. Ivan was an enthusiastic but not a brilliant cricketer.

The first ball went for six. "Keep 'em up," said Leo. The next one had plenty of air and fell even shorter. That too went for six. "For heaven's sake keep 'em up," said Leo. Ivan then bowled a great donkey-drop. Another six. Leo was perturbed. "Didn't I tell you to keep 'em up?"

And Ivan replied: "Well, I can't throw them up any higher."

Before the war the competition comprised the club teams together with Old Wesley and University. The competition was extended after the war with the addition of St. Kilda and Old School elevens such as Old Scotch, Old Melburnians, Old Xavier, Old Trinity and Old Caulfield. The competition is run by the M.C.C., and the majority of the players in all sides are M.C.C. members.

The standard is high and the play very competitive, yet sometimes like the old days there is a happy incident. Col McCutcheon, one of the hard-working playing organisers, remembers one thing that happened years ago. The Colts were playing the M.C.C. A team. Bob McKenzie, a brilliant former Melbourne footballer, was umpire. Before the start he told the senior members of the As that 16-year-old Peter Bailey of the Colts was a real prospect whom they should "have a look at." Bailey had barely reached the wicket when there was a loud appeal from Doug Reid, the bowler, for lbw. He was right in front. McKenzie said dogmatically, "Not out." Bailey went on to bat brilliantly.

Later Col said to him, "Bob, that was pretty close, wasn't it?"

"Close," said Bob, "it was plumb."

"Well, why didn't you give him out?"

"Why?" he replied. "I wanted you to see him bat. It was worth it, wasn't it?"

The club always was able to field great stars. In the 1960s one remembers particularly batsmen Ian Huntington, Jim Symons, Neil Crompton, Max Haysom, Gerry Hammond, Norm Carlyon, wicket-keeper; Graham Brown, the all-rounder Graeme Watson, Peter Bedford, Eivion Williams, Kevin Cassidy, Bob Lloyd, Claude Reid and, of course, the incomparable Test star Paul Sheahan. In the bowling we had Ian Jones, Colin Guest, M. Hill, Lindsay Kline, Ian Gribble, John McKenzie, Roger Rayson and the deadly accurate Max Walker, who in 1968–69 took 53 wickets at an average of 14.06.

In the 1970s star batsmen were Jeff Moss, keeper Charlie Dart, Greg Booth, David Broad, Robert Lamb, John Anderson, David Shepherd, and Barry Matters. Our top bowlers were Peter Twyford, Neil Williams, Glen Swan, Ian Hennig and Michael McCarthy. In the 1980s the best performing batsmen were Michael Sholly, Mark Hooper, Peter King, Warren Ayres and the explosive Test batsman Dean Jones. Our best bowlers were Cliff Wright and Dennis Hickey, but Peter King scored the triumph in the summer of 1987–88 by topping both the bowling and batting averages.

But the man who must be remembered over these decades is David Broad. He played 176 games, only a few less than the great Vernon Ransford (178) and H. C. Sandford (202) a prolific player in the 1920s. He scored 5536 runs and was our sixth highest scorer behind Amstrong (8163), Ransford (7303), Beames (7072), Sandford (7067) and Vaughan (6977).

Our best years were premierships 1972–73 versus Collingwood and 1975–76 versus Footscray. There was another premiership in 1981–82, when the club defeated South Melbourne.

Club XI cricket always has been and we hope always will be an important part of M.C.C. cricket, as shown by the enthusiasm which prevails when old meets young at one of the Cricketers' Reunions.

The XXIX Club

In October 1956 there was an important gathering at the Club. Dr. Ian McDonald, Keith Rigg, Jack Daniel, Max Haysom and Jack Green met with the idea of forming a new club. They wanted a club that would be devoted entirely to pleasant and social cricket: an extension in fact of the old teams that had previously played at various centres under the M.C.C. colours.

It would be a club open to all M.C.C. members, including members who played in other teams. It would be for young members who were just making the grade, but especially it would be for members who had played class cricket and were now past their prime. No longer could they take part in District or even Sheffield Shield Cricket, but they were loath to leave the game altogether. This would be the club for them.

On November 1 the idea was put into effect at an inaugural meeting held at the Albert Ground. Twenty-five foundation members and a committeeman attended. They decided to call it the XXIX Club. This was a recognition of the widely held belief that when a cricketer reaches 29 he never gets any older either in the spirit or in the flesh.

The first President was Keith Tolhurst; Secretary, Tom Leather; Committee: J. Daniel, C. L. Fairbairn, J. G. Green, M. R. Haysom, Dr. I. H. McDonald, Leo O'Brien and K. E. Rigg.

Three days later they had their first match against Southern Command at Broadmeadows. The first annual dinner was on July 21, 1957, when the speaker was the patron, or rather the "Permanent Backstop," Mr. R. G. Menzies.

Ian McDonald took over the presidency from Keith Tolhurst at the annual dinner in 1960. Ian Johnson proposed the toast to the incoming president, and he likened the situation to Homer's Odyssey. He referred to the shipwrecked Odysseus, asleep under the bushes and being awakened by girlish laughter. He peered through the bushes and there before his eyes were Nausicaa and her beautiful unclad handmaidens playing ball. Johnson claimed that had McDonald been in Odysseus' position at that moment his eyes would have glowed. Quite naturally his only thoughts would have been: "Ah, fielding practice. Cricket enthusiasts, surely? I might get a game out of this!"

Such was his love of cricket. He carried on the work that had been done so well by his predecessor. The Club arranged its first interstate fixture, and there was a match against International House, when players from all countries opposed the XXIXers.

In recent years the Club has extended its activities even further.

Within the overall fixture list of about 20 games per year, interstate games and games against visiting overseas teams are common and the XXIX Club itself has undertaken a number of overseas tours. They have visited the U.K. twice, South East Asia on three occasions to visit our friends at the Singapore and Hong Kong Cricket Clubs, and in 1985 they were the only team from south of the equator to compete in the International Masters Games at

355

Toronto, Canada. In 1987 they fielded a team in the Australian Masters Games, held in Hobart, and were successful in winning the gold medal.

The dinners since the XXIX Club's inception have been a feature of cricket life in Melbourne. In 1960 Jack Fingleton came from Canberra to be guest speaker. In 1961 it was the Hon. A. A. Calwell, who performed brilliantly when he stepped in at five minutes notice to replace Dr. Evatt.

Outstanding was the dinner for the West Indies team, when the "Permanent Backstop" was present, and in his role outshone in brilliance all other backstops. The backstop, the Rt. Hon. R. G. Menzies, was in regular attendance at these functions, and installed Keith Rigg in the presidential seat—a baby's chair with a convenient hole in the seat. On many occasions at club dinners Sir Robert Menzies and Mr. Arthur Calwell brilliantly sharpened their wits on each other.

The list of guest speakers since those early days reads like a "who's who" of cricket and some memorable speeches have resulted.

A significant event in the life of the XXIX Club occurred in 1985 when it celebrated its XXIXth birthday, its coming of age, and confirmation of its strength and continuing role in the history of the Melbourne Cricket Club.

Football

Australian Rules football, the M.C.C.'s main associated sport, was not played until 20 years after the first cricket match. In that period there was little attempt to play football of any kind. There was a match here and there, but they were played with no recognisable rules. As one historian put it, "they were only indulged in at festivals or holidays, just to entertain the rougher elements of the colony, and with such prizes as a barrel of porter or ale."

The code of Association or soccer football was still unknown, but Rugby already was a popular sport in England. It is curious that some attempt was not made to introduce it to Melbourne, and if there had been, the story of football in Victoria may have been very different.

In November 1850 three games of football took place, apparently with no rules whatever. This was part of the celebration arranged to mark the separation of the colony from New South Wales, and a prize of 15 guineas was offered for the winners of a match between two teams of 12 men a side. These matches were played on Batman's Hill, then a beauty spot and the playground of Melbourne. This hill was on the south side of the present Spencer Street railway station.

In 1856 T. W. Wills, who was born at Molonglo, N.S.W., now Australian Capital Territory, returned home from Rugby, where his father had sent him for schooling. He was a top class cricketer and footballer, and he played in the second Intercolonial cricket match against N.S.W. in 1857.

In that year he was appointed secretary of the Melbourne Cricket Club, and he wrote a letter to *Bell's Life*, the sporting newspaper of the day, suggesting that the M.C.C. should form a football club to keep the cricketers in condition during the winter months. This suggestion was taken up quickly, and the M.C.C. Committee instructed T. W. Wills, H. C. A. Harrison and W. J. Hammersley to meet and draw up the rules for a new game of football.

Very likely T. W. Wills was the only one who had seen Rugby football played, as he had captained Rugby College at football in England. He was very definite about not allowing the Rugby tackle in the Melbourne game, because he felt that the grounds here were too hard and there would be many injuries.

Soon after, the first match played under something approximating to Australian Rules was advertised in the Melbourne *Herald* of August 7, 1858, when it was announced that a Grand Football Match between Scotch College and the Church of England Grammar School would be played near the Melbourne Cricket Ground, commencing at 12 noon, with an interval for lunch.

It was decided to play 40 a side, and the first team to kick two goals would be the winner. But with 80 men in the game, and the goal posts nearly half a mile apart, scoring was very difficult. However, Scotch College after battling for three hours managed to score a goal, and finally darkness made play impossible. After a fortnight the match went on, but still Scotch could not get the second goal. A week later the two teams tried for a third time to finish the match, but even then the 80 players could not score a goal, and the game had to be abandoned. It was officially declared a draw.

Wills umpired part of this match, Harrison was an interested spectator, and these men soon realised that 40 a side was too many, so they cut down the teams to 20. The game was known as Victorian football and 20 a side was the rule for many years.

To play this new game of football it was necessary to have someone to play against, and Geelong was the second club formed. Then followed Richmond, South Yarra (now defunct) and Carlton.

In 1872 there was a revision of the rules: ends were changed at half time, and a central umpire decided questions hitherto settled by the captains, for no provision in the initial rules had been made for an umpire.

In 1860 Wills left for his father's property in Queensland, and he was away for nearly four years. When he returned he appeared to take little interest in football. Meanwhile his cousin, H. C. A. Harrison, a most able administrator, took over the game and guided it through its early stages. Undoubtedly there were many difficulties in launching this new game of football, but there was one splendid advantage—there was no opposition from other codes.

The Carlton club was formed in 1864, and immediately became formidable rivals to Melbourne, and they have been friendly competitors ever since. The Carlton men adopted blue socks, while the Melburnians wore red, and became known as the "Red Legs." Then with the adoption of the blue guernseys, their name was changed to "Fuchsias." "Checker" Hughes was the man who changed all that. He wanted a name with more devil in it, and they became known as the "Red Demons," and that name is never likely to be changed.

All matches in the early days were played in the park outside the M.C.G., but in 1869 application was made to the Governor-in-Council for permission to use the ground for athletic sports and other purposes of recreation besides cricket. This was granted and a match was played for charity between the Melbourne Football Club and the Police Force, captained by Tom O'Callaghan. However, the Committee still refused to believe that football would not ruin the ground, and it was many years before football on the M.C.G. became a regular thing.

Melbourne won its first football premiership in 1870.

In 1877, the Victorian Football Association was formed, with the Hon. W. J. Clarke, afterwards Sir William, as its first President, H. C. A. Harrison Vice-President, H. H. Budd Hon. Secretary, and J. A. Power Treasurer.

The game up to this date had not spread to the other colonies, but Phil Sheridan, a trustee of the Sydney Cricket Ground, became very interested. He invited George Coulthard, one of the best exponents of Victorian football, to go to Sydney with the idea of establishing it there. But Coulthard had an unfortunate experience. His host invited him to join a fishing expedition in Sydney Harbour. While sitting on the side of the boat with his coat almost trailing in the water a savage shark seized the coat tails. If he had not parted company with the coat he would have been pulled into the water. This was all too much for Mr. Coulthard and he promptly returned to Melbourne. So it could be argued that but for an unpleasant shark Australian Rules could be the major code in Sydney today.

The game appeared to be hard and tough. One reads of a player having four shirts torn from his back in a single match. Then there was the former Scotch College boy John "Specs" Binnie. He was very shortsighted and he

358

always played in glasses. It was his custom to bring six pairs to the ground on match days, give them to the umpire, and as each pair was broken he would collect another set. At the end of the match he would take the broken parts and have them repaired for the next encounter.

Uniforms worn in those days were often weird and wonderful. In a match Melbourne versus the XIV Regiment, one officer appeared in immaculate white with a belt on which his girl friend had embroidered the words "Neck or Nothing." Apparently it was "Neck" because within a minute he was carried off on a stretcher. What his girl friend embroidered next time is not recorded.

Between 1880 and 1889 the Melbourne Football Club failed badly. Members took very little interest, and in 1889 the club was in such financial trouble that it made an approach to the M.C.C. Committee. The Committee took over the club's assets and arranged an overdraft to discharge liabilities. And so the club which started the game was saved. The official name became the Melbourne Cricket Club Football Club. The energetic Major Ben Wardill took over and there was a vast improvement. Leading amateurs joined up, and once again Melbourne began to look like a football team. At this time Essendon was well nigh invincible. From 1891 to 1894 they won four premierships and lost only three games in the process. The strength of Essendon indirectly helped Melbourne. The champion from Tasmania, Fred McGinis, tried to join Essendon, but with two fellow-Tasmanians, George Vautin and Colin Campbell, starring as rovers, the Dons were not interested. So Melbourne signed McGinis. He became one of the greatest footballers the code has known, and he played a big part in Melbourne's first League premiership in 1900.

In 1897 eight Association clubs broke away from the V.F.A.—Collingwood, South Melbourne, Essendon, Fitzroy, Geelong, St. Kilda, Carlton and Melbourne. They formed the Victorian Football League, with Alex McCracken as its first president.

Three major reforms immediately improved the game:
1. The little mark was abolished.
2. Behinds were counted as one point (previously they had been scored but not counted in the actual result of the game), and
3. The system of playing semi-finals and finals was introduced and this added greatly to public interest.

Another big improvement made two years later was the reduction of the size of the teams from 20 to 18.

Melbourne's first V.F.L. premiership came in 1900, when they defeated Fitzroy in the final. Melbourne's captain was R. C. (Dick) Wardill, and among the top players was W. C. McClelland, who was to become President of the V.F.L. from 1926 to 1955, and President of the M.C.C. from 1944 to 1957. He was also captain of the M.F.C. from 1901 to 1904.

After taking the flag the team gradually declined. The game was becoming all too professional, and club scouts went all over Australia to sign recruits. Balance sheets were crafty affairs. Sums put down to items such as eucalyptus read like the national debt. The Melbourne Football Club stuck strictly to amateur ways and made little progress.

The year 1908 was one to remember. This was not only the half-century of the Melbourne Football Club but the Jubilee year of Australian football, and the first Australian Football Carnival fittingly was held on the M.C.G. The Carnival was a great success. Victoria won the championship, but the surprise was the good form of New Zealand, which beat N.S.W. and Queensland. Melbourne's representatives in the Victorian side were A. M. (Joe) Pearce and Hugh Purse. At the end of the Carnival there was a "Monster Smoke Night" in the Melbourne Town Hall, and the Prime Minister, Mr. Alfred Deakin, christened the game by proposing the toast of the Australian game of football. From that time the game has been known as Australian Rules football.

In 1911 it couldn't be disguised any longer that V.F.L. players were being paid under the lap. So the League brought in a rule making pay legal. Even so, a number of footballers continued to play as amateurs.

After the 1915 season Melbourne withdrew from the League for the duration of the war. After the Armistice the job of rebuilding was not easy. In 1919 the club did not win a match, and it was many years before Melbourne became a real threat. Melbourne was third in 1925, but the real year was 1926, a red letter one for Melbourne, and ever since the 1926 team has been used as a measuring stick for assessing club sides. The captain and coach was Albert Chadwick. Then there was Ivor Warne Smith, one of the all-time greats in football, and that year he easily won the Brownlow Medal. In the ruck there was Colin Deane, on the half-forward flank there was Bunny Wittman, on the wing Dick Taylor and, of course, there was Bob Johnson, father of the towering Bob Johnson of more recent years. Bob senior was a superb high mark. He was on the forward line with H. Davie and H. Moyes. They each kicked 50 goals for the season, something that hadn't been done before. So Melbourne won the premiership.

In 1927 Melbourne finished out of the four, and in 1928 the club had a tie with Collingwood in the semi-final and lost in the replay. That year Ivor Warne Smith won his second Brownlow Medal.

Melbourne dropped and dropped and dropped down the ladder. In 1933 the team won only three games, but then Checker Hughes and Percy Page crossed over from Richmond, and the great rebuilding plan started. Hughes was an outstanding judge of the capabilities of a player and he knew what he wanted. On the other hand, Percy Page was the organiser. He made sure that the players Checker wanted were recruited.

And he did recruit them. In 1934 he signed Alan La Fontaine, one of the most brilliant footballers in the history of the club; they found Jack Mueller, one of the best of Melbourne's big men, and another was Maurie Gibb, the brilliant half-forward. For recruiting it was certainly a vintage year, not to mention the arrival of Norman Smith in 1935.

All the planning bore its beautiful fruit in 1939, the first premiership for 13 years. Checker Hughes had gone for a big team—a team that combined both weight and pace. The system on the forward line was deadly. Norman Smith, the full forward, would drive his full back to misery. He roamed everywhere and, of course, the full back had to follow. Meanwhile, Alan La Fontaine would drive the ball forward to Ron Baggott at centre half-forward or maybe to Maurie Gibb on the half-forward flank. Then Jack Mueller would drop back into the pocket. Each understood the other as time and again they drove the ball into the open goal mouth. It was the first time such tactics had been used successfully and no counter was found to them.

Melbourne won the flag in 1940 and again in 1941, but no longer was it easy to concentrate on football. Australia was in danger of invasion and many of the best footballers were in the Services. Keith Truscott, Noel Ellis, Syd Anderson, John Atkins, Ron Barassi and Harold Ball all were killed.

Bluey Truscott, D.F.C. and Bar, became one of Australia's top fighter pilots, and the Truscott Cup donated by Checker Hughes commemorates his name. Harold Ball, Syd Anderson and Ron Barassi, father of the former Melbourne captain, also are remembered by annual trophy awards.

In 1942 Checker Hughes resigned as coach for the duration of the war and Percy Beames took over, but Hughes was back in 1946. His influence on the game was extraordinary. It would have surprised no one if Melbourne had taken years to recover from the effect of the war. Yet this year Don Cordner won the Brownlow Medal and the club lost only to Essendon in the Grand Final. Then 1948 was the year of the incredible Grand Final tie with Essendon. The season had to be extended a week for the play-off, and so the club won another premiership.

This was the end of an era for the Melbourne Football Club. Norm Smith retired as a player and Checker Hughes retired as coach, and soon all the great players like Mueller and La Fontaine had gone. When the fall came, it came

361

quickly. It was hard to believe that the time would come when teams like Collingwood, Carlton, Essendon and even St. Kilda would look forward to a match against Melbourne on the M.C.G. as almost a guarantee of four match points, but it happened in 1951. That year the Demons won only one match, the worst effort in 32 years. Something had to be done, and that something was the return of Norm Smith as coach. He had been one of the cleverest forwards the game had known, and he was able to use that cleverness as coach. But more than that, because of his amazing devotion to the club, he could pass on his enthusiasm and his skill to his players. He had few equals as a teacher. It took time. The club finished in sixth position in 1952, and dropped back to second last in 1953. But in 1954 there was an unexpected and meteoric rise. Melbourne reached the Grand Final, only to lose to Footscray.

This was a vintage year for first season players—Bob Johnson, Clyde Laidlaw, Laurie Mithen, Ian Ridley and Brian Dixon. Ron Barassi, Peter Marquis, Ken Melville, Frank Adams and Don Williams played their first games the previous year. The committee felt that the club now had the nucleus of a premiership combination, in fact one of the finest combinations ever seen in League football. There was John Beckwith, Truscott Cup winner; Denis Cordner and Stuart Spencer, both dual Truscott Cup winners. Denis Cordner was the younger brother of Don and Ted, who had already done so much for the club.

Noel McMahen led the club to its premierships in 1955 and 1956 and John Beckwith was captain when Norman Smith equalled Checker Hughes' record of three successive premierships in 1957. Of course, the dream was that the club would win four in a row and equal Collingwood's famous record. And nothing looked more certain. All the year the Demons sat on the top of the League ladder. Melbourne set the standard for League football; it was the club to beat. Yet against the predictions of all the tipsters the club went down to Collingwood in the Grand Final, and so the Magpies protected their own record.

The players were disappointed when the record slipped away at the last moment, particularly when they had beaten Collingwood in the semi-final. So they came back with more determination than ever. With John Beckwith as captain the club won the flag in 1959 and again under Ron Barassi in 1960. This time they did make League history—no other club had ever played in seven successive Grand Finals. The name of Ron Barassi was a byword, as well known as that of the Prime Minister. The football writers called him "Mr. Football" and half the little boys in Melbourne were wearing number 31 Ron Barassi Demon sweaters.

In 1961 the club finished second to Hawthorn on the League ladder. The second semi-final was the match of the year, and it was undecided almost to the finish. Hawthorn won by seven points and many a football judge felt that the Grand Final was played on that day. Melbourne had its second chance in the preliminary final, but it was defeated by a young and enthusiastic Footscray.

In this year Ron Barassi became the second Melbourne player to captain a Victorian Carnival side, the first being Bert Chadwick in 1927. Brian Dixon was the first Melbourne player to win a Tassie Medal, awarded to the best player in the Carnival.

Since the formation of the Leagne in 1897 Melbourne have won 11 premierships, and the game on the M.C.G. has attracted Australia's biggest crowds, with a keenness perhaps only equalled by great football cities like Glasgow and Buenos Aires. The record crowd was for the 1956 Grand Final between Melbourne and Collingwood—115,902 spectators.

Much of the success of the club must be credited to the very active committee, with men like A. E. Chadwick, the chairman, Tom Trumble, Denis Cordner, and the selection committee, with Ivor Warne Smith, F. V. Hughes and H. Long.

Then there is Jim Cardwell, the club's first full-time secretary. He started in 1951 and became full-time in 1958. Since he has been on the job the club has won five premierships and been runners-up twice. This is a record for any secretary, but Jim Cardwell hasn't the slightest doubt that before he is through he will be called upon to handle many more premiership flags.

All through the 1970s and 1980s Melbourne tried to recapture the dream days of the 1950s and 1960s, but the dream was all too elusive. In the days of the Cordners, Noel McMahen and Barassi, victory for Melbourne seemed automatic, so where did the club go wrong. One theory was the zoning system. Jim Cardwell as secretary had an extraordinary skill for seeking out country recruits. He had his scouts and his contacts. Should any new talent come forward in country football Jim Cardwell was the first to hear about it.

Come 1966 the V.F.L. divided Victoria into zones and Melbourne's zone was the Goulburn Valley. For the next 10 years the only champion to come from that zone was Peter "Crackers" Keenan who played part of his career with Melbourne.

A new era of professionalism came into the game. The Red Legs supporters group was launched in 1969. Originally it was just a vehicle for M.C.C. members who wanted to see an improvement in the players' performance on the field but its base broadened with the change of scene. It became a dynamic fund-raising force, whose object was to buy players and help the Demons up the ladder.

Jim Cardwell retired at the end of the 1975 season. He had been secretary for 15 years and was also known as the "Prince of Secretaries." He had been there through 11 finals appearances and six premierships. Ivan Moore who previously was associated with Hawthorn became secretary and John Mitchell, chairman.

There was another significant event in 1975; the club established a scholarship to scout for young footballers, aged 14 to 16 in the metropolitan zone. Senior players coached them on Sunday mornings. The idea was a big success. Two players who came from these scholarships were the brothers Gerard and Greg Healy.

Bobby Skilton was now the coach. The club finished 10th in 1973, 12th in 1974 and 10th in 1975. The year of agony and disappointment was 1976. The Demons at last had a chance to play in the finals and everything depended on two matches. If Melbourne beat Collingwood and Carlton beat Footscray then the Demons were in the final five. The match was almost over; Footscray and Carlton were dead even. Right on the siren R. Walls of Carlton took a mark 35 metres out right in front. He had only to kick a behind for Carlton to win. He kicked it out of bounds. Meanwhile Melbourne beat Collingwood by 15 points at Victoria Park. There was stunned silence from Demon supporters as the scores from the Footscray-Carlton match went up on the board. There was deep grief in the Melbourne changing room; particularly upset was Gary Hardeman whose career ambition had been to play in the finals.

In 1977 Melbourne won Mayne Nickless Ltd as its first major sponsor but there were worries ahead. Before the beginning of the 1978 season, Stan Alves resigned, announcing he would move to another club. The press reported that Alves was leaving because of a disagreement with coach Bobby Skilton.

"To say that I was dismayed was an understatement," said the Melbourne chairman, John Mitchell. "The demands made by the coach on Alves were no different to those made on every player in the club."

Alves wanted to go North Melbourne but North, said Mitchell, made a ridiculously low offer which was utterly unacceptable. So Melbourne took the case to the Complaints Committee and Appeals Board. The North Melbourne Football Club was found guilty of breaking a League rule and fined $2000. But it was a sweet fine for they got Alves for no transfer fee, because the rules had been changed in 1975.

Said John Mitchell: "The Melbourne Football Club, which broke no rule, lost its most experienced player with no compensation, involving a loss of $35,000 to $40,000." From now on it meant the financially strong clubs could get stronger and the financially weak clubs weaker. It was not in the best interests of the V.F.L.

Greg Wells became the new captain, Dennis Jones became the new coach and the club sank to the bottom of the ladder. The next year the former St. Kilda great, Carl Ditterich became captain and coach. Melbourne finished 11th. Wayne Reid took over as chairman.

In 1980 Richard Seddon became executive director and the club started a whole new process of re-building. Ron Barassi returned as coach. Football writers reported that he was now the highest priced commodity in the Victorian Football League and miracles were expected.

Indeed miracles were expected in all directions. This was the year the Melbourne Football Club broke away from the Melbourne Cricket Club to become the Melbourne Football Club Inc. There were many on the committee, who were not keen on the idea, including John Mitchell who had been football club chairman and cricket club representative on the football committee. After all, the Demons had always been part of the M.C.C. and it was the cricket club that invented the game of Australian Rules Football.

Furthermore this change came at a delicate time when the club was negotiating with the V.F.L. over the Grand Final. But the M.F.C. wanted to be its own master. Football in the 1980s was moving into an era of huge business. During 1979 its costs had exploded. After starting the era with a credit of $148,882, it finished with a debit of $135,645, in effect a loss for the year of $284,527. The club wanted to be able to move quickly and to act on its own initiative.

As for Barassi, the newspapers billed it almost like a "second coming." But it was a time of disappointment. The club collected the wooden spoon in 1981, came eighth in 1982, eighth in 1983, ninth in 1984, and 11th in 1985. Even the legendary Barassi could not perform his magic. At the end of the season he announced his resignation and John Northey from the Sydney Swans became the new coach. During the Barassi years Brian Wilson won the Brownlow Medal in 1982 and Peter Moore won in 1984. In 1981 Sir Billy Snedden was appointed club chairman.

Sir Billy Snedden stepped down at the end of 1985, and Stuart Spencer became the new chairman. The club finished only 11th in 1986, but at last the new coach, John Northey, was beginning to get results. He was not a man for dramatics or histrionics; he preferred to keep out of the camera's eye and the year 1987 was a wonderful season for the Demons, the best since 1964. The club won the night premiership, with wins against the Swans and North Melbourne overseas, it won the Foster's World Champions, but most aston-ishing was the surge that came at the season's end. By round 17 the ladder had an ugly familiar ring, seven losses and only four wins. There had to be some-thing better to do on Saturdays rather than watch the Demons. From here on Melbourne won eight games straight with an average winning margin of eight goals.

Melbourne beat Footscray for a place in the finals, and despite the kiss of death from most tipsters the Demons went on to record crushing victories over North Melbourne and the Swans.

The tragedy came in the Preliminary Final, in a heartbreak even greater than that of 1976. When Melbourne appeared to have the game won Gary Buckenara of Hawthorn kicked a goal after the final siren. Many thought the umpire should never have awarded the kick, indeed many hardened Demon supporters after wiping away their tears, thought it the greatest robbery since the days of Ned Kelly. Hawthorn won the match 11.14.80 to Melbourne's 10.18.78.

It was a particular grief to Melbourne's extraordinarily gifted Robert Flower, who had been captain since 1981. He had been just two points away from playing in his first ever Grand Final, now it would never happen, 1987 was his retirement year.

However members were in love with their team again. Average attendance for home and away games was 21,000, a 61 per cent. increase on 1986. They were very thirsty for another Demon flag.

Baseball

There has been baseball in Victoria since the eighteen-fifties—ever since the diggers from California played the game in the days of the gold rush. Like most sport on the goldfields, it was unorganised and there was no public interest until the U.S. Man-of-War *Enterprise* visited Melbourne in 1885. The 18 officers all became honorary members of the M.C.C.

The Americans wanted to play baseball while they were here, so the M.C.C. Committee recruited a team, provided lunch at the ground, and the first baseball match on the M.C.G. was played. It all looked so spectacular the Committee thought that here was a scheme for improving the fielding and throwing of the cricketers, and furthermore, what a happy way of keeping them fit during the winter. Tom Wills, when he was worrying about the waistlines of his cricketers, had the same idea when he suggested a football club in 1858. So the Committee asked Mr. A. G. Spalding to bring two teams to Australia. Mr. Spalding was then the top man in American baseball.

The following year the All Black Georgia Minstrels visited Melbourne. Not only were they magnificent on the stage, part of their repertoire was to play exhibition games of baseball, and because of this association, J. C. Williamson and Harry Musgrove became interested in the Spalding project. Harry Musgrove was a leading cricketer in his day and he managed the 1896 Australian cricket team in England. J. C. Williamson was an American actor who first visited Australia in 1874 and later founded the theatrical firm of Williamson, Garner and Musgrove—later J. C. Williamson & Co.

A Mr. Lynch came to Australia to complete the arrangements, then A. G. Spalding came out with his Chicago team and an All-American combination. They played their first match on the M.C.G. on December 22, 1888. Chicago defeated the All-Americans by 5 runs to 3, and 7000 people watched the game. E. Crane, the All-American pitcher, was the big drawcard. He was so good some felt that he was even like Spofforth—he could vary his pace without the motion of his arm giving the slightest indication of what he was doing. There were matches in Adelaide and then a big return match on the M.C.G.

Chicago outclassed Victoria 12 runs to 1, then the All-American team defeated Chicago, 5 runs to 1. But to give the 12,000 spectators extra value for their money there was a football match between Carlton and Port Melbourne. This was something, a football match on the M.C.G. in January! It was a draw —three goals each. Behinds did not count in the eighteen-eighties.

There was an exhibition of throwing the cricket ball, and E. Crane, the All-American pitcher, threw the ball 128 yards 10½ in., breaking the Australian record of 126 yards 3 in. The record baseball throw was then 133 yards 11 in. A cricket ball was ¼ oz. heavier than a baseball.

An aviator named Bartholomew was scheduled to make a balloon ascent and then to make a magnificent parachute leap, but a strong wind was blowing and he refused to take off. However, the crowd was satisfied; they received their money's worth.

A baseball league was formed in 1890, and the M.C.C. voted three guineas towards it. J. C. Williamson was the first president and he remained in office for six years. He was succeeded by Major Ben Wardill, who was tremendously interested in the game and already he had put on the uniform. Melbourne were premiers in 1890, 1893, 1894 and 1897, and they played everywhere, even on the goldfields in the Strathbogie Ranges.

The depression of the eighteen-nineties and the Boer War upset baseball, but in 1897 there was an ambitious plan to send a team to the United States— the first foreign team to play in America. A South Australian, A. M. Roberts, donated £1500 towards the expenses.

Frank Laver was captain, W. G. Ingleton of Melbourne was vice-captain. Other well-known cricketers apart from Laver and Ingleton to make the tour were Peter McAlister and Harry Stuckey. Then there were the Melbourne players A. Wiseman, H. Irwin and Charlie Over.

There were big hopes for this tour. It was thought that it might result in regular Test matches against the Americans, just like the cricket Tests. Sadly the tour was a financial and sporting failure. The Australians were vastly inferior to the Americans. Advertisements for the games in America carried the line, "Come and see the Kangaroos hop!" The team returned home via England, where they had a success in defeating a team of English players at the Crystal Palace. This was the only time that an Australian baseball team went overseas.

The first Intercolonial match was against South Australia in 1889 and the first Interstate match against New South Wales in 1901. This was almost a Sheffield Shield affair, with Frank Laver, Peter McAlister and Sam McMichael for Victoria and Victor Trumper, M. A. Noble, Austin Diamond and Frank Iredale for N.S.W.

After the turn of the century the club was very powerful, and there was an extraordinary run of successes, when Melbourne won the premiership seven successive times until they were defeated by Fitzroy in 1914.

In 1912 there was a baseball carnival in Victoria, and several teams came over from N.S.W. Alan Kippax was among the juniors, and Charles Simmonds, the Australian representative and catcher for N.S.W., was among the seniors. Then among the Victorians there was Vernon Ransford, right field, and Jack Ryder, left field. New South Wales won, nine runs to six.

Many stories are told about Charles Simmonds in those days. Not all of them have been substantiated, but this was interesting. On one occasion C. W. Simmonds was catching and there was a man on third. After taking a pitched ball, Simmonds inconspicuously took a white potato from his pocket and hurled it towards third base. It sailed high over the baseman's head. The runner on third, thinking it was the ball, immediately took off for the home plate with thoughts of a certain run. As he ran towards home Simmonds casually tagged him with the ball, which had been carefully concealed in his glove.

It could be a rugged game at times. One time when he was playing the M.C.C. at Rushcutters Bay, Sydney, Simmonds ducked a ball from Dr. Twiss; it hit him on the head and bounced right out of the field into the tennis-courts. Baseballers, apparently, are built for that sort of thing and he was uninjured. Another time on the M.C.G., when N.S.W. was playing Victoria, Simmonds was stealing second base. J. Balantyne, short stop, covered second base, went to tag Simmonds, but missed his body and hit him on the chin with the ball. He knocked him unconscious. Later Charles Simmonds introduced him as the only man who ever knocked him out. On the left was Balantyne, 10 stone, on the right, Simmonds, 12½ stone.

The greatest event in baseball was the appearance in 1914 on the M.C.G. of the two top American teams, the New York Giants and the Chicago White Sox, under the leadership of the famous John J. McGraw and Charles Comiskey. Baseball fans were able to see in action such immortals of the game as Tris Speaker, Larry Doyle, Fred Merkle and the incredible athlete Jim Thorpe. In 1950 a nation-wide poll of American sports writers voted Thorpe as the greatest athlete of the first half of the 20th century, as well as the greatest football player. Apart from his football and his baseball, he was the unofficial winner of both the pentathlon and the decathlon in the Stockholm Olympic Games of 1912. In one match on the M.C.G. Thorpe hit a home run from in front of the old Public Stand clean over the fence on the opposite side of the ground. The ball landed on the asphalt embankment and crashed into the booth bar on top of the bank, much to the astonishment of the drinkers. It was the biggest hit ever recorded on the M.C.G.

The class of these two teams was so superior one would have thought they were playing a different game. The Giants defeated Victoria 18 to 1, and the White Sox were almost equally destructive, 16 to 3. Hugh Trumble used to tell a story of this visit. The top-hatted, frock-coated advance agent came to his office. He gave a full-speed, non-stop oration on terms and requirements and he finished it with these words:

"We don't like to fuss around with foreign banks and foreign currency—and as we leave for Adelaide after the play, we would be glad for you to have the proceeds in sovereigns right at the gate. We will count them on the train."

In 1915 a breakaway organisation, the Victorian Baseball Union, was formed, and the club won the A grade premiership in 1916, 1919 and 1920. The club had little success from 1921 to 1924. Vernon Ransford, Freddie

Vaughan and Harry Taylor retired, and some of the famous names at this time were Mel Stokes, Charlie Macartney, Peter Gibaud, Frank Mercovich and Frank Beaurepaire.

In 1925 the League and the Union amalgamated into the Victorian Baseball Association, and the A grade competition coincided with the League football fixture list, which that year had expanded into 12 clubs. Baseball curtain-raisers to League football had been an institution right back to the years before the First World War, and this was the time when the game was most popular with the public. They were discontinued in 1947 when official football curtain-raisers were introduced. M.C.C. baseballers have since made their headquarters the Albert Ground in St. Kilda Road.

After 1929 the club steadily began to improve. There were some great occasions such as the day in 1929 when the left-hander Bill Mackay pitched a no-hit game against University, or the day in 1934 when Perry Balmer, the giant American first baseman, received the first award of the Lansdown Medal for the best player in Victoria. Perry was one of the greatest players ever to represent the club, and his death in 1937 saddened all who knew him. During the 'thirties the club was always well up in the four or just out of it. There were players of class like Bill Ponsford, Len Darling, Geoff Eustace, Ken Kennedy, Stan Quin, Les Cheong, Jack Francis, Colin Spargo and Keith Taylor. In 1939 Colin Miller won the Lansdown Medal.

The war cut down the club from 40 members to 12, but the game went on. Melbourne won the premiership in 1942 and 1943, and the club was one of the few teams to beat the powerful combination of American servicemen. In 1943 the final was a very exciting match, and the club defeated St. Kilda by two runs. A big factor in the success was the strong batting of George Meikle and Lyn Straw and the pitching of Ross Straw, backed up by the catching of Stan Quin and Bill Jost.

Jost was a gridiron footballer of some note, and he fascinated Melbourne crowds by the way he could throw a football. In one demonstration he competed against Fred Hughson of Fitzroy, and according to Fitzroy fans nobody could kick a ball further than Hughson. This day he had to kick the ball 75 yards to beat the throwing of Bill Jost.

The club again won the premiership in 1946, and it was like the old days after the First World War. It had taken four premierships and two championships in five years. The B team was also doing well, and its win in the 1947 final was an extraordinary affair. Three of Hugh Trumble's sons, Tom, Charlie and Ken, were playing. Both Charlie and Ken broke their left legs.

Ken had returned after years as a prisoner-of-war in Japan. Disaster came in the second innings when he was sprinting from second to third base. There had been some rain during the week and the turf on the M.C.G. was hard on top but soft and sticky underneath. As he went into his slide his boot dug deep into the ground and he went into a catherine wheel. When the players picked him up his foot, which should have been pointing north, was pointing south. His badly dislocated ankle was broken and they took him to Prince Henry's Hospital.

Later in the game Charlie Trumble was trying to steal from first to second. It was too dangerous. He made a mighty leap back to first base, his foot dug in, and he did exactly the same thing as his brother. Something seemed to give, but he felt no serious pain. That night he went to the hospital to see Ken, and by this time his leg was swelling. At the hospital the doctors decided to give him an X-ray. His leg was broken in two places and he was to be in plaster for 14 weeks.

The irony of it was that next day he received a note from Vernon Ransford congratulating him with the news that he had been appointed captain of the club's D cricket eleven.

In 1948 George Belfrage, who had been secretary for 30 years, was appointed chairman and Les Millis became the new secretary. George Belfrage started as a player in 1916, and when he resigned early in 1957 his association with the section had lasted 41 years. He was succeeded as chairman by Tom Trumble, who worked as a player and administrator since 1925.

During the nineteen-fifties we took the club championship of Victoria in 1953 and 1956, and with great interstate players like Max Lord, Ken Stephens, Ken Donald, Stan Matthews and Lyn and Ross Straw there was no shortage of talent. But there was a black year in 1957. The pitching went to pieces, the club sank to the bottom of the list and went into the B grade. Yet in 1958, under the coaching of Max Wishart, the all-Australian second baseman, there was a superb recovery. They went through the B grade like a hot north wind to win the B grade premiership and the club championship. Melbourne in 1959 was back in the A grade four.

Since then, with players like the speed pitcher Alan Connelly, Ken Stephens, Bernie Bryer, Eddie Illingworth, Ken Capp and David Went, the club has done well. In 1961 we lost the grand final to Malvern by only one run.

Season 1962 opened with seven teams representing the club. There was an extra senior team to absorb all the promising juniors and a third under sixteen team. All these boys are being well coached by Max Wishart assisted by Charles Gassner, ex-New York Giants; Ian Huntington and our senior players.

One has only to look at the names of Victoria's top baseballers now and in the past to see what the game has done for cricket, and the story has been the same throughout Australia with everyone from Norman O'Neill and Neil Harvey back to the days of Trumper, Ransford and Ben Wardill. The M.C.C. Committee of the eighteen-eighties showed great enterprise.

After the outstanding successes of the 1960s and 1970s the Club's performance faltered and seemed to lack purpose for some years.

As with all other sports the post-war socio-economic development of Melbourne had its effect on baseball. Housing and industrial development in the outer areas saw increases in clubs participating in the Diamond Valley, Ringwood and Dandenong Baseball Associations. Conversely, the inner suburbs with an aging Australian population and an influx of migrants from European countries saw the demise of many clubs catering for all types of sports. As far as baseball was concerned this included North Melbourne, Richmond, Carlton, Collingwood, Brunswick, East Brunswick, South Melbourne, Prahran and Flemington. The M.C.C. found recruitment of juniors living within a reasonable distance of the Albert Ground and Fawkner Park had become a problem.

In August 1976 the Victorian Baseball Association made a decision to change the season for its main competition to summer. This is the time of year in which the sport is played in the two major countries of America and Japan. Furthermore all other Australian States were playing during summer and this put Victoria at a considerable disadvantage for the Australian Championships (the Claxton Shield). The immediate impact on Melbourne was that the Albert Ground was no longer available for training or matches. Understandably the M.C.C. cricketers had first call on this outstanding ground surface.

With the benefit of hindsight this enforced move had the particular benefit of rejuvenating the junior section of the Club. It had only been through efforts of players and former players like Ken Stephens, Ron Ralph and Wayne Bishop organising groups of juniors from their own residential/work areas that the Section had been able to fulfil its V.B.A. obligation to field three junior teams. Ten years later the Club now runs its own Under-13 Centre with four teams in regular competition. In addition upwards of 20 to 30 Under-10 players learn about the game and its skills playing the modified version called T-Ball. Two Under-15 and two Under-17 teams complete a junior contingent numbering well in excess of one hundred.

After a short stay in the City of Kew the Section in 1978-79 established its home base at Macleay Park in North Balwyn. The neighbouring areas have proved to be a continual source of junior players.

372

During this period the senior teams were competitive but inconsistent as they settled down in their new home. Some outstanding individual performances were recorded. David Went was appointed Manager/Coach of the Australian team. John Hodges joined him in the national side as short-stop. Ross Arthur and Rod Chapman who had joined the Club as juniors in the early 1970s became regular members of the Victorian senior team. Ross Arthur won the V.B.A. Division 1 Best Player Award—records indicate that he is probably the only Melbourne player to achieve this honour since the War. An 18-year-old pitcher, Grant Weir, won selection firstly in the Victorian Under-18 team and then in a representative side to tour America. He has subsequently repeated this performance at senior level.

All this time the junior programme was developing momentum. An early indication of its potential was seen when the first batch of older boys combined to win the Division 1 Reserves premiership in 1981-82.

The years 1983 and 1986 saw the end of an era for the Club and, hopefully, confirmation of the beginning of another.

At the end of the 1983-84 season David Went retired after nearly 33 years association with the Club. His service included 20 years as a player (1951-71) and 17 years as senior coach (1967-84). During this time he achieved state representation as a player from 1962 to 1968 and as senior coach from 1970 to 1982. The Victorian side was successful four times at the Australian Championship whilst David was coach including a hat-trick of wins in the 1970s. Similarly he represented Australia as a player from 1962 to 1965 and in various coaching capacities from 1971 to 1982. He was Australia's first Level 3 Accredited Baseball Coach. In 1985 following his retirement David Went was made a life member of the Victorian Baseball Association.

No less a contribution, albeit largely off the field, was made by the Cavanagh family. Arch and Veronica became associated with the Demons in 1959 and then followed the Club's progress along with that of their sons (Tony, Michael and John). They became part and parcel of the administrative and social structure of the Club. Arch was elected Section Chairman in 1976 and held that position until his retirement in 1986.

The fruits of the junior programme began to be harvested in these years with pennant victories in all age groups. In particular:

1. The 1983-84 Under-13 side represented Victoria at the Australian Championships as the best club team in the State;
2. Under-13 teams under the coaching of Des Marshall won the metropolitan Lightning Premiership (one day's continuous play competition) in 4 out of the 5 years from 1983 to 1987;

3. The 1986-87 Under-17 team won the State Club Championship to confirm their standing as the best top-age junior team in Victoria.

October of 1986 saw the Melbourne Club produce a "first" in Australian baseball by hosting a dinner for the visiting American "Hall of Fame" great, Stan Musial. The evening, staged in the Olympic Rooms, was a huge success —both for the Section and Victorian baseball generally.

The Section now moves into the 1989–90 season—its Centenary Year.

It is an odd turn of history that the Melbourne Club won the first ever Victorian title—and in the 1987–88 season won the title again to return to the top Division 1 competition in their Centenary Season.

The potential for a very exciting and rewarding future now faces the M.C.C. Baseball Section.

Tennis

Long before the days of the L.T.A.A. the M.C.C. was interested in tennis. In 1878 the Committee put down an asphalt court. This was considered to be the pride of the club and one of the finest in the colony. The game then was more gentle than athletic, but it was so popular that soon the Club had to consider putting down another court. The members could hardly go to the expense of another asphalt court, so they compromised with what they thought second-best—a grass court. It was said to be far cheaper than asphalt and the bill was £60.

In the first years there were matches against Geelong, Bendigo, and, of course, all kinds of tournaments. The open tournament was for all M.C.C. members, and the matches were styled "4-handed sets." The trophies were £3 each for the winners and £1 for the runners-up. The first winners were W. H. Moule and George Wilkie. Moule, later the famous Judge Moule, toured England with Murdoch's 1880 Australian Eleven. Runners-up were A. F. Robinson, M.C.C. secretary in 1875-76, and his partner Major Ben Wardill, who always seemed to be in everything.

In 1884 there was a tournament for the ladies, and here is a description of a mixed doubles match in 1882:

> The ladies were attired in long white dresses with gem hats firmly fixed with fierce-looking hat pins, the points often sticking several inches out, in spite of persistent agitation that the points should be protected; the hair bunched high on their heads.

The men wore knickerbockers and brilliantly coloured belts, white shirts, with stiff collars and tie, skull caps and blazers. The umpire was correctly attired in a grey topper.

Two tennis balls were used, one was red and one was white, and the lady's partner placed the tennis balls in her hand and stood beside her as she served underhand. When she won the stroke, she was rewarded with a courtly bow by her partner and acknowledged it with a curtsey. At the close of play there was another exchange of bows and handshakes, in which the umpire joined, sweeping the ground with his grey topper. The glowing lady was then con-ducted by her partner to the seat where her chaperon was sitting, watching with an eagle eye for any improprieties.

In 1888 there was a crisis. There was no local manufacturer to provide tennis balls; no one had ever dreamed of the idea of changing tennis balls regularly during a match. These were plain rubber affairs, and the smart innovation of tennis balls with the white nap did not come until 1891. Because of the tennis ball shortage the 1888 M.C.C. tournament was delayed far into the summer. The same balls were used over and over again until they had practically no bounce left.

In the early days the Melbourne Cricket Club did for tennis what it did for cricket. It virtually launched tennis in the colony. It ran the first intercolonial match against N.S.W. in 1884 and the pennant competitions until the for-mation of the L.T.A.V. in 1892. For the intercolonial matches the M.C.C. paid the rail fares and expenses of practically all the selected players so that the colony could be properly represented. Until 1892 all the intercolonial matches took place on the club's three asphalt courts at the M.C.G. Then they moved to the Albert Ground and the big matches until 1907 used to take place on the cricket pitches in the centre of the arena.

That year there was a deputation by the L.T.A.V. to Mr. Edward (later Sir Edward) Mitchell, who was an interstate player and a member of the M.C.C. General Committee. The deputation asked for a strip of land at the Albert Ground. This strip was at the northern end. It ran from St. Kilda Road to Queen's Road, enough room to build eight tennis courts. The L.T.A.V. wanted to make a start with headquarters of its own. The M.C.C. very gen-erously agreed to the request. So the L.T.A.V., with no money of its own, and with only a ground rent of £50 a year to pay, won an ideal position and the future welfare of tennis was assured.

There was a rush to complete the tennis courts by the end of 1908. Aus-tralia had won the Davis Cup from England, and seeing that Norman Brookes was a Victorian player, the L.T.A.A. had offered the Challenge Round to Melbourne. So the big matches took place at the Albert Ground. It was again the scene for the Challenge Round in 1912. Here is the report that appeared in the *Australasian*:

> On Thursday, November 28, attention was focused on a single strip of green, the court that had been prepared for the Davis Cup—the crown of the meeting, the most important tourney in the world of tennis. It was top-dressed and sown in August, and months were spent in its preparation. Round it had been erected an immense temporary stand that looked like a circus and cost £900 to erect, the timber alone being worth £800. It seated amply, and more or less comfortably, 6000 people, and is the largest stand ever provided for the Davis Cup event. Surely such trouble was never before taken to render conditions perfect for the players! Thirty-one feet from base-line to the back of the court and another five to the first row of seats, ample space at the sides, a grass court absolutely level and shaved until it looked and played like a billiard table, half a dozen new balls, duly weighed and measured, for every set, and six boys to pick them up. Tennis de luxe indeed! And around all a close-packed crowd that was there to see sport and applaud the fine strokes impartially.
>
> It was little past noon when the early birds began to arrive. An elderly gentleman with a small parcel of lunch paid his half-crown, and after carefully looking over the prospect, settled down in the south-east corner to wait an hour and a half in patience; a party of girls with baskets, cushions and a Thermos flask ranged through the members' reserve and took up a vantage post. First the half-crown, then the five-shilling and finally the reserved and members' areas filled up, till quite 5000 people were present. Twice during the last five minutes the brass band broke off a comic opera number to play the National Anthem, and the two Government House parties filed in. Lady Denham wore a large hat, trimmed with roses, and a costume whose general effect was-but that is the Fashion Lady's story!

Parke of England defeated Brookes of Australia, 8-6, 6-3, 5-7, 6-2; then Dixon, the English captain, beat Heath, 5-7, 6-4, 6-4, 6-4. In the doubles Brookes and Dunlop revived the rubber with a 6-4, 6-1, 7-5 win over Parke and Beamish.

As the *Australasian* said, public opinion is very easily moved. After the first day many people had given up the Davis Cup for lost and now they came back in their thousands. On the third day there was a capacity crowd. The capacity was meant to be 6000, but they crammed in so tightly that there were over 7000 people. On the Thursday the L.T.A.A. had made a special request that the ladies should not wear white. This could easily confuse the players, so it was reported that the dressing was mostly homely, and the prevailing colour was blue. Most of the men wore straw hats, although one gentleman had a fine black silk topper which stood out like a chimney pot. The Governor, Sir John Fuller, "watched every point carefully and he clapped his yellow kid gloves with increasing vigour as the games went in favour of the British team." Brookes beat Dixon 6-2, 6-4, 6-4, to tie the series two-all, but in the final match Parke beat Heath 6-3, 6-4, 6-4. *The Times* described the victory by the British Isles as a surprise. The thought that Parke would defeat Brookes was never seriously entertained.

This was the last Davis Cup at the Albert Ground, but ever since it has been the meeting place for name tennis players. The two men who had most to do with running tennis there were Bill Daish and Harley Malcolm. Bill Daish was the club secretary from 1909 to 1930. He died in 1931. Harley Malcolm was the secretary from 1930 to 1947. These two were the power behind the Autumn Tournament, which took place in March every year. It had a tradition that went back to 1888, and sometimes there were over 900 entries.

It was such a big affair that in the twenties it rivalled even the State title, and on the big days the Albert Ground was as busy as an ant heap. The whole arena was marked off into 16 grass tennis courts and divided by nets. Bill Daish used to be the secretary and Harley Malcolm the referee. Mr. Malcolm, was always a man of very strong character. He was the M.C.C. delegate to the L.T.A.A., and a tough advocate for keeping the game as amateur as it could be. Time and again he spoke out against the players who took jobs with sporting goods companies, which amounted to very little work for the company but happy years of tennis playing in all the major tournaments of the world. Surely this was being paid to play tennis, he said.

He ruled the Autumn Tournament with a firm hand. He had to, for there were so many entries. He was no respecter of persons. If a player failed to report within 10 minutes of the allotted time he was out. Perhaps he relaxed his rule just a trifle for a Wimbledon champion, but only a trifle. Yet few administrators have ever given so freely of their time or done so much for tennis as Harley Malcolm.

The history of the tennis section is really the story of big tennis in Australia. The stars before the First World War were the Davis Cup players Alf Dunlop and Rod Heath. Then while they were playing the big tournaments a junior was coming on. Gerald Patterson started with the Club in 1910, and even before he became captain of the Scotch College cricket team in 1913 the critics were saying that he had a tremendous future in tennis. After the First World War, twice he won the singles championship at Wimbledon.

Many other Davis Cup players have been members of the M.C.C. Harry Hopman joined in 1930. His record as a Davis Cup captain and player is well known, but Harry also had an astonishing record with the M.C.C. In ten years he won the singles at the Autumn Tournament eight times. Frank Sedgman, the future Wimbledon champion, joined in the 1946-47 season, and another Wimbledon winner, Neale Fraser, was the promising junior of 1950.

Right through the 1970s the tennis section entered six teams in pennant competition and more recently, seven teams. In 1985 Dr. Donald Cordner, on becoming President of the M.C.C., retired after 12 years as chairman of the section. Peter Mitchell who had been secretary for 15 years became the new chairman and Barry Brennan replaced him as secretary.

The Club acquired a new pavilion adjacent to the en tout cas courts at the Albert Ground. It replaced the old shelter which had witnessed the play of almost every great Victorian in tennis.

Then in 1985 the section established a perpetual award for the most valuable player to be known as the Dr. Donald Cordner award. The inaugural trophy went to Ron McKenzie at the Combined Sections Dinner.

In 1987 for the first time the section entered a ladies team in pennant competition which in 1987 comprised 600 men's teams and 250 ladies' teams. Tim Straford won the Cordner Award. Tim was also the first M.C.C. player to win the V.T.A. trophy for the outstanding player in each grade of pennant.

The section has not entered an A grade team since 1983, but M.C.C. still remains the most successful club in the history of the pennant competition. The club has won 30 A grade pennants. Its nearest rival is Grace Park with 11 pennants and Royal South Yarra with eight. It is impossible to list all the names associated with those wins, but to mention a few there have been "Sos" Wertheim, Jack Clemenger, B. W. Dunlop, A. G. Dunlop, I. H. Trethowan, J. Purcell, Ian Carson, Harry Hopman, Colin Long, Frank Sedgman, Brian Tobin, Neale and John Fraser, Tony Ryan and Wil Coglan.

Perhaps it may not be long before a ladies A grade pennant is added to the club's outstanding record.

Lacrosse

Lacrosse began in America and it was played by the North American Indians at the time of Christopher Columbus. It fascinated the French, and eventually it swept Canada, becoming the national summer game by legislative act in 1867. The Indians had many names for it, but the most common was bagataway. The stick they used reminded the French Canadians of a bishop's crozier, and naturally they dubbed the game "la crosse."

The game came to Australia through Victoria, and Melbourne saw its first matches in 1874. The Melbourne Lacrosse Club was the original body, but so many members left to form other clubs it rocked under the strain, and finally it went out of existence. Some of the Melbourne members, along with players from Caulfield, formed the M.C.C. Lacrosse Club in 1896. So through those original Melbourne players the M.C.C. traces its lineage back to the start of lacrosse in Victoria.

From the beginning the club was enthusiastic and powerful. The A team won premierships in 1900 and 1901, and in those days the M.C.C. often would help the sport by paying the fares of the entire interstate team, regardless of club affiliation. In 1903 the club's interstate representatives were Penne-father, Ransford, Box and Joynt. The Ransford, of course, was Vernon Ransford. He was so good that he earned interstate representation in one year. So he had the reputation of playing for Victoria in cricket, baseball and lacrosse.

During the 1906-7 season a Canadian lacrosse team came to Australia. This was a tremendous event, a visit from the masters themselves. H. A. Relph, who was secretary of the club for many years, says the first match on the M.C.G., Australia versus the Canadian team, was almost like a football final. There was a crowd of over 30,000. The M.C.C. had one representative in H. Box, and in the match against Victoria there were Box and A. Dean. The Canadians were too strong. They won three out of the four matches against Australia.

Mr. Relph says the Canadians caused a small sensation. They ran on to the field magnificently padded with shoulder guards and padding down the arms. They looked like gridiron footballers. This had one small influence on Victorian lacrosse. Soon afterwards an M.C.C. team went to Bendigo for an exhibition match. A Bendigo player came out arrayed in this fine padding. Mr. Relph recalls that they suggested to Harry Hooper, a top M.C.C. player, that it might be fun to test this padding, and they also gave the tip to the umpire, Wally Lambert.

Harry Hooper gave the Bendigo man a few slaps on his padding. Lambert said to him: "Do that once more and you go off." Hooper did it once more and off he went. Hooper was furious—he didn't realise this was part of the joke. In lacrosse the dismissal from the field meant that the player had to stand on the sidelines for 10 minutes or so. He wasn't banished from the entire game as in Rugby. It was more like the school master dismissing the difficult pupil from his schoolroom.

The first Australian Lacrosse Carnival took place in Adelaide in 1910, and

Victoria won the championship. Since then there have been regular carnivals, now involving the Western Australians as well. Mr. Relph was a Victorian representative in the original Adelaide championship, and he says it was the only time he saw a really serious injury in lacrosse.

A West Australian threw the rubber ball and it hit Vic Sreet, the Victorian captain, in the eye. They turned him over and there was so much blood they thought he had lost it. Fortunately he had not, but all the bone around the eye was fractured.

Lacrosse closed down for the duration of the First World War, but in the immediate post-war years and the twenties the M.C.C. was very strong. It had players like the Victorian captain, Vic Sreet, and interstate men like F. Smythe, Roy Duckett, L. Davis, D. Doyle, A. McIndoe, A. Totten and Dr. G. Wright. There's a famous story told about Roy Moore. He was due to be married in 1911—on 24 August. But this was also the date of a vital game. The team asked him if he was prepared to play. Roy said, "No"; so they switched their attack to Roy's fiancee, with some success. Following the game, the wedding party (with members of the team) went to Lara, just outside Geelong, where another lacrosse friend, Hokey Pokey, was curate. (They called him "Hokey Pokey" because this was the most violent expression that ever crossed his lips.)

Undoubtedly it was one of the greatest examples of devotion in the club, and furthermore the M.C.C. won its match. In 1935 Roy Moore became president of the Victorian Lacrosse Association.

For the 1922-23 season the V.A.L.A. adopted a system of semi-finals and finals as in League football. This was the start of years of rivalry between the M.C.C. and Malvern. Always it seemed that Malvern was the team that had to be beaten. It was like the rivalry between Melbourne and Collingwood in the V.F.L. or the New York Yankees versus the Dodgers in baseball.

The club was beaten by Malvern in 1925, but 1926 was the spectacular season—the two clubs played off four times. Melbourne won the semi-final. The final was a drawn game. The replay was a drawn game. Then in the finish Malvern won the grand final by one goal.

The M.C.C. team had its revenge by winning the premiership over Malvern in 1927. However, in 1931, 1932, 1933 and 1934 the club was runner-up to Malvern four times in succession. Melbourne lacrosse players must have had nightmares about Malvern and often the play was very tense. In one grand final Frank Cantwell, the M.C.C. goalkeeper, was taken to hospital. He returned before the match was over with two superb black eyes and he looked a frightening sight. All around his eyes he had leeches to draw the blood. To him this was of no importance. The match was close and it was all the team could do to stop him from running back on the field.

One of the greatest players at this time was Arch McIndoe. He was the best and fairest of the 1929 Carnival side. Neil Robson, Jim Reid and Jim Lake all were interstate players in the 'thirties. Then in the 1938-39 season the M.C.C. had its famous "Half Ton Backline."

There was Jim Reid, 6 ft. 4 in., 19 stone; Bill Boswell, Ian McGregor and Lindsay Dawkins, all six feet and over 16 stone; Bill Grey and Roy Buckley, 5 ft. 9 in. and 13 stone. Then Keith Buchanan, the goalkeeper, 5ft. 9 in. and 11 stone, was the smallest man in the team. Keith Buchanan was for several years the section's honorary secretary.

In 1942 lacrosse was suspended, and except for an occasional match it ceased to function until the end of the war. When the game resumed the Albert Ground was needed for football, so play switched to the outer reserve in Caulfield Park. In the post-war years the club was strong, often in the finals and semi-finals, but it had not taken the flag. In 1949 the team went to Brisbane and played two matches against the Queensland State side.

The first of the international post-war events was the visit of a team of American University players. They represented the University of Virginia and Washington-Lee, and it was the first international visit since the tour of the Canadians in 1907. The M.C.C. lacrosse section acted as hosts to the Americans, and Bill Gray was in charge of the social arrangements. The matches were played on the Albert Ground and at Olympic Park.

The main event was the Test match on the M.C.G. which concluded the Australian Carnival. When some of the lacrosse veterans saw the Americans they recalled the Canadians of 52 years before. The University players looked like supermen, shoulders wider than the door with shoulder guards and padding in the Gridiron style. A few minutes before the start of the game their dressing room was cleared so that they could pray and make their personal devotions.

They had the classic American style of play, the long passing game with tear-through and blocking tactics. Also like Gridiron footballers they had many standard plays and preconceived manoeuvres to meet every situation.

On the other hand, the Australians had the short-passing game. Rather than preconceived tactics they preferred to depend on personal initiative, and with no padding they had the edge in speed. So they won 8 to 5, which was a big shock to the Americans. Never at any stage had they contemplated the possibility of a defeat.

381

There was a farewell dinner in the Members' Dining Room. George Corrigan and Bob McHenry of the American team talked of the historic value of the M.C.C., of the wonderful hospitality they had received and how sorry they were to go back. At one stage Bob McHenry was close to tears and everyone present was moved. They hoped there would be many more international visits.

The 1970s started with the senior sides fighting for bottom positions on the ladder, but this inspired a good period of reconstruction. In 1977 junior centreman Steve Delooze won the trophy for the best junior in the State and created history by winning it again the following year. The 1979 premiership in Division 2 was the first open-age grand final win by an M.C.C. side since 1927.

The club won another Division 2 flag in 1982 then 1984 saw the State League in the finals for the first time since 1960. Bill Stahmer became State League coach with M.C.C. and through him the side became a force. Greg Date broke the club State League record by throwing 11 goals in a game on two occasions.

Team performances rose even higher in 1986 when the State League team appeared in the Grand Final. Although unsuccessful it was their first crack at the pennant since World War II. The Division 3 team of old and bolds had been the chopping block for many seasons, but they won the 1987 premiership.

In 1984, State League centreman, Joe Vazzoler, club champion for three consecutive years, won the coveted Vince Healy trophy for best senior player in the State. Ken Nichols won the club best and fairest on four occasions. He was captain of the Victorian and Australian teams and won the Vince Healy trophy in 1987.

Our main problem was getting an adequate junior program together to feed into senior lacrosse. After much negotiation the Mitcham Lacrosse Club, which had been very successful in junior lacrosse, amalgamated with the M.C.C. at the start of the 1988 season. Another first for the club: lacrosse was represented in all open age divisions and all junior slots.

Bowls

The Melbourne Bowling Club at Windsor, Victoria, is the oldest existing bowling club in Australia, founded on April 11, 1864.

At a committee meeting of the Melbourne Cricket Club held at Scott's

Hotel on May 19, 1865, it was resolved that £50 should be devoted to improvements during the winter, including the formation of a bowling green. Then on January 3, 1866 the committee formed a bowls sub-committee of five to manage the new green.

No club was formed and the green was for the convenience of members. The green was in existence over two years later when Prince Alfred, Duke of Edinburgh visited the M.C.G. on November 27, 1867 to witness the cricket match, Natives v. The World. It was said: "He entered the ground by the Richmond gate and rode inside the chain fence to the bowling green, where he was received by the officials and conducted to the pavilion."

How long the green lasted we do not know. However from as early as 1874 M.C.C. members played the game on the greens at the Richmond Bowling Club, which was situated on two acres west of Punt Road, just south of the railway line in Yarra Park. It was described as "a pretty area. There was a punt across the river, and there were vineyards on Punt Road Hill which were said to be capable of producing a most drinkable claret."

At the annual meeting in 1890, a member made the suggestion that "in consequence of the large number of members who are at present prevented from taking part in the game of bowls, this meeting is of the opinion that the Committee should be requested at once to take steps if possible for the formation of a Bowling Club."

In 1894 the Richmond Bowling Club was in financial difficulties and approached the Melbourne Cricket Club, asking to be taken over "debts and all." This was agreed to, providing the greens could be moved closer to the Melbourne Cricket Ground. An application was made to the Lands Department and the Melbourne City Council for the exchange of two acres occupied by the Richmond Bowling Club for one acre adjoining the Melbourne Cricket Ground. This request was granted, subject to the Melbourne Cricket Club removing all buildings from the Richmond site, ploughing it, sowing it down, and restoring it to parkland. The club agreed and spent $2500 clearing the park and meeting Richmond's liabilities.

That same year the club joined the Victorian Bowling Association under the title M.C.C. Bowling Club and W. J. Cudden was the first delegate. He was also the first club singles champion. One five-rink green was established in November 1894 and a second five-rink green was opened by Frank Grey Smith, president of the M.C.C. in September 1895. In 1896–97 the club won the Four-Fours Pennant and the following year C. J. Hayward, one of the M.C.C. skippers, won the singles championship of Victoria. Major Ben Wardill, who was secretary of the M.C.C. from 1880-1911, was an enthusiastic participant in most of the club's sporting sections, including bowls. In 1899 the Australian cricketers, under the captaincy of Joe Darling, were in England and Ben Wardill was their manager. He was keen to organise an English visit of the Australian bowlers, so while he was there he was instrumental in the formation of the Imperial Bowling Association. Dr. W. G. Grace was interested and the final outcome was the formation in 1903 of the English Bowling Association with which the Imperial Bowling Association amalgamated and in 1905 the International Bowling Board was formed.

On June 15, 1900 Charles Wood, President of the Victorian Bowling Association, astonished the bowling world by announcing that M.C.C. was arranging to conduct the Singles Bowling Championship of Australia. The first championship was played on M.C.C. greens from 5 to 10 November, 1900 for trophies valued at £70. It was open to any amateur bowler in the world, and attracted 128 entries. The winner was J. Sheedy of the Richmond Union Bowling Club and two members of M.C.C. finished in the last eight. The event proved so successful that the first eight Australian Singles Championships from 1900 to 1907 were organised by the club and played on the M.C.C. greens at Melbourne Cup time.

M.C.C. won the V.B.A. White Pennants in 1897, 1901, 1902, 1911, 1916, 1917 and 1918. In the 1929 season play was interrupted by the rebuilding of the M.C.C. Members Pavilion when half the rinks were out of action. In 1961 the Trustees and the general committee had to fight newspaper criticism for a quarter-acre of parkland, to build the new Western Grandstand now named the W. H. Ponsford Stand. The proposed new building was to sit square over the eastern half of the bowling greens, causing the Bowling Club to move further west into Yarra Park.

Many notable personalities have been connected with the club. Edward Cordner, grandfather of the President of the Melbourne Cricket Club, Dr. Donald Cordner, was chairman of the bowls section from 1911 to 1918. Joe Cordner, a cousin of Donald's father, was secretary of the Victorian Bowling Association in 1923-24 and was succeeded in that office by his son Clem. Clem Cordner was the first full-time secretary of the V.B.A. and occupied that position from 1924 to 1943. Clem was the M.C.C. singles champion in 1934, 1937 and 1940 and represented Victoria.

Another great contributor was Joe Blair. He won the Fours Championship of Australia in 1931, the Pairs Championship of Victoria in 1923 and 1938, and the Fours Championship of Victoria in 1938. He was M.C.C. Singles Champion in 1935 and 1938, and chairman of the bowling club from 1934 to 1945. Fred Morsby's feat in winning five Singles championships in 1941,

384

1943, 1949, 1950 and 1952 has still not been equalled. In the same era Dr. Norman Speirs won the Singles championships in 1945, 1946, 1951 and 1953 and Frank Lawn in 1957, 1964, 1965 and 1967. In more recent years Billy Williams and Lindsay Williams have given us a splendid father and son performance. Billy was the M.C.C. singles champion in 1944 and 1958 and Lindsay won the Singles championship in 1970, 1974 and 1975, the club Pairs championship in 1976, 1978 and 1980 and the Triples championship in 1982.

Ken Austin has a fine record in club championships—Singles in 1977, 1978, 1980 and 1981, Pairs in 1976, 1978 and 1980 and Triples in 1983. Arnold O'Brien is the current club coach and Singles champion. He has represented Victoria in 191 interstate matches and has won the club Singles in 1985, 1986 and 1988; Pairs in 1984, 1986 and 1988, and Triples in 1984 and 1987. Only one member, Dr. Larry Skues has won all three club championships—Singles in 1971, Pairs in 1977 and Triples in 1981.

In 1988, the Australian Bowls Championships final series matches were played on the Melbourne Cricket Club Greens.

M.C.C. fields five Pennant sides of 16 players each. The number one side has maintained its place in Division 1 since season 1978-79 and for the past two seasons the three top sides have been in Division 1, 2 and 3. Over the 93 years since its inception in 1894 the Bowls Section of the Melbourne Cricket Club has had only 11 chairmen and three of these stood for only a year. The present chairman is Allan Bamford and the secretary is Charles Lux.

Rifle Shooting

The M.C.C. started its rifle club during the Boer War. It was a rifleman's war, and at the turn of the century it was the duty of a patriotic man to be a good shot. The Committee looked at a suitable place in the gymnasium, and recommended the purchase of three rifles with Morris tubes and that a target should be erected.

The club actually came into being on June 14, 1900. G. W. Lamb was the first secretary and Major Ben Wardill was a natural as the first captain. The committee voted £10 and 14 rifles were bought at 10/- each, together with 2400 rounds of ammunition. There is a suspicion that these rifles might have been elderly retired Martini-Henry rifles. Such rifles had almost a half-inch bore and a kick like an elephant.

Obviously they were not satisfactory. Next year the club bought 15 rifles at £2 each and the members had to pay them off at the rate of 10/- a month.

In 1902 the club had 50 members and 40 of them were armed with .303 rifles, and now they were shooting regularly at the Williamstown Rifle Range.

The first moves for a miniature rifle range came in 1906, and it was built in 1908 alongside the tennis courts, roughly where the scoreboard is now. It was a 25-yard range and the shooters used to crank their targets back and forth on a cable.

The President of the M.C.C., Mr. Justice Cullen, declared the range open and with the Minister for Defence, the Hon. T. Ewing, fired the first two shots. They both resulted in bull's-eyes. Then H. C. Du Rieu, who won the club championship four times in a row, showed the accuracy of the Greener rifle by putting seven in a half-inch bull's-eye.

In 1912 the club won the C.A.C. trophy. J. T. Haynes, the club championship winner for 1915-16, recorded that it rained solidly all afternoon at Williamstown. Each team had to shoot dinner plates. Ordinary 10-inch plates were placed on the ends of sticks. The first team to knock out the plates won. They started at 600 yards and worked back progressively by 50 yard intervals to 350 yards. As Mr. Haynes remembered, it took a good eye to hit a plate in the rain at 600 yards. When the club won after toiling time and again across the rain-soaked range, there was a celebration to get back a little warmth. One happy member trailed off to the railway station dragging his rifle on the ground behind him.

In 1914 Mr. Lew Armstrong won his first club championship. He was to be an outstanding member of the club. Altogether he won the championship 11 times, he was runner up 10 times and was a regular shooter until 1982. In the 1960-61 season he won the championship at the age of 72. Good shots never retire, they only mellow. He went away with the Australian Rifle Team to Bisley in 1910 and in 1928. In 1910 he won the Graphic Cup and a Bisley King's Badge and in 1928 he won the Wingrove Cup. In 1927 he won the David Syme Aggregate, the Argus and Australasian Cup, the Victorian Grand Champion and B.S.A. Championship. He has represented Australia for five Empire Matches against Great Britain and other Dominions and he has captained five Victorian State teams in Commonwealth matches.

During the First World War C. G. Meudell died on active service and the Meudell Memorial, a long-range handicap at 800 and 900 yards, was instituted in his memory. The club steadily picked up strength in the twenties, and then there was an incredible period.

Jordan Shield	1927-28-31-33-34-50-54
State Championship to be won twice.	1932-33
Lambie Memorial	1929-31-32-33-34-59
Templeton Cup	1925-27-28-29-31-32-33
Empire Trophy to be won 3 times	1930-31-32
All Australia Trophy to be won twice.	1930-31

During the 1932-33 season the club did not lose a match. It won every cup that could be held, and the triple win in the Empire Trophy was a particular success. Individual clubs shot for this contest on their home grounds, then posted the results. The contest was conducted under careful supervision; it was almost like the Olympic Games. Clubs in every capital city throughout the Empire took part. There were 10 to 12 clubs in Melbourne alone. One of the great club shots at this time was D. R. Davies. He was chosen to represent Australia at Bisley in 1924 and in the Bisley Tests shot his way into the first seven, and his fine consistent shooting throughout the meeting won him the "All Comers" Aggregate against the world's most competent riflemen, some-thing that has been achieved only twice by Australians. He won the King's Prize in Adelaide in 1931, and Walter Thompson, another club member, won it in 1930, with Davies runner-up. Les Smith won the New South Wales King's Prize in 1932. In 1934 J. King, shooting as one of the four representatives of Victoria at Sydney against competitors from all States of the Commonwealth, won the King's Medal, carrying with it the title of Champion Rifle Shot of the Commonwealth. Tom Stephens won the King's Prize in Victoria 1951 and the Syme Aggregate in 1937.

There is not space to list all the trophies won by M.C.C. members in the 1930s, but among the outstanding shots were Len and Lloyd Righetti, Lew Armstrong, L. A. Smith, W. Thomson and D. R. Davies.

With the outbreak of the Second World War, club shooting was over. All the ammunition had to go to the Services, and most of the eligible members had joined up. Lloyd Righetti lost his life in the sinking of H.M.A.S. *Perth*. Alan Righetti, a pilot officer, was shot down while serving with the R.A.A.F. but returned. John Learmonth was killed with the A.I.F. in the Middle East. S. A. F. Pond, who won a shooting blue at Melbourne University, served with the 8th Division in Malaya. After the fall of Singapore he was a Lieutenant-Colonel in charge of "F" force working party in Thailand with 700 troops under his command as prisoners of war. Many of those who survived owed their lives to his maintenance of strict discipline in appalling conditions.

It was nine years before club shooting started again. Even the clubhouse at

Williamstown was gone. This was built in 1928. During the war the anti-aircraft battery at Williamstown used it as a recreation hut. Then when the war was over the club did not get it back. The Housing Commission took it over and for years it was used as emergency housing. After all, it made quite a comfortable house.

The Government gave the club £2250 compensation and the members themselves built a finer clubhouse than before. It contained a locker room, washing room, cleaning room, kitchen and main room with plenty of space for entertaining visiting rifle teams.

In the post-war years Len Righetti, Lew Armstrong, D. R. Davies, R. W. Pearce and J. Lennox, all represented Australia at Bisley, and some very fine shooting has been done. E. S. King established a record by winning the club championship five times in succession from 1948-49 to 1952-53. Tom Griffiths won the Tasmanian Queen's Prize in 1953-54 with a record score of 337 and K. Gillam won it in 1957. He also won the club championship, and he was appointed captain of the Australian team to compete at Moscow for the World Shooting Championship—a great honour for the club.

Len Righetti, a very fine rifle shot, died in 1959. He finished on two occasions in the King's shoot and he won 11 King's Badges. For many years he was on the executive of the Victorian Rifle Association Council; in 1947 he was chairman, and he was chairman of the Commonwealth Council at the time of his death.

Many great shoots, both local and international, have gone unmentioned, so too have many famous club names, but ever since its formation the M.C.C. Rifle Club has had an outstanding record, and it ranks as one of the best clubs in the Commonwealth. In 1981 Jack Armstrong was one of the two initial winners of the Hans Ebeling Award for service to the sections.

Hockey

Hans Ebeling, international cricketer and M.C.C. senior vice-president, recommended to the Committee late in 1960 that the Club should form a hockey section.

Ready agreement was reached, and so the M.C.C. with its eighth sporting section became represented in its first Olympic sport, and one in which Australia was demonstrating a meteoric rise.

The actual formation of the section was handed over to committeeman Dr. Ian McDonald, former Victorian wicketkeeper and hockey blue. He gathered about him Stewart Jamieson, who became honorary secretary; Charlie Morley, the Australian Olympic coach, and other enthusiasts. So the section was born.

In its first season, 1961, the club fielded teams in B and C grades of the Victorian Amateur Hockey Association. To everyone's delighted surprise each team won the premiership in its grade, and the club produced interstate vice-captain Ken Clarke and Victorian Colts representative Andrew Wright. Recruiting in the early stages had admittedly been good, as Clarke was already an Olympian when he joined M.C.C., as was Geoff Bennett, while Stewart Jamieson, Des Clarke and Alan Hardman had each represented Victoria.

During 1961 the M.C.C. provided facilities for the visit of the Indian Wanderers team, and the game played at the Club's Albert Ground between that team and Victoria was generally agreed to be the finest ever witnessed in this State.

The establishment was increased in 1962 to five teams, including two junior elevens, and the club progressed beyond even the most optimistic expectations, the three senior teams each winning the premiership in its respective section, whilst the under 13 team reached the Preliminary Final.

With the winning of their premiership in 1962, the first XI was elevated to A1 grade, the pinnacle of Victorian hockey competition. The social atmosphere was already the envy of other clubs, the junior section was taking shape, supported especially by Malcolm Hull and Alan Jackson, and soon to be located as M.C.C./Box Hill in the eastern suburbs, while our "home" was confirmed as the best ever weather ground in Melbourne on the southern shores of Albert Park Lake.

Malcolm Hull went on to establish an unbeatable record, having played without a break in the first one hundred games since the club's foundation. Another original player was Ian Huntington, captain of cricket and a Victorian XI player. A natural left hander, he proved invaluable on the left wing, but it has always been a disappointment that no other cricket member has joined our ranks, though for two or three years we played an annual cricket match against the XXIX club.

There was an extraordinarily happy dedication to the new club by those who had for one reason or another thrown in their lot with us, and after 28 years, old originals like Ernie Royall, Lew Jenkins, Ken Clarke, Dave Sanders, and Ian Scott are still to be found watching, supporting, and even playing.

The advantages of the M.C.G. facilities were put to excellent use when we hosted the W.A. team in 1963. The notoriety engendered brought us several excellent interstate recruits, while our association with cricket ensnared a number of useful Oxmians, including Tony Brooker, coach during the seventies, and David Pettit the present chairman.

Coaching and training was carried out at Albert Park, the move hastening the erection of the club house in 1964 and floodlighting in 1968. Many were the arguments with the chairman of the Albert Park Trust, Senator Pat Kennelly, over these developments. We won some, we lost some. Basic to the development however was a wonderful response from the hockey members themselves, with gifts, work, and loans. Their enthusiasm and foresight was responsible for the excellent grounds which we enjoyed for so long, and which are a tribute to the indefatigable Treasurer, Lew Jenkins, as triumphant off the field as he was in battle.

After the tenth year, Lew Jenkins, the old war-horse took over the chairman's reins. The section's fortunes on the field after the initial rousing success had fluctuated, and the first XI had fallen again to B grade. More than anything it was to be Lew's responsibility to oversee the change of administration from the old to the younger players. It was a gradual transition—oldies such as Des Clarke, Les O'Connell, Ken Hearse and Alan Jackson continued to support the club strongly in the coaching area. Frank Hill took over from the inimitable Stewart Jamieson as secretary, followed soon by the new generation including John Pearce, Trevor King and Ian Ferrier.

The doyen of M.C.C. hockey, Stewart Jamieson, took over the chair in 1975, the last of the original veterans to do so. We still had the difficulties suffered by M.C.C. sides—the lack of a suburban zone from which to draw—and whilst we fairly regularly won pennants in lower grades, our elevations seemed no more frequent that our subsequent relegations.

Meanwhile Stewart's health was not good, and in 1978 he retired in favour of the fourth chairman Ken Sparks, former captain and coach for several years. Soon afterwards an encased display of hockey memorabilia was accepted by M.C.C. for permanent exhibition in the Baer Museum, dedicated to the names of Stewart and Audrey Jamieson who had done so much for the M.C.C. Rob O'Connell and Bruce Unthank continued the new era of younger generation secretaries but we still had the disturbing problem of mediocrity on the field of play, despite periods of excellence by Trevor King's first XI.

The year of 1985 could be regarded as crucial. After having been honoured early in the year by the award of life membership in the Australian Hockey Association, the master builder of the club, Stewart Jamieson, died. His memory is preserved in the award of a trophy for the most improved player.

After a seven year term, Ken Sparks passed the chair to David Pettit who found himself in the midst of rapidly changing standards. The steady rise in the professionalism of Australian teams who were consistently winning international acclaim, culminating in the World Cup in Pakistan in 1986, was mirrored at State and club level. The football club made a great contribution to the hockey section when the President, Stuart Spencer's brother-in-law, Australian squad member Tony Gillow, crossed to M.C.C. After more than twenty years we again had a coach of international class; the response was undeniably positive. Together with others like Gerard Shirley who came with him, he developed the expertise of many talented youngsters who were coming through the ranks, so that in 1986 we won the State League 3 premiership with over 100 goals scored, and the second XI was also promoted.

Promotion from 3rd grade to the top level demands a great deal of dedication, but after a near miss in 1987, everything fell into place in 1988 when both first and second XIs won their respective flags. After twenty two years we found ourselves in top company, and in a curious quirk of fate, exactly as in 1962, it was against Greensborough that we won both grand finals, and with whom we made the step upwards once again to State League 1, the modern equivalent of the old A1.

The game is now very professional if largely unpaid; one cannot relax. Our position and our prestige as our M.C.C. section will attract newcomers who will have to prove themselves not only on the field, but also in the social life of a club which has become renowned for that. In 1984, funds were swelled by selling off the red wine left after Ric Lewtons and Trevor King took charge of the bottling. That will be insufficient sustenance for the new secretary Andrew McDonald, and treasurer Gerard Shirley, for since then the widespread use of artificial surfaces has changed the cost structure of the section, and the fact that we now train and play several games on the the artificial surface of Olympic Park is our indication of the way we shall have to go to maintain ourselves in the highly competitive world of State League 1. The use of centralised grounds, artificially surfaced, will continue to strain the committee's resources to maintain social cohesion when the club has a less easily reached home base. This will be the challenge for Dr. Rob Gregor, manager Mike Robinson, captain, and all their mates.

Today the section has five senior teams, two under age and two Veterans teams and minkey, and is looking to introduce women's hockey. If the huge camaraderie bequeathed by this section's founders can be maintained, the section will undoubtedly add more pennants, sing the song more loudly, and create material worthy of contemplation.

391

Squash

When the Western Stand at the M.C.G. was designed, two squash courts and associated facilities were included. The main objective was to provide a facility for M.C.C. members to play squash at the Club.

The courts were opened in October 1968 and their popularity was immediately apparent. Shortly afterwards, Ken Mitchell—a keen competitive squash player, submitted to the M.C.C. Committee a proposal that an M.C.C. squash section be formed. M.C.C. members were informed of the proposal and the section was officially formed in December 1968.

The inaugural squash section president was Mr. Denis Cordner and Ken Mitchell was appointed secretary. Teams were organised and since its inception the squash section has represented the M.C.C. in Victorian Squash Racquets Association club circuit competitions.

Over the years pennants have been won (and lost) in all grades, from A to F. During 1987, eleven M.C.C. teams participated in pennant squash. In addition, the Section conducts two tournaments annually—the M.C.C. Squash Section Championships for Squash Section members, and a "Closed" Tournament in which all M.C.C. members are able to participate.

The current chairman is Peter Mitchell, and the Secretary is Malcolm Rumsey.

The Staff

The staff at the Melbourne Cricket Club has always been interesting. Very often the man behind a desk in an office at the M.C.G. or out on the arena has been a world champion. Just to mention the cricketers—Hugh Trumble, Vemon Ransford, Warwick Armstrong, Hunter Hendry, Len Darling, Clive Fairbairn, Bill Ponsford, Harry Hill, Jim Symons, Joe Kinnear, Tom Leather, Ian Johnson and our present secretary John Lill—all have worked for the Club. Then among the footballers we have had—Fred McGinis, Geo. Moodie, Herbert Fry, Jack Leith, Goosey Lewis, Ernie Tout, Jack House, Harry Cope, Gordon Ogden, Bill Vanthoff, Joe Kinnear, Maurice Gibb, Charlie Streeter, Eric Glass, Les Jones, Bob McKenzie, Jimmy Davidson and Hector Davidson.

The first curator at the M.C.G. was Rowland Newbury, a very careful Scot. In the old days a curator had to do everything. The story is told of how he took the takings home on New Year's Day, 1862, when the Melbourne and

Districts XVIII was playing Mr. Stephenson's All England XI. There had been a record crowd, between 25,000 and 30,000. So much money had been collected Rowland Newbury was terrified. He was sure a thief would get into the house and steal it, so he hid all the money in the kitchen oven. He neglected to tell his daughter about this, and she was just lighting the fire to bake some bread when Mr. Newbury rushed in to rescue the takings.

Since then facilities for looking after the takings have improved a good deal, with armed officials and armoured security wagons; but there was a scare in 1931 at the time of the famous Coles hold-up, when Constable Derham was shot in the head. On a Saturday evening, just after the finish of a League football match, the day's takings, all bagged up in canvas bags, were held in an area close to the main members' entrance. The men in charge of the cash were awaiting the arrival of an M.C.C. official before ordering a hire car to take the money to the bank. A plain-clothes policeman, the regular armed escort, was there. Just then a taxi driver walked into the ground. He said he was looking for a fare, which seemed odd, because everyone had gone home. The escort policeman was suspicious and he asked him several questions. Suddenly he recognised the alleged taxi driver as a man convicted of an offence a week or two earlier at the Richmond Court.

Obviously everything was all set to go into action, for 30 yards away a large black car was parked. Its doors and windows were locked and there was a slumped body, apparently asleep or drunk, over the steering wheel. However, the radiator was warm, and obviously the engine had been running a few moments before. By this time the hire car had arrived and the takings went safely to the bank. Very soon after, the spectacular Coles hold-up took place. The two gunmen who shot Constable Derham were the same men who waited outside the M.C.G. that day.

Anyone who visits the M.C.G. now will see two large lamps on brackets protruding from the brickwork of the Members' Pavilion, facing the park area outside the ground. Their installation dates from the date of the Coles hold-up. They light the area very well, and mercifully there have been no armed robberies at the M.C.G.

Rowland Newbury was the first man who had to worry about the takings, and after him came the curators W. McAlpine and Tom McCutcheon. The late Ted Morton, who was assistant to each of these curators, wrote in his memoirs, published in 1928: "The first curator of my time was Rowland Newbury, and associated with him were Sam Cosstick, Sam Borders and Charlie Dench. Occasionally a flock of sheep were let on the ground to keep the excess growth of grass in check. During McAlpine's term as curator a determined effort was made to improve the condition of the ground. Each year for a period of seven years 400 loads of Merri Creek soil were spread over the ground, the main object being to turf the ground completely and level it."

Morton says of Newbury that had he wanted to he could have taken the Aboriginal team to England. He was a burly 16-stone Scotchman, and he had been known to lift a cottage piano singlehanded into a wagon. Although he paid Bert Luttrell the tribute of making wickets to last out any of our present-day marathon Test matches, his highest compliment went to McAlpine. "He knew the temper of a wicket better than any other man I ever knew."

Bert Luttrell, who transferred to the M.C.G. from the Albert Ground, was the originator of the "Shirt Front" wicket. In his preparation of a Test match pitch he followed the theory of regular rolling for at least two weeks before the match. This was done for a period in the morning, but always for one hour between 1 p.m. and 2 p.m., immediately after lunch. The veterans at the ground can still picture him guiding the shafts of the heavy stone roller, controlling its direction with three of the ground staff on one side and three on the other. He did not favour the use of a horse fitted out in leather horse boots for wicket rolling, although he used this method for grass cutting. There were no motor mowers in Bert Luttrell's day. During the Second World War, when the M.C.G. was occupied by the Americans and the R.A.A.F., he kept the ground in good order. Yet after the years of disuse there was some deterioration in the quality of the black soil. In those years he was almost blind and he had to retire.

The arena was completely churned up for the laying down of drains and running tracks for the 1956 Olympic Games, and it had further drastic treatment in its reconstruction after the Games, which naturally affected the grassing of the arena. It was the responsibility of the curator, Bill Watt, to bring it back to its former status as the best sporting arena in Australia. Bill Watt came to the M.C.G. from the Sydney Cricket Ground.

Ted Morton, who wrote the memoirs, is another name to be mentioned. He migrated from Tasmania in 1878 and he served the Club for 50 years before he retired. Some of the older members can remember the bed of roses within the members' reserve, which used to border the arena fence. This bed, which has long since disappeared, was Ted Morton's responsibility. Then there was Austin (Goosey) Lewis, an old player with Melbourne Football Club. He used to control the watering during the summer, then in the winter he was a trainer and custodian of the football equipment. Then there were famous characters like Herbie Fry and Charlie Over. Herbie was not very advanced in such talents as reading and writing. He could hardly sign his own name, but he was a mighty footballer. He was a rover in the famous McGinis, Moodie and Fry ruck combination at the turn of the century. Furthermore, he was a fine cricket coach, a sought after umpire, a good slow bowler and a first-class wicketkeeper. Herbie retired when the ground was occupied in 1942 and the Club gave him a testimonial.

Charlie Over was a first-class spin bowler. One had the idea he could spin a ball even on a sheet of ice. With Over, Fry, Bob Crockett and others at the nets, M.C.C. members had fine practice.

Charlie Over also went away with the Australian baseball team to America in 1897.

The successor to Albert Cuttriss as assistant secretary was Mr. Maurie Gibb, a large genial man of immense patience, Maurie Gibb joined the staff of the Melbourne Cricket Club in 1934, the same year that he started tplaying with the Melbourne Football Club. He developed into one of the finest half-forward flankers the game has seen. He played with the club until 1943 and in 132 games he kicked 167 goals. He was a member of the 1939, 1940 and 1941 premiership sides.

Another great staff member was Mr. W. H. Ponsford, or as everybody knew him, Bill. He joined the staff on April Fool's Day, 1932 and left on Friday the 13th of June, 1969. As the club newsletter pointed out those were two rather strange days for a sportsman who was just as superstitious as most. He was the office manager and one of his major duties was to look after all matters relating to membership. In his time he saw full membership double from 6,200 to 13,800 and the waiting list rise from 4,000 to more than 50,000.

His cricket exploits are told largely elsewhere in this book but he started to hit the front pages in 1923 when, at the age of 22, he scored 429 against Tasmania. He outdid this in 1927 when he made 437 against Queensland. This match against Queensland was the beginning of an incomparable three weeks. In three matches played in successive weeks on the M.C.G. he scored 1,013 runs in four innings. After his 437 against Queensland he made 202 and 38 against New South Wales and a few days later he made 336 against South Australia. In all, he made 6,902 runs for Victoria at an average of 86.27.

But Bill Ponsford was such a good cricketer one tended to overlook his skill as a baseball player. He played for Melbourne and Victoria and is generally acknowledged as one of the finest baseballers Australia has produced.

Recent staff members and their stories are covered in the latter part of the book—and all are conscious of their place in the tradition of the Club.

APPENDIX II

M.C.C. Batting Averages

		Runs	Av.
1838-1844	No record.		
1845/46	H. Goddard	38	9.5
46/47	G. Cavenagh	86	12.28
47/48	W. Philpott	146	16.22
48/49	D. Turnbull	134	14.88
49/50	T. F. Hamilton	91	18.2
50/51	C. Lister	327	17.21
51/52	C. Lister	178	35.6
52/53	F. Budd	56	14
53/54	C. B. Hall	76	12.66
54/55	B. Butterworth	64	32
55/56	Captain Hotham	129	32.25
56/57	T. W. Wills	102	34
57/58	W. H. Hammersley	150	30
58/59	T. Butterworth	47	11.3
59/60	T. F. Wray	198	12.6
60/61	R. W. Wardill	167	16.7
61/62	R. W. Wardill	247	27.4
62/63	R. J. Wardill	100	20
63/64	R. W. Wardill	333	19.10
64/65	E. Fowler	197	24.5
65/66	J. L. Wilson	94	23.2
66/67	R. W. Wardill	300	21.6
67/68	R. W. Wardill	446	37.2
68/69	Josh Phillips	361	36.7
69/70	C. S. Gordon	465	35.10
70/71	V. L. Cameron	173	28.5
71/72	G. Gibson	365	22.13
72/73	G. Gibson	234	19.6
73/74	T. J. Kelly	225	42.3
74/75	W. Newing	238	21.7
75/76	G. Alexander	643	40.3
76/77	B. B. Cooper	426	35.5
77/78	J. P. Tennent	264	29.34
78/79	G. Alexander	632	33.5
79/80	A. Loughnan	233	48.20
80/81	C. J. Dunne	721	42.41
81/82	J. D. Edwards	309	44.14
82/83	T. J. Kelly	446	37.16
83/84	P. S. McDonnell	336	67.20
84/85	J. M. Blackham	429	85.80
85/86	J. McIlwraith	368	52.57
86/87	F. H. Walters	603	50.25
87/88	F. H. Walters	421	42.10
88/89	J. McIlwraith	549	91.50

		Runs	Av.
89/90	W. Bruce	640	40
90/91	R. W. McLeod	312	52
91/92	R. W. McLeod	684	76
92/93	W. Bruce	460	57.50
93/94	W. Bruce	464	77.33
94/95	C. H. Peryman	287	57.40
95/96	H. Trumble	591	65.66
96/97	W. Bruce	563	62.55
97/98	C. H. Ross	238	34
98/99	H. Graham	469	67
99/1900	H. Graham	642	49.38
1900/01	H. Graham	336	48
01/02	W. Bruce	290	41.42
02/03	W. Bruce	571	81.57
03/04	W. W. Armstrong	812	135.33
04/05	V. Ransford	655	72.77
05/06	W. W. Armstrong	840	76.36
06/07	W. W. Armstrong	825	75
07/08	F. Vaughan	543	77
8/9	F. Vaughan	425	60.71
09/10	F. Vaughan	482	60.25
10/11	F. Vaughan	444	44.4
11/12	R. L. Park	459	57.37
12/13	R. G. Johnstone	301	60.2
13/14	V. S. Ransford	442	73.66
14/15	F. Vaughan	577	57.7
15/16	W. W. Armstrong	842	93.55
16/17	V. S. Ransford	322	53.66
17/18	W. W. Armstrong	419	139.66
18/19	V. S. Ransford	577	115.4
19/20	W. W. Armstrong	700	100
20/21	H. C. Sandford	621	51.75
21/22	E. K. Tolhurst	367	45.87
22/23	V. S. Ransford	413	82.6
23/24	B. A. Onyons	385	38.5
24/25	H. C. Sandford	259	25.9
25/26	H. L. Hendry	754	107.71
26/27	W. A. Stokes	274	54.8
27/28	B. A. Onyons	473	52.55
28/29	H. C. Sandford	581	58.1
29/30	E. K. Tolhurst	533	59.22
30/31	J. Thomas	345	38.33
31/32	L. Darling	419	59.85
32/33	W. H. Ponsford	353	88.25
33/34	C. Gardner	329	54.83

		Runs	Av.			Runs	Av.
34/35	W. H. Ponsford	470	78.33	63/64	G. D. Watson	862	50.70
35/36	W. H. Ponsford	829	75.36	64/65	I. Huntington	726	60.50
36/37	W. H. Ponsford	337	56.16	65/66	N. Crompton	367	33.36
37/38	W. H. Ponsford	744	82.66	66/67	E. R. Williams	327	40.87
38/39	P. J. Beames	661	55.08	67/68	C. E. Rudd	332	41.50
39/40	N. Ley	818	45.44	68/69	R. G. Lloyd	560	32.94
40/41	P. J. Beames	363	40.33	69/70	J. K. Moss	257	28.55
1941–1945	Suspended on account of war.			70/71	G. D. Wastson	320	53.33
45/46	P. J. Beames	317	35.2	71/72	R. G. Lloyd	399	30.69
46/47	J. Green	602	50.16	72/73	C. J. Dart	303	60.60
47/48	C. McDonald	623	56.63	73/74	G. R. Booth	537	61.50
48/49	J. Green	541	33.81	74/75	A. P. Sheahan	365	60.83
49/50	C. McDonald	449	40.81	75/76	A. P. Sheahan	540	90.00
50/51	J. Daniel	485	34.64	76/77	A. P. Sheahan	383	76.60
51/52	J. Solomon	297	33	77/78	J. K. Moss	514	85.66
52/53	M. Haysom	372	37.2	78/79	J. G. Anderson	539	67.37
53/54	R. B. Stevens	440	55	79/80	D. J. Broad	448	49.77
54/55	J. Daniel	313	31.3	80/81	S. M. McCooke	434	39.45
55/56	J. Daniel	337	56.16	81/82	D. S. Shepherd	552	46.00
56/57	M. Haysom	339	48.42	82/83	D. S. Shepherd	591	49.25
57/58	P. Bailey	361	40.11	83/84	D. J. Broad	690	49.28
58/59	M. Haysom	505	42.08	84/85	J. G. Anderson	740	52.85
59/60	I. Huntington	328	65.6	85/86	P. D. King	531	59.00
60/61	I. Huntington	319	29	86/87	D. S. Shepherd	457	50.77
61/62	I. Huntington	640	49.2	87/88	P. D. King	732	48.80
62/63	N. Crompton	539	67.38				

M.C.C. Bowling Averages

		Wkts.	Av.			Wkts.	Av.
1857/58	A. M. Bruce	33	3.60	78/79	G. Alexander	93	9.82
58/59	W. J. Hammersley	7	5	79/80	P. Must	14	9.57
59/60	W. J. Hammersley	30	7.3	80/81	J. D. Edwards	42	8.50
60/61	C. Makinson	13	15.11	81/82	J. D. Edwards	25	9.52
61/62	W. J. Hammersley	23	7	82/83	W. Bruce	58	9.24
62/63	W. H. Handfield	39	5.35	83/84	W. Bruce	42	8.61
63/64	W. H. Handfield	91	5.64	84/85	W. Bruce	58	12.72
64/65	W. H. Handfield	18	6.15	85/86	W. Bruce	14	15
65/66	J. Conway	31	3.11	86/87	W. Bruce	38	7.07
66/67	V. L. Cameron	14	5.11	87/88	H. Trumble	36	6.77
67/68	T. W. Wills	97	8.37	88/89	A. Shee	17	13.94
68/69	F. E. Allan	37	4.32	89/90	R. P. Dickson	10	9.70
69/70	C. S. Gordon	44	6.17	90/91	H. Trumble	32	10.21
70/71	C. Reid	47	7.43	91/92	R. McLeod	15	14.26
71/72	R. W. Wardill	31	9.10	92/93	H. Trumble	38	11.84
72/73	E. Butler	8	4.6	93/94	C. McLeod	43	16.04
73/74	G. Alexander	17	12.5	94/95	W. Bruce	17	13.58
74/75	D. J. Cameron	38	7.5	95/96	W. Bruce	19	16.47
75/76	T. J. Kelly	73	8.26	96/97	W. Bruce	16	21.62
76/77	W. H. Moule	29	6.14	97/98	C. L. Wilson	17	25.88
77/78	G. Alexander	135	4.87	98/99	C. L. Wilson	17	19.64

		Wkts.	Av.			Wkts.	Av.
99/1900	H. Trumble	51	9.49	45/46	G. Meikle	19	17.63
1900/01	W. Bruce	9	13	46/47	A. Lovett	18	18.5
01/02	H. Trumble	19	8.89	47/48	J. Daniel	42	17.09
02/03	C. S. Gordon	15	11	48/49	J. Iverson	64	12.06
03/04	W. W. Armstrong	17	8	49/50	J. Iverson	21	11.24
04/05	W. W. Armstrong	13	15.53	50/51	J. Daniel	34	18.94
05/06	H. Trumble	25	11.24	51/52	J. Iverson	36	9.08
06/07	H. Trumble	35	6.94	52/53	H. Hill	29	15.2
07/08	A. H. Johnston	14	27.14	53/54	J. Iverson	33	6.6
08/09	G. R. Hazlitt	29	7.93	54/55	C. L. Fairbairn	32	18.06
09/10	A. H. Johnston	24	17.83	55/56	J. Daniel	34	17
10/11	A. H. Johnston	25	13.56	56/57	J. Daniel	36	13.66
11/12	A. H. Johnston	12	19.5	57/58	R. Watson	42	15.83
12/13	S. Mullett	20	15.15	58/59	L. Kline	24	10.95
13/14	W. W. Armstrong	20	7.35	59/60	I. Jones	43	15.9
14/15	W. W. Armstrong	42	8.11	60/61	C. Guest	22	20.4
15/16	W. W. Armstrong	29	18.20	61/62	C. Guest	26	15.1
16/17	W. W. Armstrong	22	18.22	62/63	I. Jones	32	16.84
17/18	W. W. Armstrong	42	8.92	63/64	I. Jones	40	18.32
18/19	H. Ironmonger	42	8.76	64/65	I. C. Gribble	26	18.19
19/20	H. Ironmonger	79	12.67	65/66	I. Jones	23	22.74
20/21	H. Ironmonger	34	11.64	66/67	M. H. N. Walker	26	16.58
21/22	W. H. McDonald	23	14.91	67/68	G. D. Watson	16	20.12
22/23	H. Sandford	11	15.90	68/69	M. H. N. Walker	53	14.06
23/24	H. I. Ebeling	34	15.76	69/70	D. S. Crow	19	15.47
24/25	R. S. Rodgerson	19	15.89	70/71	P. L. A. Bedford	16	12.81
25/26	H. I. Ebeling	47	18.38	71/72	I. C. Hennig	13	11.15
26/27	R. Jewell	14	15.78	72/73	M. H. N. Walker	16	11.94
27/28	H. L. Hendry	15	15.53	73/74	G. C. Brown	20	16.55
28/29	H. I. Ebeling	44	8.27	74/75	G. C. Brown	10	14.40
29/30	H. I. Ebeling	47	18.62	75/76	G. M. Swan	21	17.05
30/31	H. I. Ebeling	40	13.05	76/77	N. W. Williams	17	18.23
31/32	L. E. Nagel	20	11.25	77/78	R. Jamison	16	20.00
32/33	V. G. Nagel	22	7.36	78/79	M. J. McCarthy	26	20.42
33/34	H. I. Ebeling	23	11.95	79/80	N. W. Williams	37	17.02
34/35	L. Fleetwood-Smith	24	14.5	80/81	M. J. McCarthy	32	19.90
35/36	H. I. Ebeling	29	13	81/82	M. J. McCarthy	37	18.27
36/37	L. E. Nagel	71	14	82/83	C. J. Wright	40	17.55
37/38	L. E. Nagel	51	14.4	83/84	C. J. Wright	37	22.24
38/39	L. E. Nagel	32	13	84/85	J. W. Priestley	24	24.29
39/40	L. E. Nagel	86	13.45	85/86	D. J. Hickey	28	21.67
40/41	L. E. Nagel	29	14.06	86/87	S. W. Russell	26	20.34
1941–1945	Suspended on account of war.			87/88	P. D. King	28	16.78

APPENDIX III

Melbourne Cricket Club

List of M.C.C. Presidents since Club's inception

1838-1841	No record.
1841-1843	F. A. Powlett.
1844-1845	J. Stephen.
1846-1849	G. Cavenagh.
1849-1850	William Meek-F. A. Powlett.
1850-1852	G. Cavenagh.
1852-1853	T. F. Hamilton-G. Cavenagh.
1853-1854	G. Cavenagh.
1854-1855	E. P. S. Sturt.
1855-1859	D. S. Campbell.
1859-1868	T. F. Hamilton.
1868-1877	D. C. McArthur.
1877-1880	Hon. J. G. Francis.
1880-1882	Hon. W. J. Clarke.
1882-1886	Sir W. J. Clarke.
1886-1900	F. Grey Smith.
1900-1907	R. Murchison.
1907-1922	Mr. Justice Cussen.
1922-1933	Sir Leo Cussen.
1933-1941	Sir Edward Mitchell.
1941-1944	Dr. Ramsay Mailer.
1944-1957	Dr. W. C. McClelland.
1957-1965	C. W. Simmonds.
1965-1979	Sir Albert Chadwick.
1979-1980	H. I. Ebeling.
1980-1985	Sir Bernard Callinan.
1985-19	Dr. D. P. Cordner.

M.C.C. Secretaries

Honorary Secretaries

1838-1841	No record.
1841-1843	G. Cavenagh.
1844-1845	W. McVitie.
1846-1847	O. H. Gilles) F. W. Marsden)
1847-1848	A. H. Broadbent.
1848-1849	F. W. Marsden.
1849-1850	Phipps Turnbull.
1850-1853	W. H. Hull.
1853-1854	Melmoth Hall.
1854-1855	W. H. McKenzie, Jnr.
1855-1856	A. M. Dick.
1856-1857	J. W. Brookes.
1857-1858	T. W. Wills.
1858-1860	T. F. Wray.
1860-1863	R. W. Wardill.
1863-1866	W. C. Biddle.
1866-1875	W. H. Handfield.
1875-1876	A. F. Robinson.
1876-1877	R. Johnson.

Secretaries

1877-1878	C. A. Reid.
1878-1880	B. J. Wardill-C. A. Reid.
1880-1911	B. J. Wardill.
1911-1938	Hugh Trumble.
1939-1957	V. S. Ransford.
1957-1983	Ian Johnson.
1983-	J. C. Lill.

INDEX

400

401

402

McCool, C.L., 190, 194.
McCormick, E.L., 167, 171, 173, 264.
McCosker, Rick, 284–5.
McCullough, Tom, 334–6.
McCutchan, Eric, 271–3.
McDermott, Craig, 327, 341.
McDonald, Colin, Int. ix, 202, 204, 228, 231, 232, 233, 236, 238, 239, 265, 275, 309.
McDonald Cup, 327.
McDonald, Sir John, 213.
McEacharn, Sir Malcolm, 83.
McGowan, J.S.T., 108.
McIntyre, Dr. Don, 299–300.
Mackay, Ken, 228, 232, 238, 240–1.
McKay, Heather, 335.
McKenzie, G., 251, 253, 255, 256.
Mackinnon, Donald, 111.
Mackinnon, F.A., 58, 145.
Maclaren, A.C., 72, 74, 79, 87, 89, 92, 134, 229.
Maclaren, J.W., 108.
McLean, R.A., 204.
McLeay, Ken, 309.
McLeod, R., 67–8.
McLeod, C., 68, 76.
McMaugh, Peter, 299.
McVittie, W.V., 9.
Maddocks, Len, 208, 210.
Mailer, Ramsay, Dr., 96, 107, 116, 182; death of, 183; 227.
Mailey, Arthur, 96, 122, 132–33, 137, 139, 140, 141, 158–9, 161, 170, 191, 283, 335.
Makepeace, H., 133.
Maley, John, 299.
Mallett, Ashley, 276.
Mankad, V., 191, 192.
Mannix, Archbishop, 164.
Marsh, Rodney, 267, 276, 278, 280, 285, 298, 304, 320, 344.
Martin, W., 83–5.
Marylebone Cricket Club, 89, 110–1, 157–8, 199, 229, 283, 344.
Mason, J.R., 79.
Massie, R., 264, 284.
Matthew, E. "Joe", 179–80.
Matthews, Greg, 332.
May, Noel, 325.
May, Peter, 210, 228–9, 230–1, 232, 283, 344.
Mayne, E.R., 129–30, 135, 137.
Meckiff, Ian, 229–30, 246, 247.
Melbourne City Council, 305, 321.
Melbourne Football Club, 330, 359–66.
Membership, 3, 17–18, 27, 42, 92, 113, 116–7, 121, 142–3, 152, 166, 176, 254, 313–8.
Menzies, R.G., 160–1, 167, 174, 216–7.
Merriman, Bob, 323.
Messenger, H.H., 335.
Meuleman, Ken, 194, 283.
Miandad, Javed, 291.
Miller, Chris, 308.
Miller, Keith, Int. x, 122, 136, 174, 187–8, 192, 199, 202, 203, 207, 208, 226, 232, 283, 344.
Milne, Malcolm, 335.
Minnett, R., 98, 105.
Misson, Frank, 237.
Mitchell, Sir Edward, 104, 164, 170, 173; death of, 182.
Morris, Arthur, 194, 197, 202, 203, 206, 208, 231.
Mortimore, John, 231.
Moses, H., 67–8.
Mostyn, Molly, 85–6.
Mountbatten, Lord Louis, 124.
Moyes, A.G., 33, 88, 112, 116, 163.
Muhummed, S., 267.
Muldoon, R., 302.
Mullagh, J., 33.
Mundy, A., 3.
Mundy, C.F., 3.
Murchison, Roderick, 81, 89, 93.
Murdoch, W.L., 45, 58, 96–7, 118, 143.
Murray, J., 250.
Mushtaq, M., 267, 281, 291.
Museum, Cricket, 333.
Myer, Sidney, 151–2.

Nagel, L., 171, 172.
Narwaz, S., 291.
Nash, L., 156, 171.

Nash, R., 156.
Nathan, Sir Maurice, 343–4.
New Zealand, 300–3, 308–9, 327, 331, 341–2.
New South Wales, Int. ix; first intercolonial match, 18–19; 31, 38, 74, 94, 117; world record scoring match, 138–42; record 10th wicket partnership, 147–8.
Noble, M.A., 71, 72, 88, 90, 91, 92, 97, 117, 118, 121, 122, 158, 225.
Noblet, G.K., 202.
Nourse, A. David, 96.
Nourse, A. Dudley, 96, 201.

O'Connor, Leo, 144.
O'Keeffe, Kerry, 285–7.
Oldaker, Max, 180.
Oldfield, W.A., 122, 138, 158, 162, 191.
Oliphant, E.H.C., 119–20.
Olympic Games, Int. x, 212–4, 270–1.
O'Neill, Norman, 229, 232, 239, 240.
Opperman, Hubert, 144, 335.
O'Reilly, W.J., Int. ix, 156, 162, 163, 171, 175, 283–4, 332–3.
Overs, 4-ball, 45; 8-ball, 121.

Packer, Kerry, 287, 295–7.
Packer, Sir Frank, 287.
Pakistan, 1973 tour, 266–8; 291, 299, 303, 319–20, 327–8.
Park, R.L., Dr., 95, 116, 117, 120, 129–30.
Parr, George, Int. ix, 20, 28–30, 35, 37.
Pataudi, Nawab of, 253.
Parish, Bob, 282–3.
Pavey, Percy, 335.
Pearce, A.M. "Joe", 117.
Peate, E., 118.
Pellew, C., 122.
Penfold, Capt., 85–6.
Phadkar, D.G., 191.
Phillips, Jim, 142.
Philpott, W., 11, 12, 18.
Pitch, 289, 292, 298–301, 340–1.
Pollock, G., 263, 264.
Pollock, P., 247, 263.
Ponsford, W.H., 134, 136, 139, 140, 141, 142, 144, 146, 152, 155; retirement of, 166; 171, 243, 275, 335, 338.
Porter, C; "Chilla", 223.
Powlett, C. Rev., 3.
Powlett, F.A., 2, 3, 6, 8, 11, 15, 283.
Prince of Wales, 258–9.

Queensland Cricket Association, 107.

Rackemann, Carl, 319.
Rai, Singh, 192.
Ramadhin, K.T., 200.
Rangachary, C., 193.
Ranjitsinhji, Prince, 71, 79, 92, 143.
Randall, Derek, 285–6.
Ransford, Vernon, 93, 94, 96, 97, 98, 104, 111, 148, 173, 176, 178, 180, 225–6; death of, 226; 277.
Ratcliffe, A., 141.
Redpath, Ian, 247, 267, 276, 280–1.
Reed, Curtis, 42.
Reid, Bruce, 341.
Rest of the World side, 263–6.
Richards, David, 282.
Richards, Viv, 298, 304, 319, 320, 327.
Ridings, Phil, 175, 302.
Ridley, Ian 276.
Rifle shooting, 385–8.
Rigg, Keith, 155, 167, 169, 171, 283, 344.
Ritchard, Cyril, 156.
Roberts, Andy, 303.
Robertson, Sir Macpherson, 164.
Robins, R.W.V., 169.
Rorke, G., 230, 232–3.
Rose, Murray, 334–5.
Rostron, F., 209.
Royle, V.R., 58.
Rush, H.R., 107, 110.
Russell, E., 250.
Russell, R., Int. xi, 2, 3, 7.
Ryder, Jack, Int. x, 114, 116, 117, 122, 139–40, 146, 150, 151, 152, 153, 260, 282.

404